STYLE ICONS

ART NOUVEAU

STYLE ICONS

ART NOUVEAU

TODTRI

A QUANTUM BOOK

Published in the United States by
TODTRI Book Publishers
254 West 31st Street
New York, NY 10001-2813
Fax: (212) 695-6984
E-mail: info@todtri.com

Visit us on the web!
www.todtri.com

This edition printed 2002

ISBN 1-57717-252-3

QUMSIAN

This book is produced by
Quantum Publishing Ltd.
6 Blundell Street
London N7 9BH

Printed in Singapore by
Star Standard Industries (Pte.) Ltd.

Contents

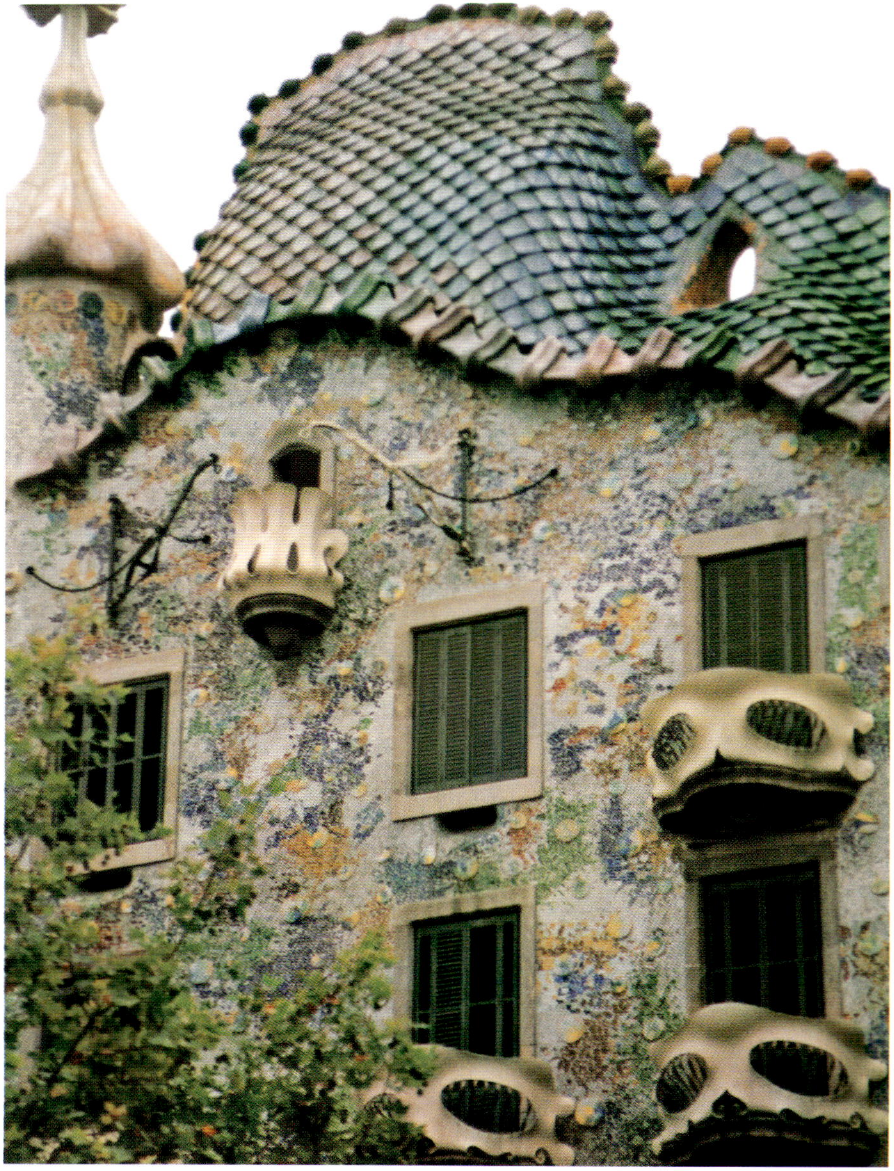

Art Nouveau Architecture and Furniture

THE ART NOUVEAU STYLE

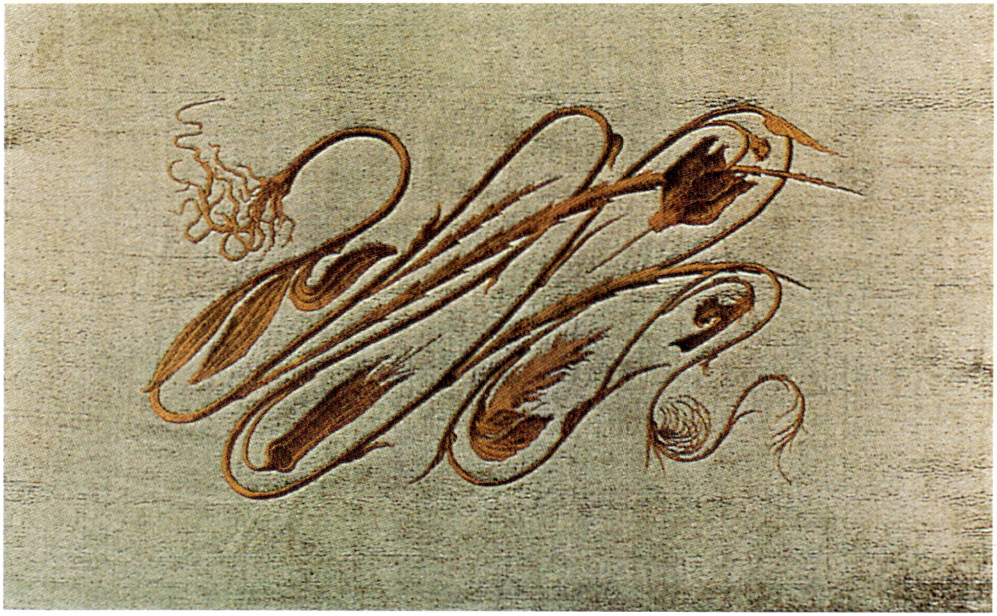

The 1800s had seen enormous changes in society in both Europe and the United States, with the spread of industrialization resulting in the creation of great wealth concentrated on the new industrial and commercial cities. The mass production methods of factories not only created a whole new class of workers, but also made a vast range of goods more widely available than ever before. Art Nouveau, which reached its zenith in the early years of the 1900s, began as a reaction against the horrors of mass production, reintroducing skills and craftsmanship which were fast dying out.

Far left: Embroidery by Hermann Obrist. The love of the undulating line is the purest expression of Art Nouveau.

The essence of Art Nouveau is a line, a sinuous extended curve found in every design of this style. Art Nouveau rejected the order of straight line and right-angle in favor of a more natural movement. Whether these lines were used in realistic descriptions of natural forms, or as abstracted shapes evoking an organic vitality, the emphasis was on decorative pattern and also flatness, a surface on which this concern for the linear, the line of Art Nouveau, could be exploited. This curving, flowing line brought with it a feeling of airy lightness, grace, and freedom.

The characteristic curving forms of Art Nouveau first appeared in England, yet they were to spread rapidly throughout Europe to a wide range of cities, each with a distinctive interpretation of the style: Paris and Nancy in France, Munich, Berlin, and Darmstadt in Germany, Brussels, Barcelona, Glasgow, and Vienna all became focal points for the style that was soon universal in Europe, and — with centers in New York and Chicago — equally influential in the United States.

ORIGINS OF THE NAME

The term itself, Art Nouveau, derives from a Parisian shop of the same name run by a

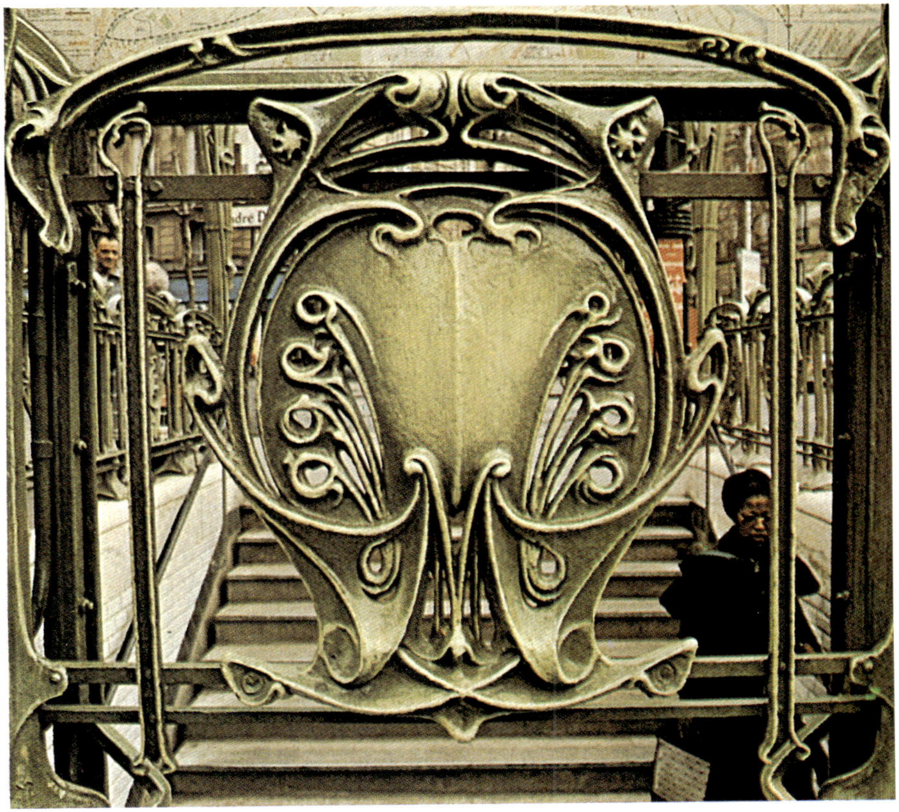

Below: Paris Métro, Victor Hugo, by Hector Guimard, 1900.

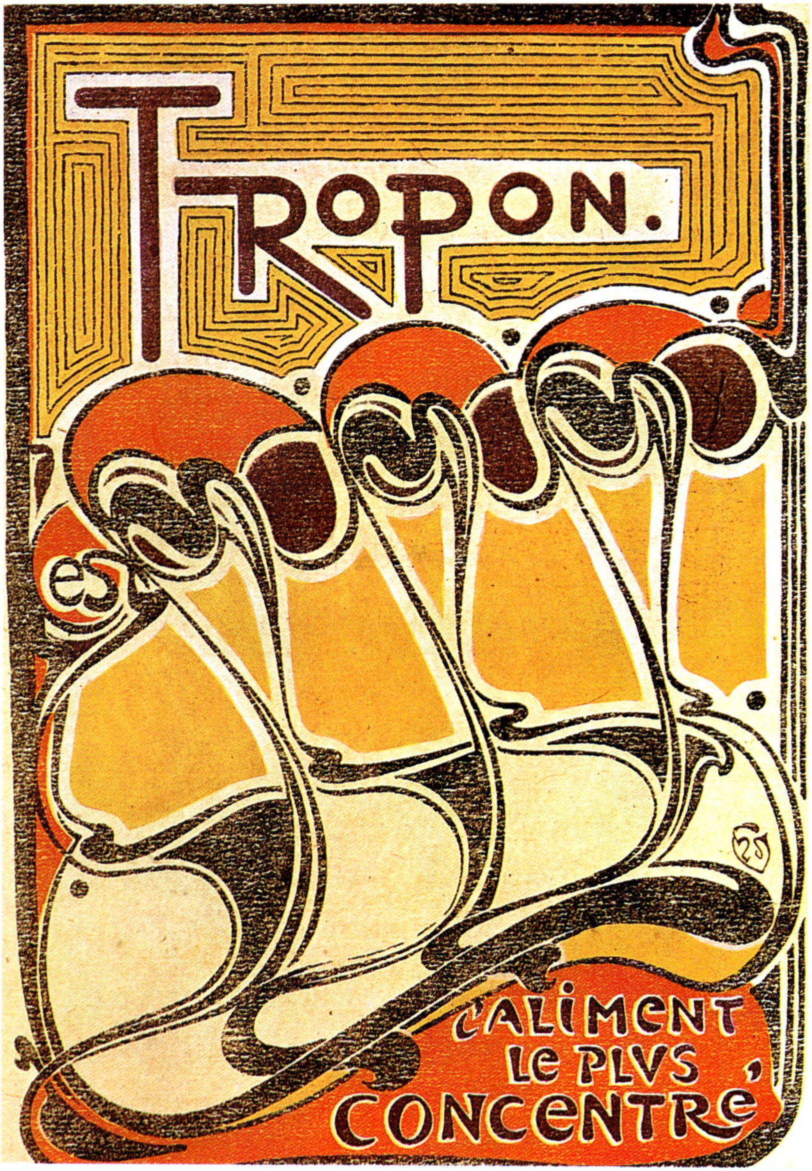

German émigré, Samuel Bing. Bing had been trading for ten years in Japanese art when, in 1895, he reopened his premises as La Maison de l'Art Nouveau and started to show the work of contemporary designers as well as painters and sculptors. The mixture of gallery, shop, and showroom became the Parisian base for the new style, encouraging Bing to commission works for the shop and to promote his artists and craftsmen abroad. Another Italian term for the style, *Stile Liberty,* was attributed to Liberty & Co., the London department store that sold the designs of progressive British craftsmen.

SPREADING THE NEW STYLE

Art Nouveau was not restricted to a few enlightened retailers. The style was also spread by the great international trade fairs of the era. The depth of interest shown by the public in the new fashions in art — and particularly the decorative arts — was also reflected in the huge numbers of new magazines and periodicals devoted to these trends which appeared in the Art Nouveau era.

TRADE FAIRS

The international trade fairs were products of the great age of industrialization, for they were descended from the 1851 London Great Exhibition, housed in the Crystal Palace, which had been held to demonstrate the possible applications of new technology. These exhibitions soon became an increasingly important feature of international commerce, at which the new styles of decorative art could be displayed. Particularly important events in the develop-

Left: The "Tropon" poster by the Belgian designer, Henry Van de Velde, from 1898.

ment of Art Nouveau were the international exhibitions of 1899 and 1900 in Paris, and of 1902 in Turin, while that of 1905, held in Liège, marked the end of the style's importance.

ART MAGAZINES

In Germany, it was the influential Munich-based journal *Jugend* (youth), which gave the name *Jugendstil* to the German version of Art Nouveau. At the same time, however, the widely read English, and later American, periodical *The Studio* also led to the style being called *Studiostil*. Equivalent influential publications were *Pan* from Berlin and *Ver Sacrum* from Vienna. The German language periodicals also included contemporary literature, poetry, and criticism, but as in all such journals of the time, the main coverage of the new style came not in specific articles, but in the actual design of the publication itself. The title page, typeface, and illustrations were all the work of Art Nouveau graphic artists.

Such periodicals had a wide circulation beyond the limited circle of craftsmen, but there existed, too, journals such as the influential *Art et Decoration* from Paris, which concentrated more exclusively on the decorative arts, and included many photographs. Thus, through exhibitions, shops, galleries, and magazines the Art Nouveau style spread rapidly through Europe and the United States, both feeding off and stimulating the public's interest.

ORIGINS OF THE STYLE

Because of the wide range of regional styles which resulted in a confusion of different

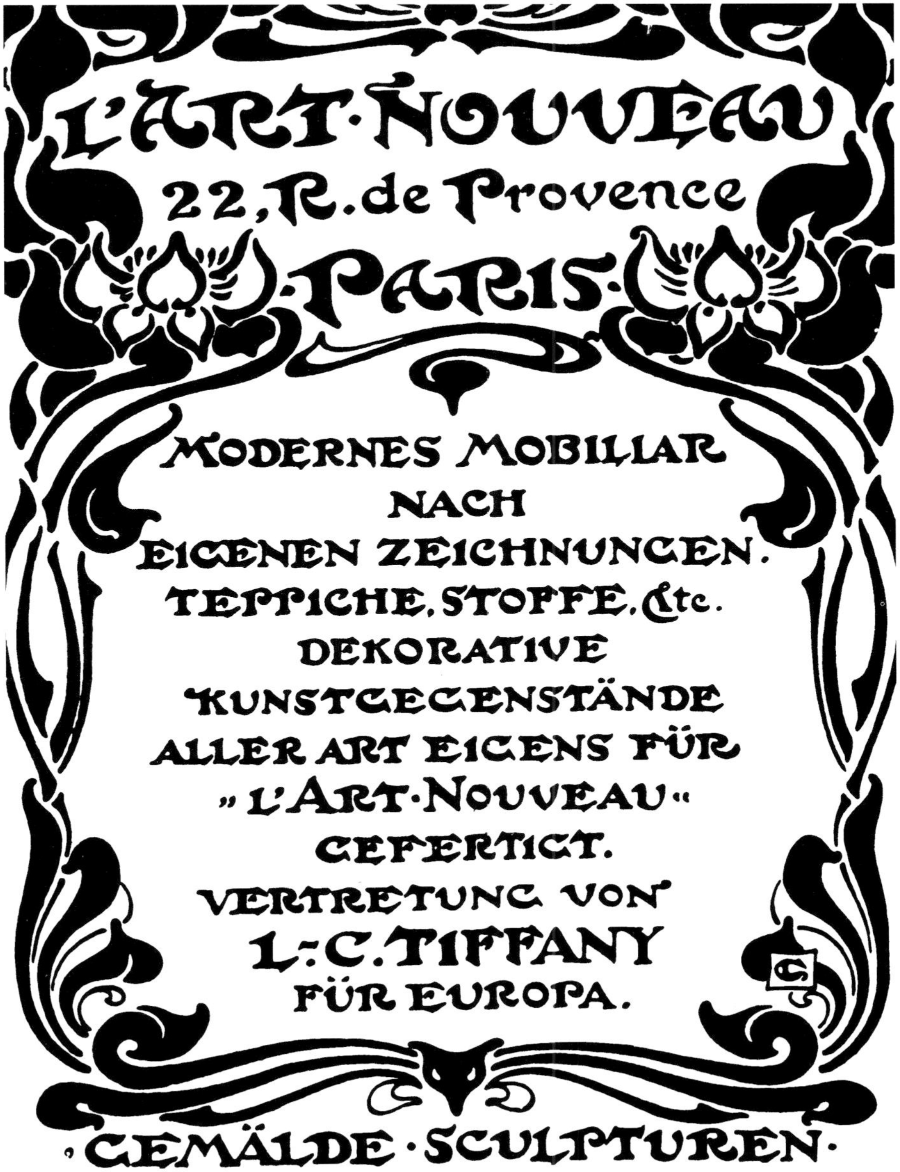

Right: German advertisement for Bing's gallery and shop, La Maison de L'Art Nouveau, which gave the movement its most popular name.

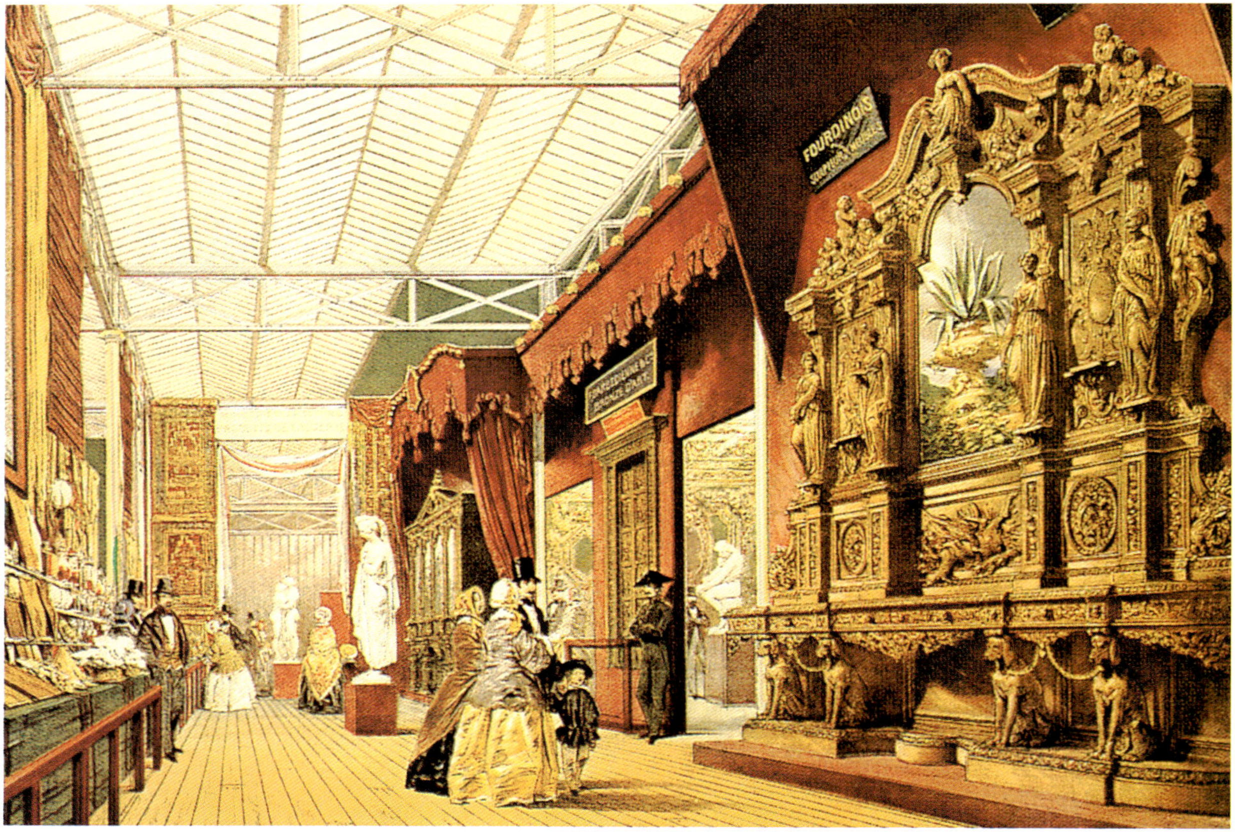

Above: Part of the French section of the Paris Exposition Universelle of 1900. While technologically advanced, the quality of design had stagnated or even regressed. Bombastic, clumsy, revivalist pieces, such as this furniture, horrified critics such as Ruskin and Morris.

names for the style — *Art Nouveau* and *Modern Style* in France, *Modernismo* in Spain, *Stile Liberty* and *Moderne Stile* in Italy, or even a reference to a place as with *Belgische Stil* (Belgian Style) in Germany — there was no clear idea as to common origin, nor shared characteristics, until Art Nouveau was in decline. It is only with hindsight that a more coherent view of the period has been formed.

The origins of Art Nouveau lay mainly in Britain, where the Victorian ornamental designer Christopher Dresser was one of the first to recognize the potency of eccentric curves. In 1862 he wrote: "A section of the outline of an ellipse is a more beautiful curve than that of an arc since its origin is less apparent, being traced from two centers."

By common consensus, the first true example of Art Nouveau design was the title page by Arthur Mackmurdo (1851-1942) for his book *Wren's City Churches*, published in 1883. The floral designs of William Morris and the

Arts and Crafts Movement were also influential in formulating the Art Nouveau look.

MORRIS AND THE ARTS AND CRAFTS MOVEMENT

Morris began his career firstly as a painter, as a follower of the Pre-Raphaelites and their dreamy interpretation of the medieval past. However, Morris had a more practical view of that period when it came to his attempt to recreate its idyll of painters, architects, and craftsmen working together, often on the same tasks — in 1861 he founded a company to produce the type of objects he wanted to see in every home. This became Morris and Co., and Morris was able to effect a genuine bridging of the divide between artists and craftsmen by employing his Pre-Raphaelite painter-friends to decorate cabinets and bureaux, and to design tapestries, fabrics, and chairs.

The actual appearance of these goods was often reminiscent of medieval models, particularly in furniture, but in fabrics, carpets, wallpaper, and decoration the Morris style was derived largely from natural sources, inspired by plant, bird, and animal forms. The use of hand-crafted, natural materials made these goods too expensive for ordinary people, yet despite this, Morris still hoped that his products would become widespread enough to improve the quality of the lives of as many people as possible. Like the influential writer John Ruskin, Morris hoped to free the working man from the drudgery of factory labor and, through craftsmanship, enable him to gain pleasure from his work.

The example of the Morris Company encouraged other similar enterprises in Britain, usually referred to under the general term "Arts

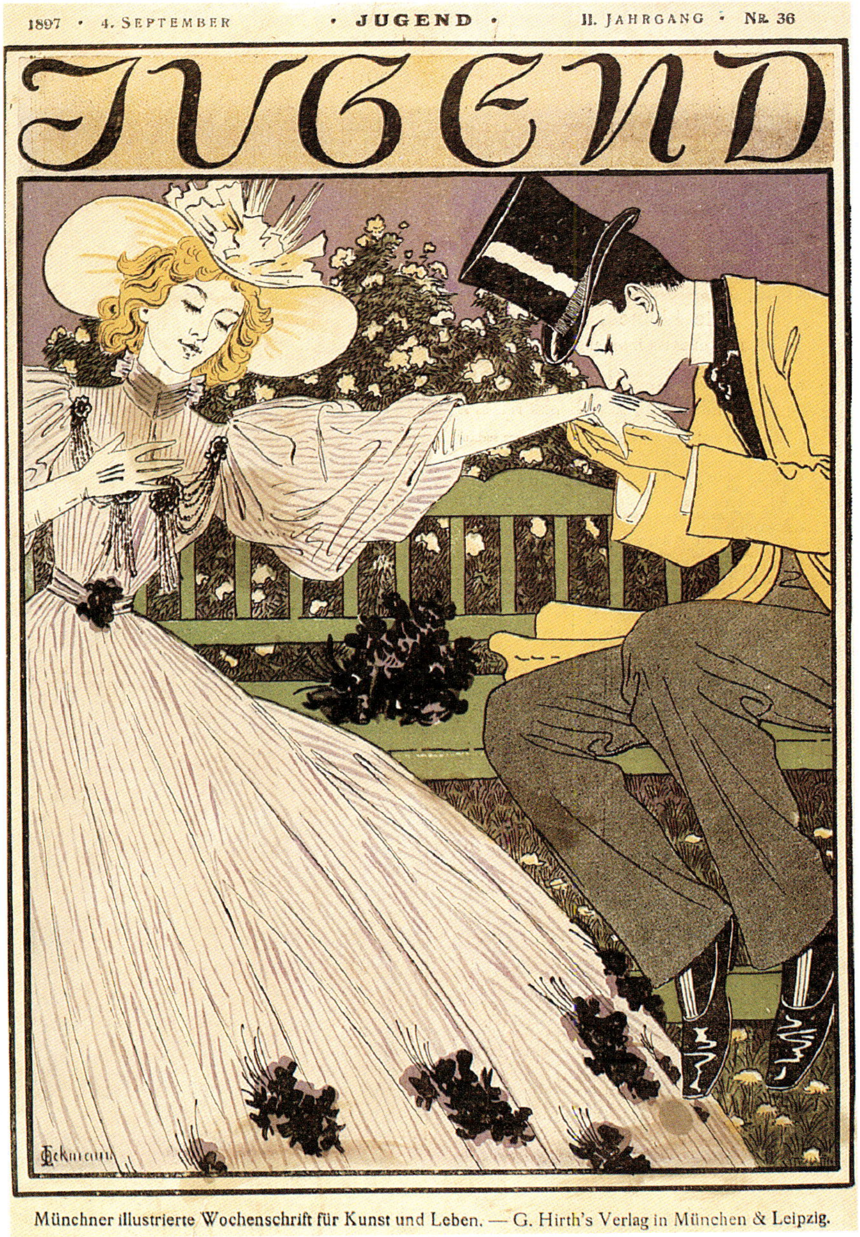

Right: The German magazine Jugend, *with cover design by Otto Eckmann.*

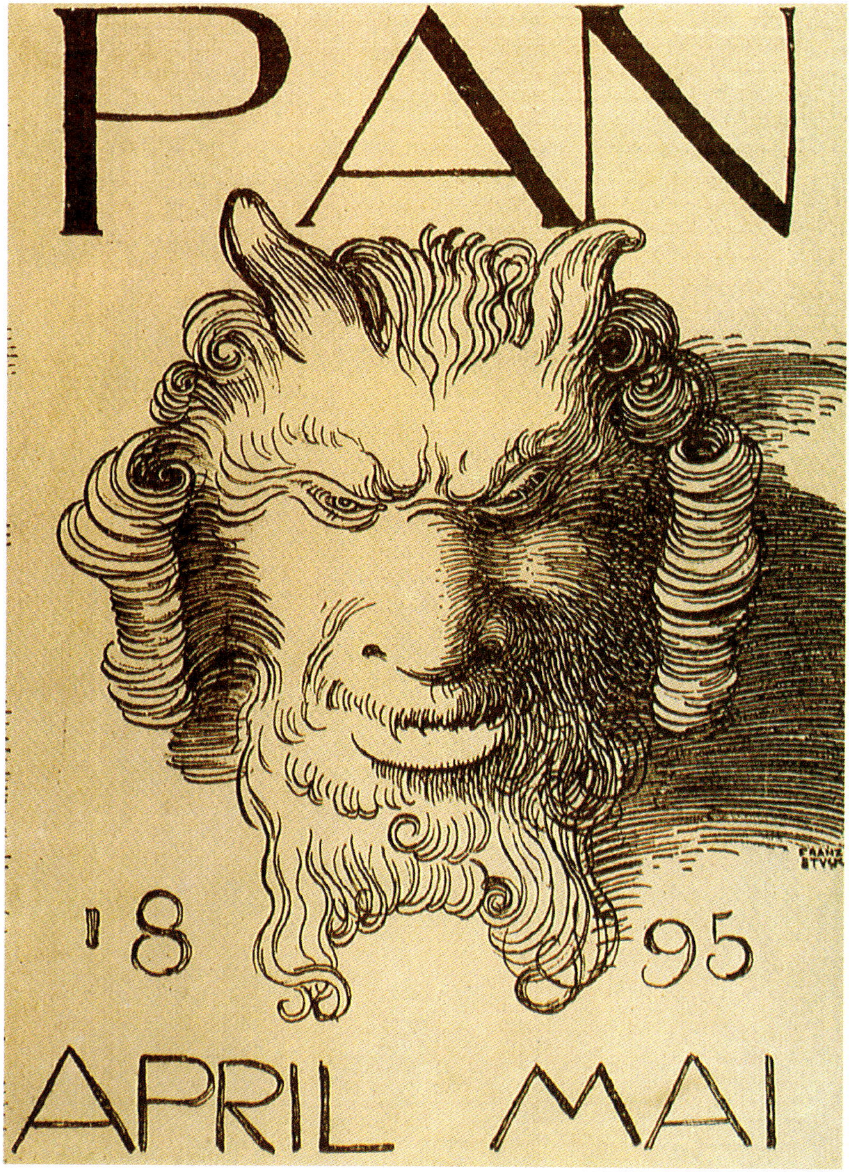

and Crafts Movement." Chief among these was the Century Guild formed in 1884 by Arthur Mackmurdo. Influenced by the flowing, natural forms of Morris, Mackmurdo developed these shapes into elongated, increasingly elegant patterns, and was the first to produce the characteristic vocabulary of sinuous flame-like shapes that were to be the hallmark of Art Nouveau for the next 20 years.

NATURE AND NATURAL FORMS

Nature was to be the ultimate source book of the Art Nouveau artist, particularly the plant world, for many artists had a scientist's depth of knowledge of botany. Flowers, stems, and leaves were chosen for their curving silhouettes. Naturally, lilies, irises, and orchids were favored, although any and every form, from palm fronds to seaweed, offered potential for development into an animated pattern.

Insects and birds of color and grace lent themselves to the same stylizing and refining process — dragonflies, peacocks, swallows, or creatures such as snakes or greyhounds. These decorative possibilities could also be developed from the curves of the female body, particularly when combined with long, loose, flowing hair which could be arranged into a fantasy of curls and waves. As the style developed, the quest for more novel forms grew.

HISTORICAL INFLUENCES

Despite the novel qualities of Art Nouveau, some of its stylistic features can be traced to past styles. The Gothic revival served in some ways as an inspiration, for the fervent examination of medieval art of the 1800s had

Left: Pan, *the Berlin magazine which covered the same combination of visual arts and literature as* Jugend *did in Munich.*

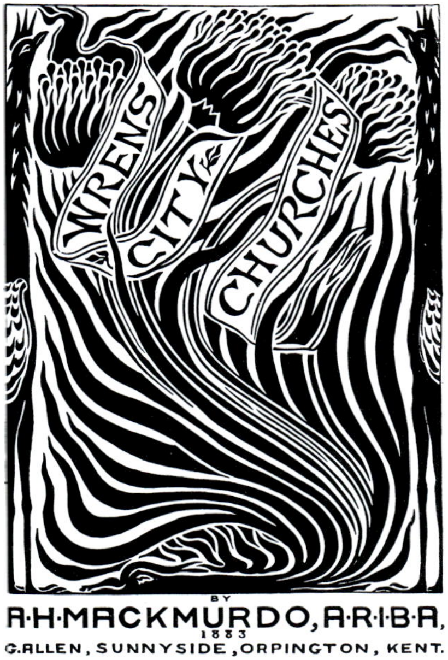

Above: The title page for Arthur Heygate Mackmurdo's Wren's City Churches.

Left: Cover for Deutsche Kunst und Dekoration, *designed by Margaret Macdonald Mackintosh.*

emphasized the value of curving, organically-inspired shapes seen in the architecture, sculpture, and stained glass of the Middle Ages. As appreciation of the Gothic grew, so too did the awareness that this term encompassed a number of different styles, from the chaste, plain lines of its early period, to the flamboyant fantasy of later medieval art. It was this form of the style that was to inspire Art Nouveau. The late Gothic style was plundered not to afford pedantic historical detail, but as a

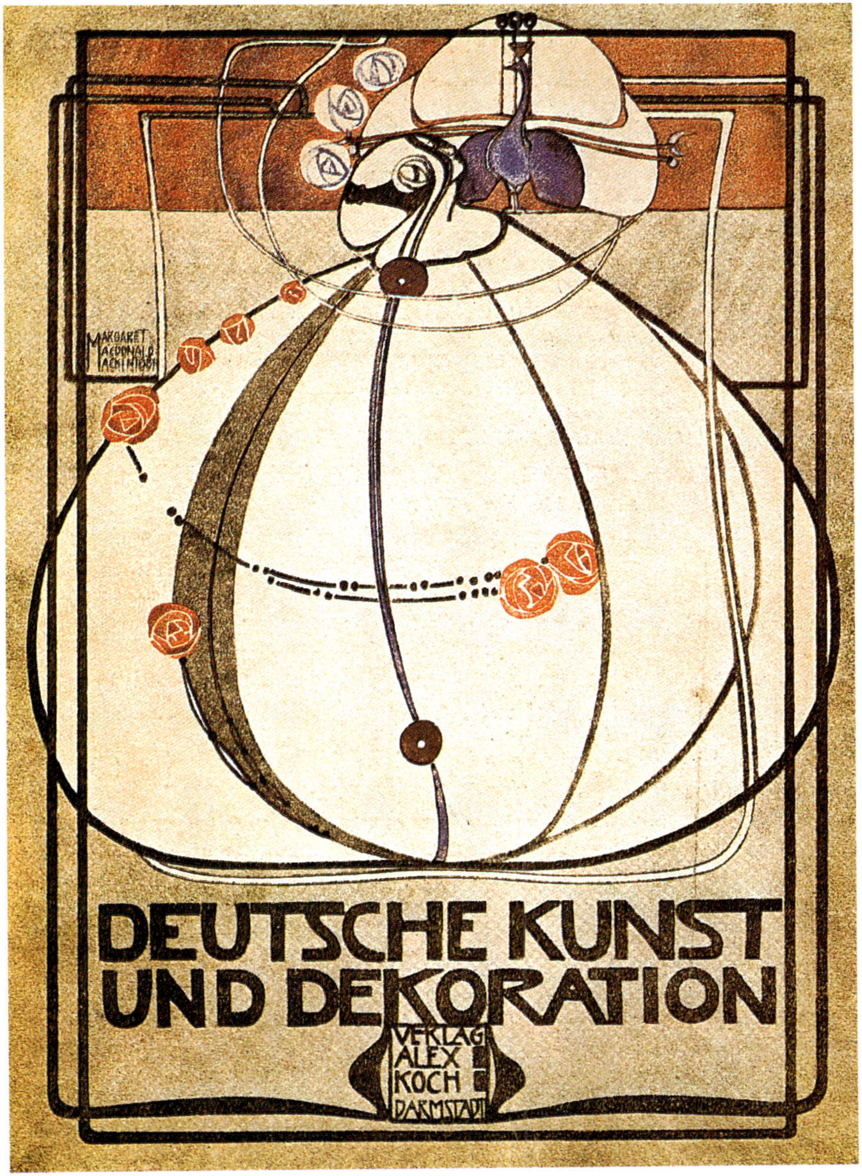

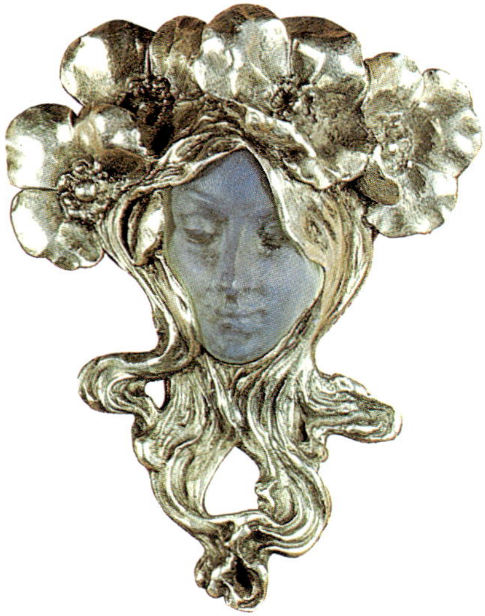

Above: Silver and glass pendant-brooch by René Lalique, ca 1900.

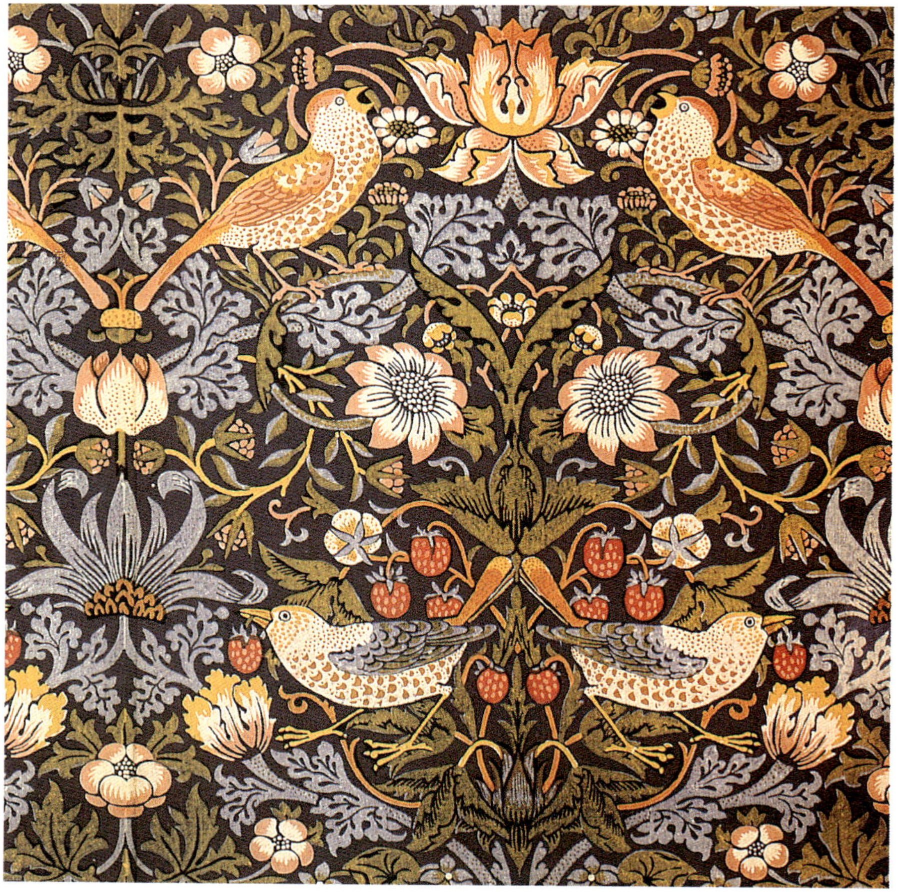

Right: "The Strawberry Thief," a Morris textile design from 1883. Unlike the more abandoned lines of Art Nouveau, the curving natural shapes here are more symmetrically ordered.

sourcebook for new ideas.

If flamboyant, late Gothic provided an example of the creative use of the past by Art Nouveau, then so too did the inspired re-examination of the 18th-century Rococo style in France. This style had become one of the many open to revivalists of the next century, but rather than resurrect it completely, Art Nouveau observed its forms and characteristics with an independent eye. Rococo had been more broadly associated with the use of capriciously cavorting, light, and delicate line as an ornament in all the decorative arts. This was very close to the line of Art Nouveau, and the connection became clear when in France the designers of the regional Nancy school began to incorporate references to Rococo in their work.

The common source of natural forms of plant and wave in both Art Nouveau and Rococo made the blend harmonious. The Rococo taste for light, high-keyed color in interiors was also pursued by Art Nouveau, in reaction to the heaviness and solemnity of somber Victorian interiors. While at its strongest in France, Munich had also been an important outpost of Rococo in the 1700s, and it is no coincidence to find that the lightest, wittiest, and

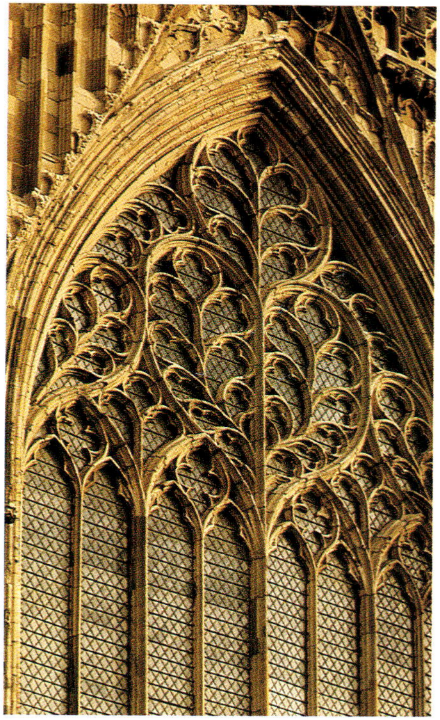

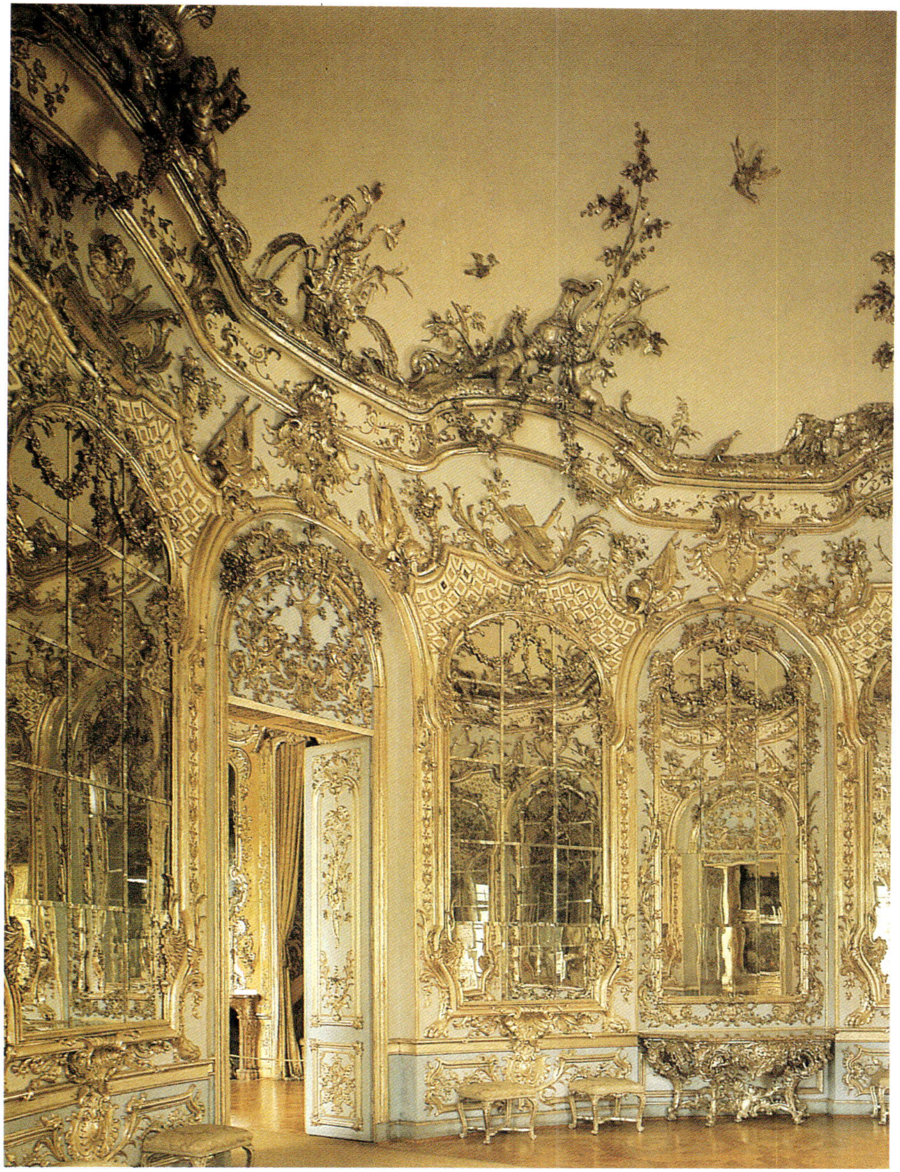

Above: The flamboyant late-Gothic style served as an inspiration to Art Nouveau.

Right: The restless line of 18th-century Rococo influenced many Art Nouveau designers.

most fanciful forms of Jugendstil were later to be found in that city in the work of Hermann Obrist (1863-1927) or August Endell (1871-1925).

Some stylistic revivals of the late 1800s were partly inspired by the growing nationalism of the time, which was tinged, as ever, by a romantic idea of the past. Some of the

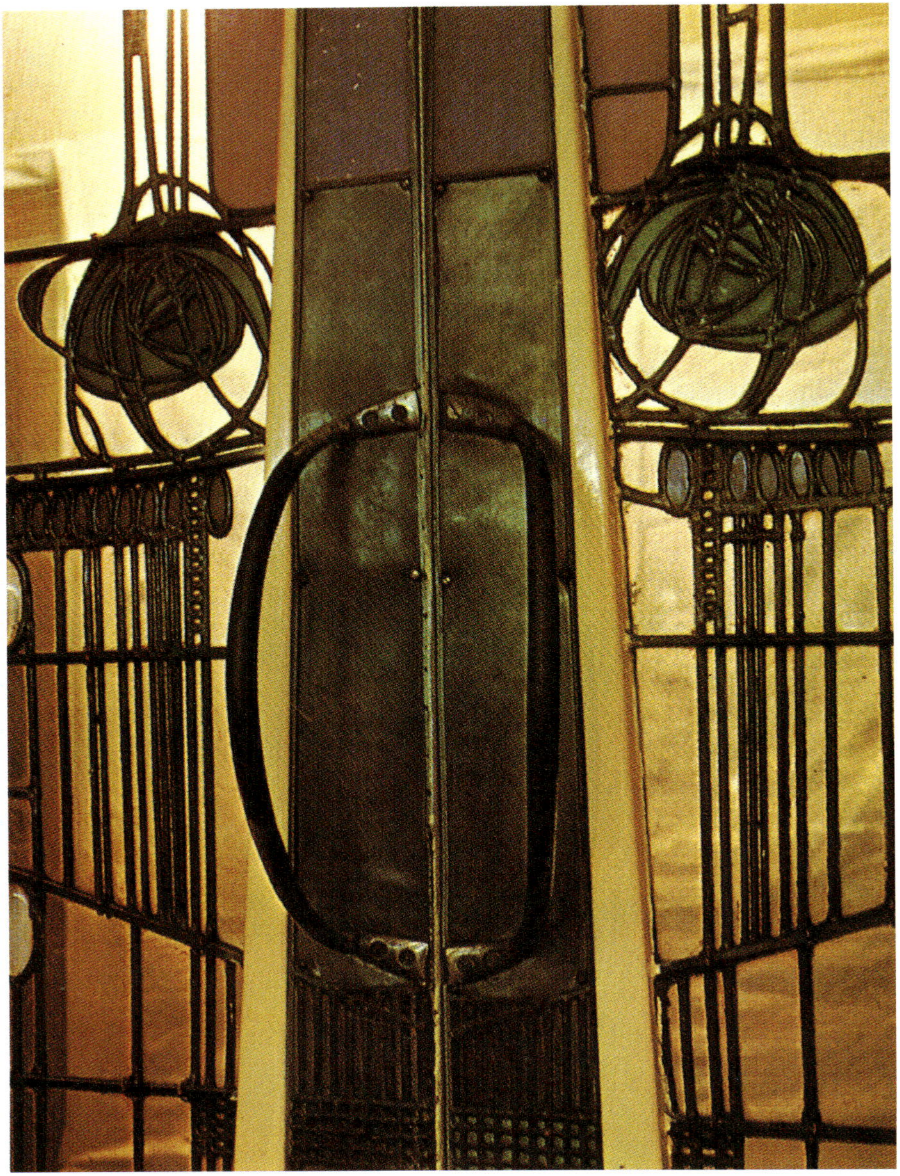

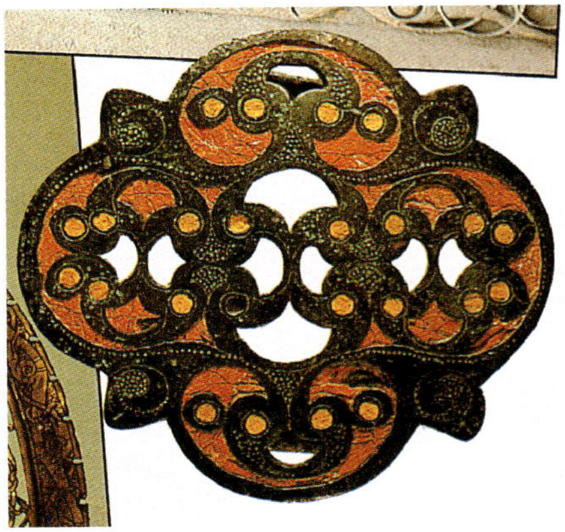

Above: Detail of a Viking wood carving.

Left: Detail of the doors for the Willow Tea Rooms, designed by C.R. Mackintosh.

revivals of national artistic consciousness also percolated into Art Nouveau and helped to form its many regional variations. An important influence on the Glasgow school and on its most renowned figure, Charles Rennie Mackintosh, was the revival of interest in early Celtic art.

Celtic jewelry and the ancient gospel books of Durrow, Lindisfarne, and Kells revealed precisely their elaborately curving and twisting decoration, the combination of stylization and the natural inspiration that typified Art Nouveau itself. More particularly, the use of lavish ornament confined within strict limits and contrasted with more open areas had strong parallels with the work of the 19th-century Glasgow designers.

With its capricious use of past and peculiar mixture of styles, Art Nouveau could not be anything other than a uniquely novel style.

Belgium and France

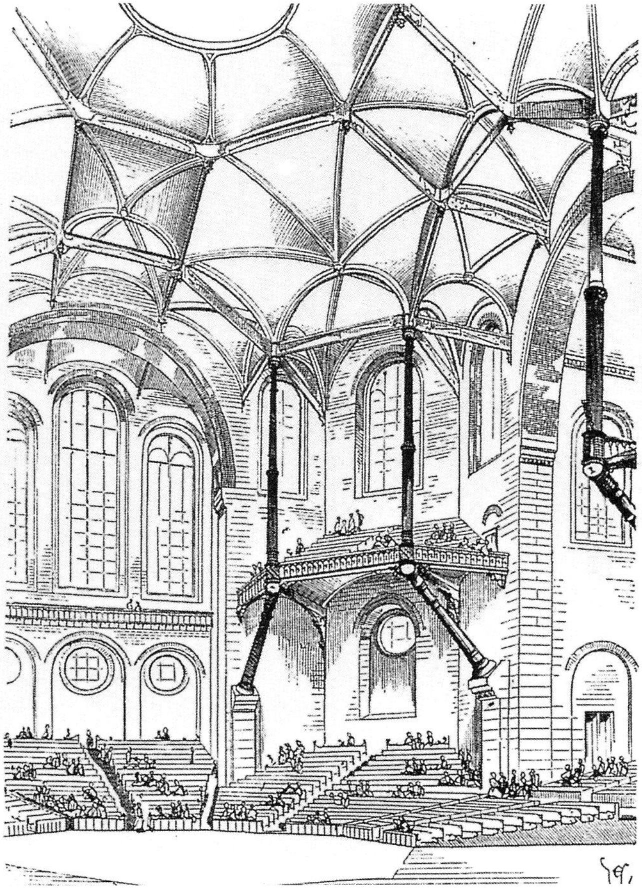

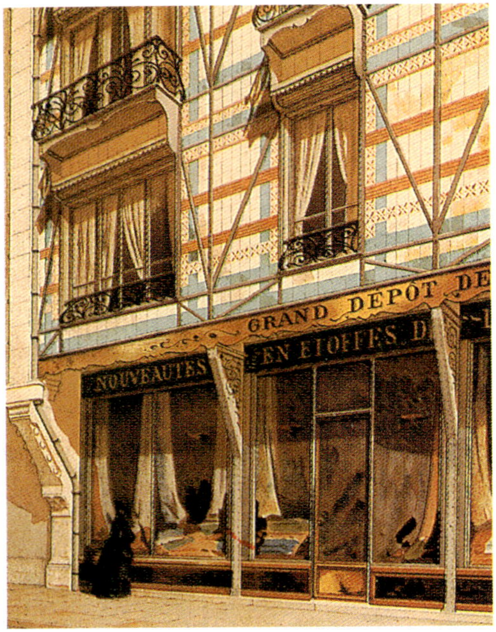

Above: Iron was used not only as a decorative element on the balconies, but also as a structural framework.

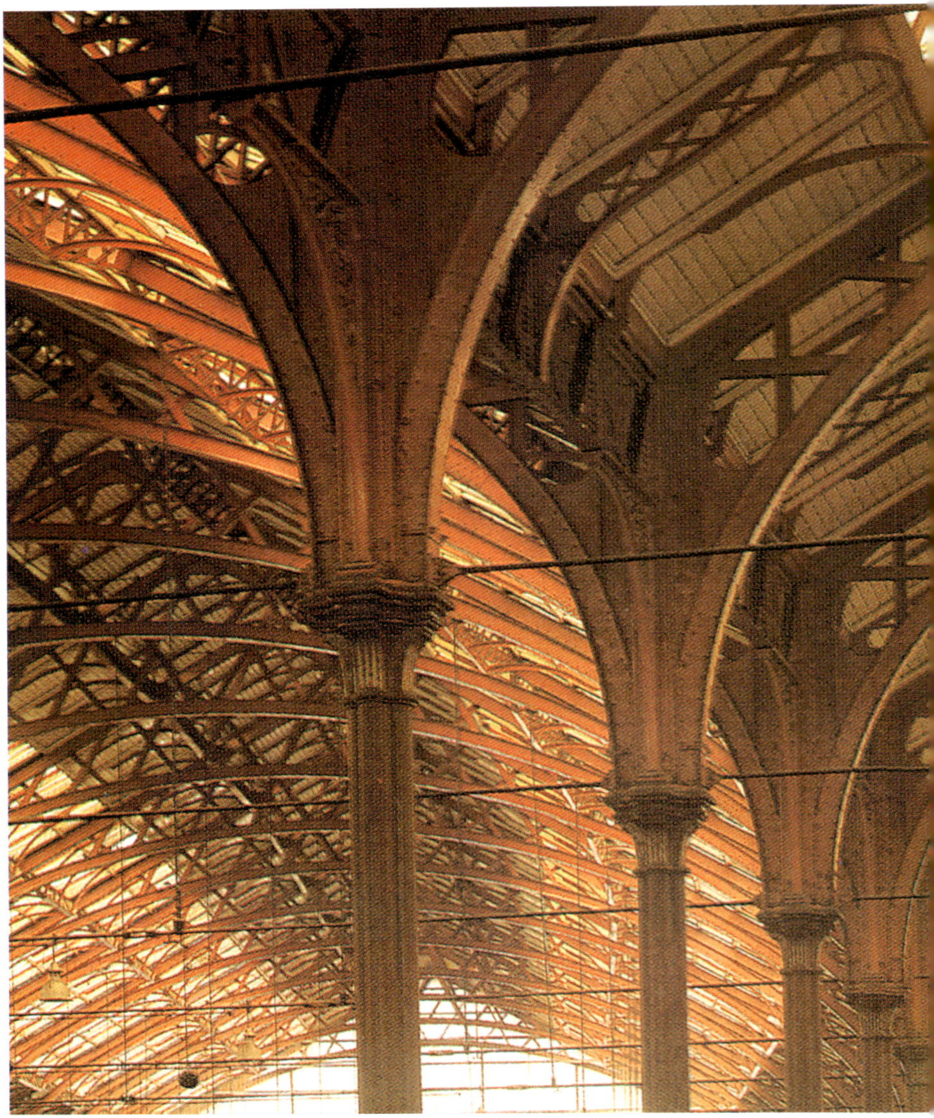

Right: The iron and glass vaulting of Brighton railway station typifies the use of these materials by engineers before they entered the mainstream of Art Nouveau architecture.

Overleaf: The vaulted hall from Viollet-le-Duc's Entretiens sur l'Architecture.

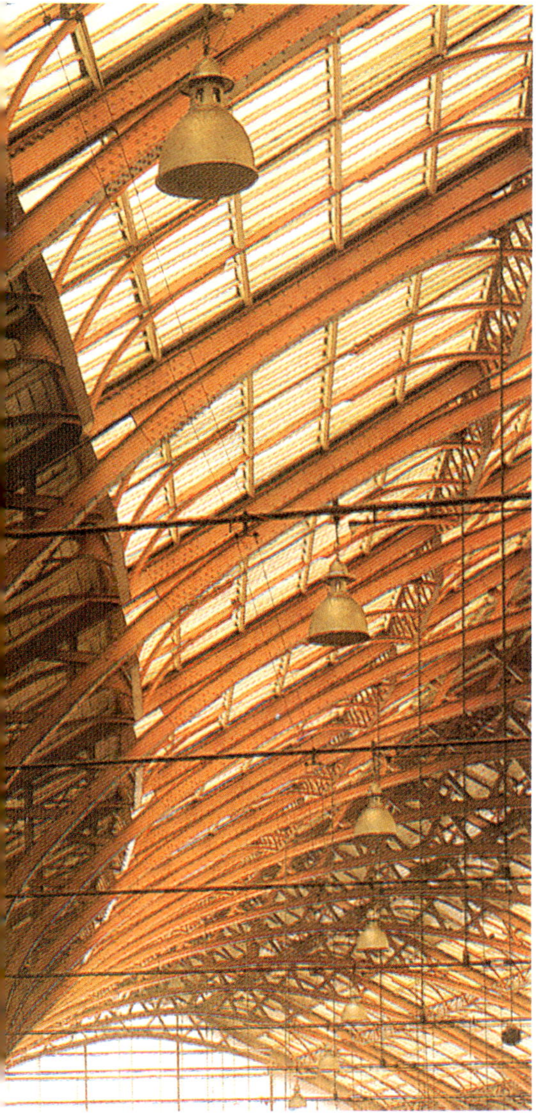

Architecture provides the backdrop against which all the varied creations of Art Nouveau can be set. The interdependence between the fine and decorative arts in Art Nouveau is best seen via the works of the major architects of the time, who required fittings in keeping with their domestic architecture while their fellow craftsmen needed the appropriate setting to display their work. From among the fine arts, it is architecture that has the strongest technical craft base, and when the conventional crafts were in decline in the face of industrialization, architects were at the forefront of their revival. Not surprisingly, the leaders of Art Nouveau were also architects: Horta, Guimard, Van de Velde, Behrens, Mackintosh, Gaudí, Gaillard, and Grasset.

MODERN MATERIALS FOR A MODERN STYLE

While the architects of the Arts and Crafts movement looked back to a nostalgic pre-industrial era of simple brick and stone homes inspired by the rich traditions of English architecture, the architecture of Art Nouveau began from an opposing premise. Instead of rejecting the industrially-produced materials of iron and glass, now more readily available and so dramatically demonstrated in the Crystal Palace, erected for the 1851 Great Exhibition in London, the architects of Art Nouveau eagerly embraced the possibilities these modern materials suggested. Consequently, Art Nouveau architecture was to become an important basis for later 20th-century developments, and paved the way for the Modern Movement.

FROM ENGINEERING TO ARCHITECTURE

The use of iron to provide strong and comparatively light frames for buildings was first developed in the architecture of the railways and other related industries. It was clear that its strength would inevitably lead to its use in more traditional architecture too, but in England, where iron had been most dramatically used, the development was tentative. The art critic John Ruskin's distaste for industrial materials was a strong influence, and when iron was used, its structural role was hidden as much as possible by the more conventional brick and stone.

GOTHIC STYLE

In France, however, the architect and theorist Eugène Viollet-le-Duc had no qualms in recommending the open use of iron-work in his writings, realizing its suitability for the high vaults of his favored Gothic style and, very significantly, suggesting ways in which it could be shaped to create foliage patterns to embellish its role as a structural element. Excited by the industrial architecture he saw, Viollet-le-Duc was prompted to write in his *Entretiens sur l'architecture* about the further uses of iron, and to produce a design for the combination of iron and stained glass. This combination of materials used to create lightness and color recommended it to the proponents of the new style, while the exploitation of the initial malleability of iron

Right: A detail of the base of the Eiffel Tower, Paris, showing some of the ornament that embellishes what is still today, a great feat of engineering.

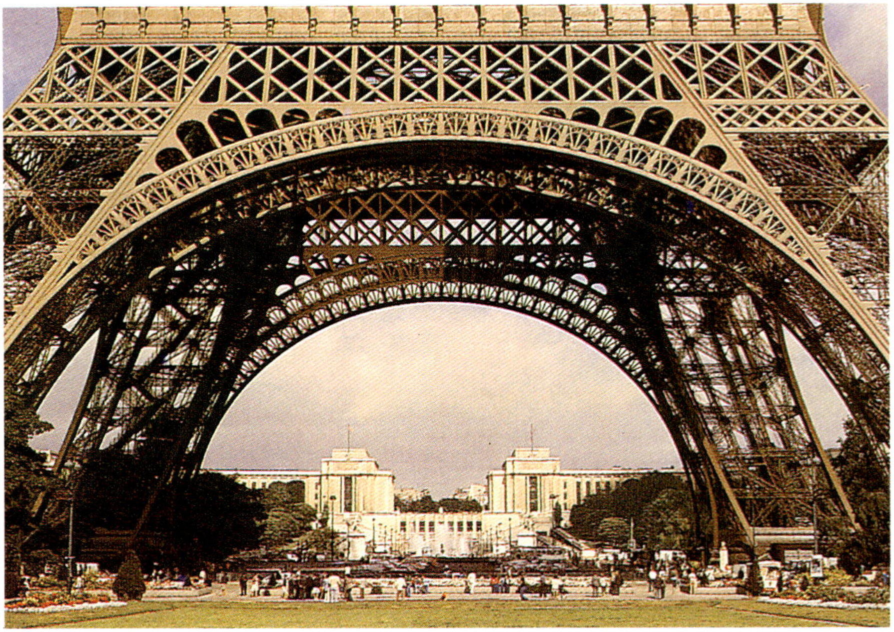

to create naturalistic ornament was to be of the greatest significance for Art Nouveau architects.

GUSTAVE EIFFEL

The great engineer Gustave Eiffel also carried the influence of English engineering to France. Increasingly involved in the design of pavilions at the numerous international exhibitions, Eiffel allowed more and more of the supporting metal frame to be revealed. It was for the Paris Exhibition of 1889 that his most famous and daring creation, the Eiffel Tower, was produced. When this was allowed to remain after the dismantling of the exhibition, the tower became an important, if controversial, monument to the possibilities of the new medium. In the manner of Viollet-le-Duc, Eiffel had also attempted to embellish his engineering masterpiece with some decorative flourishes in iron.

ART NOUVEAU EMERGES

It was in the fast expanding, and highly developed artistic climate of the Belgian capital of Brussels that an architectural style began to evolve in the works of the highly influential architect Victor Horta (1861-1947). Horta's early work had been with his employer, the academically classical architect Alphonse Balat who had built the imposing Musée Royal des Beaux-Arts.

In 1892, Horta began his Tassel House at 6 Rue Paul-Emile. The Tassel House could not contrast more strongly with the ponderous official architecture. In the interior, Horta exposed the iron columns in the hall and stairwell that carried so much of the building's weight, and refused to conceal them with brick or plaster. The slender forms of the columns were given a treatment entirely Art Nouveau in character. Instead of molding them into conventional Gothic or classical columns, Horta shaped these supports to resemble the stems of some fantastic vegetation. At capital level, Horta attached numerous twisting and turning metal fronds, as if the main column had sprouted growths. The design of the metal was echoed in the linear tendril decoration of the walls and ceilings and repeated again, in the mosaic pattern of the floor. These features and the pale color scheme gave the building an air of freshness, vitality, and movement.

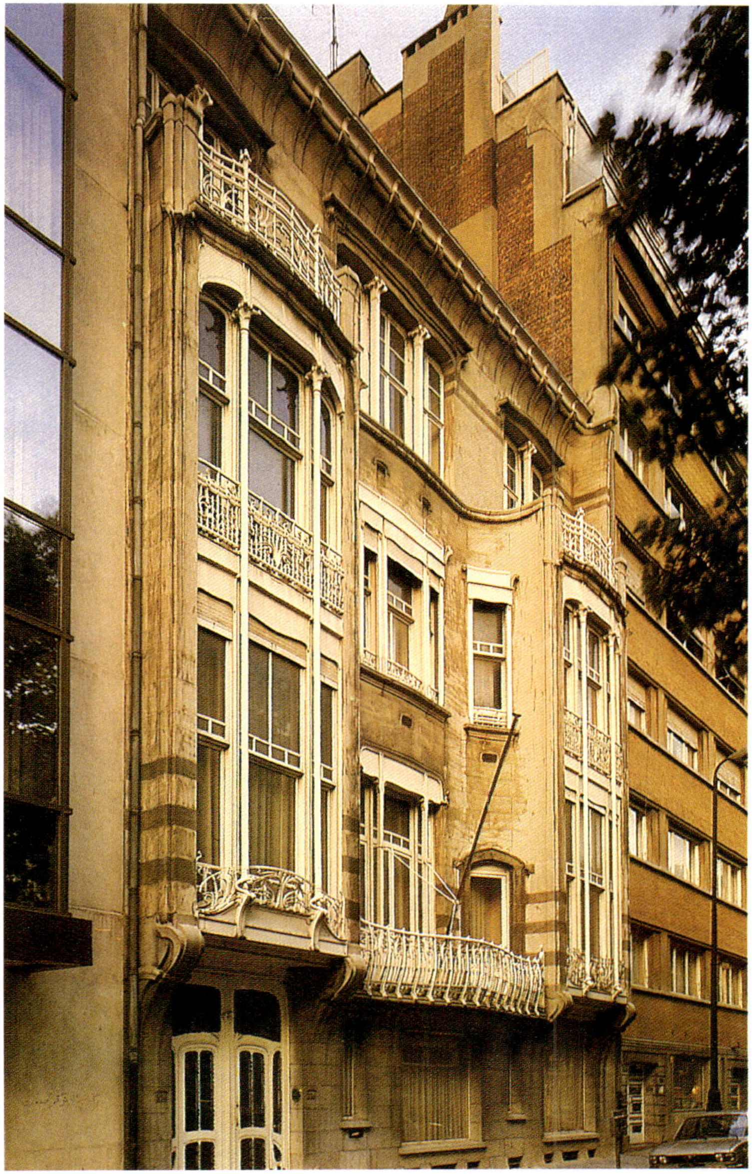

Right: The gently curving facade and the large windows of Victor Horta's classic Art Nouveau Hotel Solvay. The ironwork of the balconies and window mullions provides the only decoration.

Some of the furniture designed by Horta for the Tassel House was, however, less innovative than the building itself. A buffet, for example, with glazed cupboards at each end surmounted by S-scroll pediments and carrying a pair of candelabra with several curling arms, would not have looked out of place in a Rococo setting. On the other hand, the profusion of curved stretchers and supports under chairs and tables were pure Art Nouveau.

Having mastered the "whiplash" line in the Tassel House, Horta began to develop his style through a number of commissions. The Hotel Solvay (1894), originally designed as a private residence, is the most successful of his surviving facades. Essentially, it is a gentle curve between two framing bays supported by exposed iron columns, and is almost entirely glazed. Horta tried to lighten the effect of his architecture as much as possible with large windows, wide doorways, and open stairwells, giving an impression of open, airy space to his interiors. Now commonplace, it is easy to overlook the immensely refreshing effect that these rooms must have had after the gloom of a Victorian interior.

There is little decoration on the exterior stonework of the Hotel Solvay. Instead, it is the ironwork of the balconies that embellish the building, while their curving effect is continued in the panels of the main door and inside, with the banisters, handles, and light fixtures all designed by Horta. The latter fall from the ceiling like inverted creepers whose flowers are the shades for the electric light-

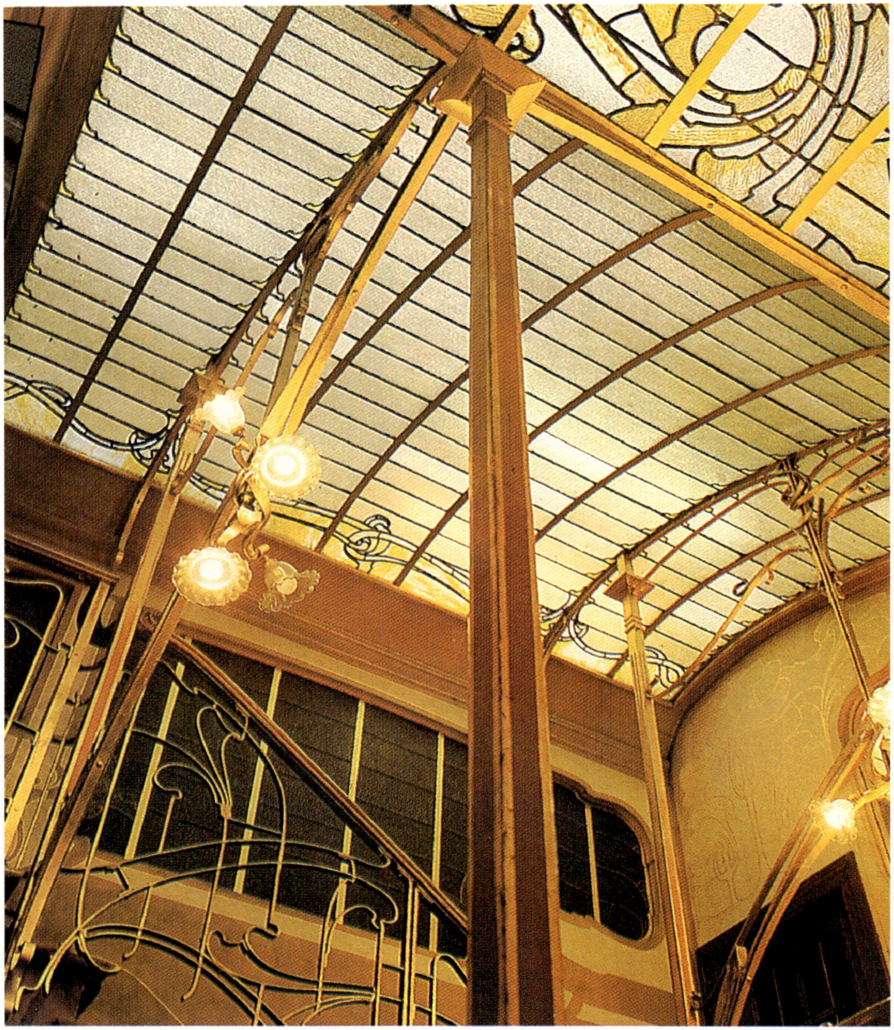

Above: Horta's airy interiors were achieved by the use of glass ceilings and splendid iron columns.

bulbs. Horta's attention to detail was such that all the fittings in the house, right down to the furniture and the locks for the doors, continued the organic, curvilinear theme.

Between 1898-1900, Horta designed his own studio and house, the Atelier and Maison Horta — now the Musée Horta in Brussels. At the same time, his structural and exterior design became increasingly adventurous, and his most ambitious work of this period is the now demolished Maison du Peuple of 1897. A vast social center, the large auditorium of this building was supported on a metal frame that was entirely exposed — a daring and modern device that was balanced by the smooth curves of the iron ribs, beams, and balconies. Built almost entirely of metal and glass, the facade was a sweeping concave of interlaced ironwork and massed elliptical windows.

Horta's style moderated progressively through the 1890s, and by 1905 he had virtually abandoned the Art Nouveau style. His furniture, however, is characterized by its abstract forms derived from nature and by its somewhat thin, spindly structural members. Horta also created the idea of built-in furniture, which became such a typical feature of the Art Nouveau interior that the French writer Edmond Goncourt invented for it the sobriquet "Yachting Style" — a banquette, for example, would run along one wall, turn a corner, and finish as a display case.

VAN DER VELDE

Another Belgian, Henry Van de Velde (1863-1957), first experimented with the Art Nouveau style through typography and book decoration. He progressed to interior decoration with the Hotel Otlet in 1894, and a year later built his own house at Bloemenwerf near Uccle, for which he designed all the furniture himself.

In marked contrast to Horta's flamboyant townhouse, it incorporated Art Nouveau lines into a rural idiom, with striped gables and shuttered windows. The furniture incorporated features derived from Arts and Crafts practices, and Horta's curvilinear style. Some pieces were made of oak, and some were simply constructed, rush-seated side chairs. But more elaborate pieces were decorated with carved ornament in a forceful Art Nouveau idiom.

Van de Velde went on to design interiors for Bing's Paris shop, office furniture for the German art critic Julius Meier-Graefe, as well as pieces for the German firm of Loffler, before moving to Germany, where he set up the Weimar School of Arts and Crafts which subsequently became the Bauhaus.

THE FRENCH MASTERS

In France, the official training college for architects, designers, and fine art students, the Ecole des Beaux-Arts, represented the old historicizing tendency at its coldest and most academic. The compulsion to imitate is encapsulated in Charles Garnier's Paris Opera House, built between 1861 and 1876, which is regarded by its more vehement critics as a worthless exercise in plagiarism. The theories of Viollet-le-Duc regarding the "honest" use of iron — leaving it exposed rather than hiding it with terracotta and other fake masonry — were to prove particularly influential to French architects of Art Nouveau. Of these, the greatest exponent was Hector Guimard (1867-1942). While Horta limited his plant-like decoration mostly to interiors, and even treated it with a certain coolness, Guimard allowed fantasy to dominate his work.

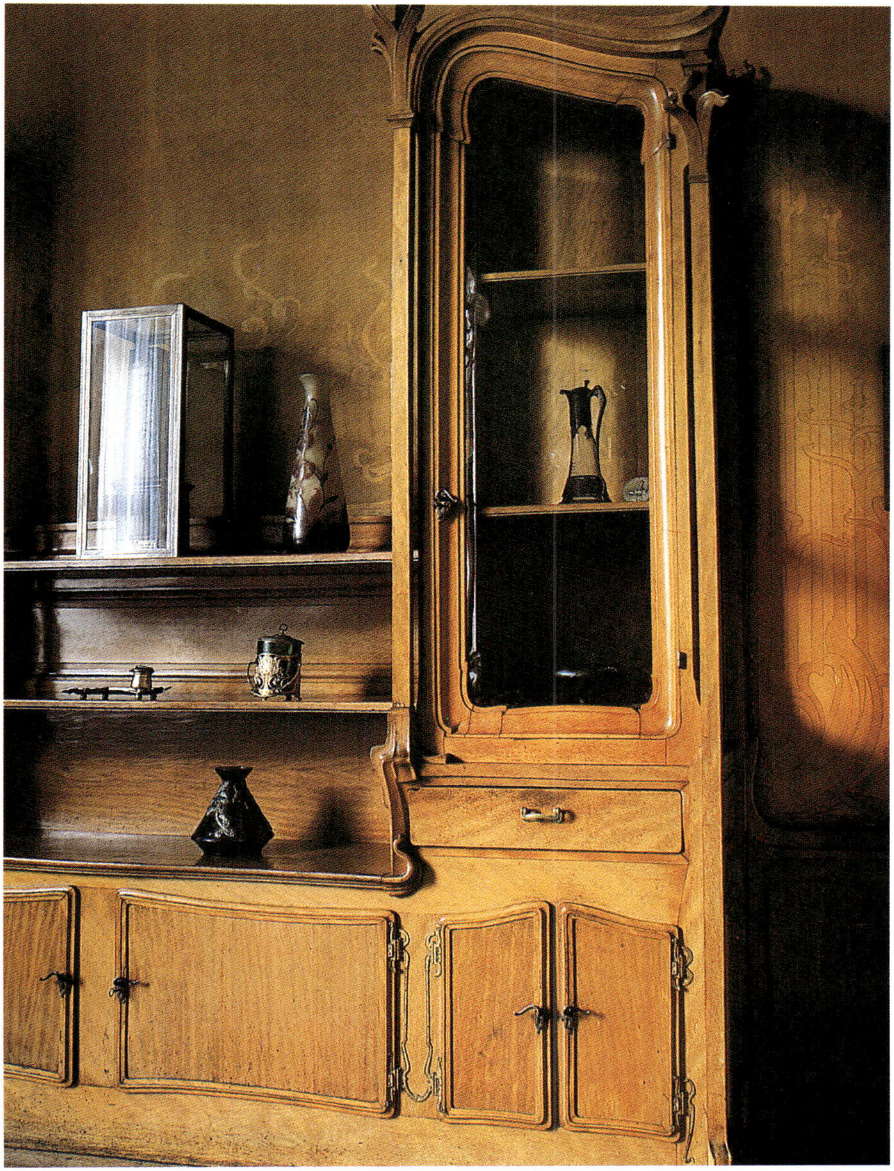

Right: A cabinet by Horta for his own house in Brussels.

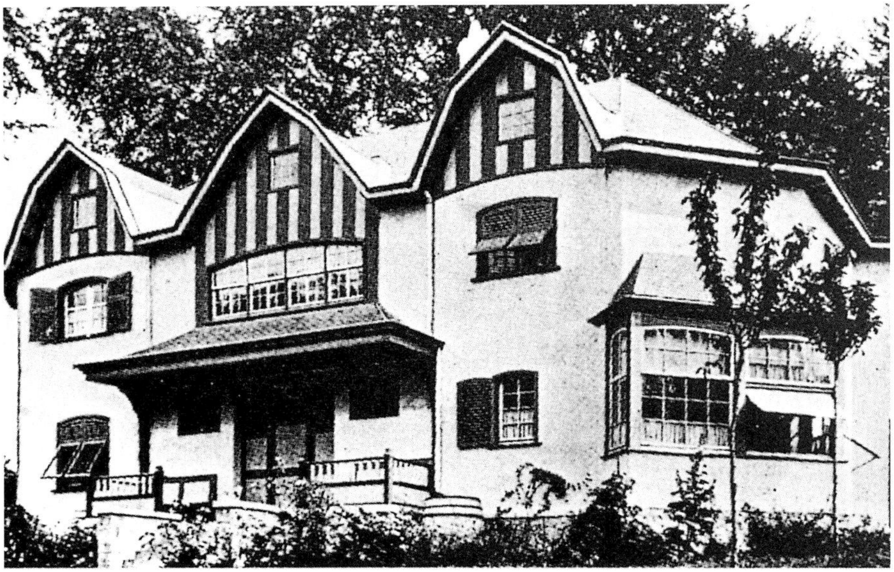

At times he seemed to be deliberately challenging the accepted limitations of his medium, whether it was iron, wood, or stone.

Based on the ideas of Viollet-le-Duc, but without using any form of overtly Gothic style, Guimard produced quaint, rustic chalets such as the Castel Henriette, with pitched roofs and a restless sense of movement in the forms of gables, doors, and windows. The informality of his out-of-town architecture is also well demonstrated in the Villa Henri Sauvage, built for the designer Louis Majorelle, outside Nancy. The house, with its high gables, assertive asymmetry, and details of chimney pots and balconies, approaches a fairytale whimsy. Only hinted at here, the verticality of Gothic was often very near the surface of French Art Nouveau architecture, as in the work of Charles Plumet who liked to use steeply-roofed dormer windows and pointed arches, or in the

Above: Bloemenwerf, Van de Velde's residence in Uccle, Brussels, 1895-96.

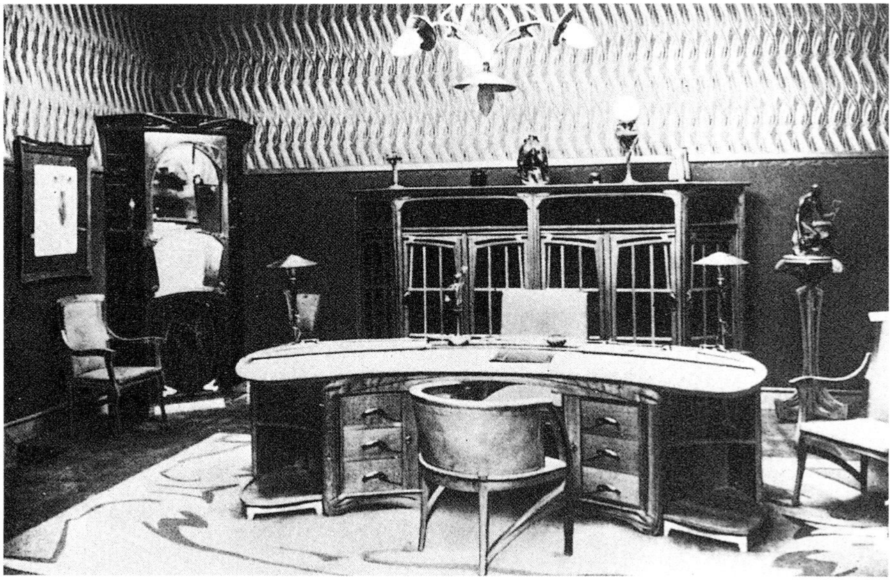

Right: Interior of the Paris shop, La Maison Moderne, designed by Van de Velde for Julius Meier-Graefe in 1898.

town house that jewelry designer René Lalique created for himself by adapting the vocabulary of French chateaux architecture.

If Guimard's country villas had a kind of rural quaintness, then his Parisian work is more forceful. In building his own house on the Avenue Mozart, he carved the stonework into the most dramatic forms, no longer simply just natural in origin, suggesting trees and plants, but exaggerated into a more artificial fantasy and elegance.

Guimard's concern for detail was equal to that of Horta. In this house as well as in his major apartment block, the Castel Beranger, finished in 1898, his designs in metalwork and stained glass are particularly notable. In these, he created purely abstract forms, emphasized by the terracotta panels decorating the entrance of the building, which ooze and flow across the walls as if they were still molten.

The furniture that Guimard designed for the Castel Beranger reflects his adherence to the principles of rational design taught by Viollet-le-Duc. Its construction, although visually flamboyant, is always justifiable in terms of strength and utility. The wave-like linear decoration carved in low relief is abstract, but clearly inspired by natural forms.

Style Métro

Unlike Horta, Guimard worked in cast as well as wrought iron, and it was the former that provided the basic material for the numerous Métro entrances and ticket offices he designed from 1900. Inspired works of fantasy, the entrances for the Paris Métro gave Guimard his most public prominence, and even resulted in a local variation of Art Nouveau, the Style Métro.

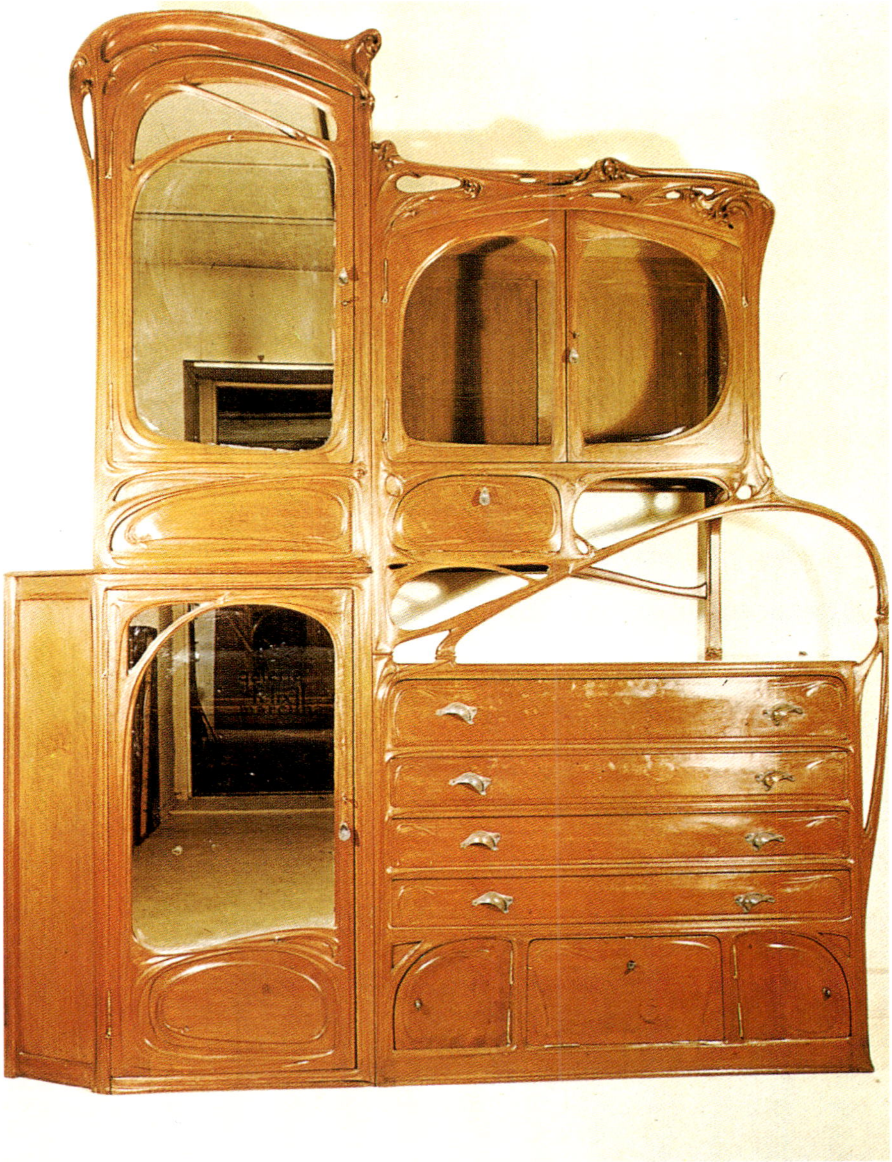

Right: A pearwood cabinet designed by architect Hector Guimard, ca 1900.

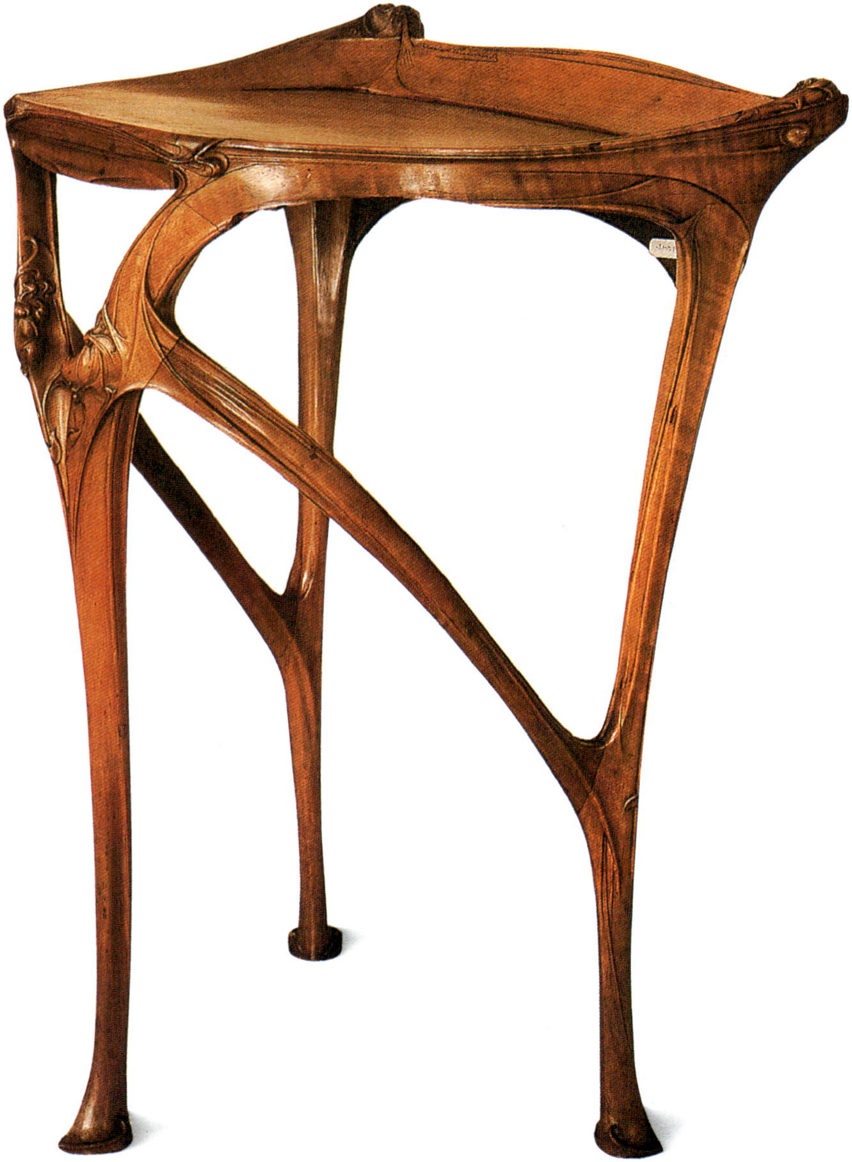

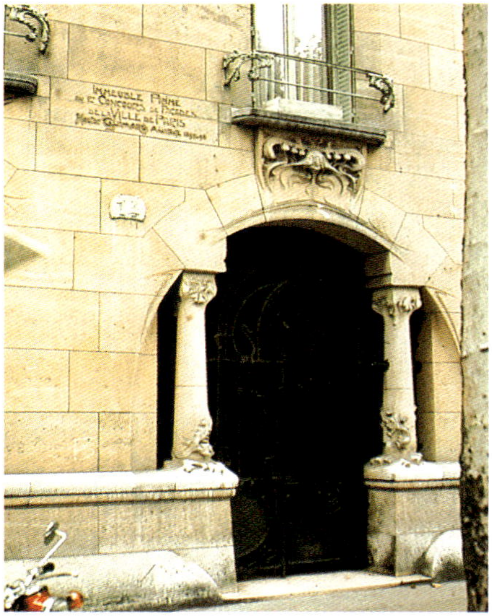

Above: The entrance to Guimard's Castel Beranger, where stone is carved to create the impression of a malleable material.

Left: An occasional table by Hector Guimard showing the same sinuous shapes as his entrances for the Paris Métro.

While the overhead structures of the Métro in the suburbs had been given a thoroughly conventional treatment — incidentally earning a decoration for their architect — Guimard was commissioned to produce shelters and archways for the entrances to the underground sections. These were so startlingly Art Nouveau that they provoked considerable controversy.

In keeping with the modernity of the new underground railway, Guimard restricted himself to the use of iron, enameled steel, and glass. The iron elements were produced in a large number of standard parts, making their assembly into a huge variety of arches and pavilions a tribute to Guimard's inventiveness and versatility. The treatment of the ironwork was typically curvilinear, with barely a straight line to be seen in the whole design. Lamps sprouted from metal branches and the word "Métropolitain" itself was carefully composed into harmonious Art Nouveau forms. Some of these amazing ironwork shapes, although organic in feel, had an angular tension strangely reminiscent of bones, and lacked the fluid grace of much of Guimard's interior designs, and of French Art Nouveau as a whole.

MÉTRO

While best known for the Métro entrances, Guimard's masterpiece was in fact the Humbert de Romans concert hall, built in 1898 and destroyed just seven years later as Art Nouveau quickly went out of fashion. Its crowning glory was a domed roof composed of steel ribs supporting a cupola pierced with windows of yellow stained glass.

ARCHITECTS: DESIGNERS AND CRAFTSMEN

Art Nouveau furniture bears all the variety of the regional styles of the movement. True to the spirit of Art Nouveau, few craftsmen specialized exclusively in furniture, and most had been trained in other arts or crafts. Most Art Nouveau furniture makers had been, or remained, architects, concerned to extend their control over the interiors of their buildings. The same tensions between ornament and structure, form and function were as evident in furniture-making as in architecture.

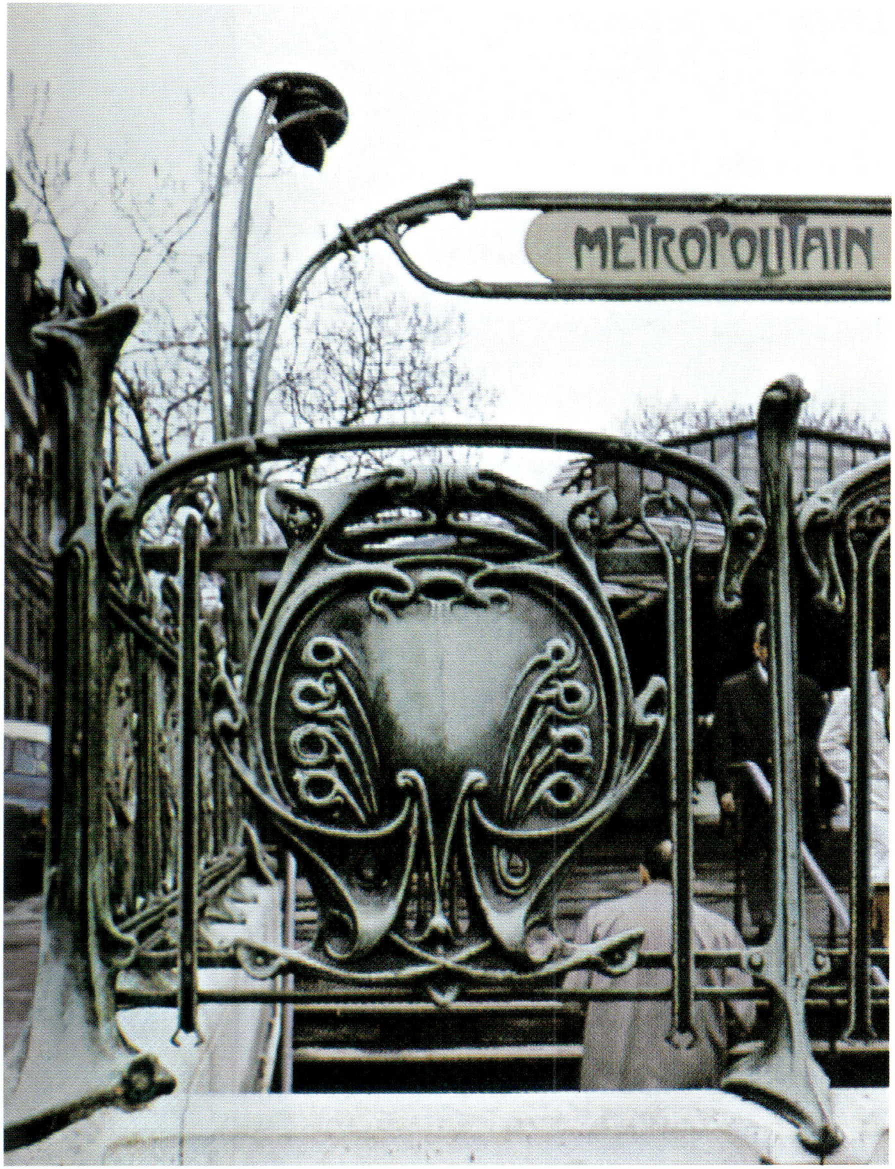

Right: The sculptural forms of the Paris Métro entrance by Hector Guimard, 1900.

Right: Side chair in walnut by Eugene Gaillard, ca 1900. The forms are inspired by nature, but are not in direct imitation of it.

Far right: Console table by Georges de Feure. The forms are pure Art Nouveau, but the gilding betrays an 18th-century inspiration.

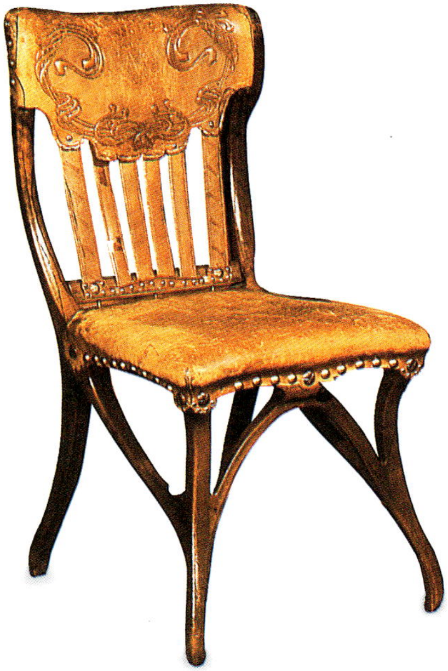

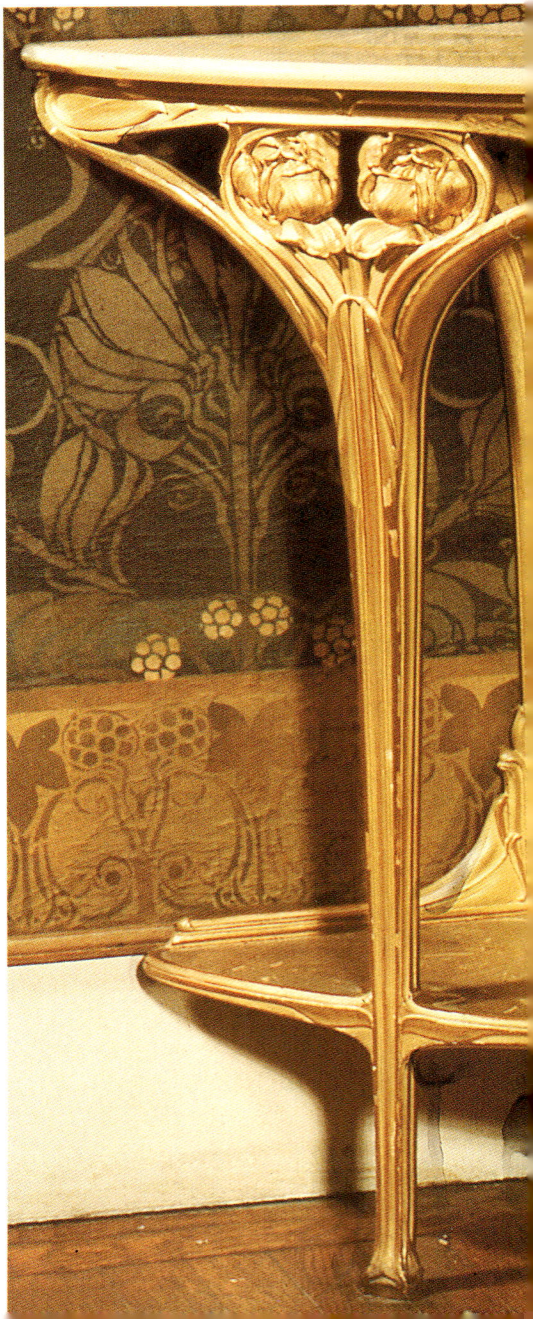

Les Six

In 1897, a group of artists calling themselves *Les Six* held an exhibition in Paris which included furniture designed by the architect Charles Plumet and the brothers Pierre and Tony Selmersheim. Their work was Art Nouveau in style, often with a strong flavor of the Rococo in its sinuous lines and gilt metal fittings which often alluded to natural forms. Another member of Les Six, the sculptor Alexandre Charpentier, (1856-1909) was a furniture designer who achieved his main effects by the treatment of wood, with gilt-bronze reliefs and color. The wood was carved to give it a molten, sometimes almost liquid, appearance; the relief panels, handles, and lock-plates represented female nudes; and the wood itself — usually hornbeam — was waxed to give it a yellow tint, somewhere between gold and honey.

Jean Dampt, another sculptor who belonged to the group, was a disciple of John Ruskin and an admirer of the English Arts and Crafts Movement. His furniture is Art Nouveau with Neo-Gothic touches.

Samuel Bing's Galerie de l'Art Nouveau

In Paris, Samuel Bing's Galerie de l'Art Nouveau was the principle showcase for Art Nouveau furniture, as for other crafts. Reflecting the nationalism fashionable at the time in France, Bing encouraged the craftsmen who worked for him to study the great French tradition of "grace, elegance, purity, and sound logic," and principally the refined poise of 18th-century work. Bing showed a great range of work, but he favored a nucleus of three furniture makers — Eugène Gaillard, Georges de Feure, and Edward Colonna.

Gaillard represents the functional side of Art Nouveau furniture; he studied the problem of function in design and produced pieces of an increasingly light, almost classic, simplicity. His chairs were concerned with comfort, had molded backs, sometimes padding at the shoulders, and leather or fabric-covered, coil-sprung upholstered seats.

The Paris World's Fair

Georges de Feure, a painter and poet, was something of a dandy. He was a keeper of grey-

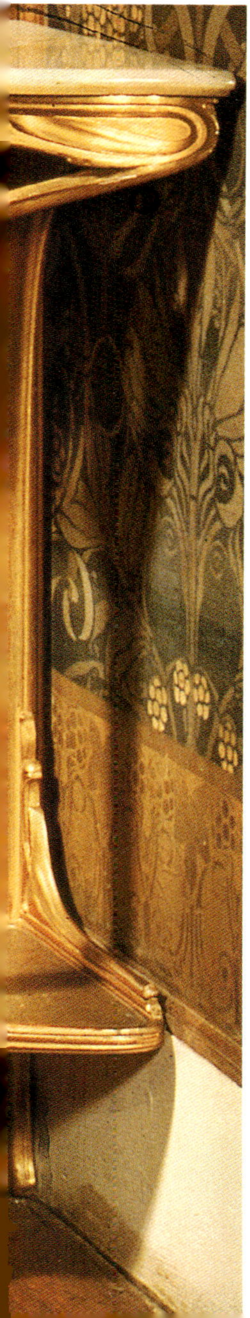

hounds, which he admired for their fine Art Nouveau lines. He brought more color and decoration to his furniture, with gilding and colored lacquer, as well as the kind of carved detail rare in Gaillard's work.

The third, Edward Eugène Colonna, had emigrated from Cologne to the United States where he worked under Tiffany, before returning to Europe to continue his career in Paris. Colonna's furniture, like de Feure's, was part of a larger output including porcelain and fabrics, and had a delicate, attenuated elegance also close to de Feure's style. When Bing was honored with his own pavilion devoted to Art Nouveau at the 1900 Paris World's Fair, these three designers were given the task of decorating and furnishing it.

THE NANCY SCHOOL

Aside from Guimard and his contemporaries working in Paris, France had a second school of Art Nouveau architects working at Nancy in Lorraine in eastern France, at a colony led by the designer Emile Gallé (1846-1904). Its outstanding achievement in architecture was the Villa Majorelle of 1900, which was designed chiefly by Henri Sauvage.

Nancy was historically the home of the glass-making industry, and Gallé, heir to a small ceramic and glassware business, became the leader of the Art Nouveau revival of the city's main industry. In the 1870s, Gallé had traveled to England and had been caught up in the growing enthusiasm for the decorative arts. He also studied the oriental collection at the Victoria and Albert Museum in London and, with his newfound knowledge of Chinese and Japanese techniques, he returned to Nancy.

Gallé also possessed a specialist's understanding of botany and entomology, his other amateur passions. Thus he was equipped with a very detailed first-hand knowledge of leaf, flower, and insect forms, which, when combined with the decorative, abstract tendency of the Japanese, combined to form the Art Nouveau blend. A third ingredient, Rococo, was already evident in Nancy, which had many fine houses and decorations in that style.

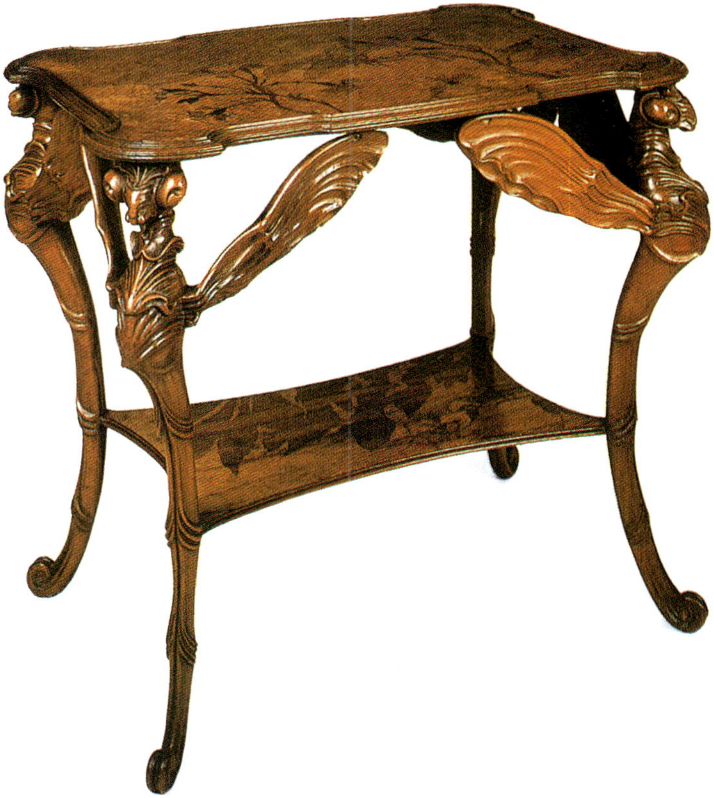

Above: A rare use of fantastic grotesques by Emile Gallé. Characteristically, the whole table leg is given over to their form.

GALLÉ AND FURNITURE DESIGN

In 1884, after some years designing in glass and ceramics, Gallé started designing and producing furniture. At first his designs were somewhat ponderous, but were invariably enlivened

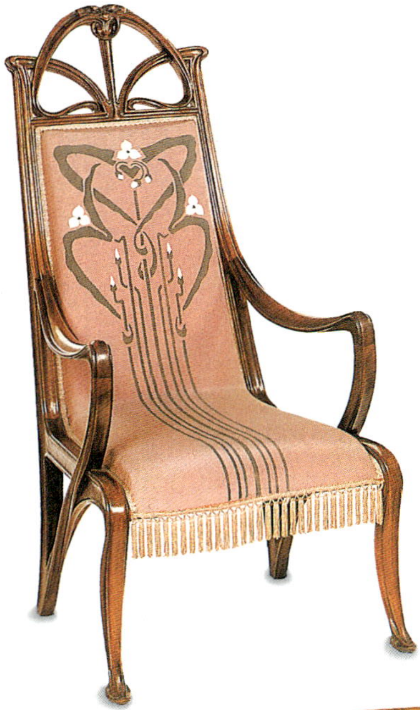

with vivid natural details. Success came at the 1889 Paris International Exhibition, where Gallé was acknowledged as an innovator who had created a new style in reaction to the unimaginative revivalism of most contemporary French furniture.

Gallé's work became increasingly lighter and more ornate. Natural forms were not restricted to details — whole arms, legs, and backs were carved in plant or insect forms, curving and twisting to animate the whole and seeming to defy the nature of the wood itself. Although stylized, those graceful shapes were always clearly identifiable plants of species known to Gallé. His favorites were local plants including cow-parsley, water lilies, orchids, and irises, though he also used exotics, such as bamboo.

Gallé preferred soft woods, of which he had a very thorough knowledge, to facilitate the creation of his effects, which included his remarkable revival of the art of marquetry. Most of the surfaces of Gallé's furniture became fields for the most intricate inlays, featuring plants, insects, or landscapes in what could become an overloading of effects. So fine was the craftsmanship though, that Gallé's own willowy signature could be reproduced on his pieces.

Left: An armchair, ca *1900, by the Nancy cabinet maker, Louis Majorelle.*

Below: A carved fruit wood and marquetry tray, ca *1900, by Emile Gallé.*

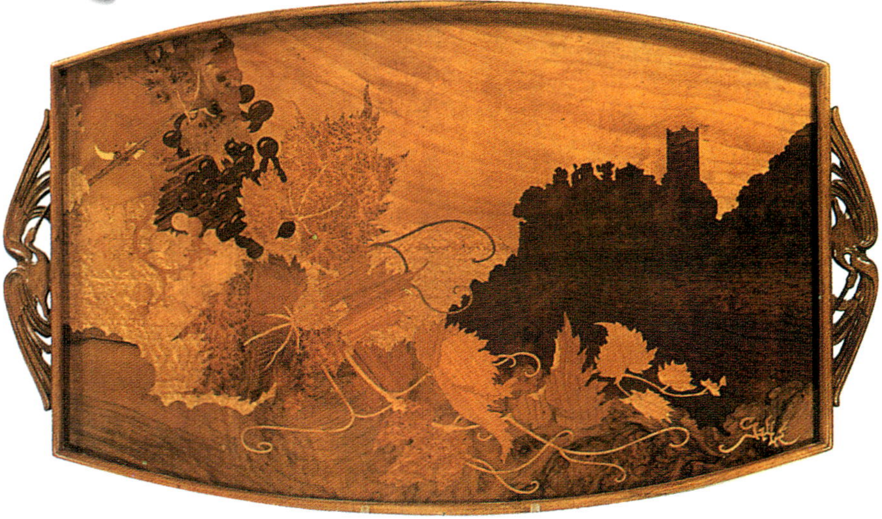

MARQUETRY

Gallé's mastery of marquetry opened the way to the expression of poetry and literary themes in his furniture. He liked to include suitable quotations and, as a mark of the fusion of the arts and crafts in Art Nouveau, he gave some pieces names in the manner of paintings or music. A console he created became *Les Parfums d'Autrefois* (Perfumes of the Past) and his last masterpiece, a bed he designed while dying of leukemia, *Aube et Crépuscule* (Dawn and Dusk). This latter piece is evidence of Gallé's increasing restraint in his late style, simplifying forms and eradicating much of the over-intricacy of his earlier work, as well as being a tour-de-force of marquetry. The dark shadows of dusk are enveloped in the drooping wings of the fantastic insect on the headboard, while at the foot of the bed, the rising wings of another huge insect are depicted in lighter woods and mother-of-pearl.

Second to Gallé at the Nancy School was Louis Majorelle (1859-1929). Majorelle began designing in an 18th-century style until Gallé persuaded him to inject more vitality and naturalism into his work. His pieces are, nevertheless, rather more solid than Gallé's, partly because he favored the use of harder, more exotic woods. The more sculptural elements in Majorelle's pieces were in the ornamentation, which, still partly inspired by the baroque and Rococo, he added in gilt, copper, or bronze. Majorelle equalled Gallé in his use of marquetry, but generally his style differs in its smoother lines. Majorelle was consequently able to make a successful transition to the simpler style of the 1920s.

CABINET MAKERS

Other cabinet makers in Nancy worked for either Gallé or Majorelle, and occasionally both. Victor Prouve (1858-1943) specialized in marquetry work for both masters as well as designing his own pieces. Eugène Vallin (1856-1925) worked for Gallé and produced pieces of far greater weight than those of his master. Vallin's work eschews intricate natural detail and instead concentrates on broad, swaying, linear rhythms anticipating the end of his career when he took up architecture and used cast concrete for his effects. Jacques Gruber produced designs for Majorelle and was also Professor of Decorative Arts at the Ecole des Beaux-Arts in Nancy. His furniture shares the same flowing forms as that of Vallin, and is removed from Gallé's Rococo touches.

Through a range of Art Nouveau furniture, it is possible to see designs stripped down to the most elegant bare curves, as well as those which are adorned with carving, brass, gilt, or ivory. A similar contrast exists between designs that are obviously designed for comfort and utility, and those that come close to sacrificing both these concerns for the sake of effect. What gives coherence to this variety are the irrepressible curves and sense of idiosyncratic inventiveness. Occasionally

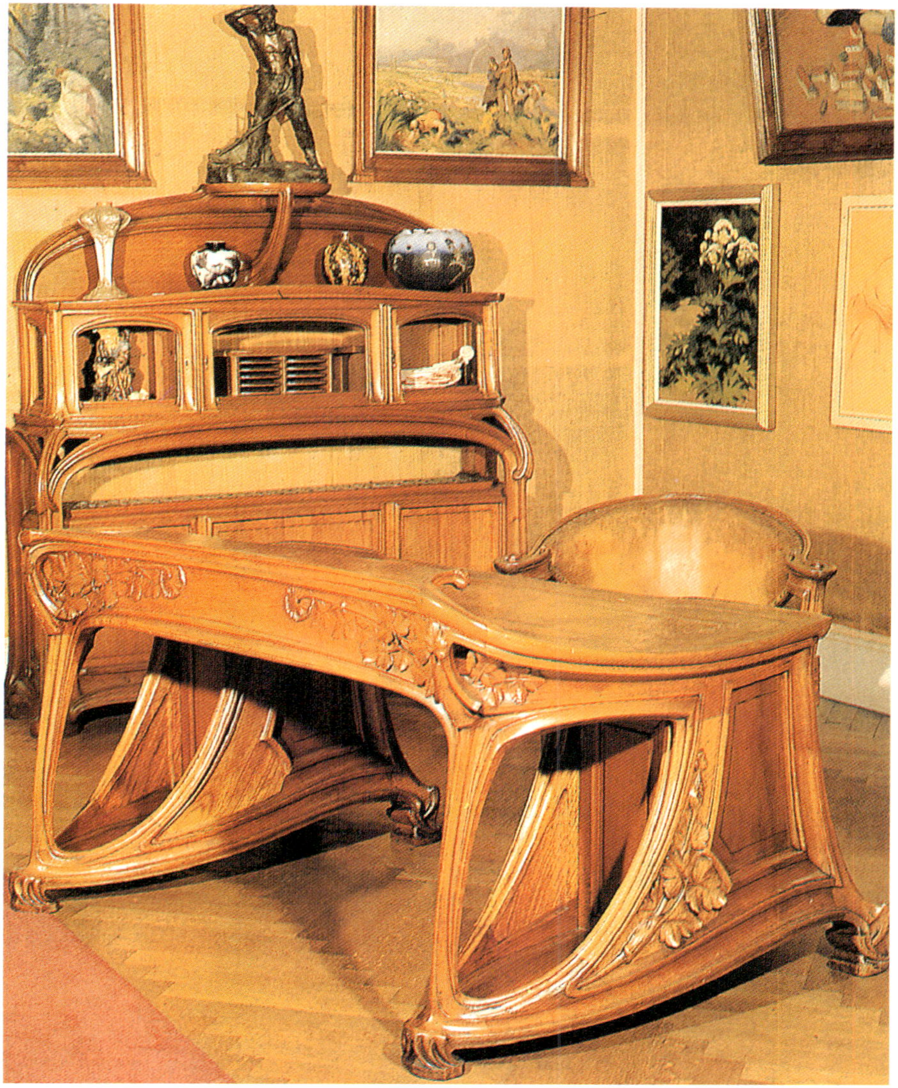

Above: Office suite by Eugene Vallin in exaggerated Art Nouveau style.

these had to be curbed especially when designs were intended for mass production. The attention to detail and the manipulation of the materials generally meant that Art Nouveau furniture was unsuitable for any mode of production other than that of the individual craftsman. As in the Arts and Crafts Movement in England, the Art Nouveau designer was forced to accept the fact that his work was primarily an expensive luxury for an élite. Factory-produced Art Nouveau furniture inevitably lost much of its natural vitality and was a coarsened version of the hand-worked equivalent. Art Nouveau architects might have been eager to embrace the new materials of iron and steel, but when they turned to designing furniture their style was fundamentally unsuitable for modern production techniques.

Below: Furniture designed as part of a unified environment by the Parisian Georges Hoentschel.

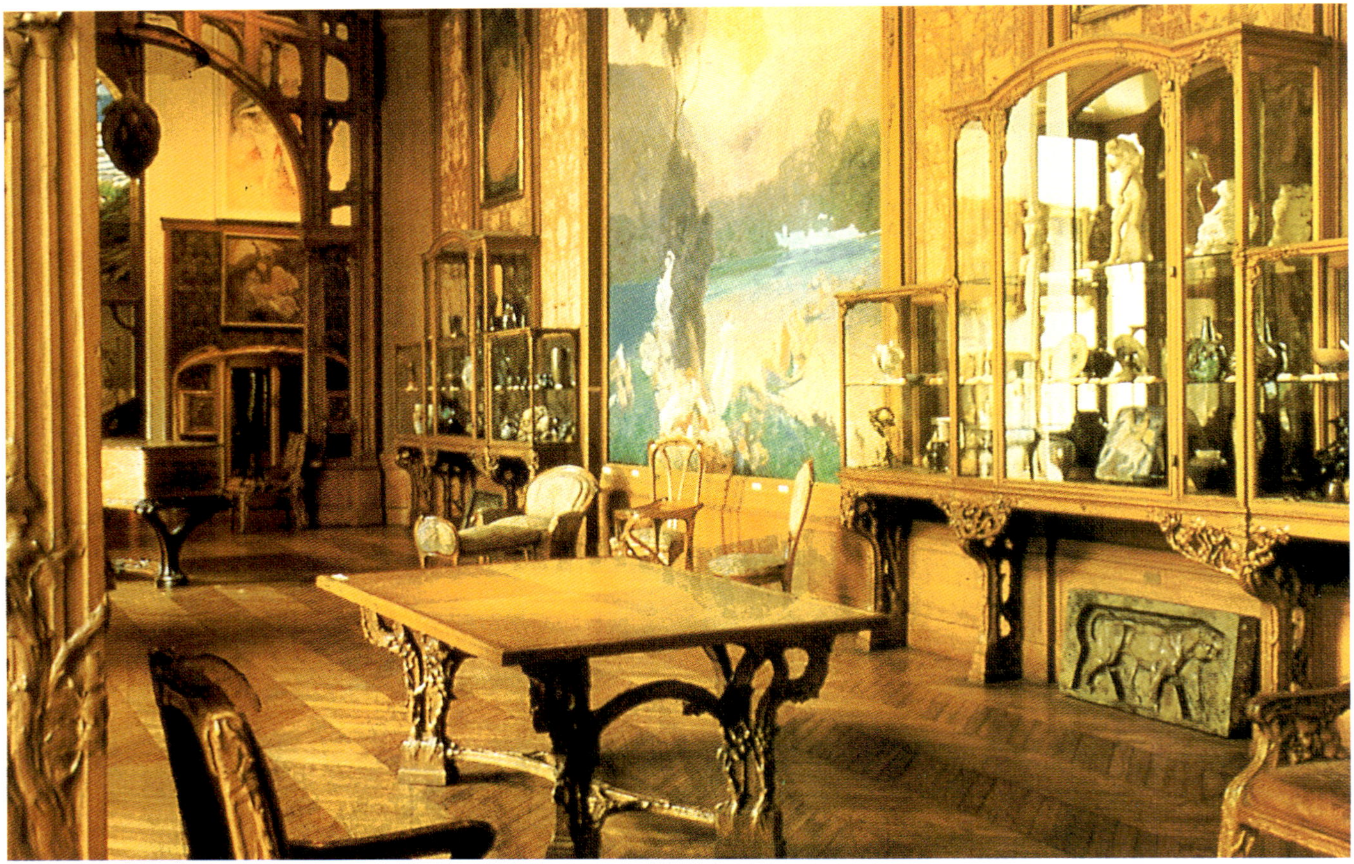

BRITAIN, AUSTRIA, AND GERMANY

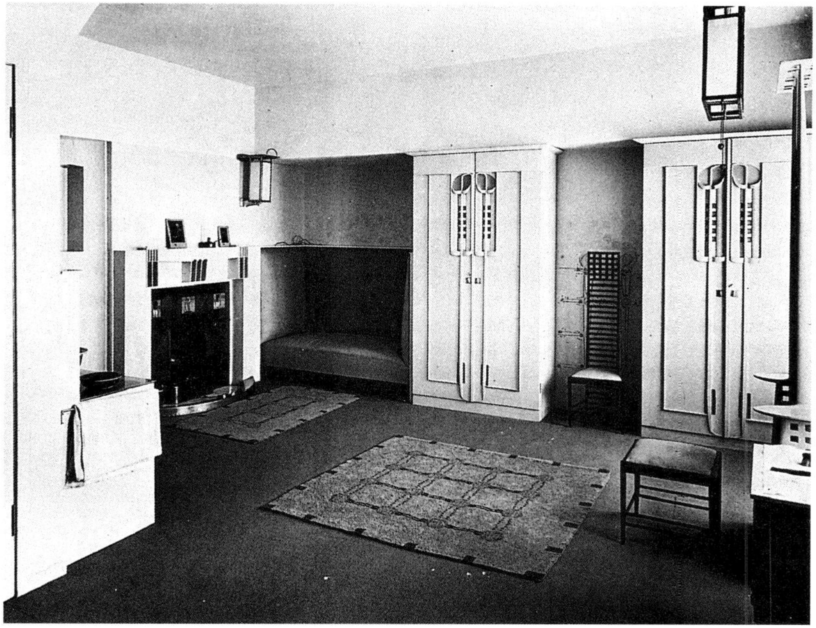

Unlike the French and the Belgians, the architects and designers of Britain, Austria, and Germany used the languid curves of Art Nouveau with great austerity, and in harmonious counterpoint to grid-like patterns of horizontal and vertical lines.

Overleaf: Interior of Hill House, Dunbartonshire, Scotland designed by C.R. Mackintosh, 1904.

Below: Oak side chairs by E.W. Pugin, ca 1870, conform to the principles of simplicity and clear construction advocated by his father, the architect and critic A.W.N. Pugin.

THE INFLUENCE OF THE ARTS AND CRAFTS MOVEMENT

From the 1860s onwards, Britain rose to a prominent position in European decorative arts. The founding of Morris, Marshall, Faulkner & Co. in 1861 had been the beginning of a new movement in reaction to the allegorical flourishes of design in the 1851 Great Exhibition. The Arts and Crafts Movement, absorbing the tenets of the Gothic Revival, was committed to honest and simple design for domestic use. Inspired by the teachings of John Ruskin and Pre-Raphaelite artists, the majority of the designers were professional architects. It was also an intellectual movement, which successfully captured the imagination of the time.

Arts and Crafts furniture laid stress on the honest presentation of materials, structure, and production, taking as its highest principle

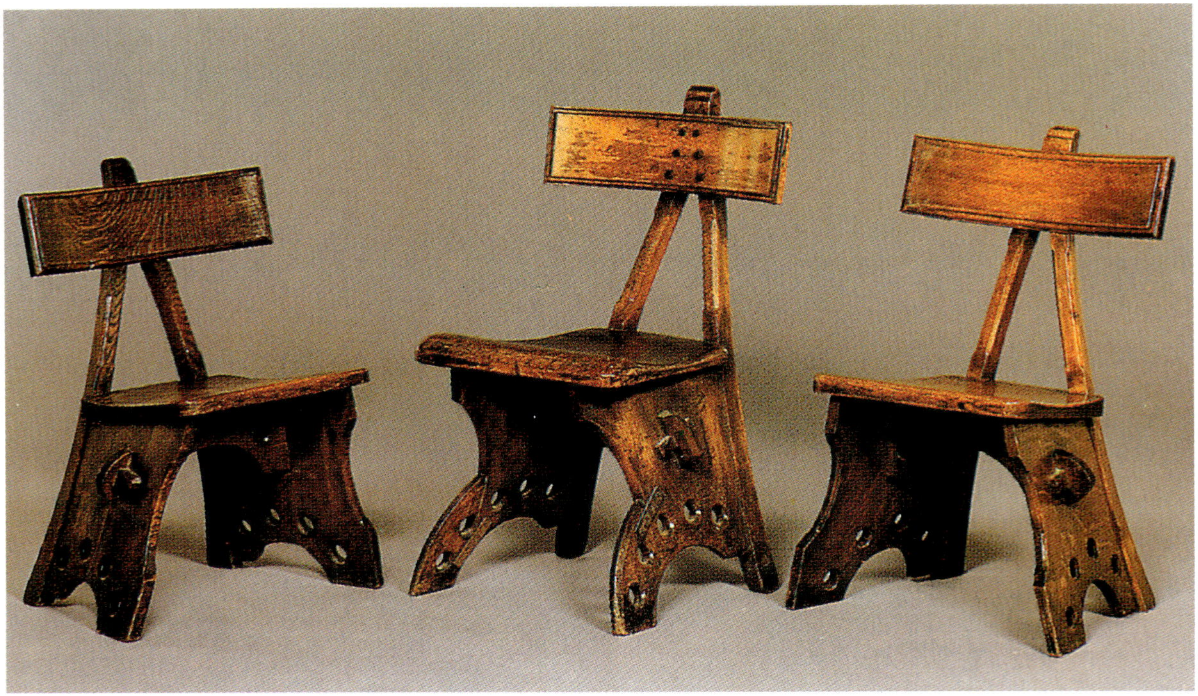

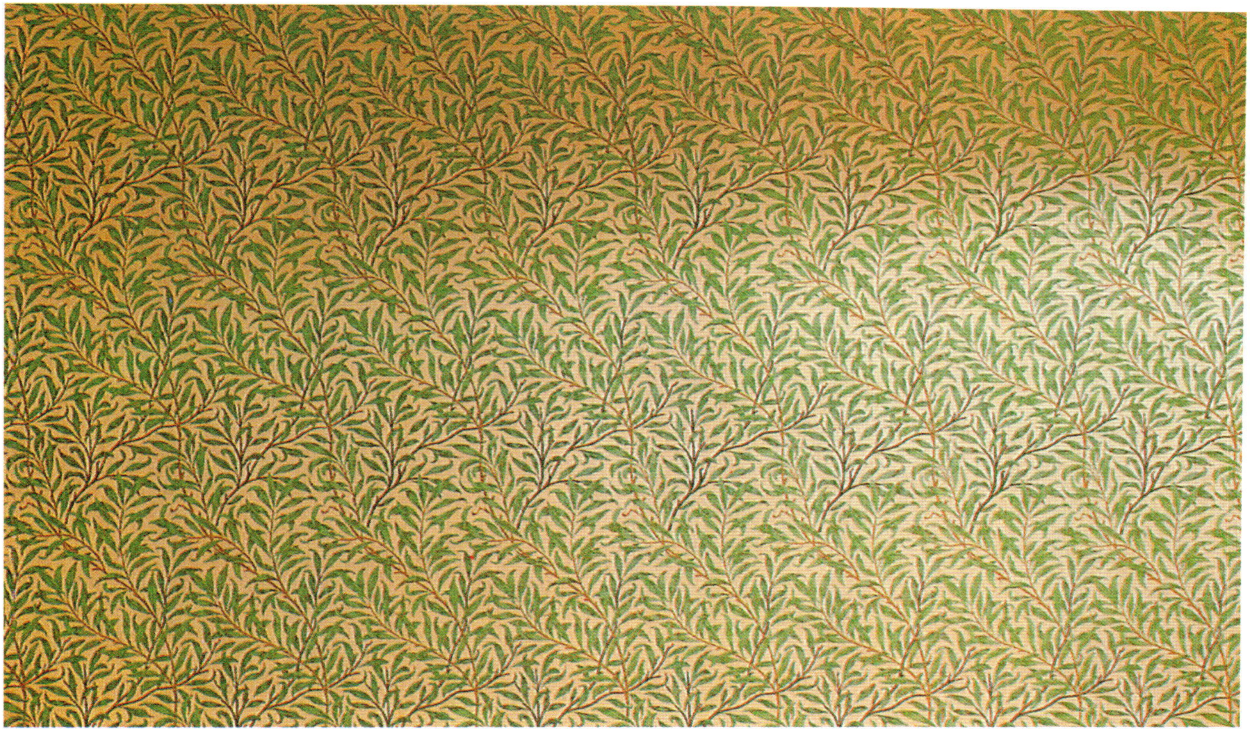

Ruskin and William Morris's belief that only the highest good could come from man transforming his own environment with his own hands. The machine was despised, as was any decorative idiom which slavishly copied past styles. Handicrafts flourished, especially in the fields of embroidery, metalwork, stained glass, and art pottery.

All over the country, handicraft guilds were founded to involve both the working man and the hitherto unemployable young lady in the practical creation of their own environment. The most influential of these guilds were the Century Guild founded in 1882 by Arthur Mackmurdo, the Art Workers' Guild founded in 1884, Charles Robert Ashbee's Guild of Handicraft formed in 1888, the same year as the Arts and Crafts Exhibition Society, and, in 1900, the Birmingham Guild of Handicraft.

SPREADING THE STYLE

The original impetus of the Arts and Crafts ideals gave rise to considerable activity which was chronicled in the pages of *The Studio*. The magazine was frankly propagandist for the movement, and through its pages the inspiration of British design was made known in Europe and the United States. In 1898, the

Above: "Willow Boughs" wallpaper, designed by William Morris in 1887. Such a wallpaper emphasizes the flatness of the wall and avoids a false illusion of depth.

Right: The Honeysuckle Room at Wightwick Manor. Carpets, wallpaper, tiles, and furniture by Morris & Co.

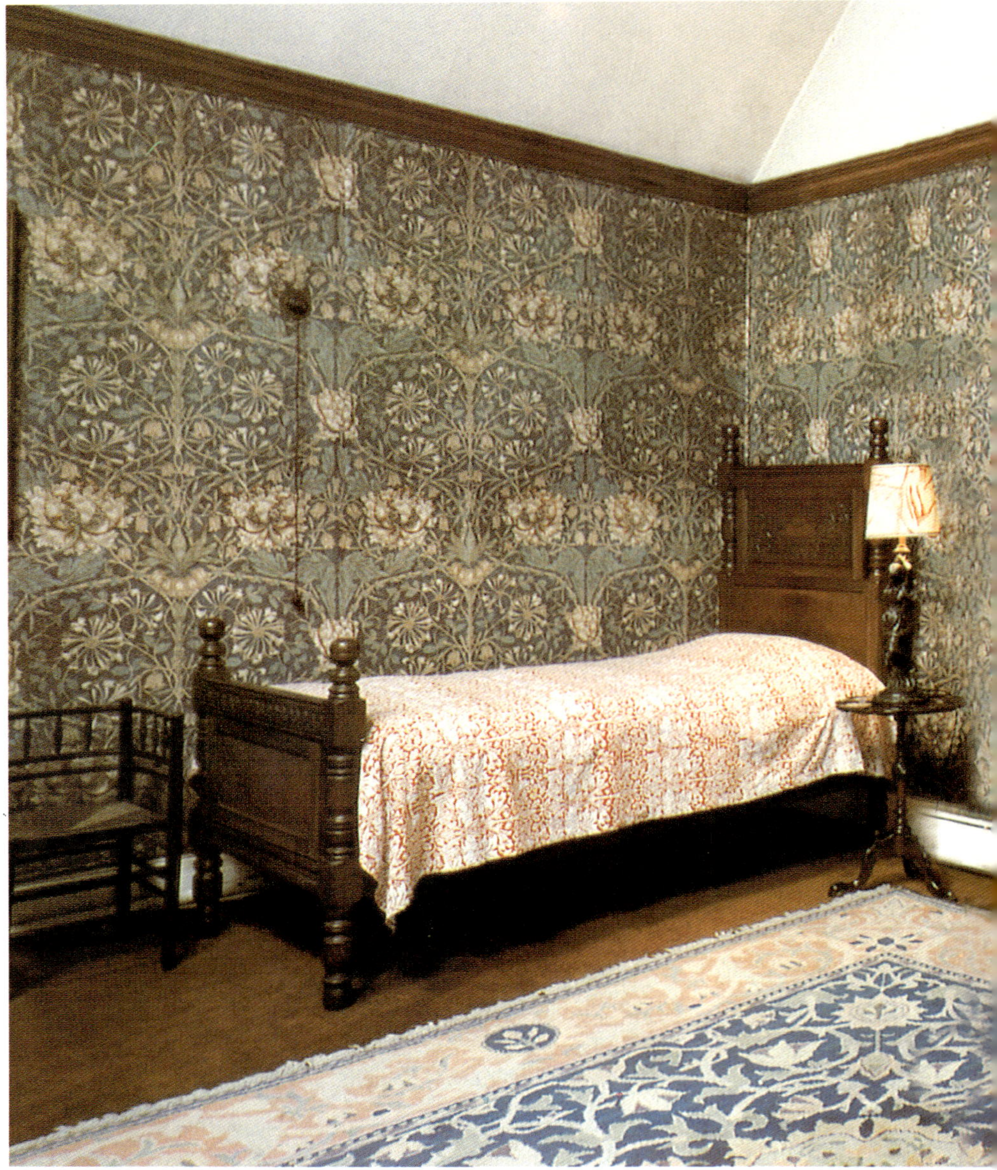

Grand-Duke of Hesse commissioned designs from Charles Ashbee and M.H. Baillie Scott for furniture, made by the Guild of Handicraft, for the artist's colony set up at Darmstadt. Britain's lead was beginning to take effect abroad.

Yet despite leading the way in the decorative arts, Britain, however, was to strongly oppose any new influences such as Art Nouveau, and remained firm in her adherence to the simple, functional lines and country morals of the Arts and Crafts Movement. Innovative artists such as the Glasgow Four, who were acclaimed abroad, were to be virtually ignored by both critics and public alike at home.

Charles Rennie Mackintosh and the Glasgow Four

The Glasgow Four were Charles Rennie Mackintosh, his wife Margaret, Herbert MacNair, and Frances Macdonald (Margaret's sister, who married MacNair), all of whom studied at the Glasgow School of Art in the early 1890s.

Mackintosh (1868-1928), an architect, had produced his first furniture designs in the early 1890s, and this early work already shows an avoidance of reference to period design and a sparseness in the absence of applied decoration. Mackintosh's designs were dictated by the problems of the arrangement of interior space and he laid stress on vertical elements, his high-backed chairs giving a variety of height within a room, despite the acknowledged criticism of their impracticality.

In 1896, the Four were invited to send fur-

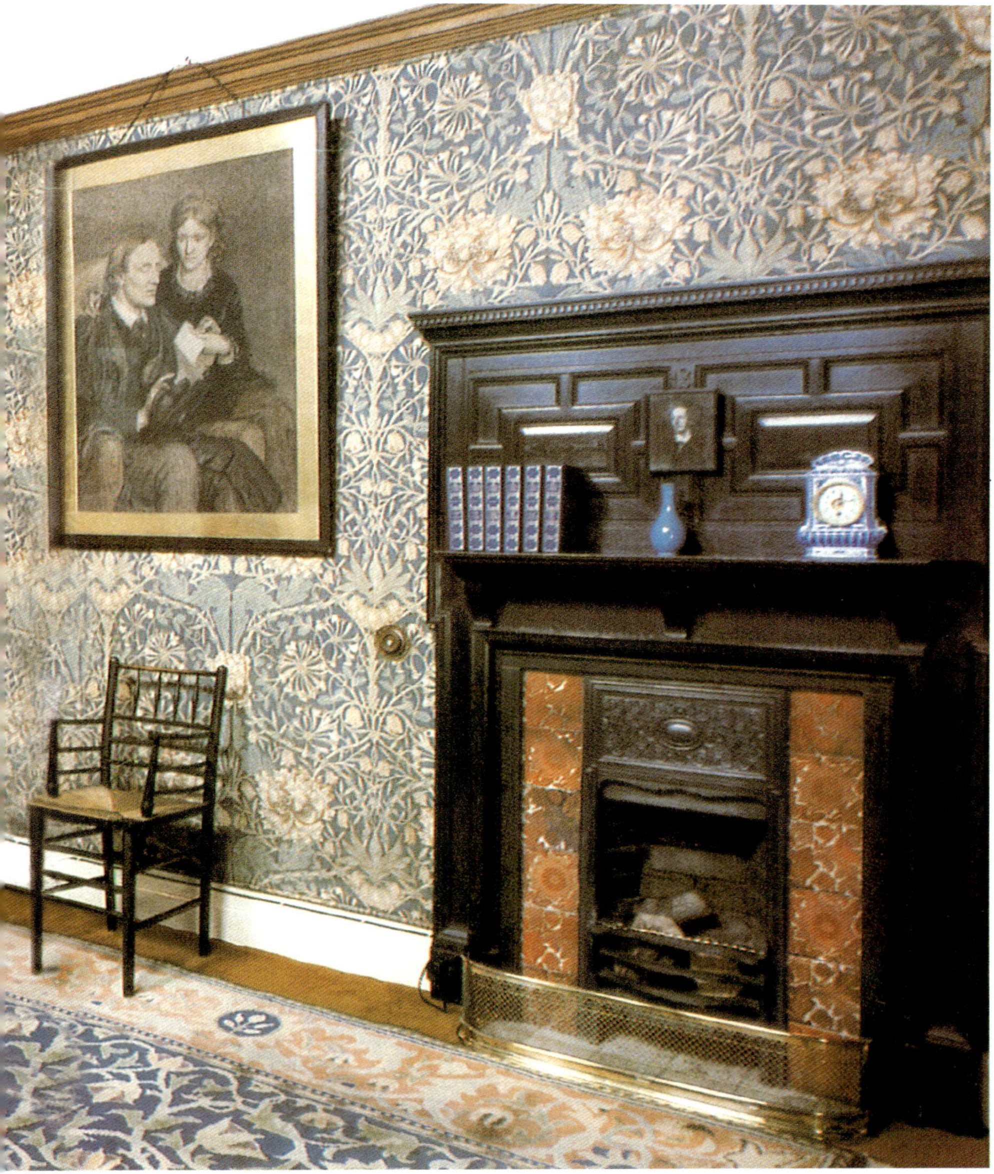

niture, craftwork, and posters to the Arts and Crafts Exhibition Society show where their work, especially the posters, met with a puzzled and shocked reaction. The editor of *The Studio,* however, made a visit to Glasgow and in 1897 published two appreciative articles on their work. This was quickly picked up in Europe, and the following year, the Darmstadt magazine, *Dekorative Kunst,* contained an article on the Glasgow School.

MACKINTOSH AND VIENNA

Earlier in 1895, work from Glasgow Art School had been sent to the Liège Exhibition where it was received enthusiastically, although Mackintosh himself never favored the Belgian and French excesses of Art Nouveau. It was in Vienna that he found like minds.

In 1900, he visited the 8th Vienna Secessionist Exhibition, which was devoted to the work of foreign designers, including Mackintosh and his wife, Charles Ashbee, and Henry Van de Velde. There he met Josef Hoffmann with whom he was to remain in contact for many years, warmly supporting the decision to found the *Wiener Werkstätte*. Mackintosh received two commissions in Vienna, including the design of a music room for the banker Fritz Waerndorfer, who was to finance the Werkstätte, where a dining room was commissioned from Hoffmann. Mackintosh also exhibited successfully at the Turin Exhibition of 1902. It must have been a sore disappointment to Mackintosh to find his work received so sympathetically abroad while being almost ignored in Britain. Despite being a very influential figure in late European Art Nouveau, Mackintosh's architectural career is largely confined to the Glasgow School of Art, the series of tea rooms designed for Miss Cranston, and a handful of private

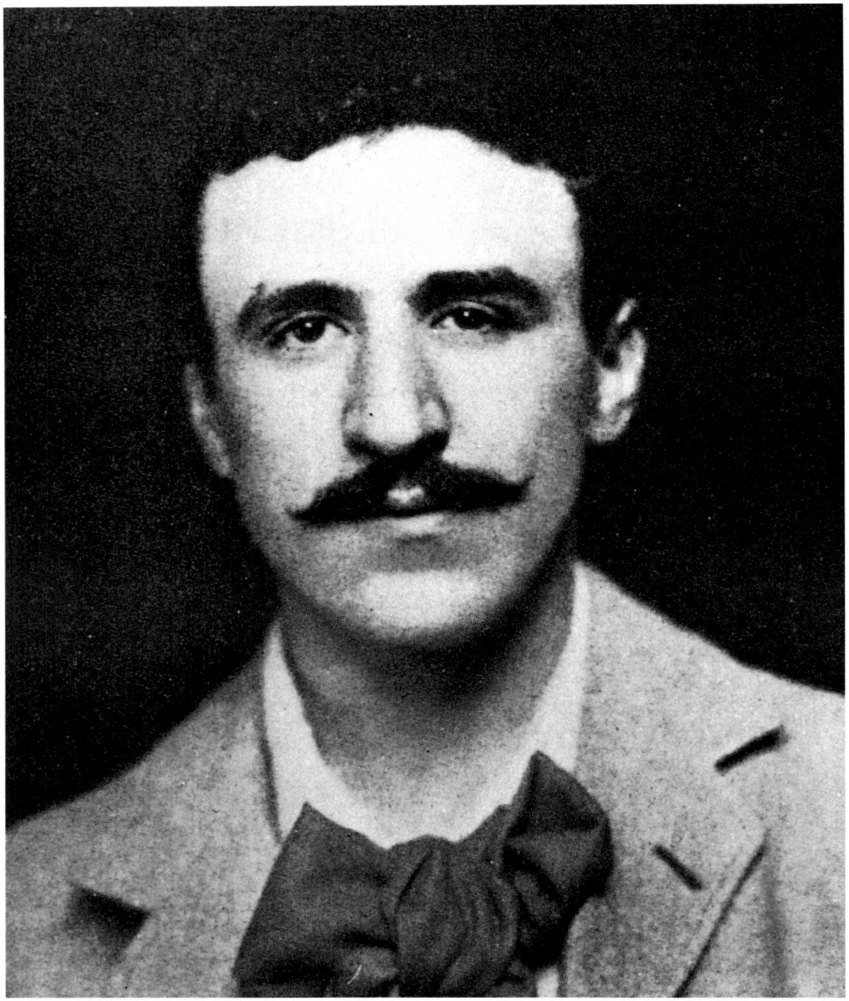

Above: Scottish architect and designer, Charles Rennie Mackintosh (1868-1928).

houses for Scottish patrons, notably Hill House, Helensburgh (1902), built for the publisher Walter Blackie. These projects, where he designed almost every element — from the cutlery for the tea rooms to the rugs for Hill House — demonstrate his remarkable creation of a distinctive style totally removed from the influences of the preceding century.

MACKINTOSH'S ARCHITECTURE

Mackintosh's first important commission came in 1896, when he won a competition to design a new School of Art for the city of Glasgow. At first sight, the building that he constructed over 12 years bears little resemblance to Art Nouveau works elsewhere.

The asymmetry and the hint of the turrets evident in the front entrance refer to Mackintosh's early enthusiasm for the Gothic revival. In the starkly-mullioned, huge windows of the north-facing studios and the apparent simplicity of the whole, there is evidence of the uniquely British Arts and Crafts architects with their Tudor references.

IRONWORK

Yet Mackintosh is a figure of European significance in Art Nouveau, and his importance extends beyond the local. The curving stonework in the center of the main facade, and the stylized elongation of the windows of the west front display the refinement of Art Nouveau, and the connection becomes stronger in the details of the building. The carving over the entrance has the curving, Celtic lines of Art Nouveau graphics and metalwork of the Glasgow school, and the ironwork indulges in more abstract curves. This is used to contrast with the harder lines of the stone background in a way reminiscent of Horta's Hotel Solvay. The ironwork, resembling buttresses against the main studio window, is rounded off in intricate, loosely-bound knots of metalwork, almost like enlarged pieces of jewelry. The strange decorations on the railings at street level, and the bundles of arrow shapes supporting patterned dishes, derive from Japanese heraldry, which emphasize the wide internationalism of Mackintosh's references and his affinity with the orientally-inspired refinements of Art Nouveau.

The simplicity and elegance of Japan are again recalled in the interior of the school's library, completely designed by Mackintosh. He was reluctant to experiment with structural ironwork, so wood is used throughout to support the galleries. Mackintosh's fascination with beams and joints was a typically eclectic Art Nouveau fusion of his Japanese and Gothic interests, and is seen again in the open rafters elsewhere in the building. The use of dark stained wood also gives the library an oriental sobriety. By opening out a continuous, airy central space, Mackintosh created slender, vertical beams, which are echoed in the delicate light fittings. It was a variation on one of the great themes of Art Nouveau architecture — the open, light, and spacious interior, in this case lit by the long, triple bay windows of the west facade.

MACKINTOSH'S FURNITURE

In furniture, as in architecture, it was Mackintosh's work that dominated British Art Nouveau. Mackintosh's furniture is intended to be seen as part of a whole interior design with secondary work often produced by other artists and designers. Mackintosh's designs show a virtuosity that is breathtaking, if sometimes self-indulgent. It is easy to understand why his furniture was not well received in England, where it was regarded with suspicion for being too stylised or "aesthetic."

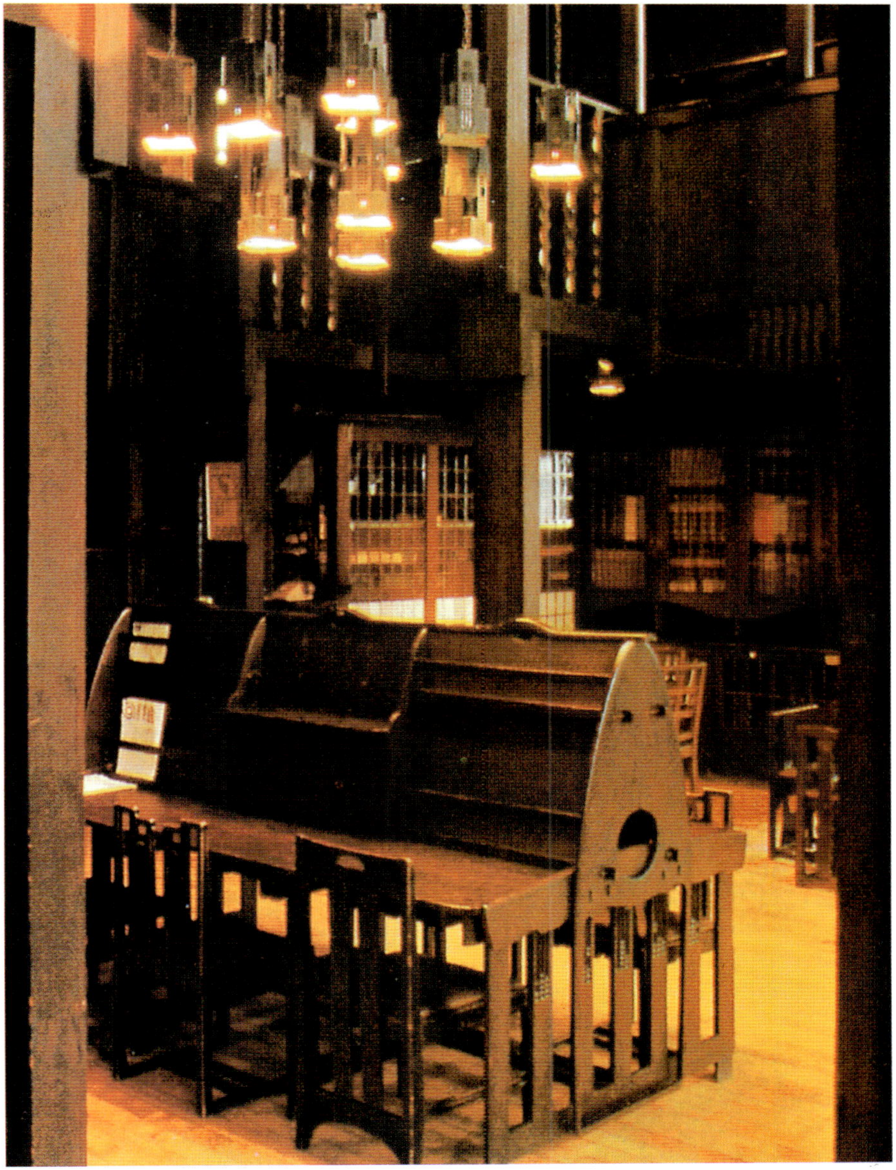

Right: Library, Glasgow School of Art, Glasgow, Scotland, 1877–99, 1907–09, Charles Rennie Mackintosh.

Right: Wall panels and mirrors with stylized plant motifs for Miss Cranston's Willow Tea Rooms in Glasgow, designed by C.R. Mackintosh in 1904. For this project, Mackintosh designed almost every element, from the cutlery to the furniture.

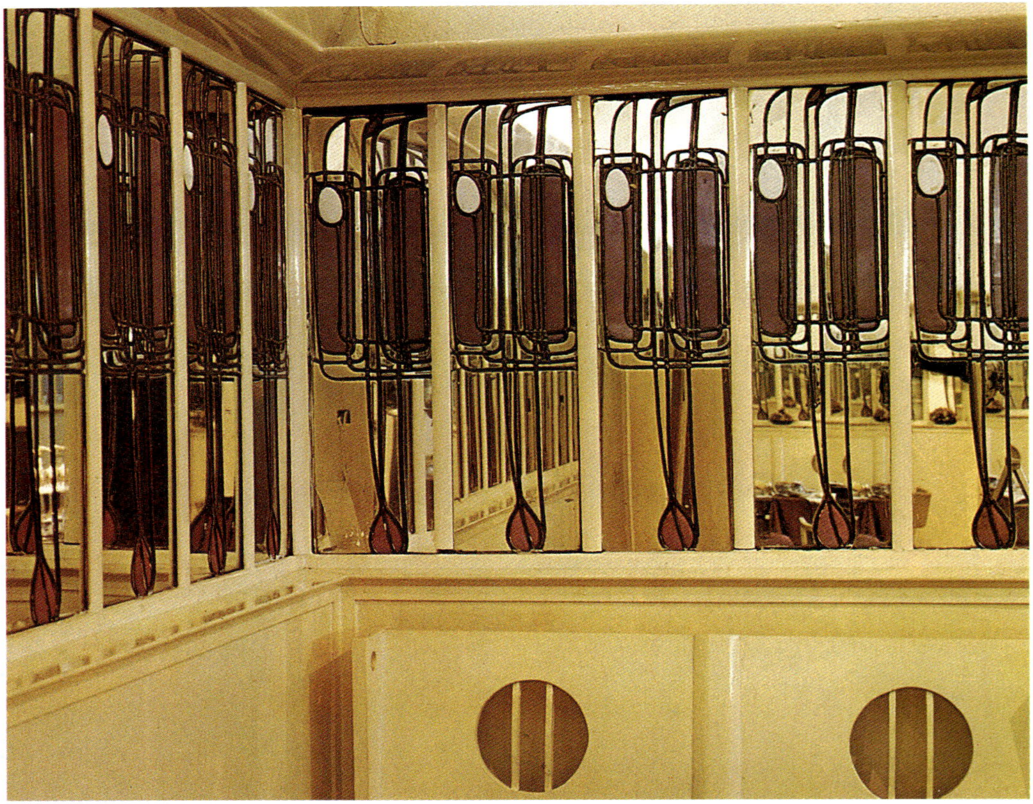

Simplicity was sacrificed to sophistication, tradition was flouted, and scant respect was shown for materials. As in his architecture, he concentrated upon the extremely elegant, exaggerated verticals, particularly in the backs of his chairs which could be exceptionally tall and slender. These were cut into ovals, grids, or ladderbacks that descended down to the floor. Curves might occur, but with Mackintosh, they were primarily used to underline the rigidity of the verticals.

Furniture was made from various woods, including oak, cypress, pine, and mahogany, which were rarely left untreated. Mackintosh felt uncomfortable with the natural grain of the wood and attempted to minimize it by deep, dark staining and eventually by lacquering or ebonizing it into matt black. He explored a converse neutrality by painting other pieces white to act as a suitable background for lilac and silver harmonies. On lighter furniture, Mackintosh stenciled stylized designs.

While he received great recognition in Germany and Austria (especially among the architects of the Secession) Mackintosh's greatest achievement may have been to point a path forward from the decorative excesses of Art Nouveau, which found itself fading in popularity after the first five years of the 1900s and was laid to rest by the horrors of World War I.

GERMANY AND JUGENDSTIL

Jugendstil (Youth Style) was the German term for Art Nouveau. In Munich during the 1890s, a number of architects, painters, and sculp-

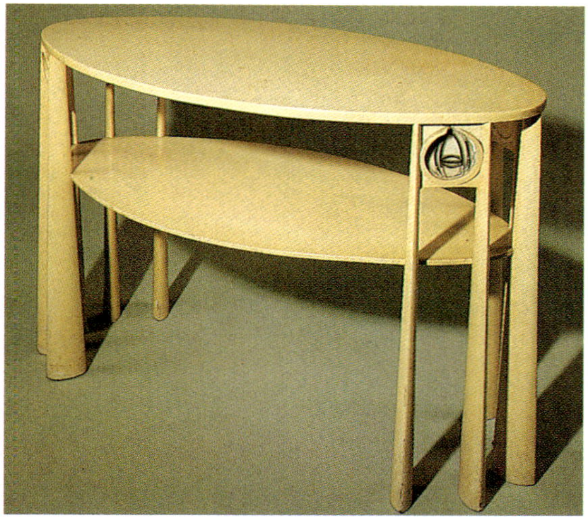

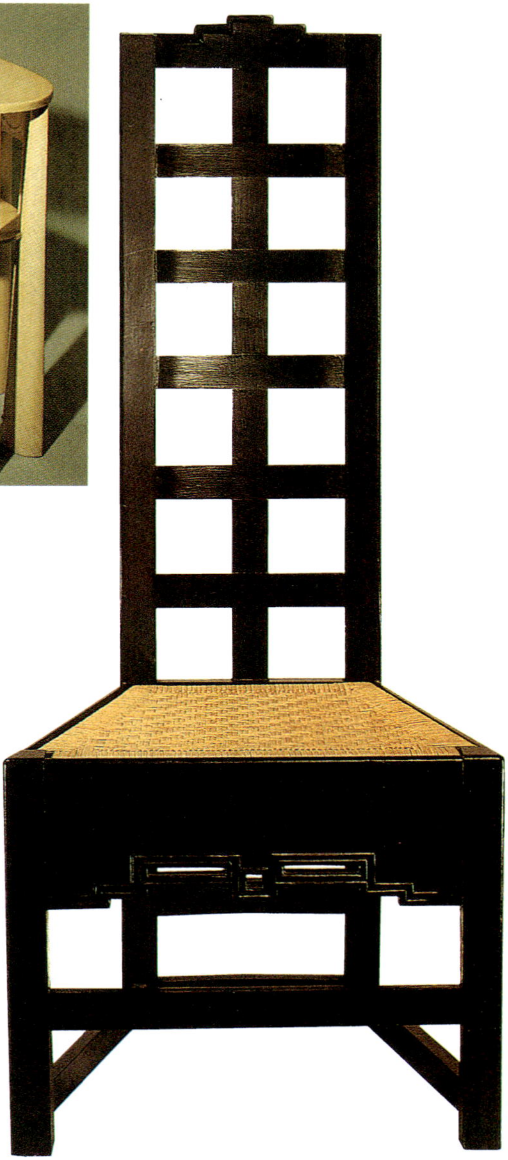

Far left: A white-painted table by C.R. Mackintosh. Mackintosh felt uncomfortable with natural grain in wood and attempted to minimize it by staining, lacquering, ebonizing, and painting the surfaces of his furniture.

Left: A black chair by C.R. Mackintosh. Mackintosh used extremely elegant, exaggerated verticals, particularly in the backs of his chairs that could be exceptionally tall and slender. They were often cut into ovals, ladder-backs that descended to the floor, or, as in this example, into grids.

tors including Hermann Obrist (1863-1927), August Endell (1871-1921), Richard Riemerschmid (1868-1957), Bernhard Pankok (1872-1943), and Bruno Paul (1874-1954) turned their attention to the applied arts. In 1897, these five, among others, founded the *Vereinigte Werkstätte für Kunst im Handwerk* (United Workshops for Art in the Handicrafts). Obrist and Endell designed furniture in flowing natural forms that were determined by a theory of interaction between physical appearances and psychological reactions. Obrist's furniture was made of oak, and Endell's of elm, while Pankok's designs, which were also based on natural forms, were made of oak, pearwood, walnut, and spruce.

NEO-GOTHIC STYLE

Richard Riemerschmid's earliest experiments in furniture were some pieces he designed for his own apartment in 1895. They were in the Neo-Gothic style, made of stained and painted pine and decorated with elaborate wrought

Right: The Atelier Elvira, 1897-1898, Munich, by August Endell (now destroyed).

Bottom: Table and chair with stenciled back, ca 1901, by C.R. Mackintosh.

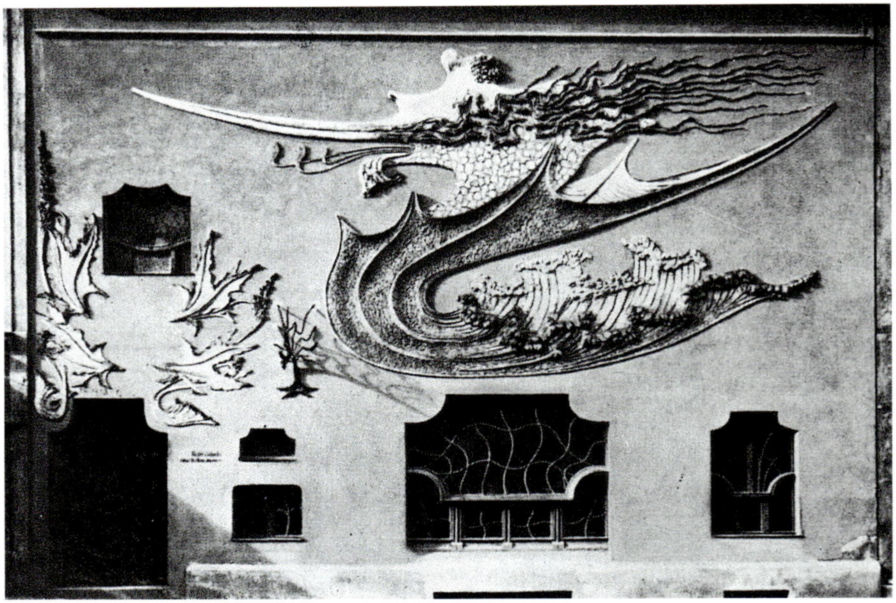

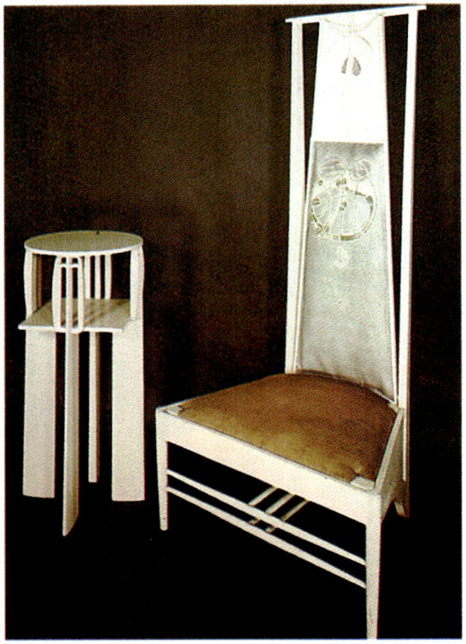

iron hinges and foliate ornament carved in low relief. However, Riemerschmid's style was to change, as a result of seeing an exhibition at Dresden in 1897 of Van de Velde's furniture. His abstract Art Nouveau style made a great impact on all the Munich artists, including Bruno Paul, whose work was characterized by elegant curved lines and was free of any ornamentation. The following year, Riemerschmid designed an oak side-chair, its backrest carried on supports which descend in a sweeping curve to the feet of the front legs.

THE DRESDEN WORKSHOPS

One of the intentions underlying the work of the Munich artists was to create furniture cheap enough for a much larger public than could afford the hand-built furniture produced by the leading avant-garde designers of Paris, Nancy, and Brussels. When selecting the forms their furniture would take, the Germans took into account the new woodworking machines being developed at the time. The leader of this tendency was Karl Schmidt, Riemerschmid's brother-in-law, who had trained as a cabinet maker and in 1898 opened the *Dresdner Werkstätte* (Dresden Workshops). At an exhibition of industrial art held in Dresden in 1899-1900, Schmidt showed an apartment of two living rooms, a bedroom, and a kitchen, inexpensively furnished with simple modern furniture. Five years later, the Dresdner Werkstätte produced a range of machine-made furniture designed by Riemerschmid.

THE GERMAN WORKSHOPS

In 1902, Adelbert Niemeyer, an artist, and Karl Bertsch, an upholsterer, founded a workshop

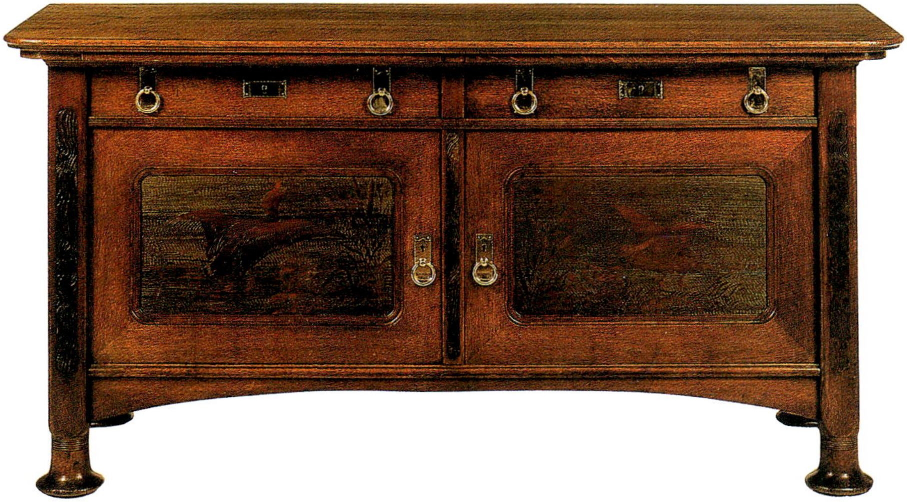

Left: An oak sideboard by August Endell, ca 1900. Endell believed that the shape of an object could induce feelings of serenity.

Below: Dining chair designed by Richard Riemerschmid, ca 1900.

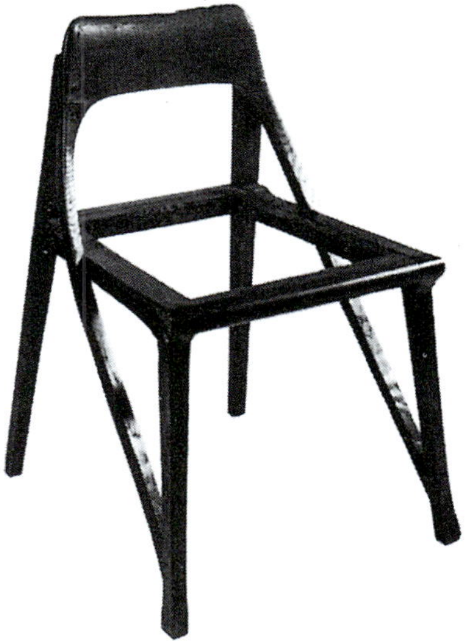

in Munich for the manufacture of furniture and other items of interior decoration. In 1907, the workshop merged with the Dresdner Werkstätte and the two became known as the *Deutsche Werkstätte* (German Workshops). This should not be confused with the *Deutsche Werkbund,* which was an association of designers, craftsmen, manufacturers, and retailers promoted by the German government and founded in the same year. Niemeyer continued to design furniture for the Deutsche Werkstätte until his death. Other designers who occasionally worked for the Dresden concern include Baillie Scott and the Austrians Josef Hoffmann (1870-1956) and Kolomon Moser (1868-1918).

THE DARMSTADT DESIGNERS

Having been frequently illustrated in *The Studio* magazine, Baillie Scott's work was well known on the continent. These illustrations had caught the eye of the Grand Duke Ernst Ludwig of Hesse-Darmstadt, who in 1897 had had a drawing room and a dining room in his palace at Darmstadt furnished by Baillie Scott and Charles Ashbee. The Grand Duke encouraged the establishment of an artist's colony in Darmstadt and donated some land for it. Seven artists were invited to join the colony, and by 1900 their homes were being built. For his house, Peter Behrens (1868-1940), an architect who had been working in Munich during the 1890s, designed furniture which was close in style to the work of Van de Velde. Josef Maria Olbrich (1867-1908), although from Vienna, was another Darmstadt colonist who created furniture for his own and other artist's houses in a style which was a successful blend of organic shapes and geometrical ornament.

AUSTRIA AND THE SECESSIONISTS

In Austria, the Art Nouveau style was called *Sezessionstil*, after the Vienna Secession which was formed in 1897 both as a reaction

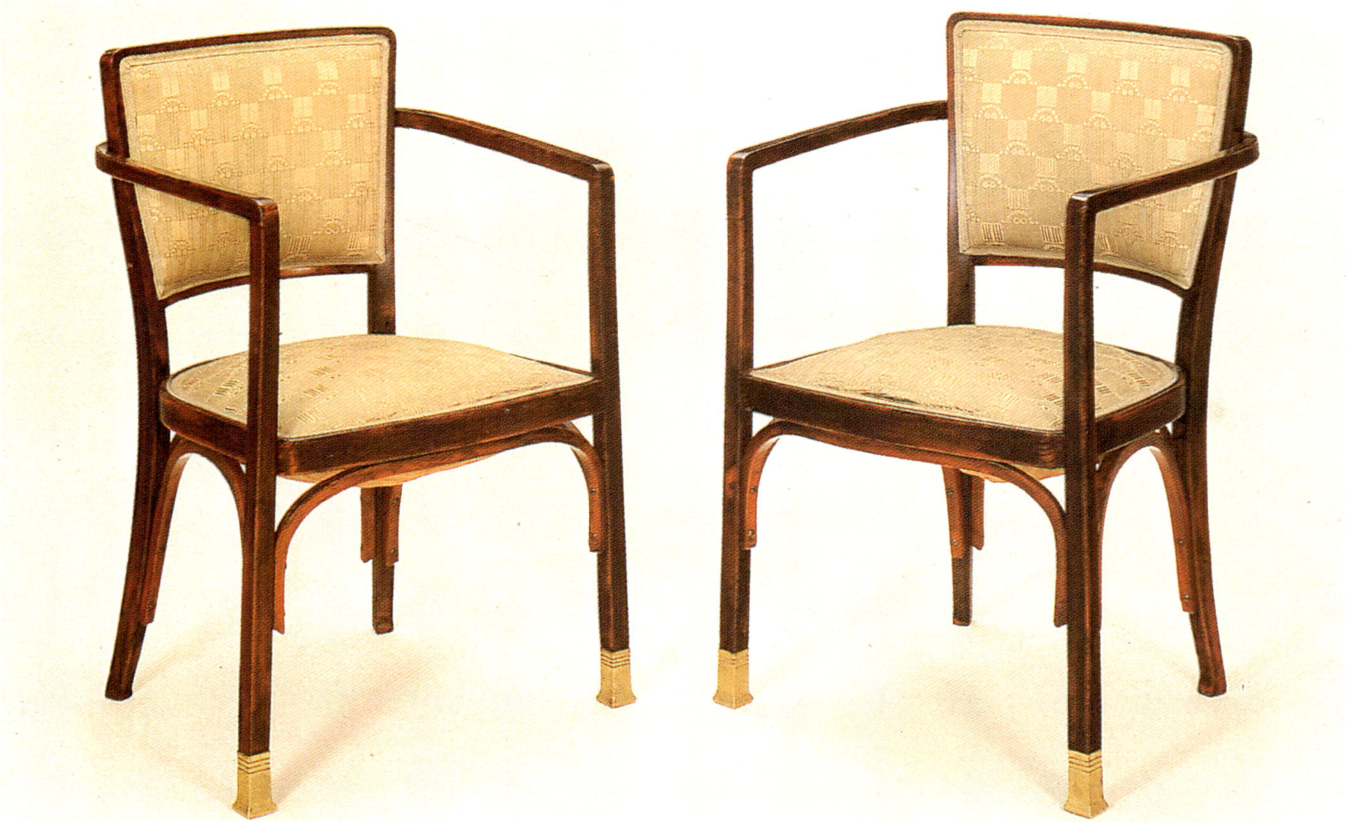

Above: Chairs by Kolomon Moser of the Viennese Secession movement, showing the great restraint of the style, partly inspired by Charles Rennie Mackintosh.

against the tired revivalism of academic artists and as a celebration of modernity. It was therefore almost inevitable that the work of its members should directly reflect the influence of the Art Nouveau style which by then was fully developed in Western Europe. Beginning as something of a local variant on Art Nouveau, this late flowering of the style was to prove a turning point between Art Nouveau opulence and 20th-century austerity. Even in their earlier works, the Austrian architects preferred a framework of straighter lines to set off the opulent curves of Art Nouveau. They were particularly appreciative of these qualities in Mackintosh's style, which helped to form their own, and of the English Arts and Crafts architects, who by this stage were opposing the sensuality of Art Nouveau.

OLBRICH AND THE SECESSIONHAUS

Just as the Arts and Crafts practitioners had lauded the merits of simplicity and honesty in architecture and design, so too did the group of Austrian architects, painters, and sculptors who seceded from the official artists' organization and held their own exhibitions in the Secessionhaus designed by Josef Maria Olbrich in 1897-99. As a founder member of the breakaway group, Olbrich felt it necessary to make a strong architectural statement. The main structure of the building — reputedly inspired by a rough sketch by the painter Gustav Klimt — is substantial, and complete with concrete facing, but the detailing with animal and vegetable life is an all-important aspect of the building, particularly on the tracery of the iron dome. Like the spires of Cologne's medieval cathedral, the perforated structure lightens the "weight" of the building. Much of the Secession's work in all art forms, achieved this type of effect through well-controlled contrast, rather than by an unbridled release of free flowing forms.

OTTO WAGNER'S ARCHITECTURE

One of the older Secessionists, Otto Wagner (1841-1918), was an influential writer and theorist. His architectural career had not brought him a great deal of public success, but the Secession supported his pupils Olbrich and Josef Hoffmann. In 1899, Wagner himself became a full member of the Secession, largely severing his connections with much of his own generation and the Vienna Akademie's school of architecture.

MAJOLIKAHAUS

The year before, Wagner had publicly shown his allegiance to the Secession style by his treatment of the facade of an apartment block he had designed, aptly dubbed the "Majolikahaus." In essence, this consisted of

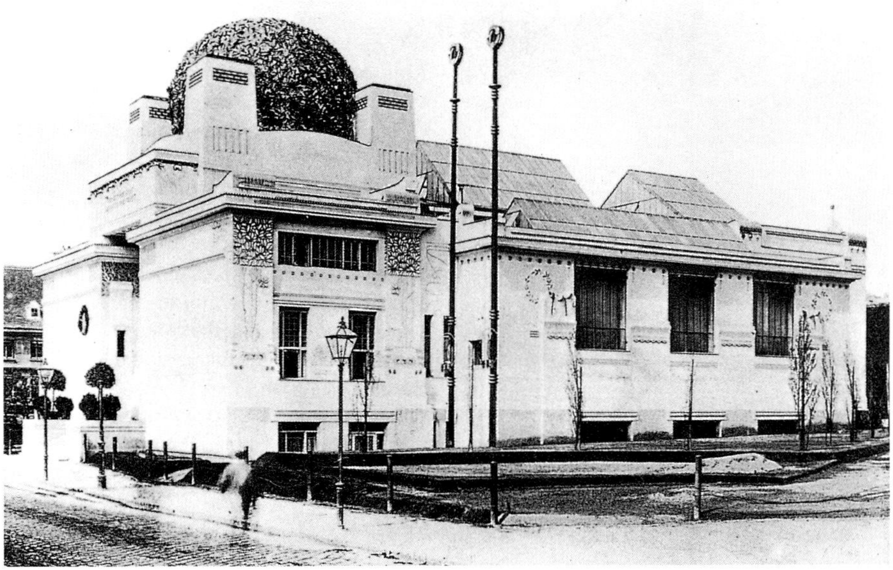

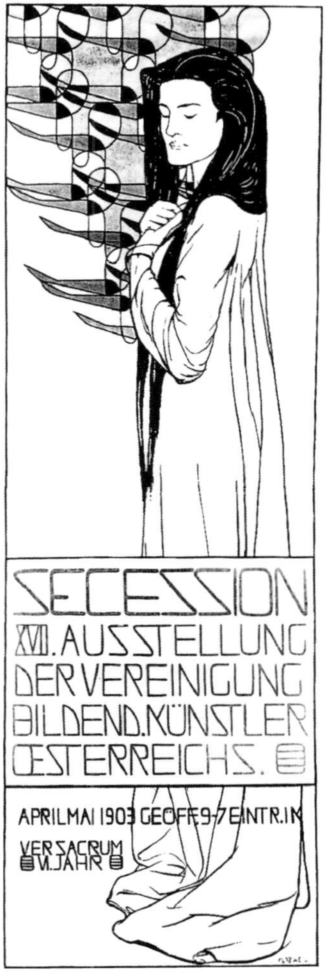

Above: A poster advertising one of the annual exhibitions held by the craftsmen of the Vienna Secession.

Left: The Exhibition Hall of 1898 designed by Josef Olbrich for the Secession in Vienna.

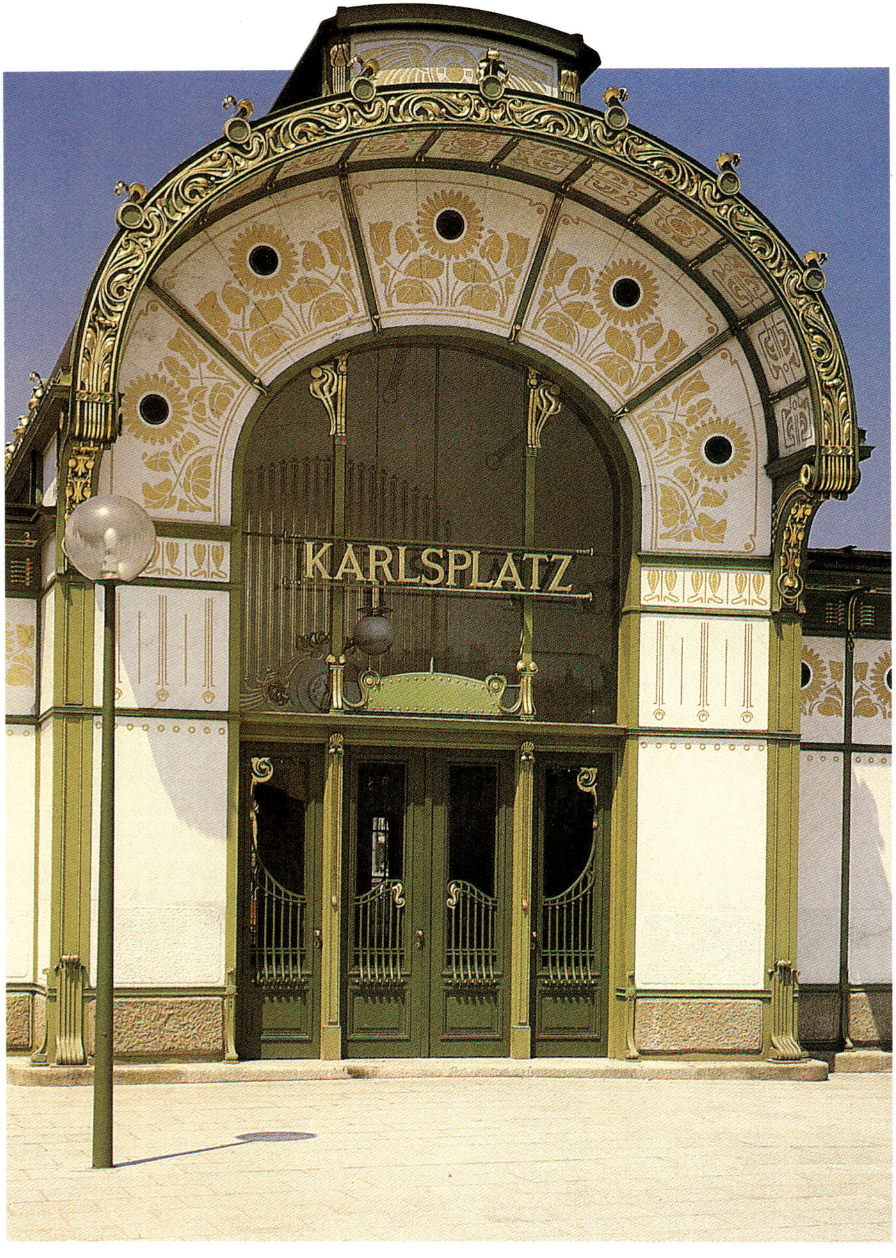

a completely regular grid of windows, devoid of any architectural or sculptural decoration. However, to counteract the austerity, Wagner decorated the whole facade with brightly-colored majolica, floral patterned tiles that seem to grow up from the second floor, and gradually enveloped the whole building in the light, sinuous lines of Austrian Art Nouveau.

STADTBAHN

Before the establishment of the Secession group, Wagner, with Olbrich as his assistant, was appointed architect to the new Viennese underground and suburban railway, the Stadtbahn. The design of the Stadtbahn stations immediately invite comparison with Guimard's work for the Paris Métro. Wagner's stations lack the free-flowing fantasy of Guimard, yet they have a somewhat Rococo grace and lightness, with abundant floral detailing, which is the closest point in Austrian architecture to the French style of Art Nouveau.

The speed with which Art Nouveau was acknowledged was equaled only by the speed with which it came under criticism. Wagner's Post Office Savings Bank, built between 1904 and 1906 in the center of Vienna, reveals a completely new aesthetic, based soundly on "truth to materials." With austere ornamentation, its structural components such as rivets and nuts provide a wealth of decoration. Here, Wagner created a building using up-to-date methods of construction and materials such as steel, aluminum, glass, and concrete to create a large, airy main hall. To the contemporary eye, the interior of the building must have appeared somewhat spartan, but in the attention to every

Left: The magnificent Karlsplatz Station of the Vienna Stadtbahn (subway train), designed by Otto Wagner.

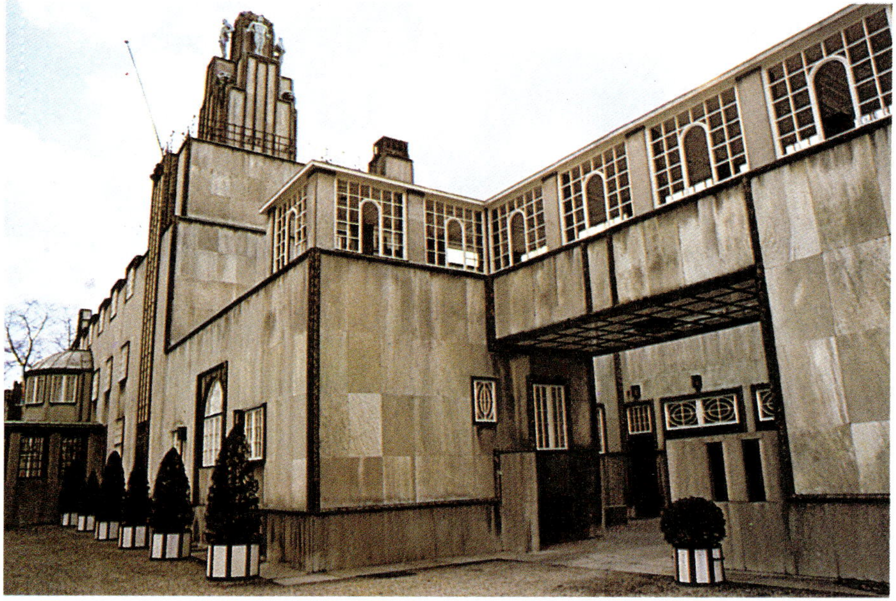

Left: Exterior view of the Palais Stoclet, Brussels, designed by Josef Hoffmann and begun in 1905.

detail of furniture and fitting, the light, glass roof, and particularly the elegant tapering piers supporting the gently curved vault, all suggest the remaining echoes of Art Nouveau.

THE WIENER WERKSTÄTTE

Wagner's former pupil, Josef Hoffmann, appreciated craftsmanship and believed that ornament had an important role in architecture. Together with Kolomon Moser (1868-1918), Hoffmann established the *Wiener Werkstätte* (Vienna Workshop), a workshop dedicated to the production of functional but beautiful objects.

Hoffmann's Purkersdorf convalescent home (1903) reveals structural sincerity — his designs for the Palais Stoclet in Brussels (1905-11) however, allowed him to put his theories fully into practice. Stoclet, a wealthy financier, commissioned Hoffmann to build a palatial home that should also serve as a suitable setting for his art collection and for entertaining. What Hoffmann designed was a house of great distinction, combining elements of formality (strong horizontals and verticals) with great informality (an irregular floor plan and a facade that did nothing to hide the irregularity of the room arrangement within). The very asymmetry of the design coupled with the unusual shapes and positions of the windows points strongly to Mackintosh's work.

HOFFMANN'S FURNITURE

Many of Hoffmann's furniture designs also show the influence of Mackintosh, but he maintained a high level of personal inventiveness. Characteristic of Hoffmann's furniture are lattice-like chair backs and table aprons, and small spheres of wood for decoration at points of structural significance. Hoffmann's style gradually became more retrospective, using some Neo-classical and Biedermeier (an informal 19th century style) forms.

The same influence is evident in the furniture created by two other Wiener Werkstätte designers, Otto Prutscher and Josef Urban (1872-1933). While some of the pieces designed by Moser were richly decorated with marquetry or inlaid metals, others, like Mackintosh's in Glasgow, were simply painted white.

ADOLF LOOS

The Viennese architect Adolf Loos (1870-1933) did not join the Secession and criticized its members for the ornament and deliberate artiness of the furniture they designed. Loos greatly admired Roman architecture and

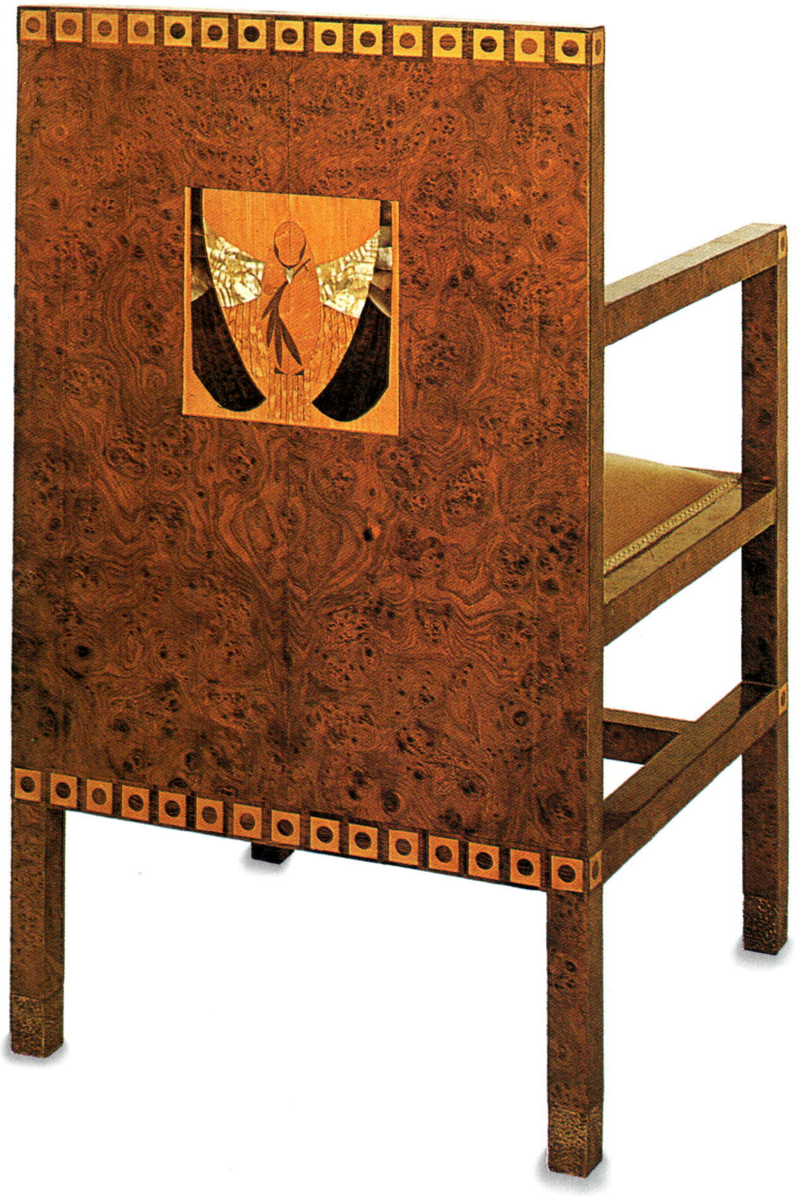

inherited from his stonemason father a deep respect for "raw" materials.

He traveled to the United States in 1893, the year after Louis Sullivan had published his *Ornament in Architecture*. Three years later, Loos settled in Vienna, bringing with him a belief in the rejection of ornament (summed up in his essay "Ornament and Crime" of 1908). Perhaps because of his outspoken stance, large-scale commissions were slow to arrive, his most notable piece during this early period being the Kartner Bar of 1907. The apparent harshness of its geometric order is dissolved by the richness of shiny metals and lavish leather seating. Loos also designed bentwood chairs manufactured by Thonet for the Café Museum. He had been impressed by the work of the English Arts and Crafts Movement and several pieces he designed were of simple, paneled construction, marked by elegant proportions and a judicious disposition of simple reeding and metal fittings.

Loos designed a house for the Steiner family in Vienna in 1910 and this commission provided him with the opportunity to manifest his principles. The house is outstanding, not least because it is one of the first examples of domestic architecture to use reinforced concrete. Externally, the building consists of smooth, flat walls of solid geometric blocks pierced by plate-glass windows (which are mainly horizontal), and a flat roof. Internally, the same geometric order prevails, but around an essentially traditional plan.

Loos went on to design many private villas before settling in Paris where he designed a house for the Dadaist, Tristan Tzara, in 1926.

Left: Armchair veneered in amboyna wood, designed by Kolomon Moser in 1904.

SPAIN AND THE UNITED STATES

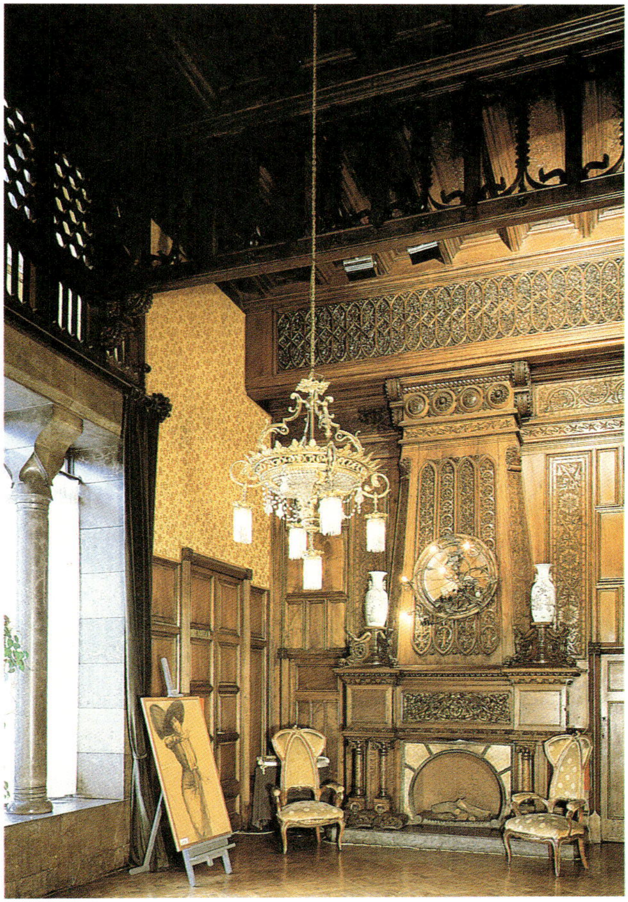

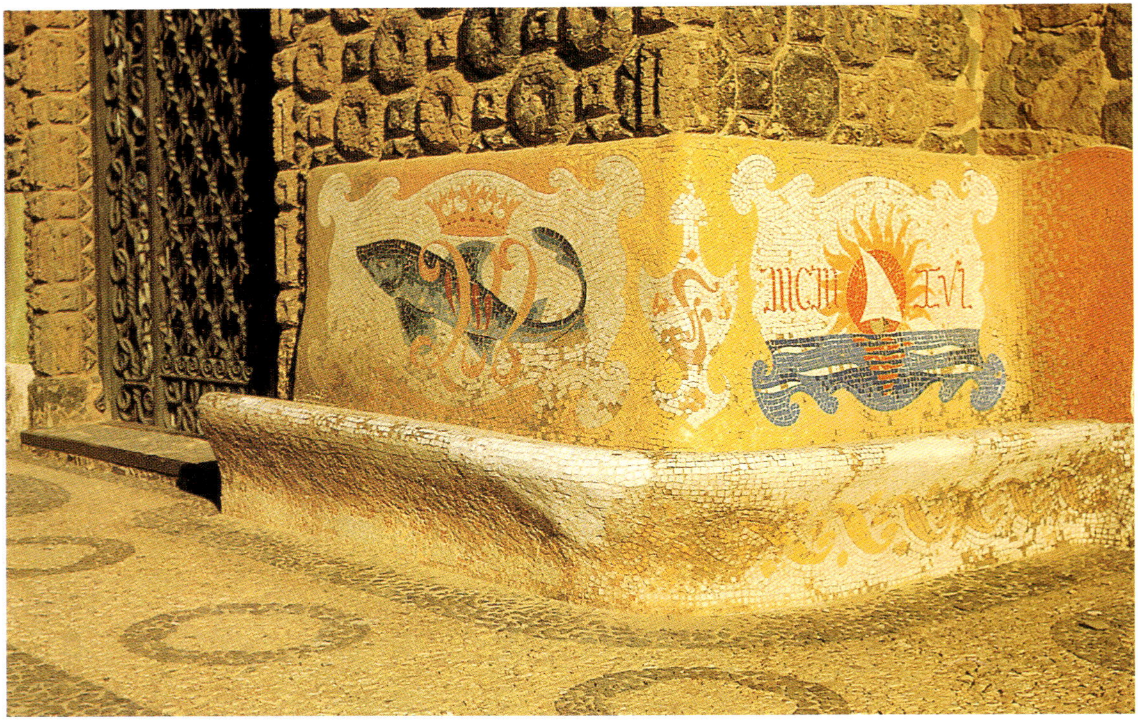

Above: Details of the polychromatic decoration which incorporates the Güell family monogram and coronet, by Catalan architect Antoni Gaudí.

Overleaf: The interior of Gaudí's mansion for Don Eusebio Güell. The interior shows the architect's interest in the ornate Gothic style, as well as Moorish-inspired design. They combine to produce a unique variation of the Art Nouveau style.

One of the strongest features of Art Nouveau was its very diversity. The remarkable set of characters, linked by common Art Nouveau traits, sets the short-lived movement apart from homogeneous previous styles, arid and easily transferred from master to pupil. The blossoming of Art Nouveau in Brussels, Glasgow, Paris, Munich, New York, Barcelona, and so many other centers was a unanimous rejection of excessive uniformity.

GAUDÍ AND MODERNISMO

In both Belgium and France, there were a number of architects working along similar lines, and Art Nouveau could lay claim to being a movement of sorts. In Spain, Antoni Gaudí (1852-1926) worked in virtual isolation, and his only direct influences came from reading the works of Viollet-le-Duc, Ruskin, and others. Yet Gaudí was arguably one of the most original and accomplished of all Art Nouveau architects.

Born in Tarragona, Gaudí moved to

Barcelona, the capital of Catalonia, around 1869, where he met his main patron, Eusebio Güell. Aside from the Neo-Gothic theories of Viollet-le-Duc, he was influenced by traditional Moorish and Moroccan styles, and by a mission to create a new Catalan architecture. His buildings were consequently more exotic than those of his contemporaries in northern Europe. In Gaudí's work, one confronts one of the strangest variations of Art Nouveau, so firmly embedded in the peculiar local conditions that it is almost possible to see it as a purely local style. Indeed, it even had its own name, Modernismo.

CATALAN TRADITION

Catalonia in particular had its own traditions. It was the wealthiest and most modern part of Spain, with its own industries and the thriving port of Barcelona, and was immensely proud of its trading history. These were vital to Catalan identity at a time when the central government in Madrid was attempting to integrate the region more completely into Spain, partly by discouraging the use of the native Catalan language. In this context of spirited Catalan patriotism, Gaudí began his architectural career as a Gothic Revivalist, but more specifically as a revivalist of the local Gothic style. This had its own element of fantasy, which Gaudí managed to emphasize through his study of the Moorish architecture of southern Spain and North Africa. To this, Gaudí added his knowledge of Viollet-le-Duc's work, with its light, almost tent-like forms of iron-supported Gothic vaults. He was also inspired by John Ruskin's ideals of the unity

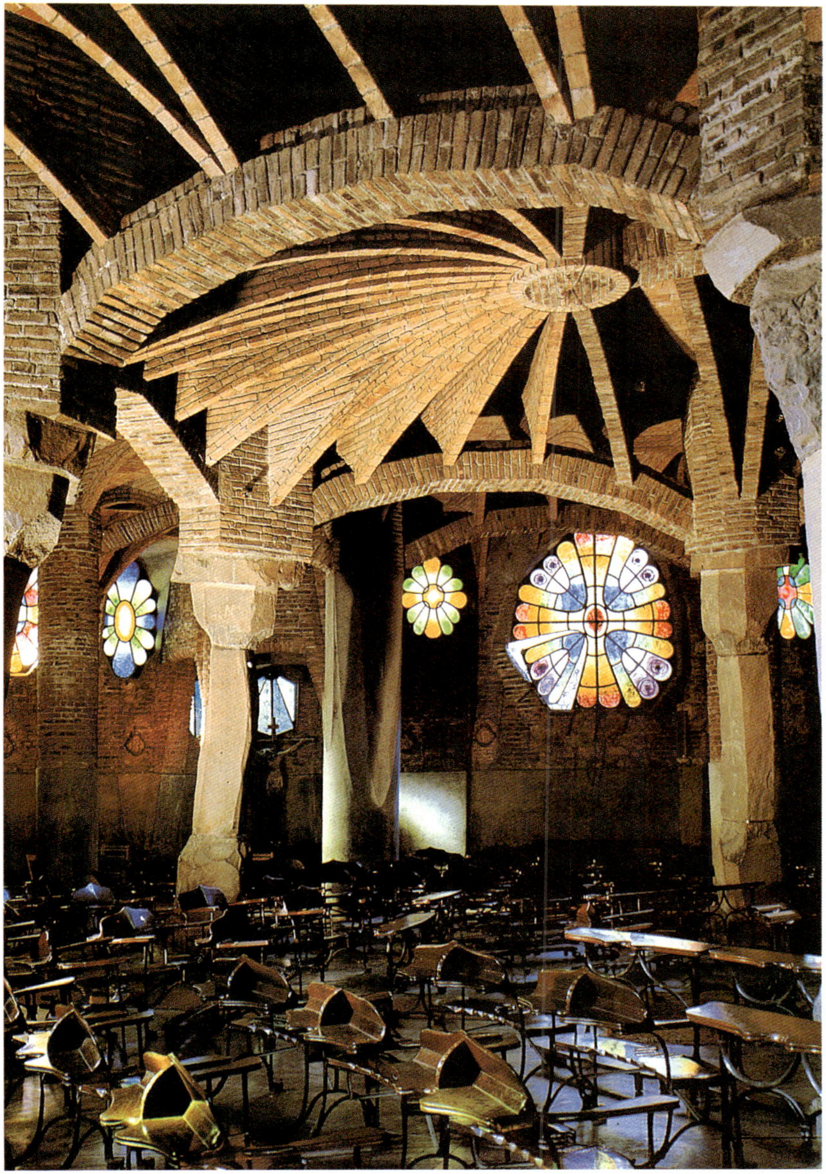

Right: Inside Gaudí's Church, Santa Coloma de Cervelló, for which he also designed the furniture.

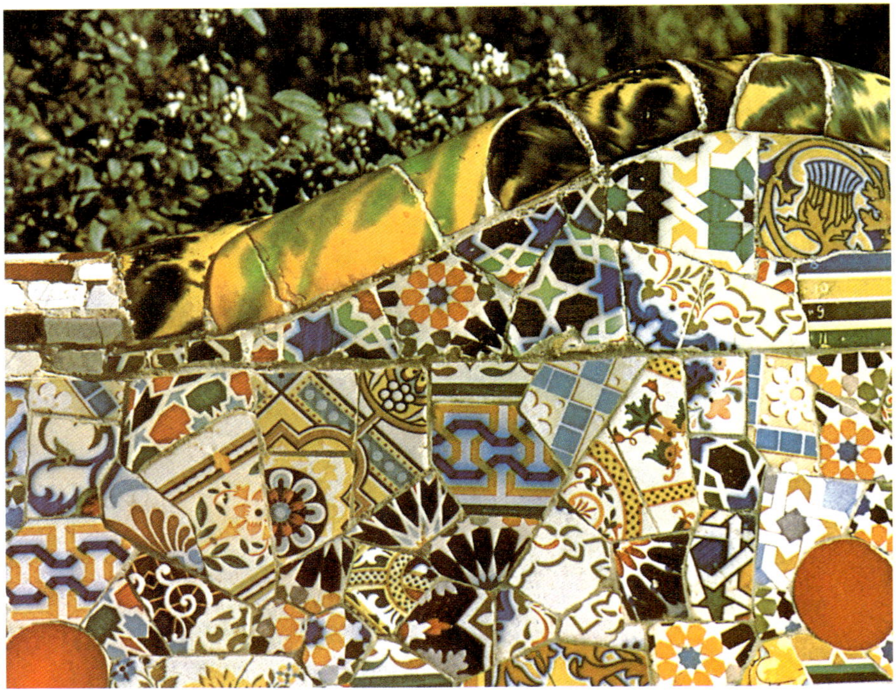

Right: Mosaic decoration at the Parc Güell include broken tiles and old crockery.

Below: The ceramic, mosaic-covered "snake-bench" in the Parc Güell, designed by Antoni Gaudí.

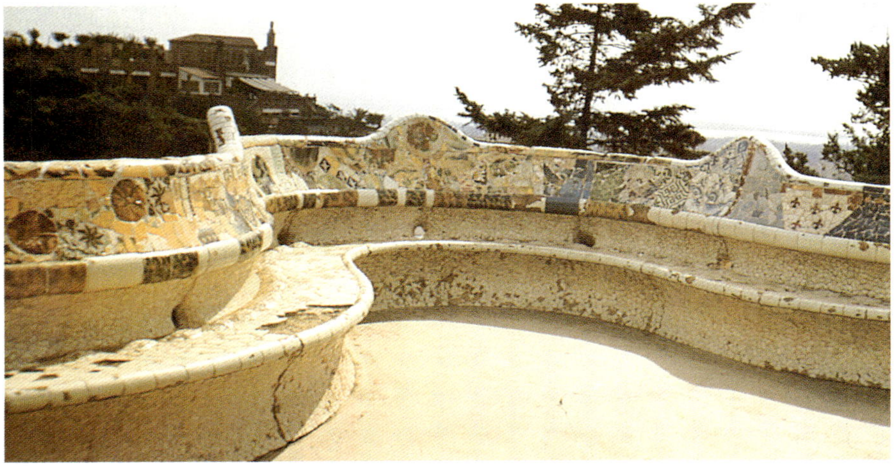

of the arts and architecture making use of color and carving more for its effects.

EARLY PATRONAGE

Gaudí was fortunate enough to have an outstanding patron for much of his work. The wealth of local shipping magnate Don Eusebio Güell allowed for very ambitious schemes. Gaudí's development was slow at first — his first work was the Casa Vicens, a city mansion built between 1878 and 1880, in which the most striking feature was the two massive parabolic arches of the portals filled by wrought-iron railings and gates modeled on a pattern of palm fronds. This was some of the most free-flowing ironwork decoration seen before Horta and Guimard.

Five years later, he started the Palacio Güell, an extravagant townhouse in which the decorative ironwork was accompanied by polychromatic glazed tiles and banded brickwork, and in which the first of Gaudí's twisted roof protuberances appeared.

The Chapel of Santa Coloma de Cervelló, begun in 1898, incorporated a fantastic, rather nightmarish interior in which the jagged asymmetry was enhanced by leaning monolithic pillars, uneven vaults, and a variety of raw textures and materials. This theme was continued in the Parc Güell of 1900, while Gaudí took the principles of Art Nouveau to their architectural extreme in two apartment blocks begun in 1905, the Casa Battló and the Casa Milà.

THE PARC GÜELL

Perhaps inspired by the flowering of Art Nouveau in the rest of Europe, Gaudí's work of the 1890s began to develop into something unique, much more than just the sum of his early influences. Equally liberating must have been the scale on which he was invited to work by Güell.

A development of worker's houses did not get very far, but the centerpiece of a parallel scheme for a middle-class neighborhood, the Parc Güell, exists today as a municipal park. The Parc Güell could be seen as a rare opportunity for the Modernismo artist to display his art against its source. Since this was a landscaping commission, Gaudí was able to employ the stylized, sinuous forms of Art Nouveau against the very natural shapes of the trees and flowers that had, in part, inspired them.

Serpentine paths did indeed weave throughout the park, but the centerpiece was a vast covered market roofed under a forest of mas-

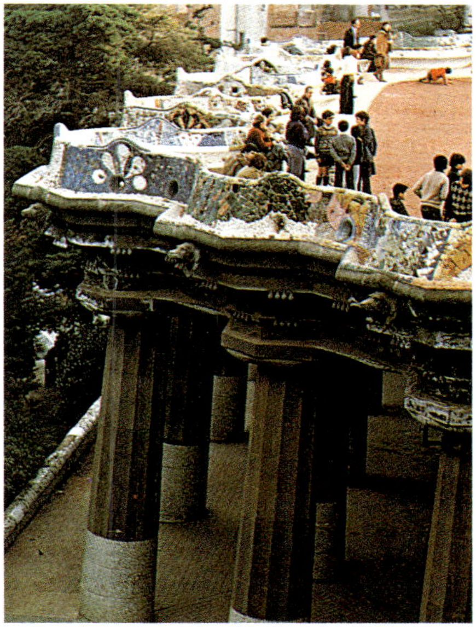

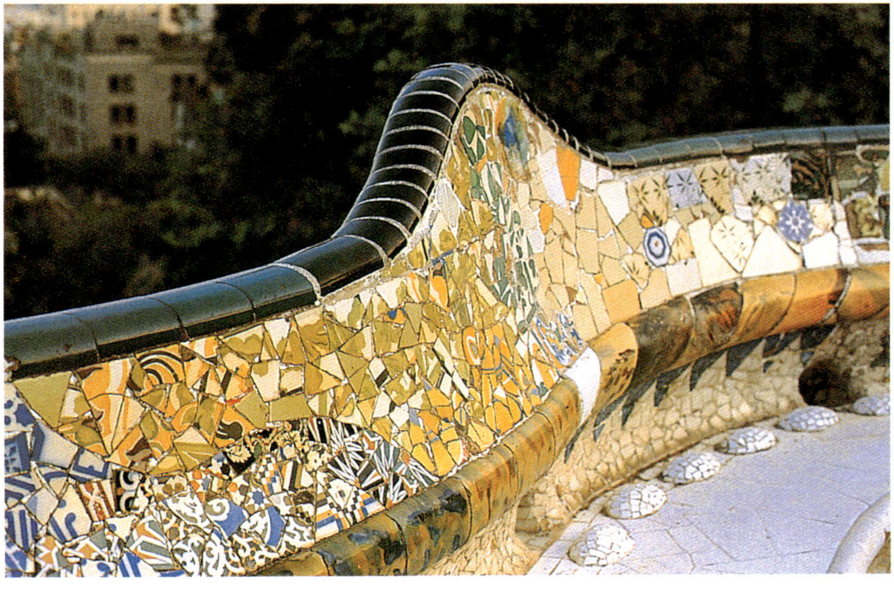

Above: The "snake-bench" frames a public space which is supported by a series of columns.

Left: Detail of the wall of Gaudí's Parc Güell. The whole complex was designed at the behest of local ceramics manufacturer, Eusebio Güell. Gaudí's solutions are as potent expressions of the Art Nouveau style as seen anywhere in Europe.

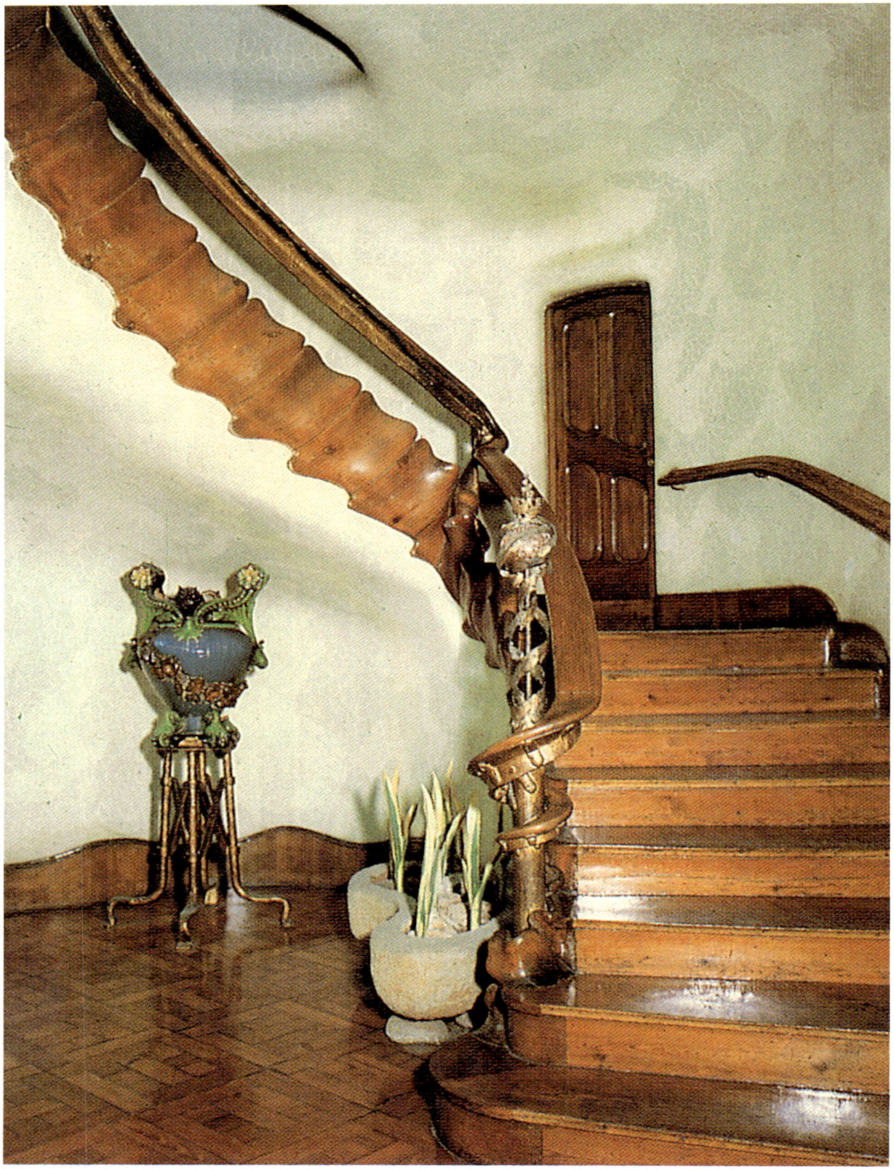

sive columns. On the plateau created above this area, Gaudí placed benches arranged in an almost continuous, undulating line from which the view of the city could be enjoyed. The backs of the benches were decorated with a mosaic of broken tiles arranged, either in patterns or haphazardly, to create a dazzlingly colorful display.

The same theme was continued on the roofs of the pavilions within the park, and, with further grottoes and concrete buttresses seemingly in the form of petrified tree trunks, the overall effect of the park is that of a strange mix of the subterranean and the maritime, perhaps appropriate for a city set between the sea and the mountains.

CASA BATTLÓ

The forms used within the fantastic realms of the Parc Güell have justly been likened to enormously magnified versions of the Art Nouveau creations of Horta and Guimard, amplifying the air of strange, in this case, oversized, biological mutations. An interest in polychromatic effects gained through a combination of media, as in the Parc Güell, was a frequent concern of Art Nouveau, with characteristic ensembles of wood, metal, and stained glass.

This interest was pursued by Gaudí in his Casa Battló apartment block of 1905-7. The commission involved remodeling an existing block and the emphasis was inevitably on the facade. Gaudí had to contend with rectangular windows, already a part of the building and totally at odds with the shapes of Art Nouveau. In order to distract attention from them, as well as exploit the shimmering light

Left: The amazing and unique staircase of the Casa Battló with its bizarre vertebrae silhouette.

of a coastal city, colored tiles were used again to create a flowing pattern throughout the facade, which was finished with a steep roof of titles colored orange to blue-green. The brilliant color effects enabled Gaudí to move away from the more symmetrically-composed facades of the neighboring houses. By means of a rather exotic turret and the fabric-like folds of the roof, the Casa Battló also managed to rise above its companions in the street.

The base of the building was reworked by using a stone cladding whose flowing lines and softly modeled protuberances seemed closer to underwater life than to architecture. Some of the remaining windows on the upper stories received bizarrely shaped iron balconies, somewhat resembling fish skeletons.

THE CASA MILÀ

While the Casa Battló was concerned with a rather two-dimensional presentation, the Casa Milà apartments, completely designed by Gaudí, received a much more plastic, virtually sculptural treatment. Rapidly named "La Pedera" (the quarry) by the locals, Casa Milà seems to allude to many natural sources. Like a cliff face or a rock outcrop eroded by the wind into a collection of grottoes or tunnels, it seems to have been converted to human habitation only at some late stage in its history.

Even in plan, the Casa Milà appears like some cellular organism rather than the work of an architect, and the internal structure was indeed only resolved at a late stage by the use of partitions.

As Gaudí's career developed, it is possible that he increasingly abandoned architectural drawings and worked first-hand with his crafts-

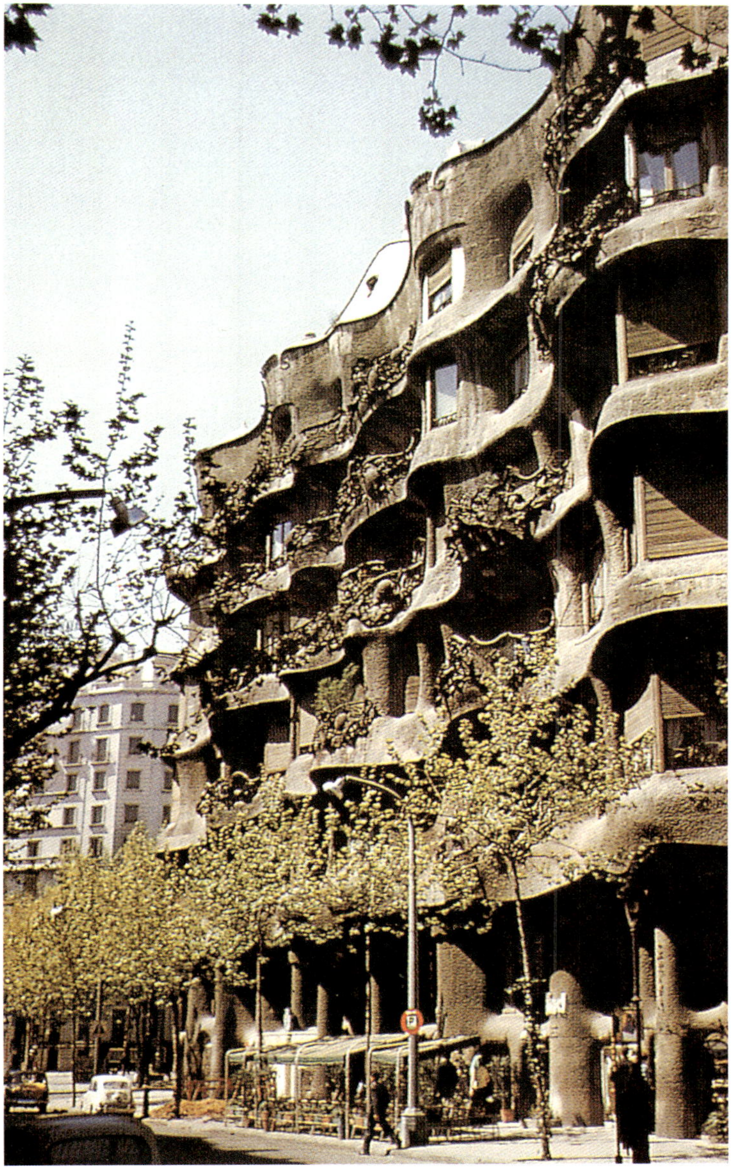

Right: The Casa Milà, with its wrought-iron balconies that recall tangled seaweed.

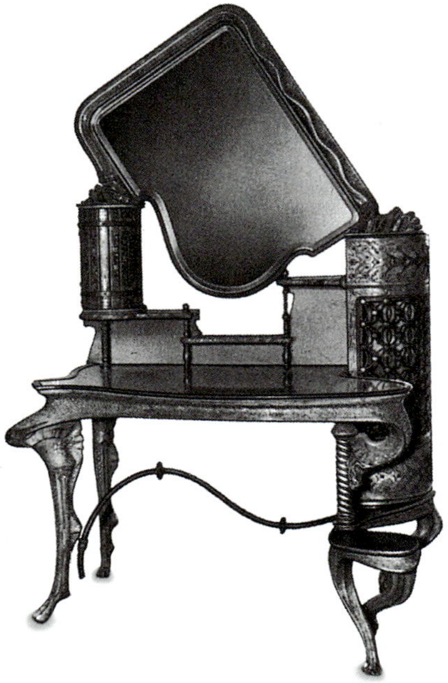

Above: Dressing table designed for the Palacio Güell, Barcelona, by Gaudí, 1890.

Right: The honeycomb surface of the (still unfinished) Cathedral of the Sagrada Familia in Barcelona.

men, like a latter-day William Morris. Certainly, he became much less reliant on iron and glass than Horta or Guimard, as is evident in the Casa Milà. Instead, the effect of erosion is produced by careful carving of each block of the stone facade. In total contrast to this softness is the ironwork of the balconies,which is molded into intricately twisted plant forms, like seaweed hanging from a cliff face before the next wave breaks on it.

SAGRADA FAMILIA

Gaudí's great Barcelona church, the still-to-be-finished Sagrada Familia, occupied him for his entire career, and like the Casa Milà, it is an example of extreme Art Nouveau fantasy enlarged into monumental three dimensions. It is also a typical combination of the reactionary and revolutionary, stemming from Gaudí's extremely devout Roman Catholicism, here given a form of unique novelty — Gothic seen through Art Nouveau eyes of the late 1800s.

GAUDÍ'S FURNITURE

For many of his buildings, Gaudí designed equally extraordinary, idiosyncratic furniture. Among surviving examples are pieces designed for the Chapel of Santa Coloma de Cervelló, the Casa Calvet, built from 1898-1904, and for the Casa Battló.

The style of the furniture is consistent — organic "shell-and-bone" forms are the most obvious. One extraordinary piece, (the authenticity of which is doubtful, however), is an ornate prayer stool believed to have been part of the furnishings for the Casa Battló. The rich "acajou et bois de loup" base of the stool, with upholstered platforms for the knees and elbows, was surmounted by an edifice of stained glass embellished by five large gilt-

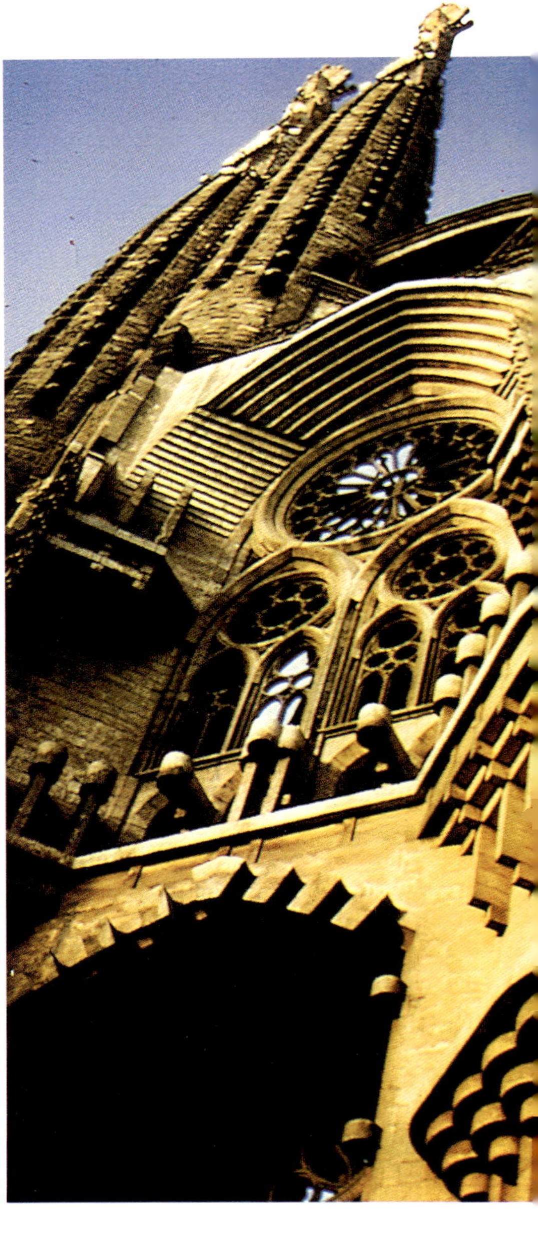

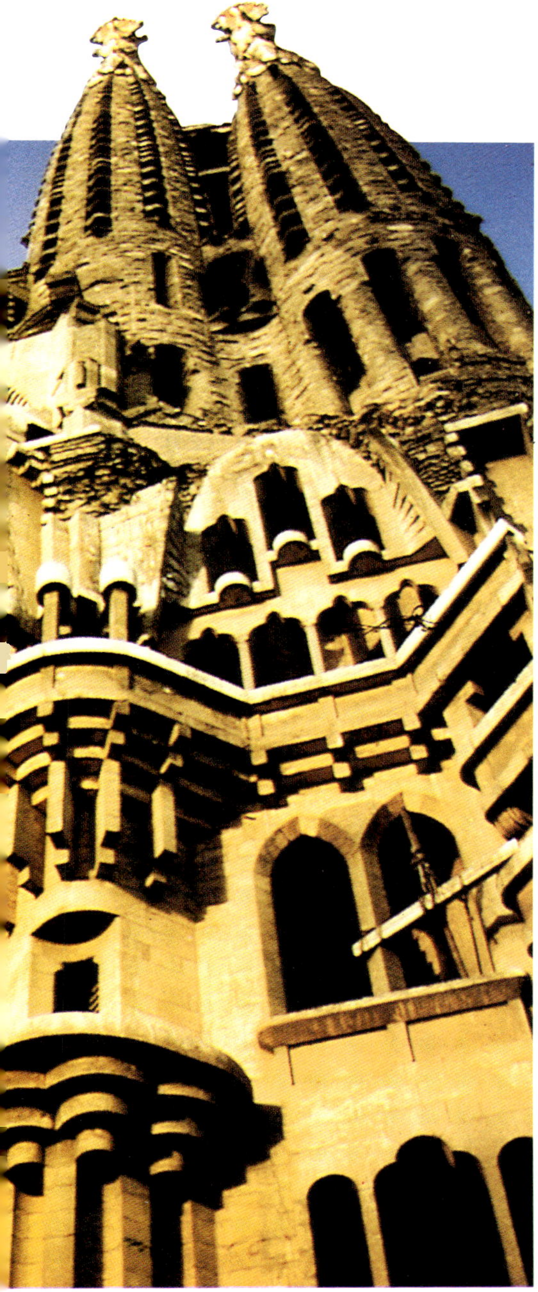

bronze roses. Although very Spanish in feel, the piece bears little resemblance to known examples of Gaudí's furniture.

ART NOUVEAU IN THE UNITED STATES

In the main, the decorative arts in the United States in the 1800s took their lead from Europe, whether from Greek classicism or Louis-Quinze, and these revivalist tendencies were also adopted in architecture. But the United States led the world in technical virtuosity and in the far-sightedness of many of its designers and patrons.

Contemporary movements in Europe tended to reach the United States somewhat anachronistically and haphazardly. The Gothic Revival of Ruskin reached the United States merely as a style to be adopted by a few designers, and lacked both the emotional and nationalistic fervor of the English movement. The opening up of Japan, however, and the resultant Aesthetic Movement, did capture America's artistic imagination.

ARTS AND CRAFTS IN THE UNITED STATES

By 1890, the most important foreign importation of style was the Arts and Crafts Movement of Morris and Ruskin. Many Americans had visited England and met Morris personally before returning home, fired with his ideals, dedicated to handicrafts and the rejection of the machine in art. Publications such as *International Studio, House Beautiful, The Ladies Home Journal,* and *The Craftsman* spread the word to an even wider audience.

The Arts and Crafts Movement was important in the United States not only for the fine workmanship it encouraged from individuals, but also for the growing awareness it developed among Americans that they should also find a truly national art.

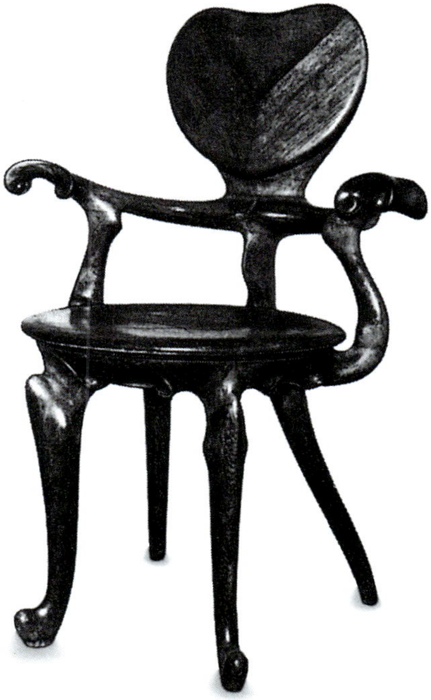

Above: A wooden armchair designed by Gaudí for the Casa Calvet, Barcelona, in 1902.

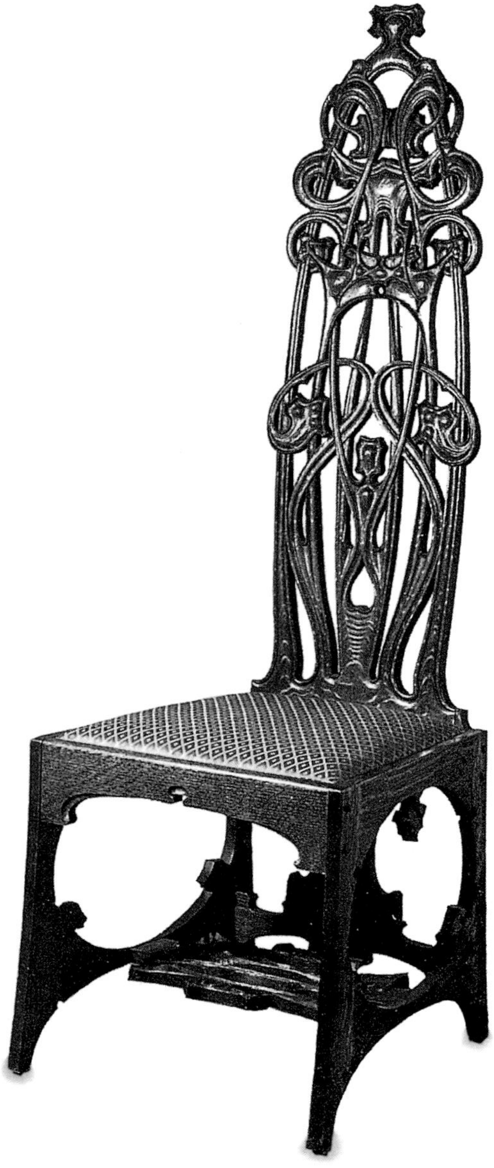

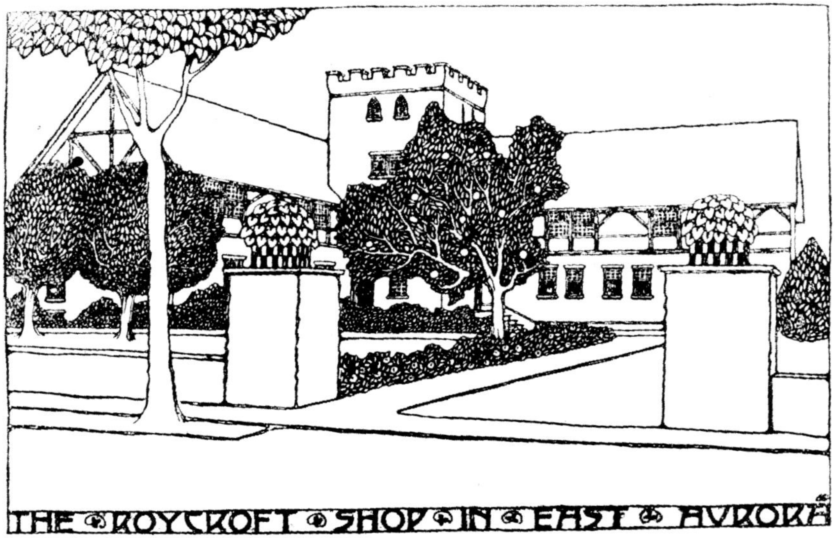

Left: Oak chair by the American designer Charles Rohlfs, 1898.

Above: Print of the Roycroft Shops of Hubbard's crafts community in East Aurora, near Buffalo, New York.

But the concepts of national art did, in fact, differ across the country. On the East Coast, Morris-inspired communities were founded and furniture and other decorative items were made which had a direct resemblance to the British movement. On the West Coast, however, the climate and the landscape led to different interpretations. Morris's romantic return to the medieval European past was supplanted in California by the recognition of its own past in Spanish-Mexican and Native American culture.

CRAFTSMEN COMMUNITIES AND WORKSHOPS

One of the first to assimilate European trends in design was Charles Rohlfs, who opened a small workshop in Buffalo in 1890. His work reflects both the "Mission Style" of California and Art Nouveau in elaborate carving and detailing, mainly in oak. Rohlfs often lectured at the Roycroft community at East Aurora, which had been started by Elbert Hubbard in 1895.

Roycroft was run along business lines, beginning with a press and book bindery, and gradually incorporating other crafts. Around 1901, the furniture shop was started. Solidly and honestly made, generally in oak or mahogany, early works were heavier versions of chairs by Morris & Co., while later pieces resembled the Craftsman style of Gustav Stickley (1857-1942).

Stickley and *The Craftsman*

Following his debt to Ruskin and absorbing the principles of his architecture, in 1901 Stickley founded *The Craftsman* magazine in which he upheld the social aims of the British Arts and Crafts designers and called for a truly democratic national art. Stickley believed in a quasi-psychological view that more simple surroundings would lead to spiritual regeneration, especially in industrial cities, and his solid, severe furniture seems to reflect his social aims.

The Chicago School

A genuine American style was to be forged through the work of Louis Sullivan (1856-1924) and Frank Lloyd Wright (1867-1959) in Chicago. Sullivan had introduced Art Nouveau forms in a system of architectural ornament, holding that the outward form of a building should be expressive of its function. Sullivan's best work was for office buildings, but his ideas were taken and expanded by Wright into residential buildings.

Wright believed in integral design for his houses, and his furniture was designed to solve specific problems within a particular interior, as in the Hanna House where the polygonal furniture reflects the hexagonal design of the house. Each house also had a particular ornamental theme and any added decoration was to echo that chosen motif — decoration for Wright generally relied on positioning geometric shapes.

Perhaps the most important center of Arts and Crafts activity was Chicago. In an area

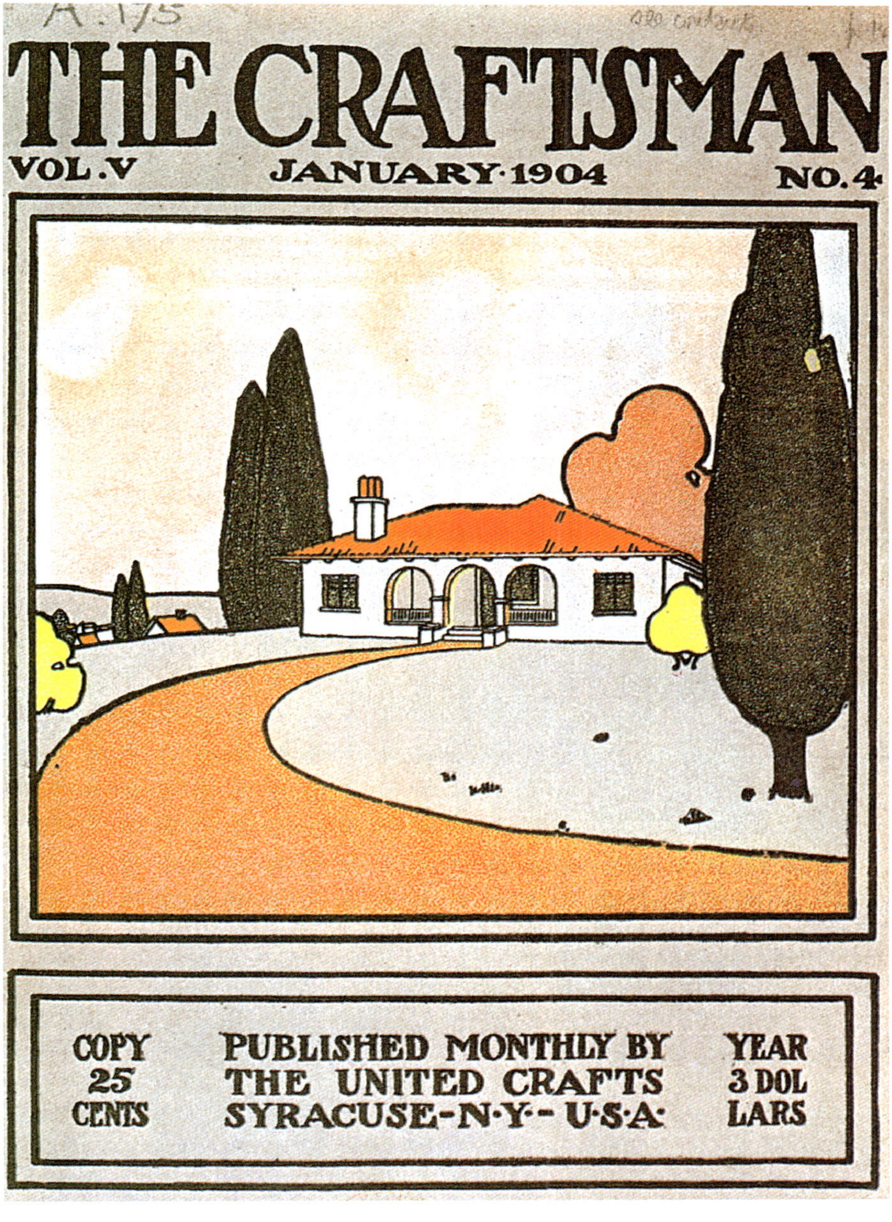

Right: A cover of The Craftsman *magazine.*

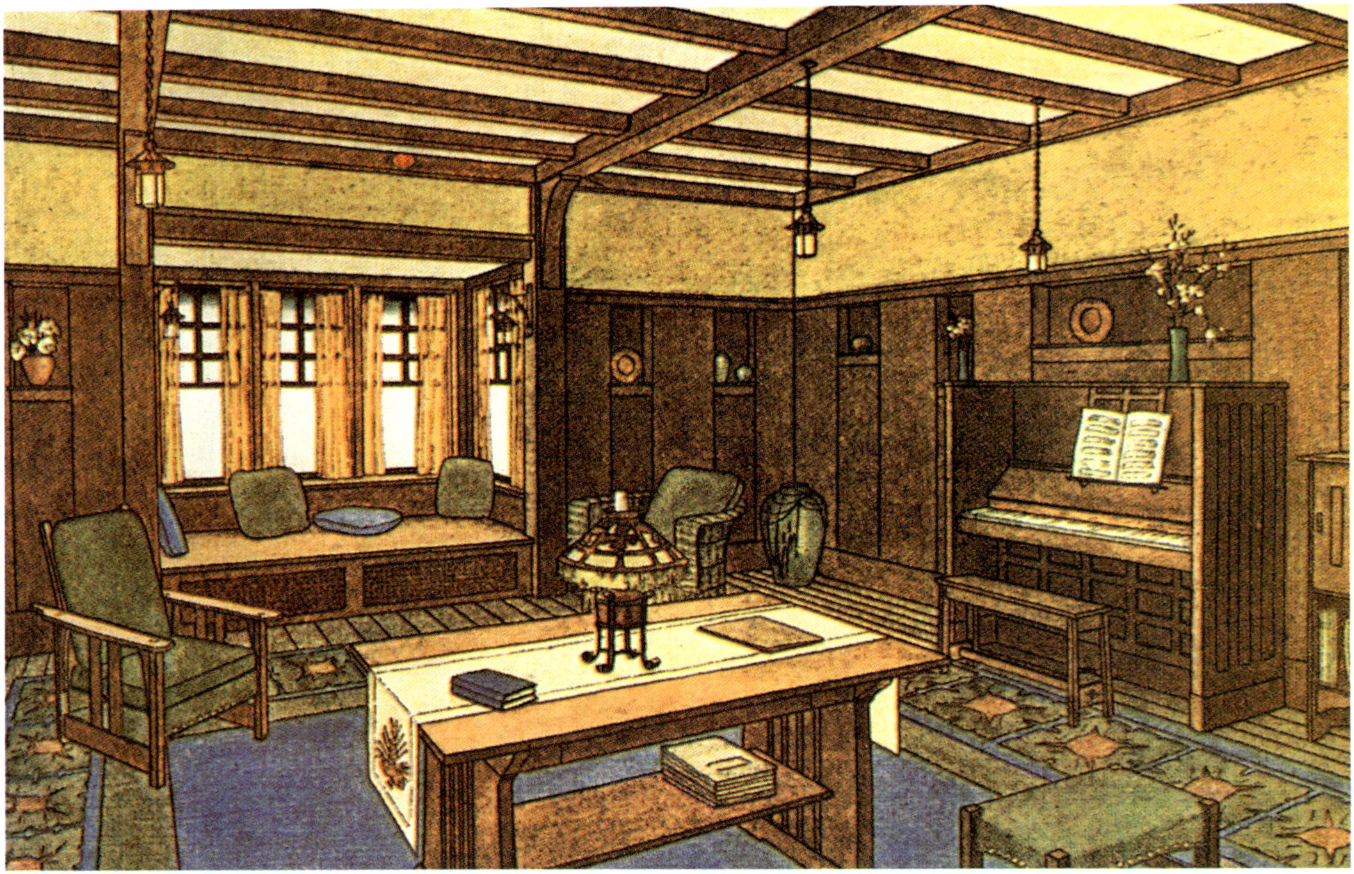

Above: A Craftsman living room as illustrated in the magazine, The Craftsman, *which was founded by Gustav Stickley in 1901.*

most affected by frontier concepts, a style had to be evolved which no longer took its lead from the commercial and organizational centers of the East Coast, rooted as they were in European traditions. The Midwest relied on modern machines and means of communications for its survival, and could not, even in the 1890s, afford to espouse the microcosmic ideals of the Arts and Crafts Movement. The movement did, however, supply the impetus for a freedom of style.

Louis Sullivan

Louis Sullivan was the leader of the innovative group of architects based in the booming city of Chicago, and his importance as a pioneer of 20th-century architecture extends well beyond the isolated decade or so of Art

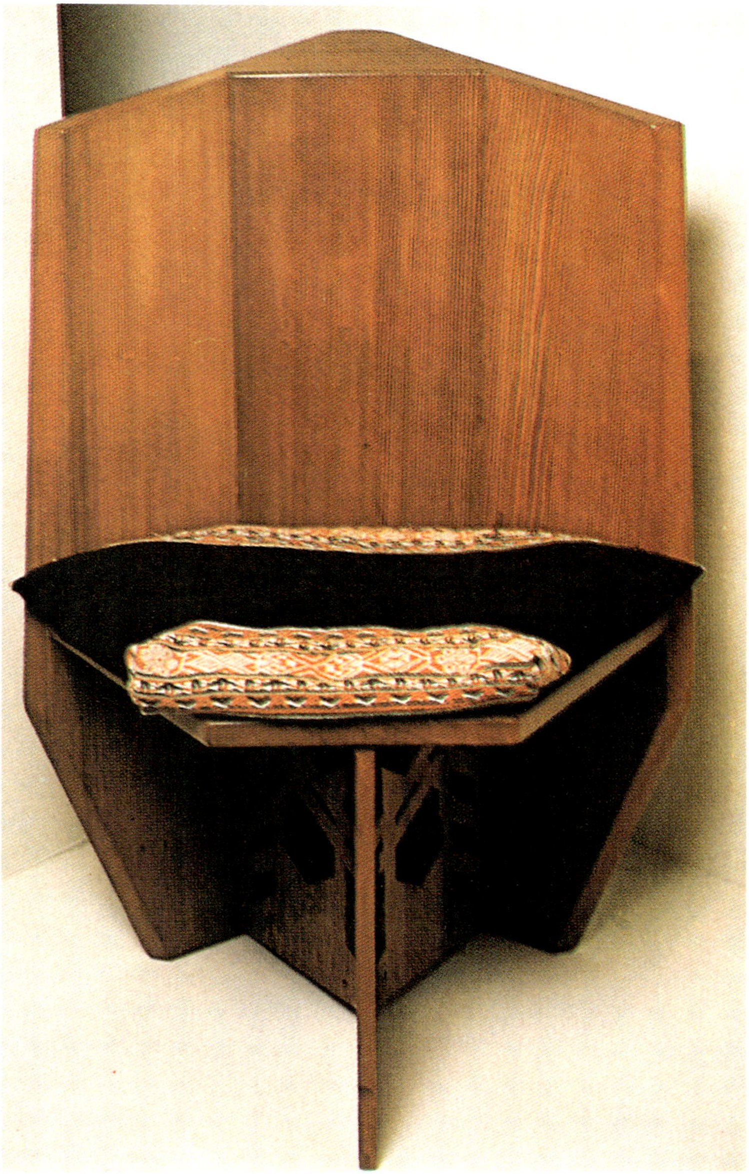

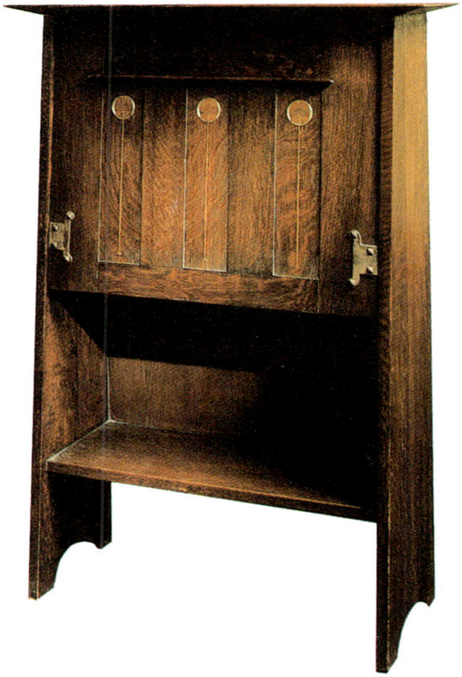

Above: Stickley is best known for his strong, sturdy designs intended to evoke the "simple life" of the early pioneers. This fall front, wooden desk is typical of his work.

Left: A redwood side chair by Frank Lloyd Wright for the Paul R. Hanna House (The Honeycomb House) in Palo Alto, California, 1937.

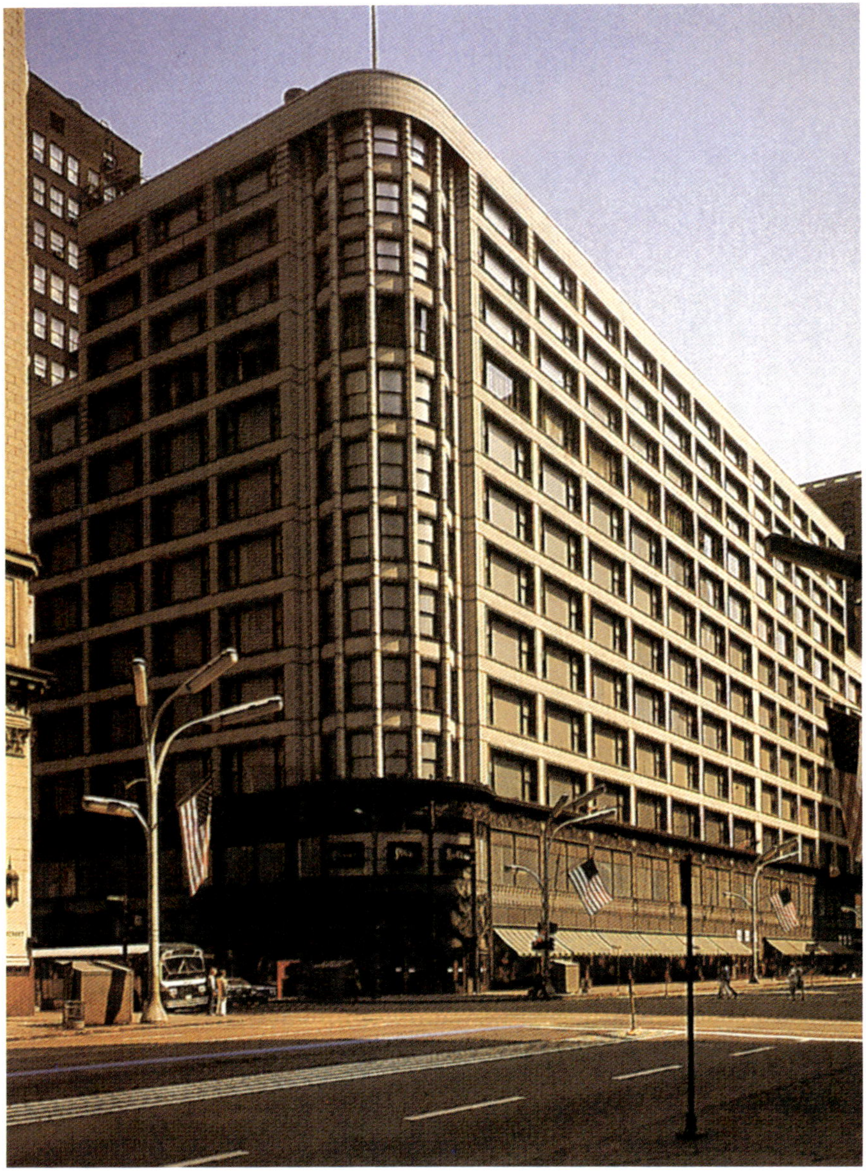

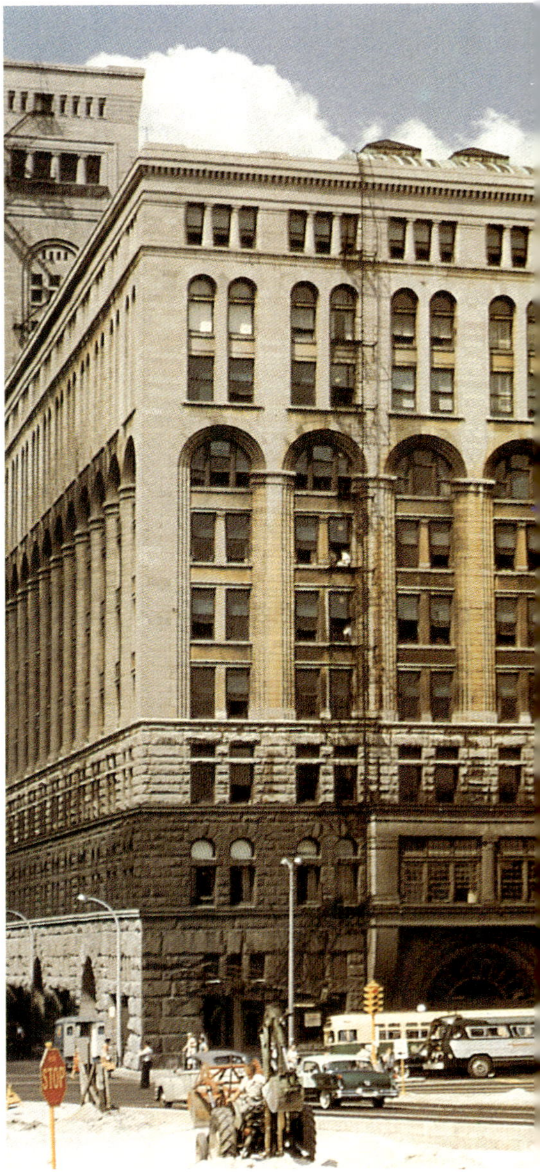

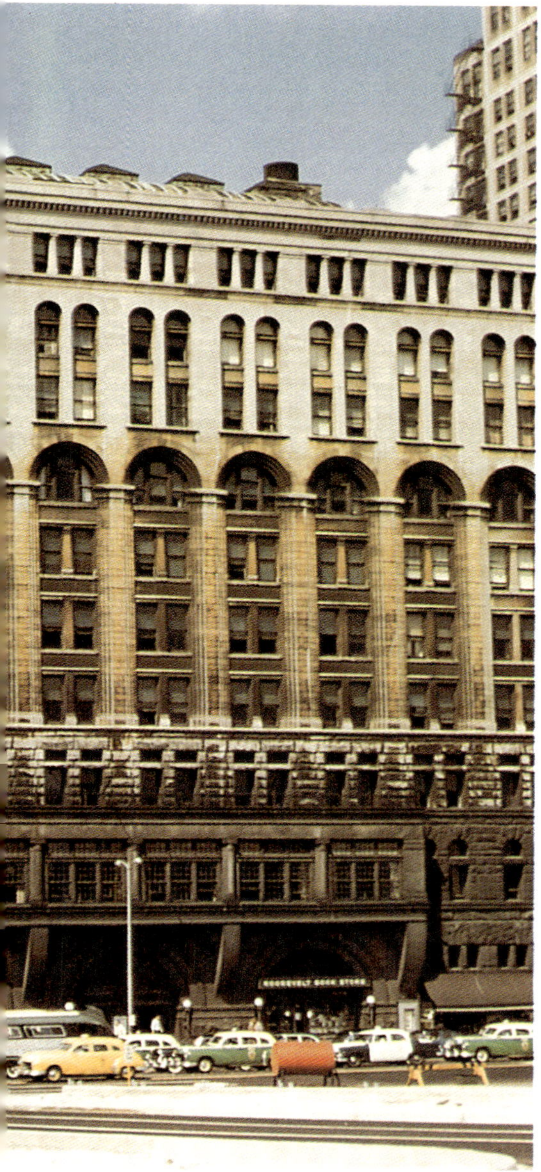

Nouveau. Sullivan led the movement towards the exploitation of the new steel-framed structures, which, with the development of the elevator, enabled him to produce some of the most successful early skyscrapers.

Structural skeleton

Sullivan's architecture is more concerned with expressing the structural skeleton of a building, by allowing a very simple grid-form to appear as the basic design, and by hollowing out the ground floor until it rests on just a few reinforced columns. These innovations of Sullivan's were eventually to become commonplace in modern architecture throughout the world.

Ornamentation

Yet Sullivan remained very much a man of his time in his attitude towards the embellishment of his buildings. His theories on the subject were highly developed, and he saw the contrast between the rectilinear and the curvilinear as parallel to the division between intellect and emotion. Throughout his architectural career, he tried to maintain a balance between the two.

The actual form of his ornament was often reminiscent of oriental abstractions from nature, but just as frequently he used more overt natural forms of intertwining leaves and branches which became very much a Chicago version of Art Nouveau — home-grown, but with very strong formal links with the style as it had developed in Europe.

The bar interior of the great Auditorium Building, a complex of opera house, hotel, and offices, shows an opulence of detail and the involvement of the architect in every small feature which is characteristic of Art Nouveau. Nor was Sullivan averse to turning his bare, exposed vertical beams, part of his grid facade, into rather exotic tree forms by using a flourish of foliage at the top, as in the facade of the Gage Building of South Michigan Avenue in Chicago.

More frequently, Sullivan preferred to contain very lush and flowing natural ornament within quite rigid limits, as in the Wainwright Building in St. Louis, where it serves to articulate the horizontal beams set against the plain verticals, and to embellish a very ornate cornice which caps the whole composition.

The natural forms of Sullivan's decoration not only recalled those of French Art Nouveau, but also had symbolic importance for him. The energy of organic growth was what Sullivan was attempting to evoke, and in particular, its application to the rapidly developing cities of America. Just as Art Nouveau was self-consciously the "modern style," so Sullivan was attempting to create a powerful, growing architecture.

Gothic fantasy

His Guaranty Building in Buffalo, New York, extends this Art Nouveau concern for growth beyond the decoration itself, into the structure as a whole. Linked by arches at their peak, the great verticals of the building seem to be enormous stems pushing up to the cornice which curls over in a gentle curve reminiscent of growing form. In this case, the

Far left: In structure, Louis Sullivan's Carson, Pirie, Scott department store in Chicago, Illinois, anticipates much of 20th-century architecture.

Left: Louis Sullivan's Auditorium Building, whose austere facade contrasts with the lavishness of some of the interior decoration.

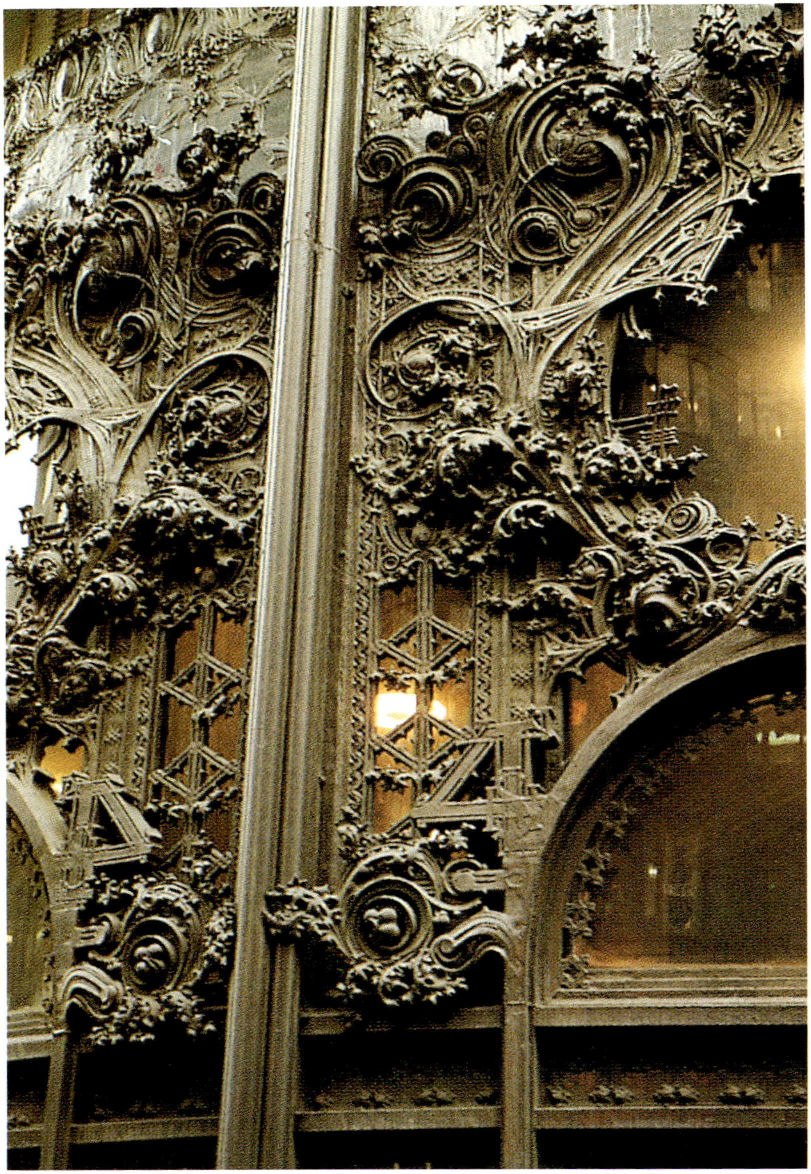

ornament makes the analogies more explicit.

Sullivan's last work, the then Carson, Pirie, & Scott department store in Chicago, seems for the main area of the facade to be too plain for any reference to Art Nouveau to be made, yet in the first two stories, and particularly around the corner entrance, there is relief work of Gaudí-like extravagance, which, even in this unlikely context, recalls Sagrada Familia. This seems largely based on an elaborate Gothic fantasy, yet its tense spider web lines and twisting foliage can ultimately only be seen as a personal Art Nouveau composition.

Left: The decorative metalwork over the Carson, Pirie, Scott store recalls the florid exuberance of Art Nouveau.

Art Nouveau Jewelry and Metalwork

HALLMARKS OF ART NOUVEAU

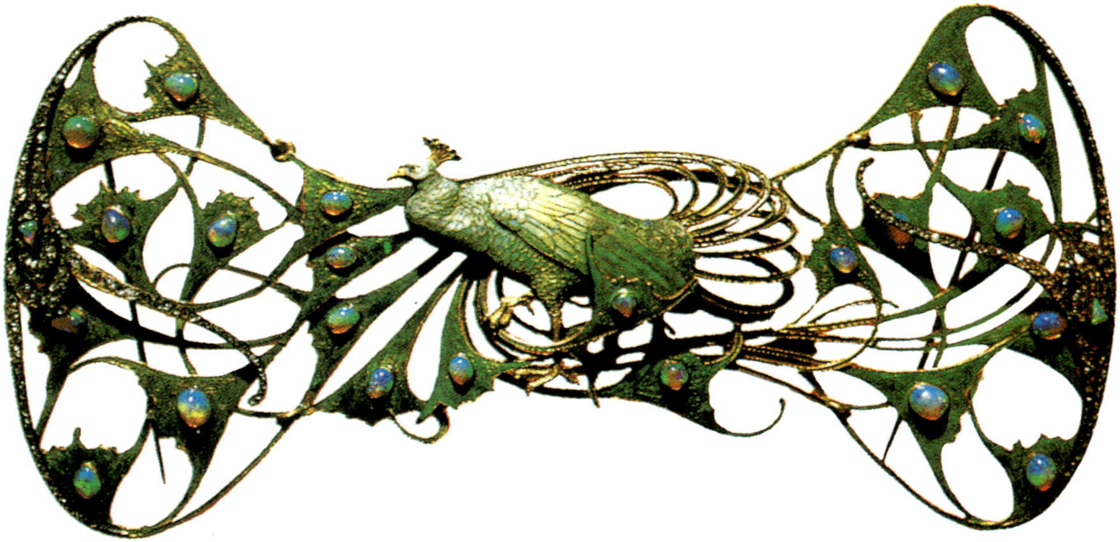

Art Nouveau, which means "new art," seems an appropriate description for an art movement that bridges the psychological gap between the 1800s and 1900s. As the 1900s dawned, the historicism inspired by the Arts and Crafts Movement began to give way to a new, forward-looking approach. Art Nouveau, which spanned the period roughly from 1895 to 1905, was caught between the joint influences of the old and new and, stylistically, owes something to each. Many designers and craftsmen seeking new sources of inspiration, looked back to earlier times and outwards to exotic cultures, and with new methods of production and novel materials, they created exciting new objects d'art.

Far left: A peacock corsage ornament, ca 1898-99, in gold, enamel, opals, and diamonds by René Lalique.

Below: Wrought iron from the staircase of Horta's Hotel Solvay in Brussels.

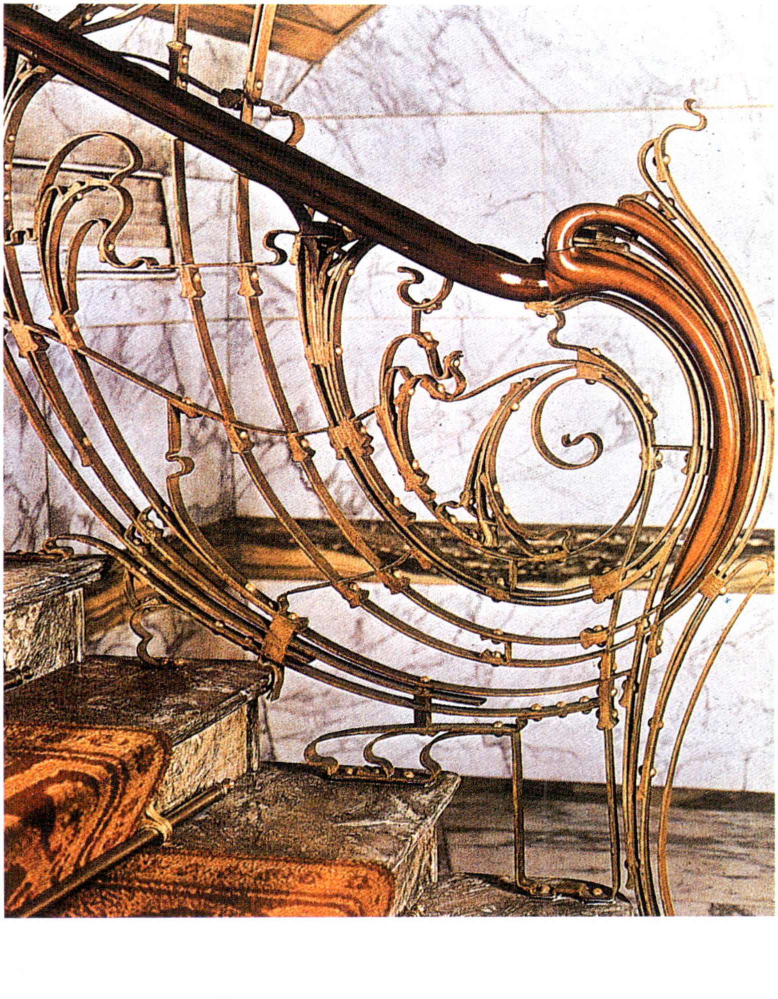

SYMBOLISM

One of the major influences on Art Nouveau was the Symbolist movement which had begun in the 1880s in reaction to the optical realism of the Impressionists. The Symbolists sought to depict the "idea in sensuous form" and, in protest against the increasing industrialization of society, drew their subject matter from legend, literature, religion, and even the occult. Distinguished by a shared attitude rather than a common style — the movement included artists as diverse as Gustav Moreau, Odilon Redon, Puvis de Chevannes, and Ferdinand Khnopff — Symbolist paintings recorded not the observation but the sensation. In both the aim to communicate emotion, and in the subject matter employed to do so, much Symbolist art is closely allied to Art Nouveau — the use of undulating line, the many representations of the nude female figure with, long flowing hair, insects, peacocks, flowers, and water-inspired iconography.

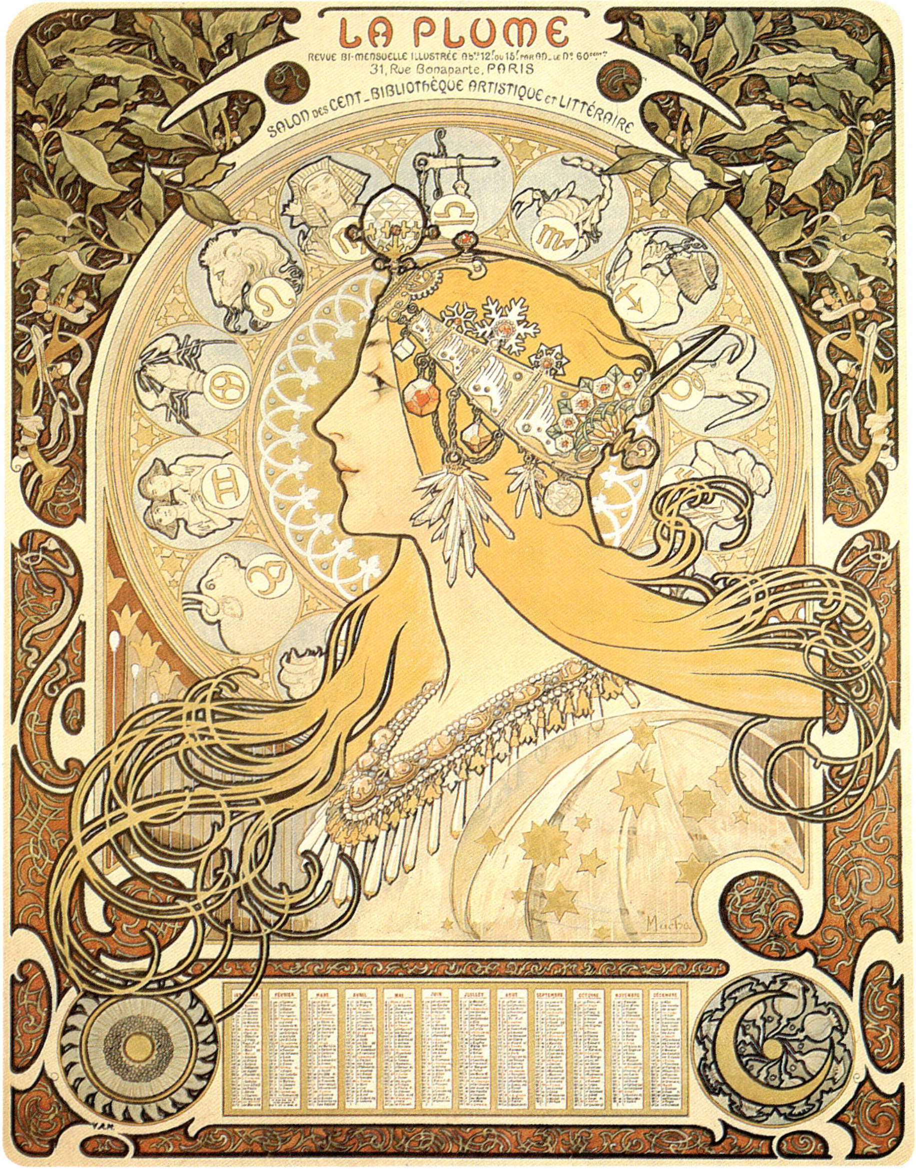

The decadent elegance of Symbolism was, in many places, to become the hallmark of Art Nouveau — it informs the graphic work of Alphonse Mucha, the glass of Emile Gallé, the jewelry of René Lalique, the ironwork of Hector Guimard, and the furniture of Louis Majorelle. But the flowing, flaring, asymmetrical lines, and the motifs largely drawn from nature and natural forms employed by Art Nouveau designers were also linked to a variety of different sources.

INFLUENCES FROM ENGLAND

Many of the origins of the Art Nouveau style are to be found also in Victorian England. Here, one discovers not only the sinuous decorative line that was to characterize the appearance of Art Nouveau, but also many of the ideas that were to become its theoretical base.

The Great Exhibition of 1851 held in the Crystal Palace in London's Hyde Park, had been intended not only to demonstrate new technology and promote international trade, but also to advertise what were generally held to be the finest examples of design. The standards of the exhibits on display, however, were to attract a great deal of harsh criticism, from the influential writer and art critic, John Ruskin in particular.

Ruskin hated the mass-produced and shoddily made products that he had seen, and called for a return to craftsmanship. This was largely inspired by a somewhat romantic vision of the Middle Ages through which Ruskin hoped to develop an alternative to the horrors of factory labor and in which he saw as a means of improving the quality of everyday objects.

Above: La Plume calendar by Alphonse Mucha. The jewels recall his work for Fouquet.

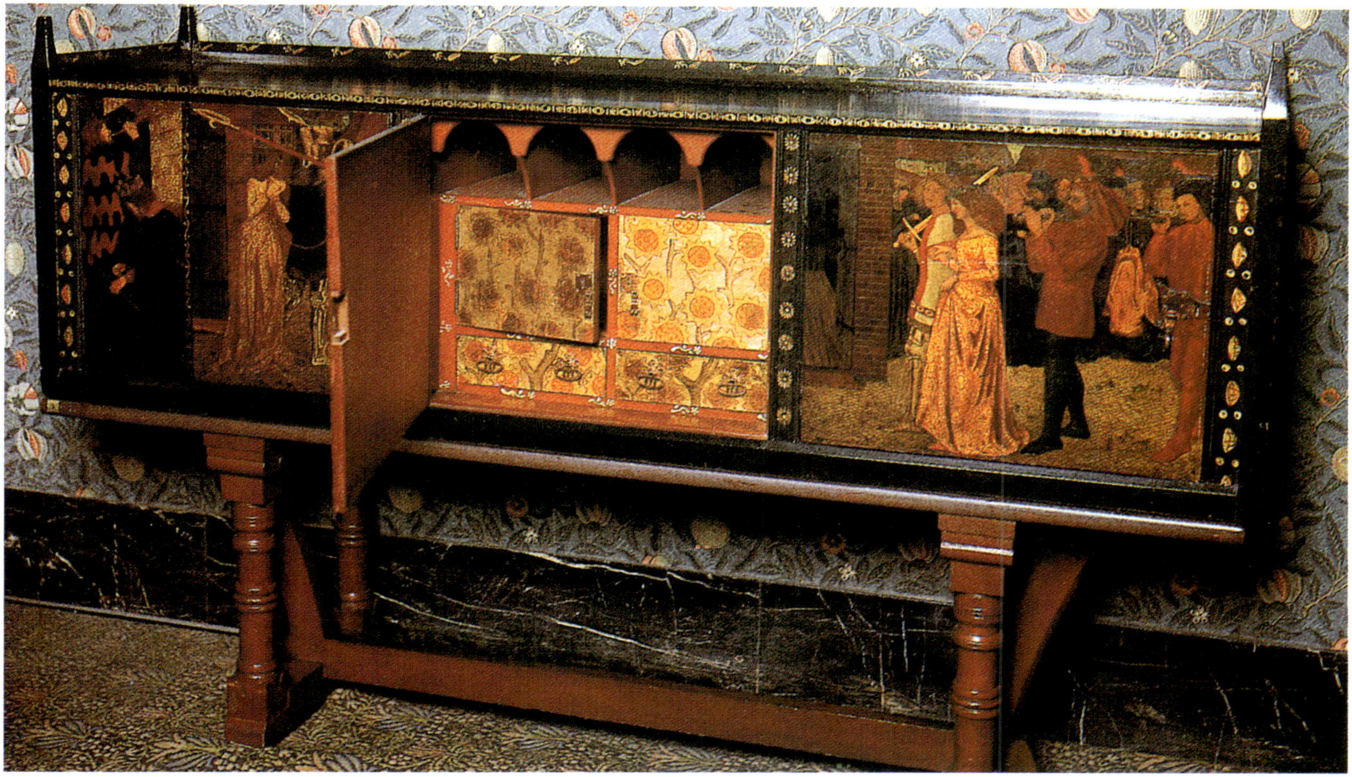

Above: Cabinet decorated with scenes from the life of St. George, painted by William Morris. The medievalism of the piece is typical of the furniture produced by Morris & Co. during the 1860s.

Ruskin advised craftsmen and designers to look to nature for their forms and cast off the historical forms common in Victorian revivalism.

MORRIS AND CO.

Ruskin's ideas were taken up by William Morris, who as a student had developed a profound affection for the culture of the Middle Ages — not only its architecture, art, and craft, but also the artistic cooperation which had fostered their creation. At Oxford, Morris met several others who shared his passion — the architect Philip Webb and the painters Edward Burne-Jones and Dante Gabriel Rossetti, who were later to become members of the Pre-Raphaelite group.

In his attempt to recreate a medievally-inspired idyll of artists and craftsmen working together on the same tasks, Morris founded a company in 1861 to produce the types of objects he wanted to see in very home. This became Morris and Co., and by employing his Pre-Raphaelite friends to design and decorate furniture, textiles, and furnishings, Morris's company was able to produce a complete range of products to furnish a home in a uniform

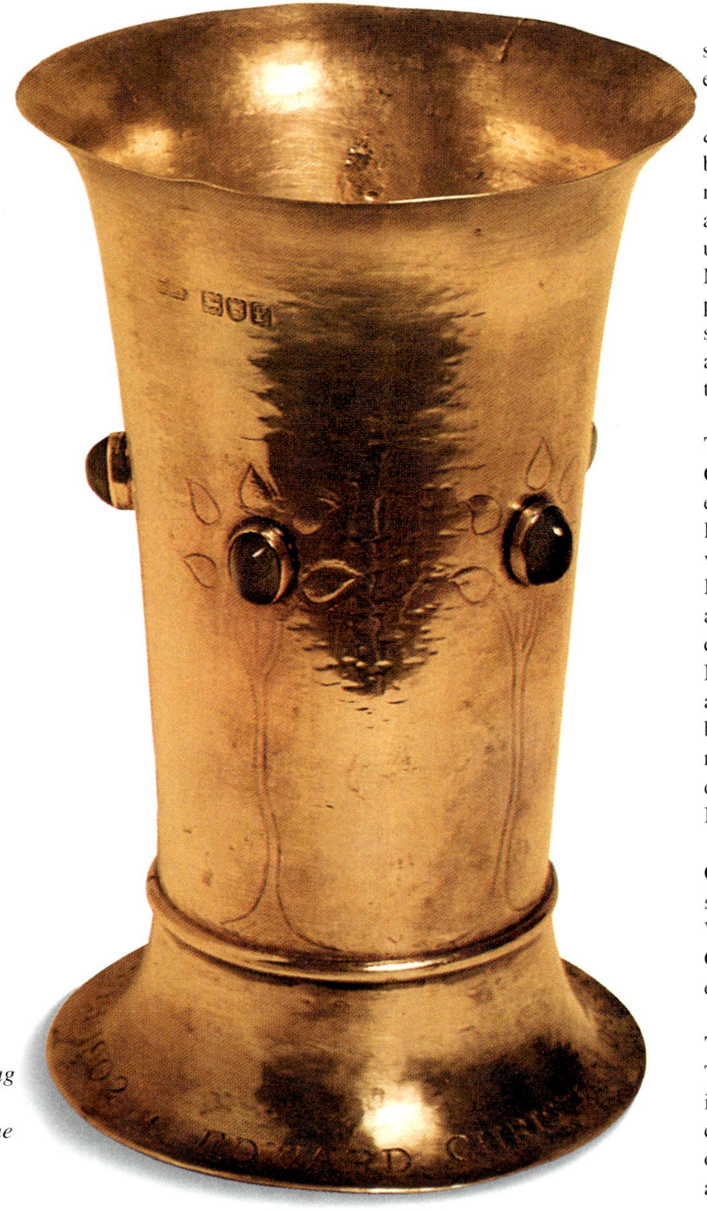

Right: Christening mug for Lord David Cecil (1902) produced by the Guild of Handicraft.

style that achieved an overall harmony of effect.

The appearance of the goods made by Morris & Co. was reminiscent of medieval models, but the style was also largely derived from natural sources inspired by plant, bird, and animal forms. The use of hand-crafted, natural materials, however, inevitably made Morris's goods too expensive for ordinary people, but his example encouraged a number of similar groups of designers to develop. These are generally referred to under the name of the Arts and Crafts Movement.

THE CENTURY GUILD

One of the most important of these enterprises was the Century Guild founded by Arthur Heygate Mackmurdo in 1882. Mackmurdo developed the natural forms that had inspired Morris into elongated, increasingly elegant lines and patterns, and as such, was the first to produce the characteristic vocabulary of Art Nouveau. The new style made its first appearance in the title page design of Mackmurdo's book, *Wren's City Churches,* and the sinuous, rippling pattern of the plants as if they are underwater, were to be the hallmark of the Art Nouveau style for the next two decades.

The theme was rapidly developed by the Century Guild and a number of other bodies such as the Art Workers' Guild, founded by Walter Crane and Lewis Day in 1884, and Charles Ashbee's Guild of Handicraft, founded in 1888.

THE GUILD OF HANDICRAFT

The work produced by the Guild was simple in design. Its metalwork, in the form of jewelry, flatware, plates, and vases was, again, often inspired by medieval sources, with the addition of semiprecious stones and decorative devices. Ashbee was one of the first designers in the Arts and Crafts Movement to experiment in jewelry.

Initially, there were few trained jewelers involved in the Guild, though many of the craftsmen involved were experienced metalworkers in copper and silver. Ashbee's own designs were in part inspired by the Celtic Revival which encouraged the use of Celtic-inspired interlaces and colored enamels, and in part by the work of Benvenuto Cellini, perhaps the greatest goldsmith of the Italian Renaissance. To these sources, Ashbee added motifs of his own and produced a range of metalwork and jewelry that included covered cups, salvers, and ceremonial spoons, and brooches, buckles, necklaces, and even buttons decorated with peacocks and flowers, and enhanced with blue and green enamels and semiprecious stones.

SPREADING THE STYLE

Public interest grew, largely due to the exhibitions of craftwork organized by the Arts and Crafts Exhibition Society and the widespread publicity given to the Arts and Crafts Movement by art journals such as *The Studio*. The business of Liberty & Co., established in 1875 by Arthur Lazenby Liberty, modified the handicraft guild's original ideal of solely producing hand-crafted goods into another direction by exploiting both markets and machinery. Technically, Liberty's factory made commercial products, and although some were hand finished, they cannot be deemed Arts and Crafts. Yet many of their designs relate to the spirit and style of the movement. Liberty &

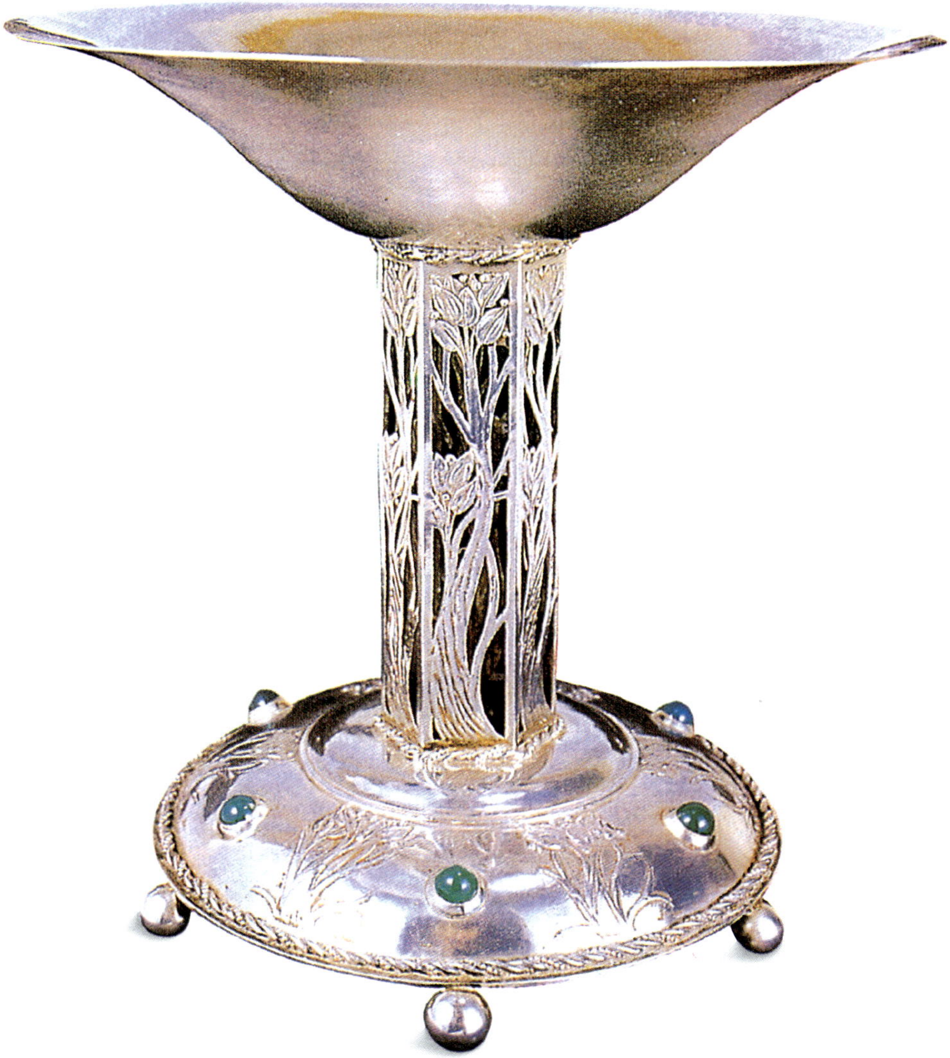

Right: A late 19th-century silver and chrysoprase bowl on stand by C.R. Ashbee.

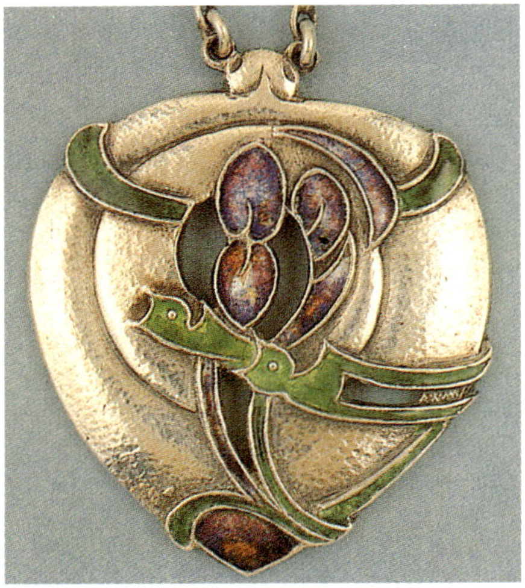

Co. managed to produce and distribute couture, fabrics, furnishings, metalwork, jewelry, and furniture to a wider public than either Morris or his followers. Despite the fact that individual handicraft and creative expression often disappeared under Liberty's policy of anonymity for his designers, his employees did include some of the most prominent names in the Arts and Crafts and Art Nouveau design of the time — Charles Voysey, Jessie M. King, Arthur and Rex Silver, Georgina and Arthur Gaskin, and Archibald Knox.

ART NOUVEAU ABROAD

This mixture of commerce and art was not restricted to England. The term "Art Nouveau" itself in fact derives from the Parisian shop of the same name run by a German émigré, Samuel Bing. Bing had been trading for some years in Oriental art and in 1888 had launched a monthly magazine, *Le Japon Artistique*. Japan was a relatively new discovery for the west, having been opened up to trading by the American Commodore Perry as recently as 1853. Artists such as Gallé, Lalique, and Tiffany owed a debt to this "japonisme."

The formal links between Japanese art, in particular, Japanese prints and Art Nouveau are strong: the emphasis on decorative line, creating flat, patterned work and the delicate balance between decoration and background were immediately found to be sympathetic. The curving, flowing Japanese line was drawn from observation of nature, filtered

Above: A pendant in enameled silver by Jessie M. King for Liberty & Co., ca 1902.

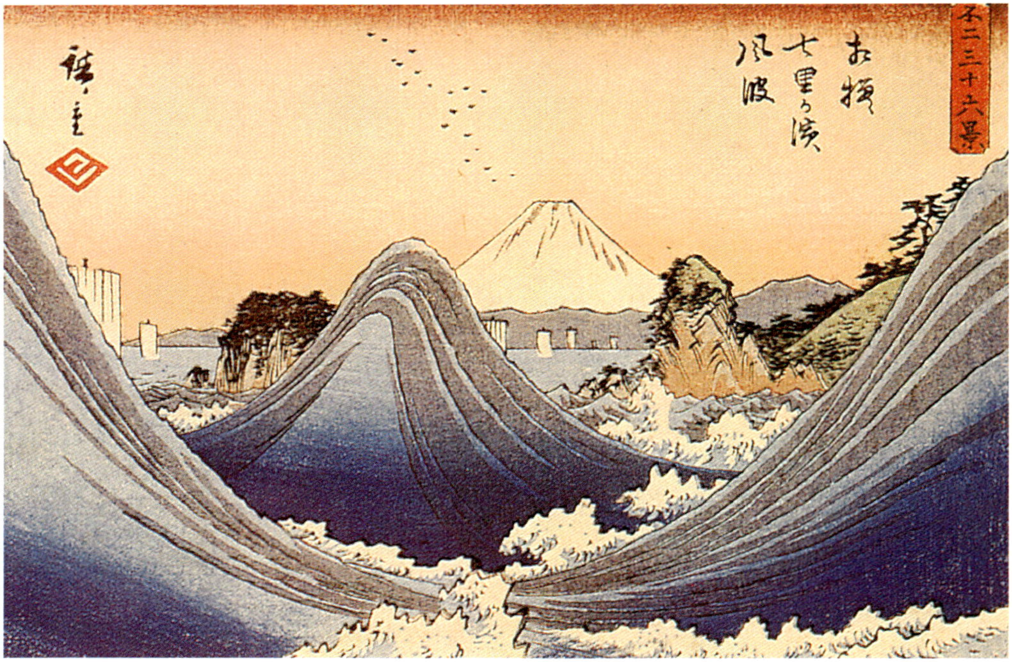

Right: Print by Hiroshige. The Japanese use of expressive line and a combination of simple, flat shapes inspired the painters and designers of late 19th-century Europe.

Far right: A lady's sitting room in Bing's Pavillion de l'Art Nouveau, by Georges de Feure, 1900.

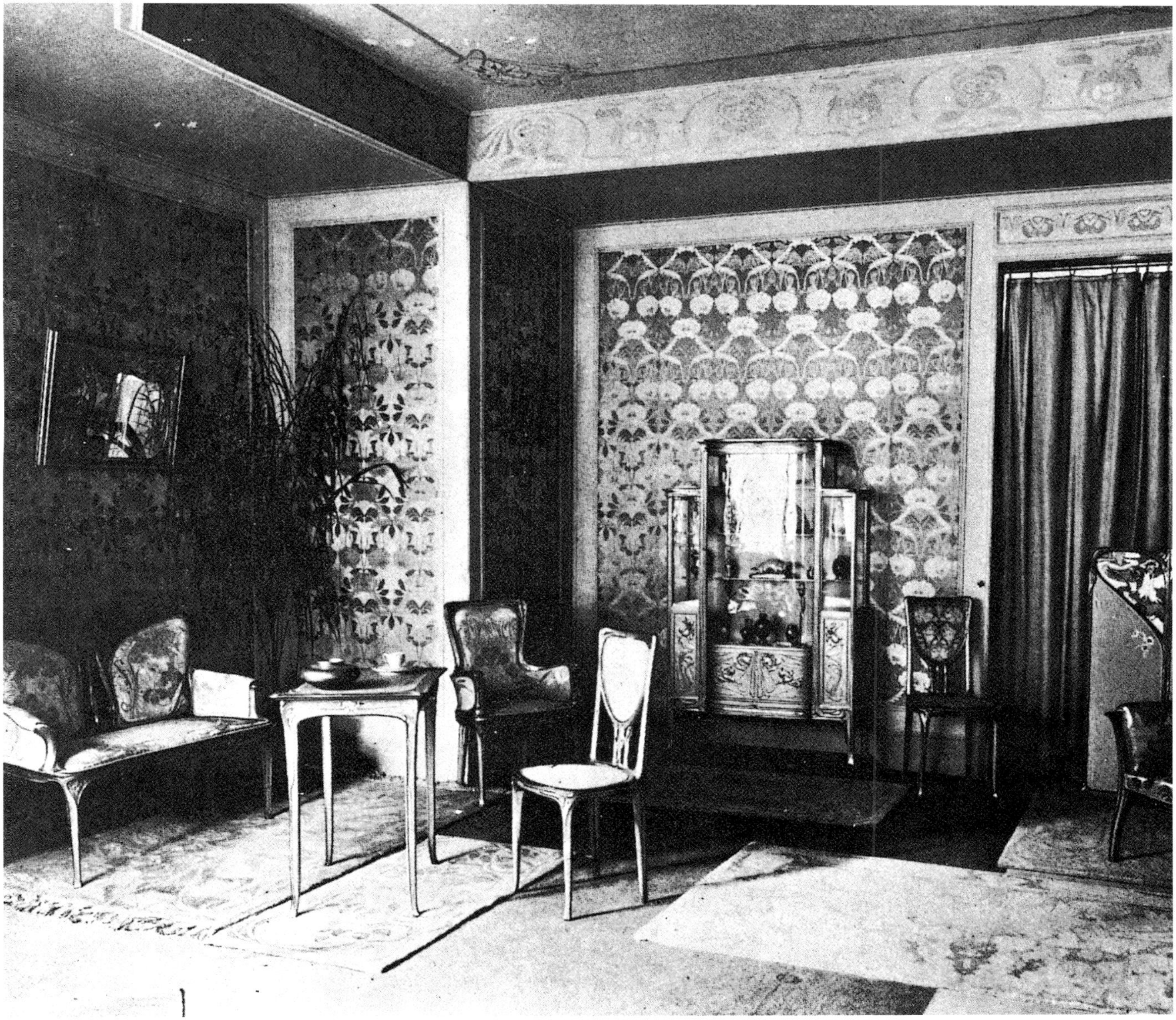

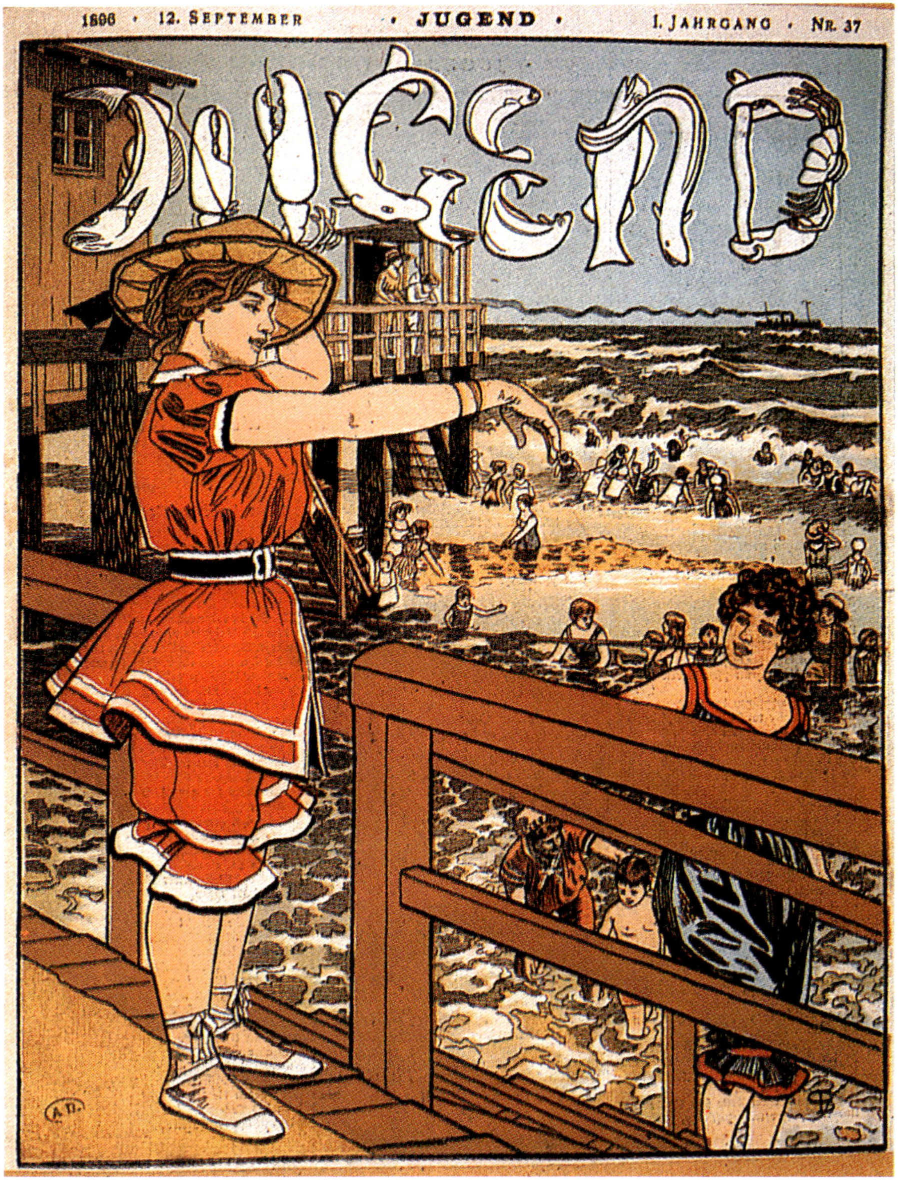

through a developed design sense to create more abstract forms and patterns with the precise degree of artificiality that the Art Nouveau artists found so appealing.

LA MAISON DE L'ART NOUVEAU

When he relaunched his shop as La Maison de l'Art Nouveau in 1895, Bing exhibited the work of contemporary designers and artists including Tiffany, Aubrey Beardsley, René Lalique, and Emile Gallé. Bing's mixture of gallery and shop was to become the Paris base for the new style of Art Nouveau, and his reputation was sufficient for him to be allotted an entire pavilion at the Paris Exposition Universelle of 1900.

International exhibitions throughout the 1800s and early 1900s became an increasingly important feature of international commerce and in the dissemination of the new style. The depth of interest among the public in new fashions in decorative art were also reflected in a growing number of magazines and periodicals devoted to the new trends.

VARIATIONS ON A THEME

In Germany, the influential Munich-based journal *Jugend* would lend its name to the German version of Art Nouveau, Jugendstil. Sometimes here the style was also called "Studiostil," after the widely read English, and later American, periodical *The Studio*. In 1907 the Deutsche Werkbund, partially inspired by British Arts and Crafts models, was formed by Henry Van de Velde and Hermann Muthesias to promote an alliance between art and industry. The Werkbund was not only interested in applying good design principles,

Left: Jugend *magazine, the German journal established in 1896.*

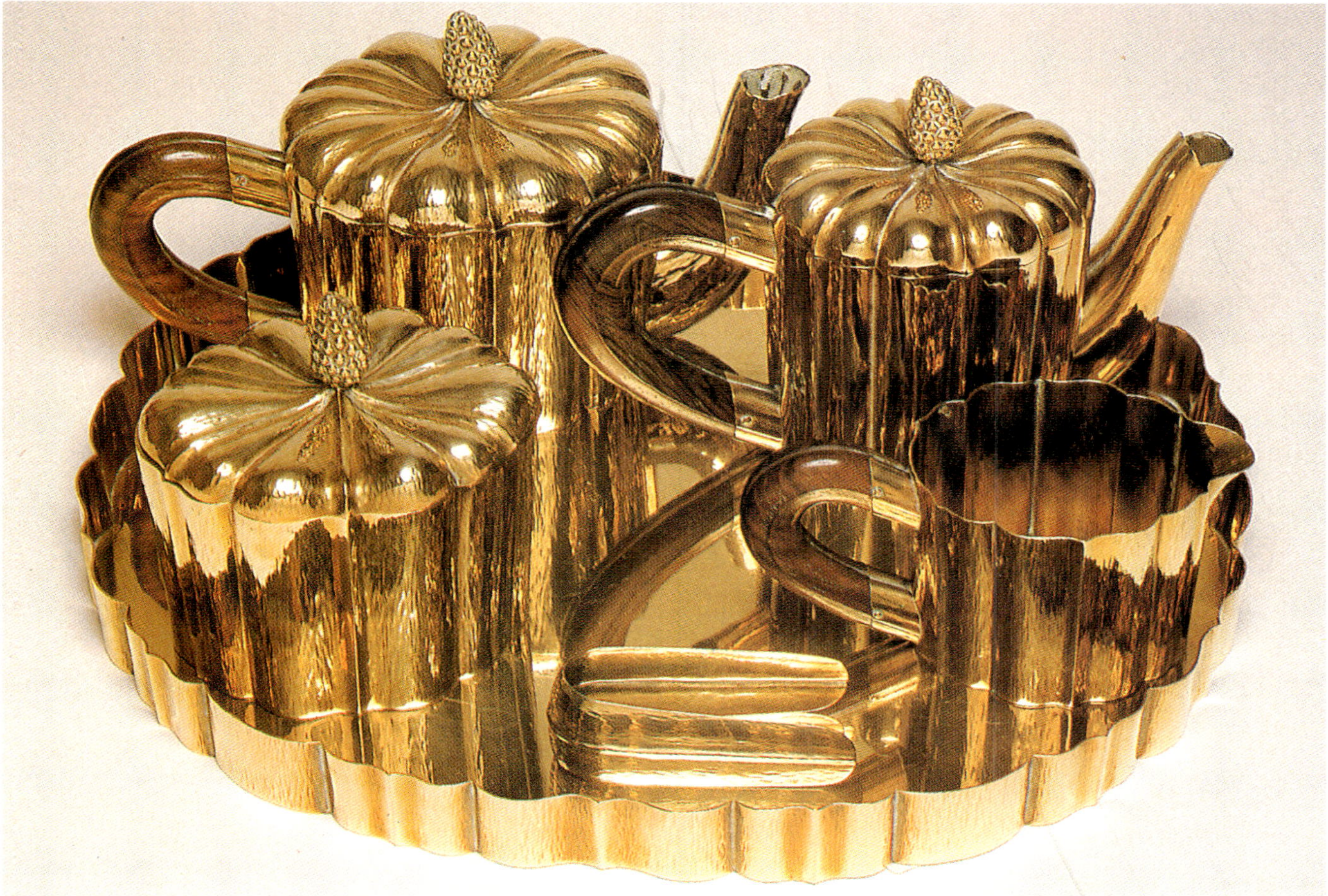

but also in educating the general public to appreciate these principles. Their ultimate goal was to shape the economic and cultural identity of Germany.

AUSTRIA

In Austria, the leading organs for Art Nouveau were the periodical *Ver Sacrum* and the members of the Wiener Werkstätte. The search for a new style at the beginning of the century was led by Josef Hoffmann and the members of the Secessionist group founded in 1897. The main objective of this group was to improve the status of the decorative arts, and in 1903 they established the Wiener Werkstätte, a small colony of artists who wished to promote the

Above: A tea set designed by Josef Hoffmann in typical Wiener Werkstätte style. The forms are more traditional than most Art Nouveau ceramics.

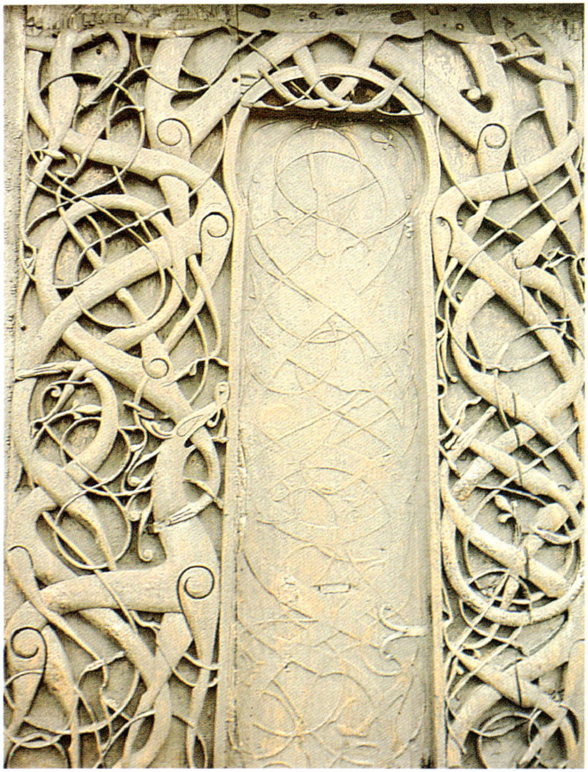

Right: A Viking wood carving in an intricate interlaced design.

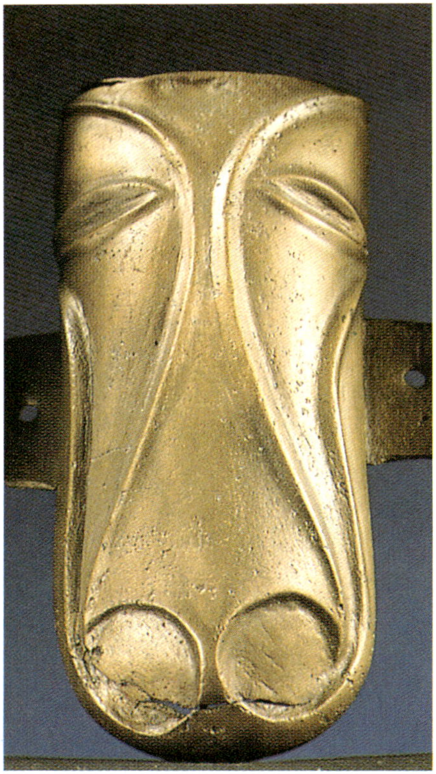

Far right: A bronze fitting from a Celtic chariot in the form of a horse's head. The combination of stylization and natural inspiration typified Art Nouveau itself.

individual creativity of the designer.

NORDIC COUNTRIES

In their search for an aesthetic formula that was in keeping with their cultural traditions, the Nordic countries of Sweden, Denmark, Finland, and Norway also drew on the idealized democratic principles of craft production espoused by Ruskin and Morris. Returning to their own indigenous folk art for inspiration, the intricate curves and spirals of this tradition found their way into the local form of Art Nouveau that was even occasionally called the Dragon Style in deference to its Viking sources.

In the United States, as in England, the Arts and Crafts Movement inspired many individuals to turn to the professional practice of their particular craft. The Arts and Crafts Movement was important in the United States not only for the fine workmanship it encouraged, but also for the growing awareness it fostered among Americans of the need for a truly national art.

Much of Art Nouveau's vitality derived from these and other centers. Paris and Nancy in France, Munich, Berlin, and Darmstadt in Germany, Brussels, Barcelona, Glasgow, Vienna, New York, and Chicago were all focal points for a style that was capable of accommodating diversity in regional variations.

Art Nouveau Jewelry in France

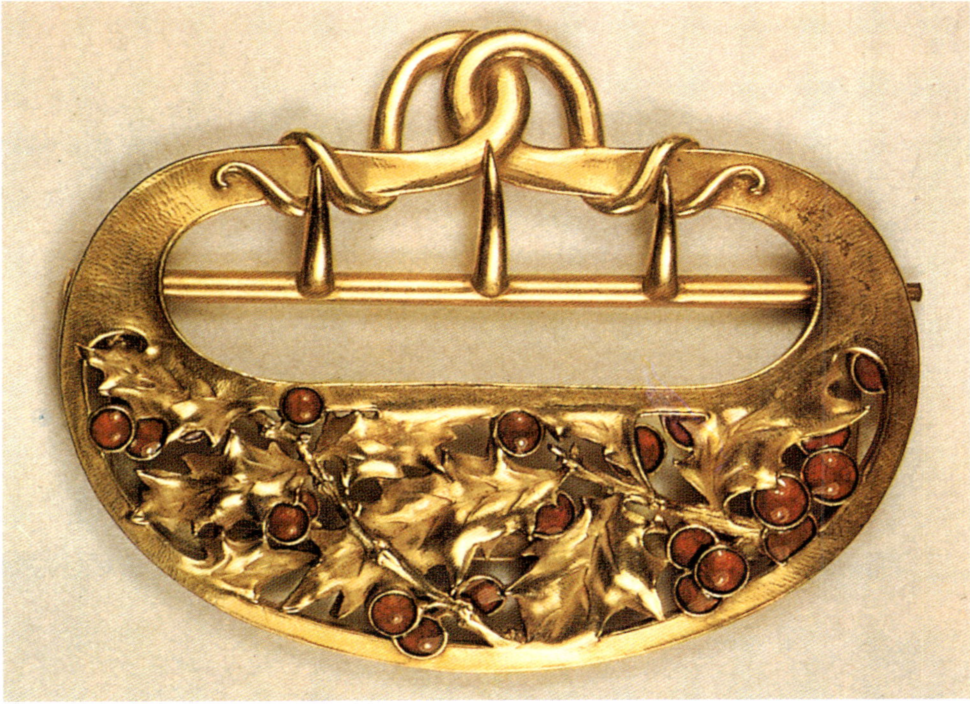

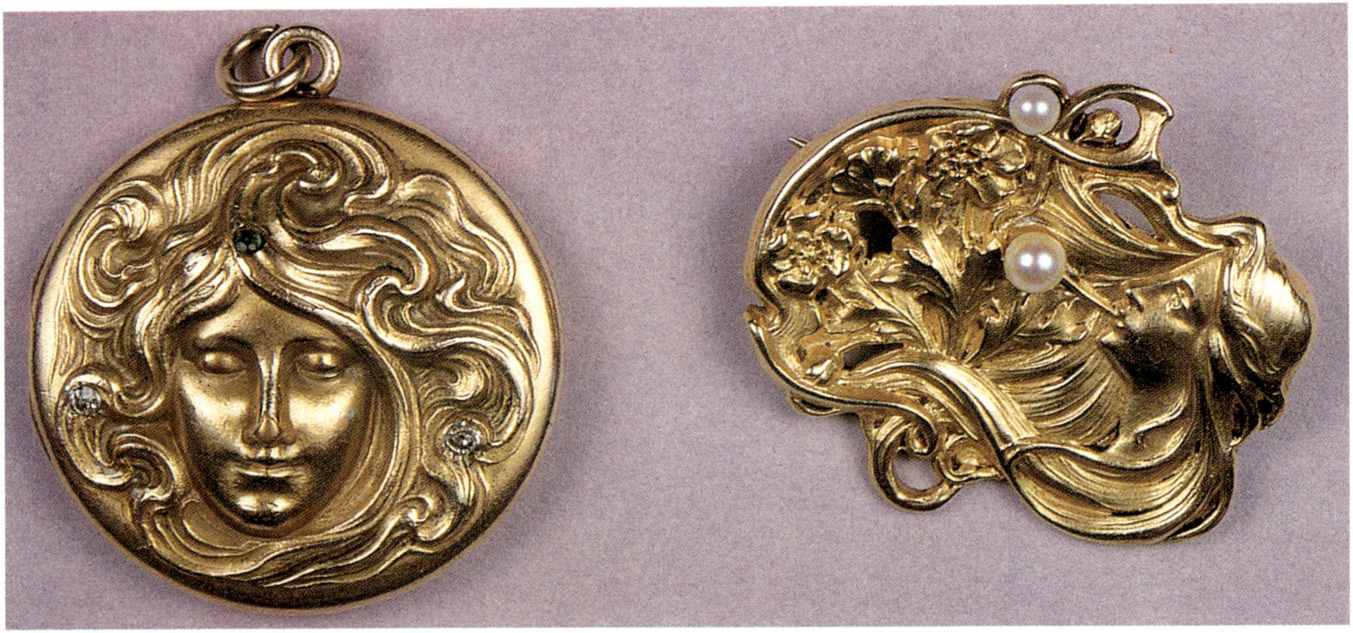

Above: Pendants in gold and diamonds. Two anonymous examples of Art Nouveau design featuring the "femme fatale."

Overleaf: A gold and enamel belt buckle. French, from around 1900.

The standards of French craftsmanship in the area of jewelry were extremely high, and perhaps unrivaled in any other country. In a period rich in its constant variety of invention, the tastes in jewelry were susceptible to the vagaries and whims of fashion, and serve as an expressive mirror of the period, reflecting the decadence of the fin-de-siècle. In France, Art Nouveau jewelry had its origins in the work of the French goldsmiths whose creations were to become the inspirations for other European craftsmen and women. The most influential among the French artist-jewelers was undoubtedly the glass maker René Lalique.

Art Nouveau jewelry

Most characteristic of Art Nouveau is a tendency to asymmetry, producing a sense of instability which is heightened by the use of the whiplash curves and tendril forms. Another ubiquitous image is of woman, either in the form of the *femme-fleur* (woman as flower) or the dangerous, man devouring, *femme fa-*

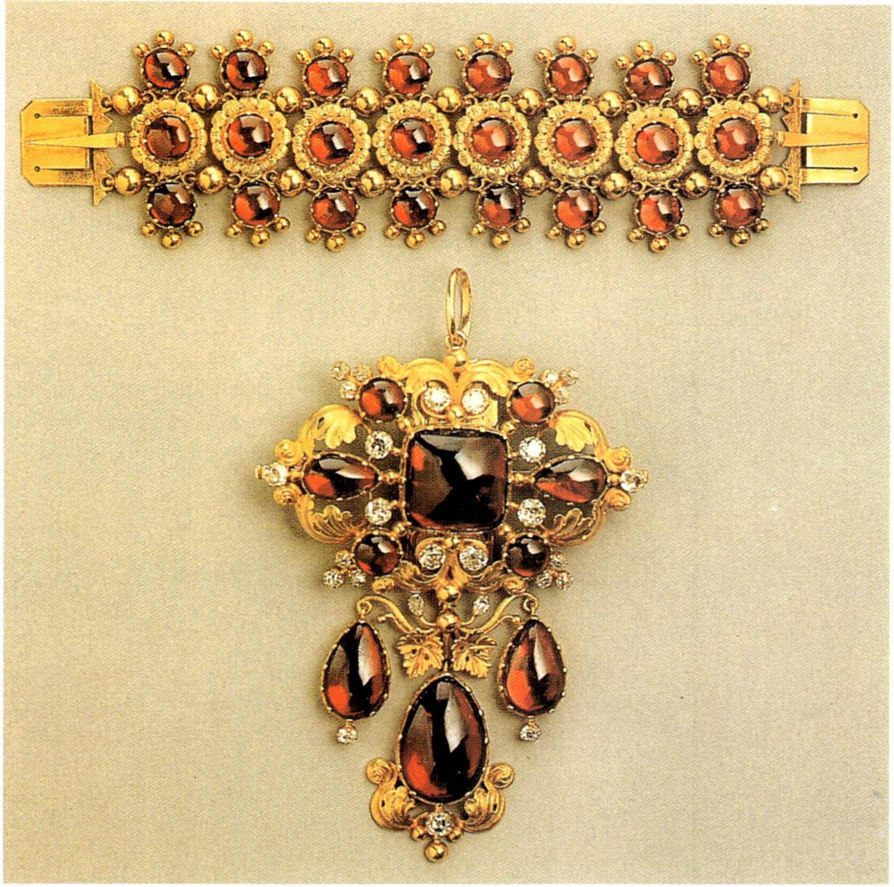

Left: The more traditional style of jewelry seen in a matching bracelet and pendant from ca 1835 in gold, diamonds, and garnets.

tale. Much of the imagery in Art Nouveau comes from mythology, whether in the form of winged serpents, the gothic horrors of bats and vampires, or more ethereal creatures, such as peacocks, butterflies, and dragonflies.

Goldsmithing in France

The goldsmith's work that was produced in France, and throughout most of the west before the Art Nouveau period, essentially followed a long, established line of classical, baroque, and Rococo jewelry. It was opulent and ostentatious, and often rather unimaginative, although one principle that many of the turn-of-the-century goldsmiths did adopt was of the jewel as a miniature work of art. On the whole, goldsmiths generally subjugated whatever innovative talents they might have had in favor of manipulating the precious gems at their disposal — namely, the diamond. In the wake of South Africa's "diamond rush" of the 1860s, there was a strong demand for cut diamonds throughout Europe and the United States, and most goldsmiths tended to work exclusively with these cut stones.

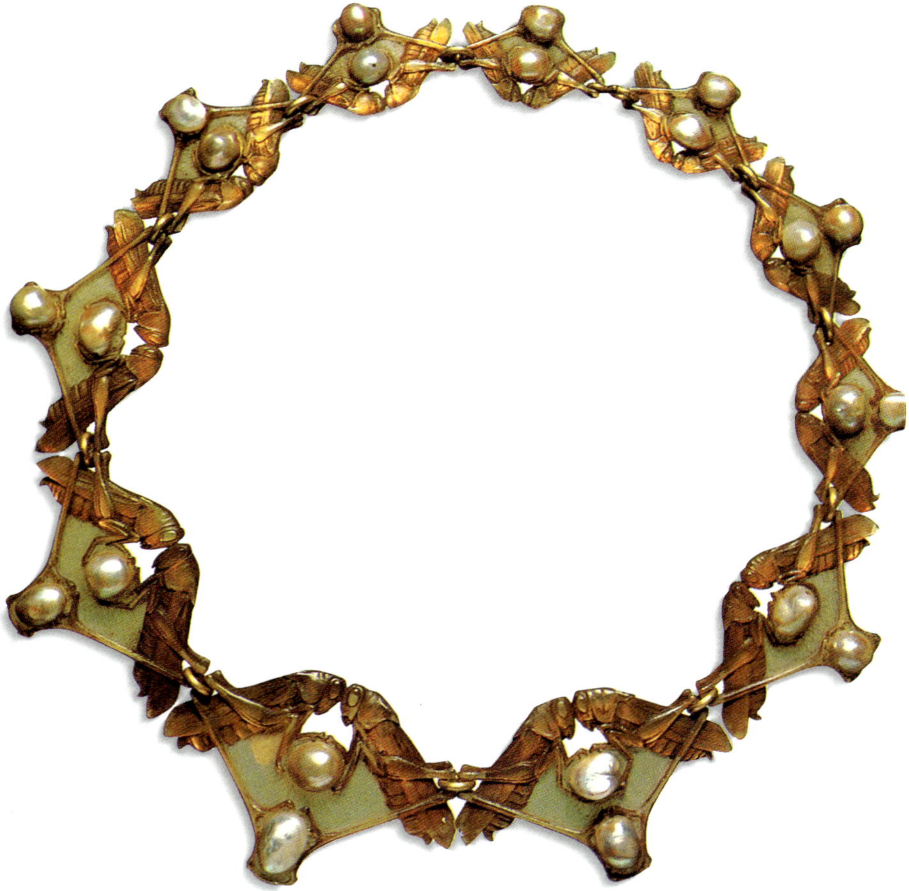

Above: Grasshopper necklace, with horn and pearls, ca 1902-04. A popular motif in Art Nouveau, the grasshopper appeared on several Lalique jewels.

LALIQUE AND JEWELRY

The jewels of Lalique are among the richest and most telling of all Art Nouveau creations. The myriad brooches, pendants, necklaces, diadems, lorgnettes, hair combs, watch cases, and other bijouterie bearing this master's signature comprise a single oeuvre shaped by a vivid imagination and honed by virtuoso technical skills. Lalique's innovative combination of previously underutilized, even scorned "lesser materials" like glass, horn, and tortoiseshell, with rare gems and metals, (such hybrid confections are called "bijouterie," as distinguished from all-precious "joaillerie") as well as his use of natural, fantastic, neo-classical, and literary images in a sublime way, makes his work an outstanding achievement in the history of Art Nouveau and in the goldsmith's art. Lalique did not forsake precious stones like diamonds, sapphires, and topaz altogether, but it was his genius to rediscover semiprecious colored stones such as opal, chalcedony, agate, jade, chrysoprase, and moonstone and to use them in exciting combinations with pearls, translucent, opalescent champlevé, and *plique-à-jour* enamels.

LALIQUE'S CAREER

Lalique's background was the perfect blend of art and craft. In 1876, at the age of 16, on the death of his father, Lalique was apprenticed to the celebrated goldsmith Louis Aucoc, whilst simultaneously pursuing his studies at the Ecole des Arts Decoratifs in Paris. Aucoc was a high-priced goldsmith whose wealthy and modish clientele demanded exactly what was fashionable at the time. This was primarily neo-Rococo jewelry with heavy and showy cut gems dominating their precious metal settings that was neither technically nor stylistically innovative.

A two year period of study in England, at Sydenham School of Art at Crystal Palace in south London, completed his education, and on his return to France in 1880, he found that the Parisian climate was becoming more sympathetic to the creation of finely crafted objects d'art. In the midst of the machine age, interest had been reawakened to in individual workmanship, an echo of the Arts and

Crafts Movement that Lalique had witnessed in England.

Lalique worked freelance for the prestigious houses of Cartier, Boucheron, Renn, Gariod, Hamelin, and Destape. By 1885, he had taken over Destape's workshop, and in the following five years, had expanded the premises. Although he had been exhibiting his jewels as early as the Exposition of 1889, (anonymously, under the names of the large companies for which he was freelancing) it was not until the Paris Salon of 1894 that Lalique displayed his work under his own name. Immediately, he won lavish praise and gained numerous commissions from the "grandes dames" of the Third Empire. Lalique was well on his way to becoming the most prominent master in his field.

Having opened his own firm, Lalique was free to design jewelry as he wanted, without any restrictions from employers or clients. His designs, which were regularly reproduced in the trade magazine *Le Bijou*, inspired both praise and imitation from numerous colleagues, including Alphonse Fouquet and his son, Georges, who took over his father's firm in 1895 and became a well-known Art Nouveau jeweler.

SARAH BERNHARDT

By this time, Lalique had begun to design jewels for his most famous female client, the actress Sarah Bernhardt, and it was she who provided Lalique with the opportunity to apply his talent to relatively large-scale, often audacious, pieces that could be easily seen by the theatre audiences she performed to. Bernhardt commissioned luxurious diadems, necklaces, belts, and other stage "props," which he tailored perfectly to the roles she was playing, such as the Theodora crown of 1884, and parures for the parts of Gismonda and Iseyl.

Despite the boldness of his theatrical extravagances, Lalique's ruling notion was that a jewel worn by a woman should contribute to the harmony and total effect of her entire ensemble. The stage pieces for Bernhardt and the 140 or so "museum-pieces" designed for the collector Calouste Gulbenkian, which were never intended to be worn, were exceptions

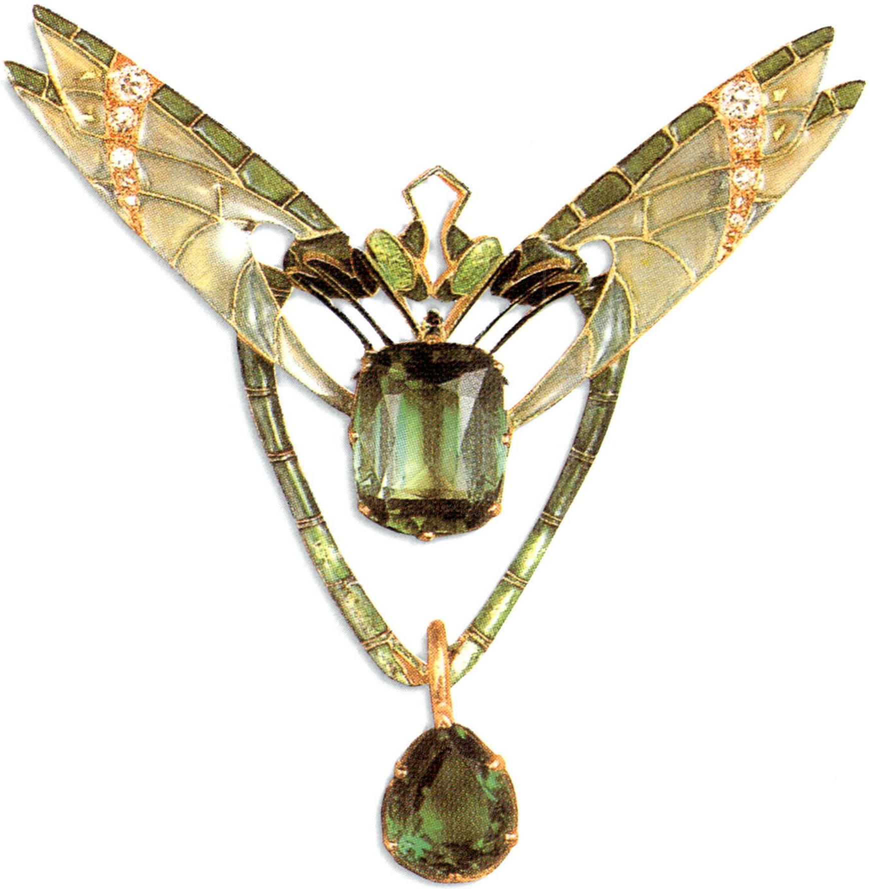

Above: Lalique pendant brooch in diamond and tourmaline offset by rich plique-a-jour *enamel.*

Right: Lalique's studies for pendants and brooches of dragonflies and butterflies as decorative devices.

Below: A medallion by Lalique of the actress Sarah Bernhardt, ca 1900.

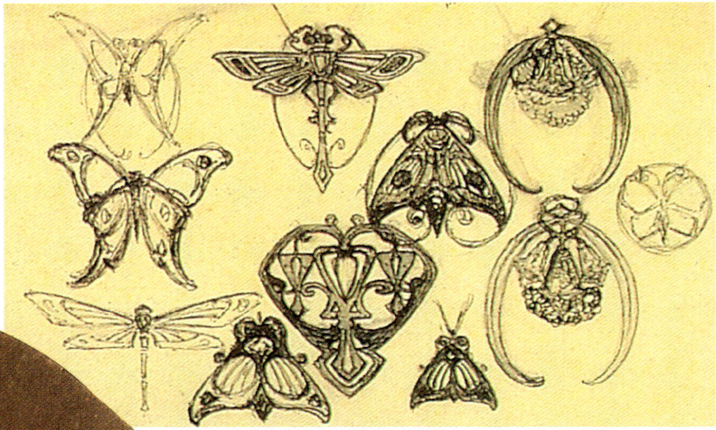

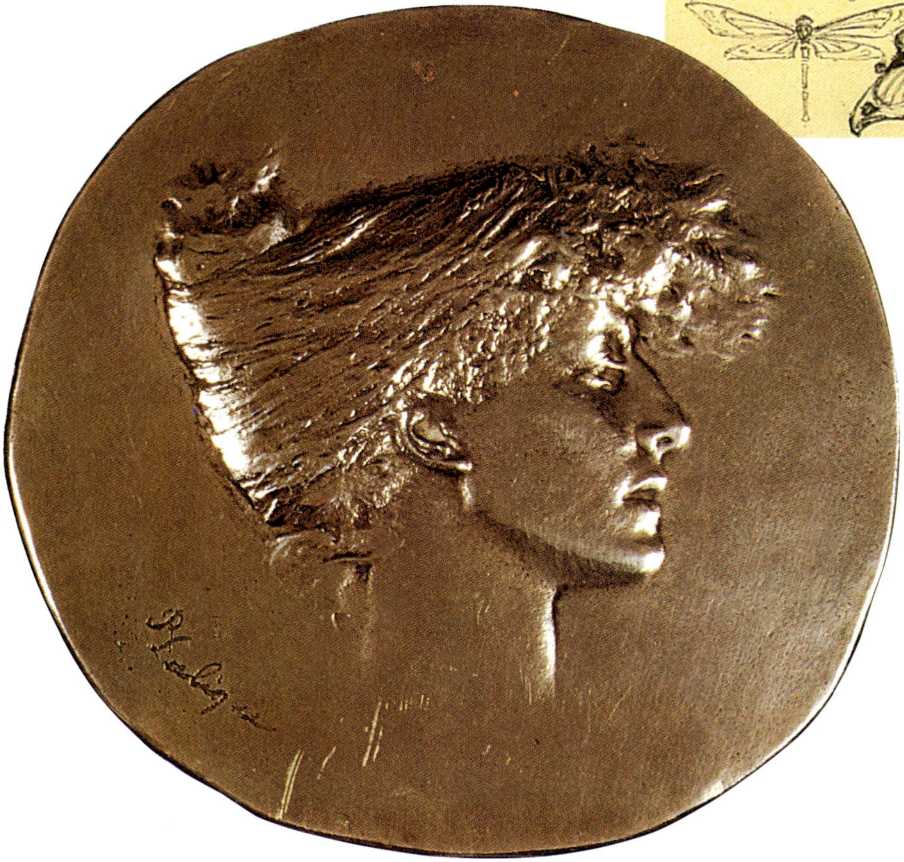

to this rule, and they were outnumbered by hundreds of subtler, though no less striking, pieces of bijouterie he produced.

OFFICIAL RECOGNITION

Throughout his three decades as a goldsmith, Lalique continually experimented with new materials and new techniques. He used horn in place of tortoiseshell and elevated that material to a near-luxury status; he employed embroidery techniques on metals, and applied enamels to a variety of surfaces. As his reputation grew, his rebellion against the more usual proliferation of diamonds in joaillerie came to be officially approved by the board of jewelers. By order of the Chambre Syndicale de la Bijouterie de Paris, the use of precious stones or materials alongside semiprecious or "vulgar" stones and materials was officially sanctioned for the first time.

Without a doubt, the Exposition Universelle of 1900 in Paris, which welcomed the dawn of the new century and commemorated the 30th anniversary of the Third Republic with displays of recent technological achieve-

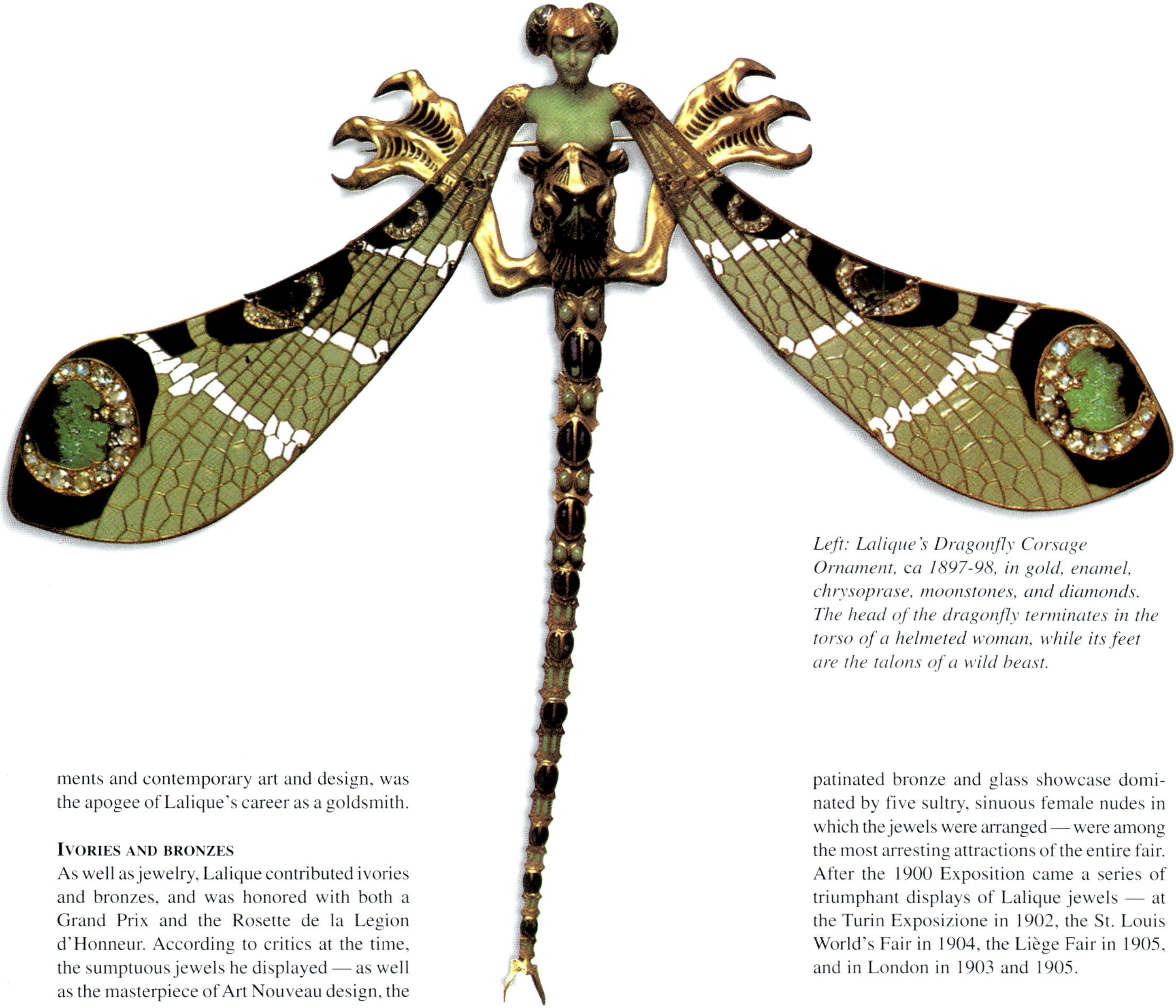

Left: Lalique's Dragonfly Corsage Ornament, ca 1897-98, in gold, enamel, chrysoprase, moonstones, and diamonds. The head of the dragonfly terminates in the torso of a helmeted woman, while its feet are the talons of a wild beast.

ments and contemporary art and design, was the apogee of Lalique's career as a goldsmith.

Ivories and bronzes

As well as jewelry, Lalique contributed ivories and bronzes, and was honored with both a Grand Prix and the Rosette de la Legion d'Honneur. According to critics at the time, the sumptuous jewels he displayed — as well as the masterpiece of Art Nouveau design, the patinated bronze and glass showcase dominated by five sultry, sinuous female nudes in which the jewels were arranged — were among the most arresting attractions of the entire fair. After the 1900 Exposition came a series of triumphant displays of Lalique jewels — at the Turin Exposizione in 1902, the St. Louis World's Fair in 1904, the Liège Fair in 1905, and in London in 1903 and 1905.

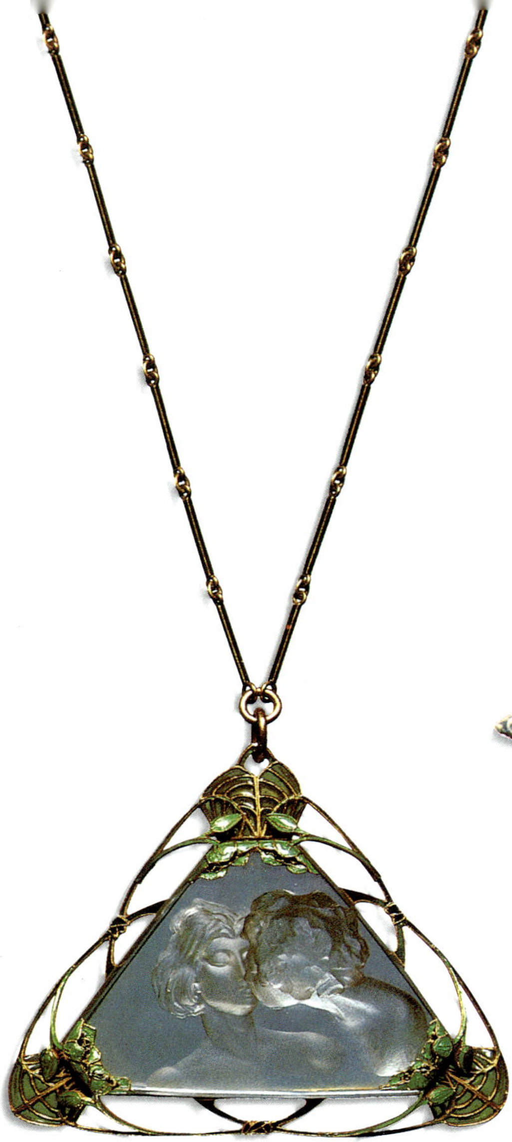

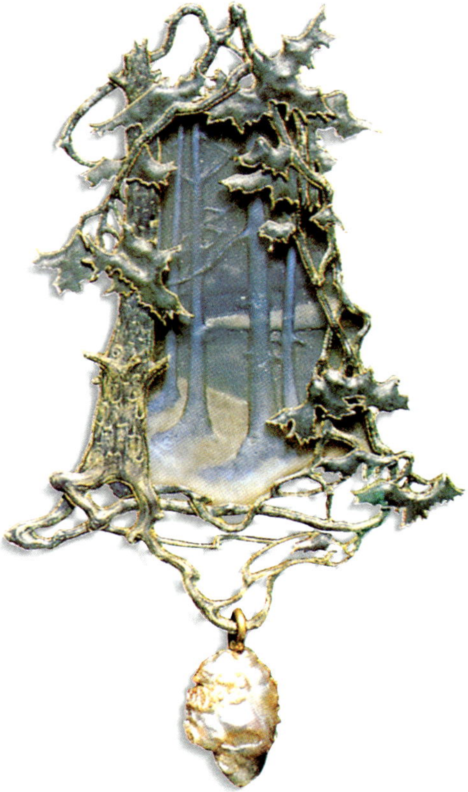

Above: Lalique's Winter Woodland pendant from 1899-1900. Several of Lalique's jewels depict miniature landscapes in great detail.

Left: Lalique's "The Kiss" pendant, 1904-05. Similar kissing couples appear on other works.

Symbolist themes

What was most striking about Lalique's jewelry — and indeed, the multimedia works of art he also created — was the fertility of their graphic creation. Lalique's motifs reflected perfectly the often morbid aspects of fin-de-siècle taste. He devised refined, graphic designs from the Medusas, the Ophelias, the drugged, poppy-wreathed maidens, the grotesque creatures, half-animal, half-human, of symbolist literature and painting. He froze into jewelry form, the literary world of Des Esseintes, the hero of Huysman's *A Rebours* (Against Nature), and the visual world of Khnopff, Redon, and Schwabe. And always, whatever the motif, Lalique's graphic ability created distinctly personal linear patterns that could also be visualized as an abstract art in themselves.

Lalique's output

Lalique's output embraces the entire repertory of Art Nouveau themes and inspirations — brightly plumaged peacocks and glistening, shelled beetles, coiled enameled serpents, realistically rendered flowers and trees, women (either devastatingly devouring or innocently dancing), and tightly embracing couples all make their appearance in his jewelry. There are also more complicated, multi-dimensional pieces, such as miniature wooded landscapes fashioned from gold, enamel, opals, and brilliants which could be attached to a collar; or an ivory carved pendant of a horseman whose steed tramples a nude below, with the entire scene surrounded by three equine heads with stylized manes. Like many of the painters of the second half of the 1800s, such as Whistler, Klimt, and some of the Pre-Raphaelites, Lalique created both the work of art and the frame enclosing it, a concept that was revolutionary in the goldsmith's art.

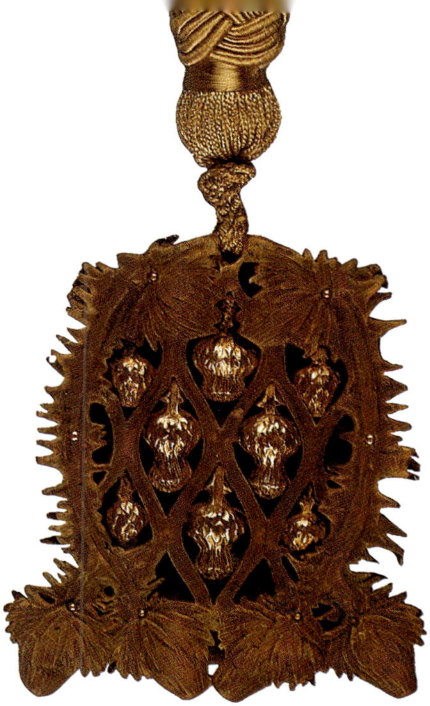

Above: *A thistle-inspired pendant by René Lalique.*

MOTIFS FROM NATURE

The subjects Lalique chose for his bijouterie mostly came from nature. At a young age, he had been a shrewd observer of flowers, trees, and animals in all their guises and stages of growth. Lalique's floral vocabulary is perhaps his richest, and in the main, the most faithful to nature. Works ranged from a simple hat-pin consisting of three silver birch leaves in horn, their gold seed cones enameled in a complementary autumnal hue, to a bracelet of five, bluish-violet champlevé enamel irises on gold, all on a carved opal background, as well as a lovely diadem in the shape of an apple tree branch which, but for its composition of horn, gold, and diamonds, might just have fallen from the tree.

Flowers and other plant forms are displayed on various brooches, bracelets, and pendants, though more often than not, these also incorporate insect or other animal life. The animals Lalique depicted in his jewels spanned nearly all the species of the zoological kingdom from grasshoppers to polar bears, to mythical dragons, sphinxes, and bizarre hybrid beasts. Insects, amphibians, reptiles, birds, and mammals were all subject to his scrutiny and his craftsman's technique. There was a decided emphasis on creatures favored by all Art Nouveau designers — the curvilinear swan, seahorse, and snake; the brilliantly hued butterflies, peacocks, and beetles, as well as more fearful creatures of the night, like bats and serpents.

The snake is one of the strongest subjects in Lalique's Art Nouveau repertory, and the masterpiece among his "serpent jewels" is the Knot of Serpents pectoral from 1898, comprising nine interlacing snakes whose silver-gilt champlevé enamel bodies of blue, green, and black fan out from a top knot, their jaws agape. Originally, each serpent was represented as spitting a row of baroque (misshapen) pearls out of its mouth.

BIRDS

Birds of various types — but especially peacocks, roosters, and swans — figure in

Below: Rose branches corsage ornament by René Lalique in gold, glass, amethyst, and enamel.

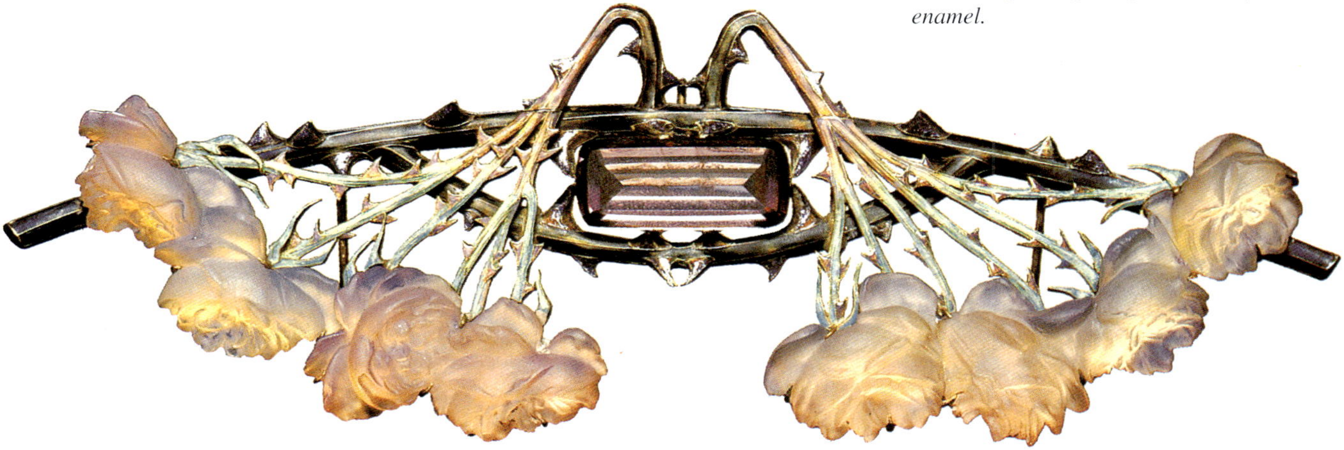

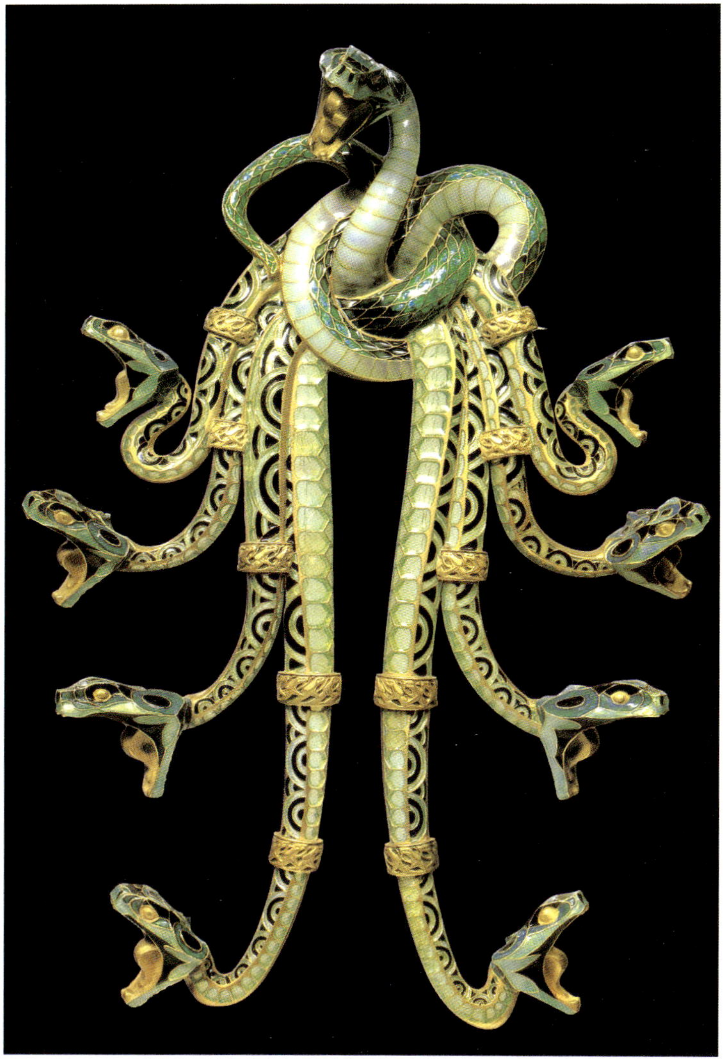

Above: The Knot of Serpents corsage ornament, the masterpiece among Lalique's jewels.

Lalique's jewelry designs as they do in his glass. One of his best-known jewels (and perhaps one of the most unwieldy) is the diadem in the shape of a cock's head. Never before in western art and design had such a lowly barnyard fowl been treated so luxuriantly. The cock's golden beak grasps an amethyst and its open-work gold and enamel comb is as delicately wrought as a spider's web. The cock motif was one that Lalique obviously found interesting for it also appears on a belt buckle. Here, two cock's heads in enameled copper are placed in profile, beak-to-beak.

The peacock had been a motif popular with artists from the Aesthetic Movement such as Whistler, but designers such as Morris and Tiffany chose to depict only its brilliantly hued feathers, often to the point of near abstraction. Lalique however, was eager to display the bird in all its glory. He created a stunning chest ornament in which the bird's enamel and gold tail feathers, richly studded with opals, swirls around its body in a bow-like pattern.

Female figures

The figure of woman also stands out in Lalique's work. Indeed it is she, almost to the total exclusion of the male sex, that dominates Art Nouveau. She appears as the long-haired seductress or the flower-crowned innocent. Lalique is believed to be the first goldsmith since the 1500s to represent the female nude in jewelry, and he did so frequently. He carved them in ivory and coupled them in erotic dances; he veiled them in vines and blossoms and he represented them as shameless pagan nymphs sometimes paired with birds and beasts, and even, the occasional male figure!

Lalique's female figures are not always nude — there is Ophelia reclining under a willow

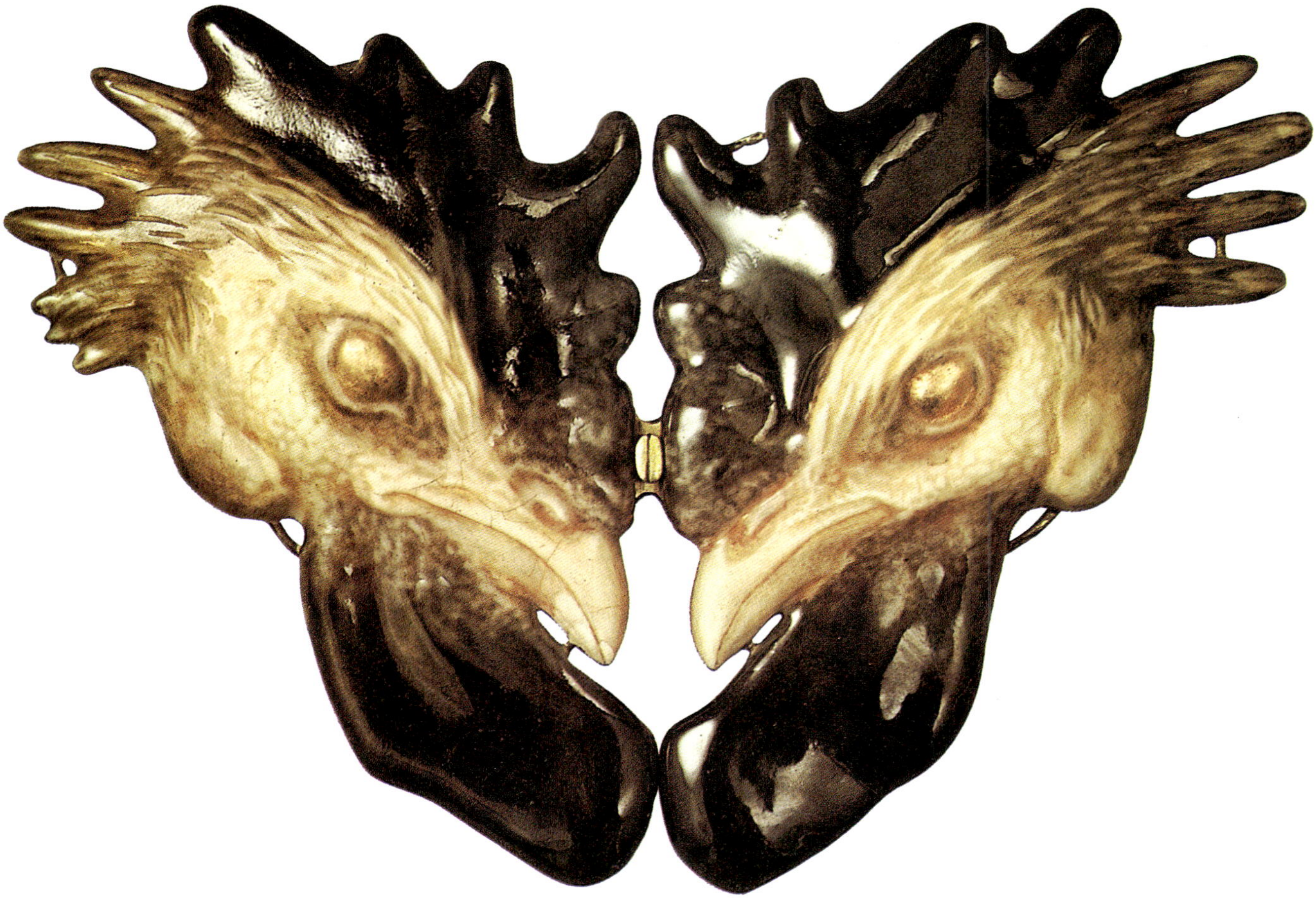

tree, angels deep in prayer, regal women with strongly carved profiles, Breton peasants in traditional costume. And even when he does not depict women directly, her spirit is often present, for the animals, plants, and flowers he used were often Symbolist allegories of woman in her various guises.

LITERARY INFLUENCES

On occasion, Lalique interpreted literary characters. The Owls bracelet from around 1900 was inspired by the poem "Les Hiboux" from *Les Fleurs du Mal* (The Flowers of Evil) by the Dandy poet Charles Baudelaire. Along a five part gold frieze, four molded frosted-glass

Above: A belt buckle in the form of two cocks' heads by Lalique. Enamel on copper and gold clasp, ca 1900.

owls, symbols of darkness and the night, are perched among pine cones and branches. A collar of 16 strands of tiny pearls surrounding a central rectangular plaque that features a profile of a smiling young woman, may well tell the story of the Frog Prince, for her head is crowned with a huge green enamel frog, while a host of frogs fill the open work field surrounding her. Most of Lalique's creatures are, however, without specific literary allusion and can be appreciated for their sheer beauty, the delicacy of their execution, and the imaginative way in which the elements are arranged.

JAPONISME

The combs, diadems, and other hair ornaments that Lalique produced, mostly of horn embellished with gold, enamel, ivory, glass, and stones, are the most realistically nature-laden of his works. In these designs, Lalique was strongly influenced by the irregular design system of flowers which characterized japonisme. The borrowed Oriental style was, thanks to Samuel Bing's efforts in bringing it to public attention, in vogue at the turn of the century.

GULBENKIAN COLLECTION

One comb in the Gulbenkian collection, Wisteria, exhibits a device often used by Lalique — certain carved areas are left "blank," that is, in their original hued state, whereas other primary areas are built up or emphasized by means of vividly colored enamels. One of the most obvious borrowings from Japanese art is a necklace from 1890 made of nine spherical *ojime* in ochre lacquer carved with a stylized wave motif and embellished with mother-of-pearl insets. Ojime are part of the traditional Japanese costume and are bell-shaped toggles which separate the little seal container called *inro* from the carved *netsuke*

Below: A bracelet with figures of women in intaglio-molded glass, diamonds, gold, and enamel by Lalique, ca 1895.

Bottom: The Owls Bracelet by Lalique ca 1900-01, inspired by Charles Baudelaire's poem, "Les Hiboux."

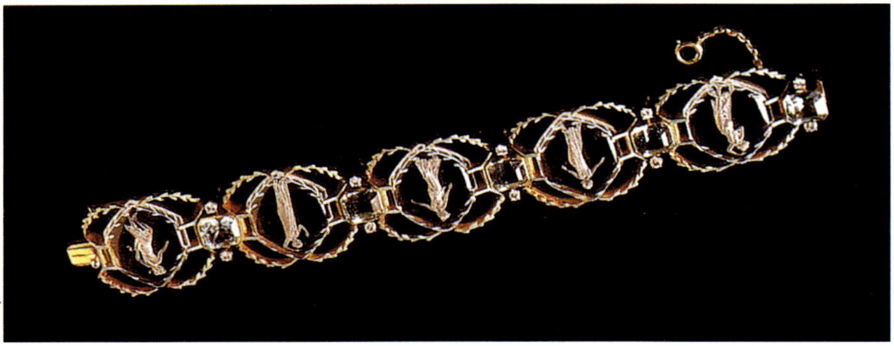

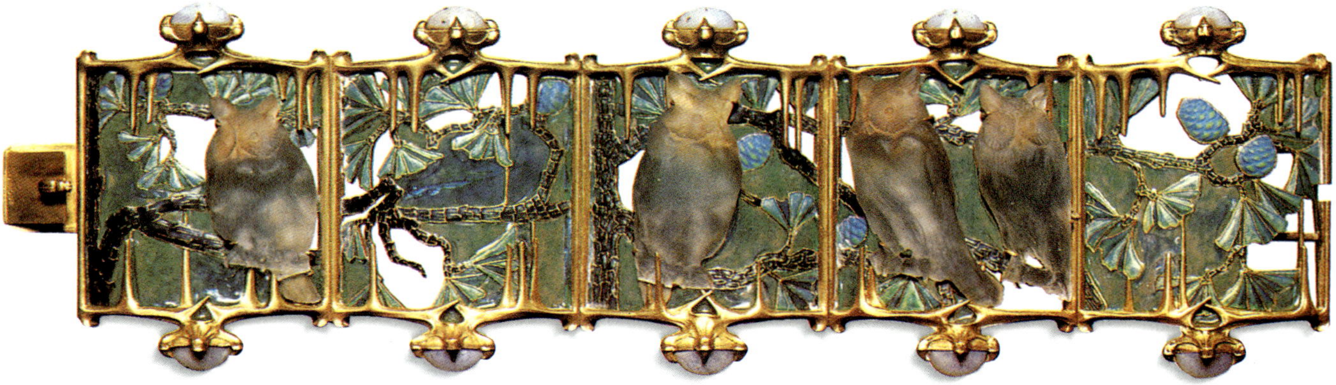

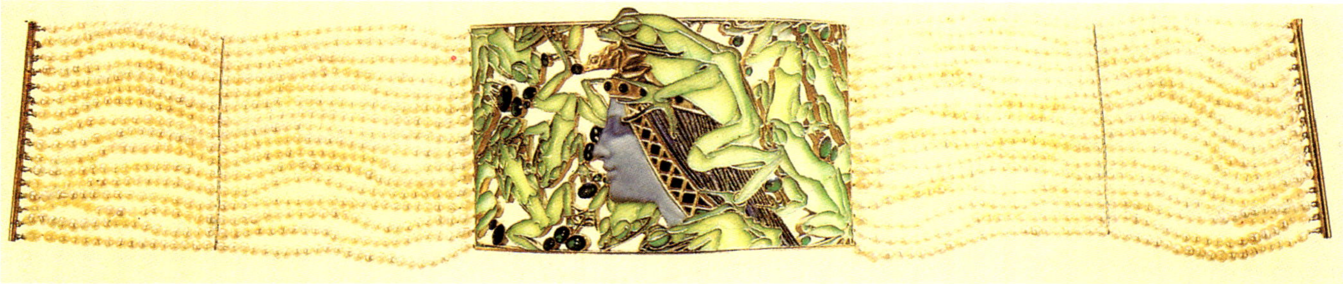

Above: Dog collar depicting the "Frog Prince" in gold, enamel, glass, and pearls by Lalique, ca 1900.

from which it hangs. In Lalique's piece, the ojime beads alternate with 20 pairs of dark green enameled, twisted links. Noteworthy not only for its obvious borrowing of Japanese forms, the necklace also translates the common Japanese motif of crested waves into the curvilinear Art Nouveau vocabulary.

Gold

Looking at the extensive and varied output of Lalique's career as a goldsmith, it is not difficult to understand that there was a talented genius at work. An innovator, arbiter of taste, and perfectionist, Lalique the Art Nouveau jeweler was all these and more. But during the years that he was establishing his reputation in bijouterie, Lalique was feeling the pull of another challenge in a material that he had already begun to incorporate into his jewelry, namely, glass. The possibilities for endless shapes, colors, and shadings in this material were endless and he was eventually to devote himself fully to its production. Amazingly, after just a few years, the most acclaimed goldsmith at the 1900 Exposition Universelle in Paris was to become the maître-verrier of the 1900s.

Right: A delicately enameled dragonfly hairpiece by Lalique set against a pendant by Philippe Wolfers.

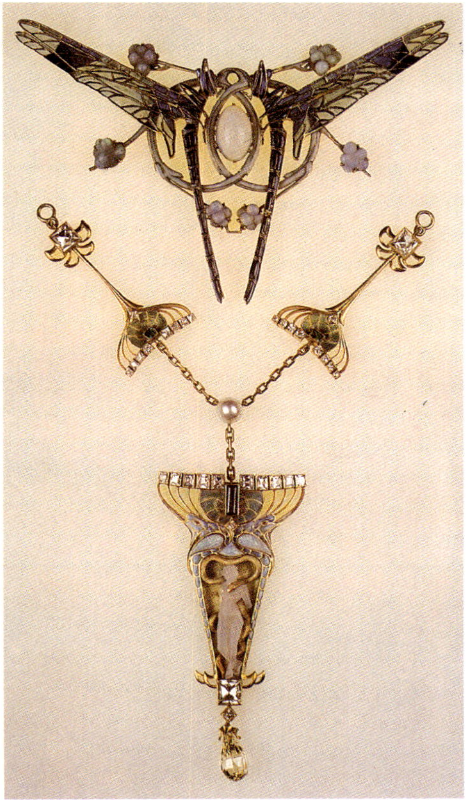

Lalique's followers

Writing in *Les Modes* in 1901, the critic Roger Marx noted that Lalique had laid open new and unknown possibilities for jewelry, and that the evolution of design in that area owed its sole debt to him. Lalique's work did indeed inspire a number of designers at the turn of the century in Paris. The brothers Paul and Henri Vever and Lucien Gaillard were among the most gifted.

Inheritors

The Vever brothers were the inheritors of a family business, and first attracted attention at the 1900 Exposition Universelle. They exploited the style and the techniques made fashionable by Lalique, and their workshops became particularly adept at enameling, especially plique-à-jour work, where enamel is contained within a framework of metal but has an open back. This allows light to pass through the enamel and the effect is a bit like that of a stained-glass window. The Vever brothers acted as entrepreneurs and many of their designs were commissioned from leading Art Nouveau designers such as Eugene Grasset and

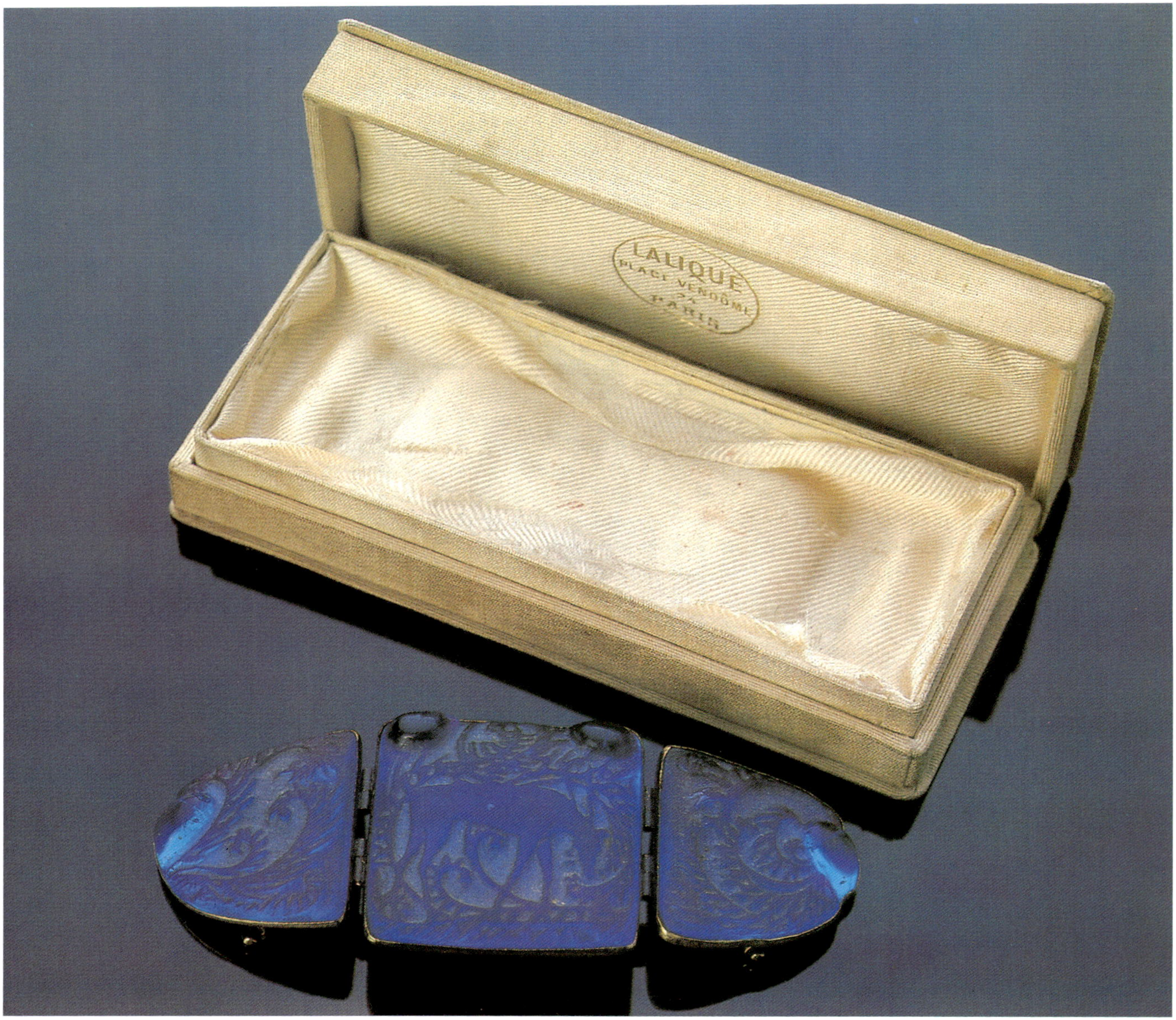
LALIQUE
PLACE VENDÔME
24
PARIS

Edward Colonna, whose jewelry designs, usually asymmetrical creations in silver and gold decorated with enamel and stones, were also sold at Bing's Maison de l'Art Nouveau.

Gaillard

Lucien Gaillard became director of his family's firm in 1892, and his primary interest was in metalwork. Around 1900, the example of Lalique encouraged him to design jewelry, and despite the evident Lalique influence, Gaillard's jewelry was very successful, winning him first prize at the Societé des Artistes Français in 1904. His most distinctive work is a series of horn hair combs carved as stylized sprays of honesty and mistletoe and often set with small baroque pearls as flower heads or berries.

Fouquet

Georges Fouquet, who took over his family firm in 1895, was anxious to express himself in the fashionable Art Nouveau idiom, and found an ideal collaborator in the Moravian-born artist, Alphonse Mucha, whom Fouquet had commissioned in 1901 to design his new shop in Rue Royale. The combination of Mucha's luscious and refined graphic sense with Fouquet's ability to translate the artist's designs into exquisite works of art produced only a limited number of jewels, but they are amongst the most extraordinary works created in the Art Nouveau period. The major examples of this fruitful collaboration are works of pure fantasy and are jewels of theatrical proportions. Chief among them is the bizarre bracelet conceived for Sarah Bernhardt, a grotesque enameled and articulated gold griffin which encircles the forearm and hand, and incorporates a ring. There is also a giant parure de corsage, incorporating a carved ivory head surrounded by carved ivory and gold arabesques of hair, an enameled halo, pendant baroque stones, and a pendant painted panel of watercolor on ivory within a gold border.

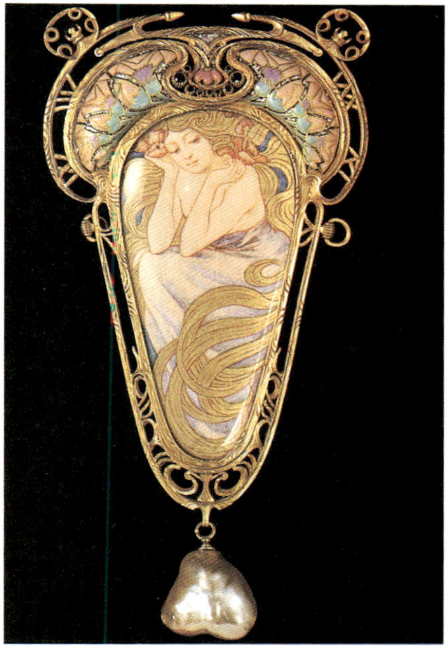

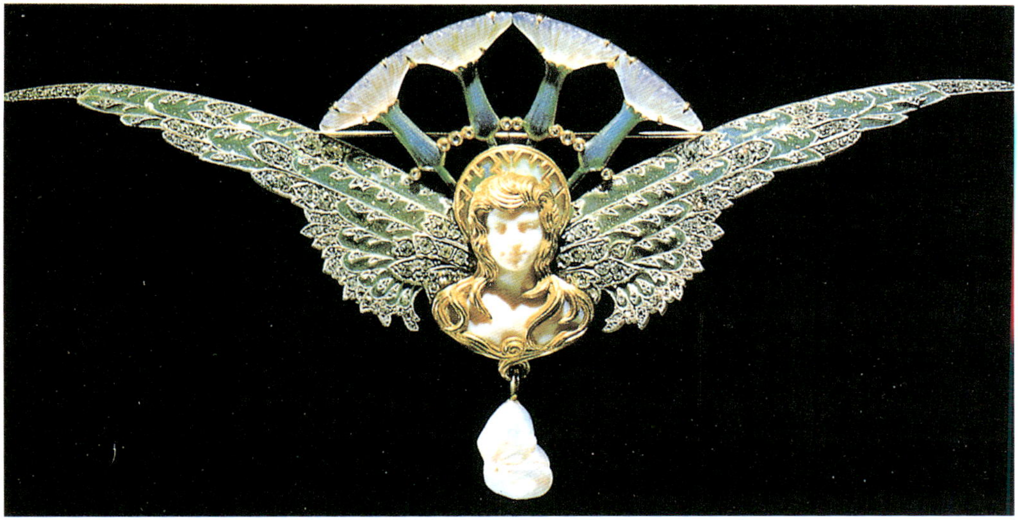

Above: Parure de corsage designed by Alphonse Mucha and made by Georges Fouquet in gold, enamels, emeralds, watercolor, and metallic paint on ivory, ca 1900.

Left: Brooch by Georges Fouquet, ca 1904.

Far left: A buckle/clasp with grazing stag design by Lalique in glass and metal, ca 1908.

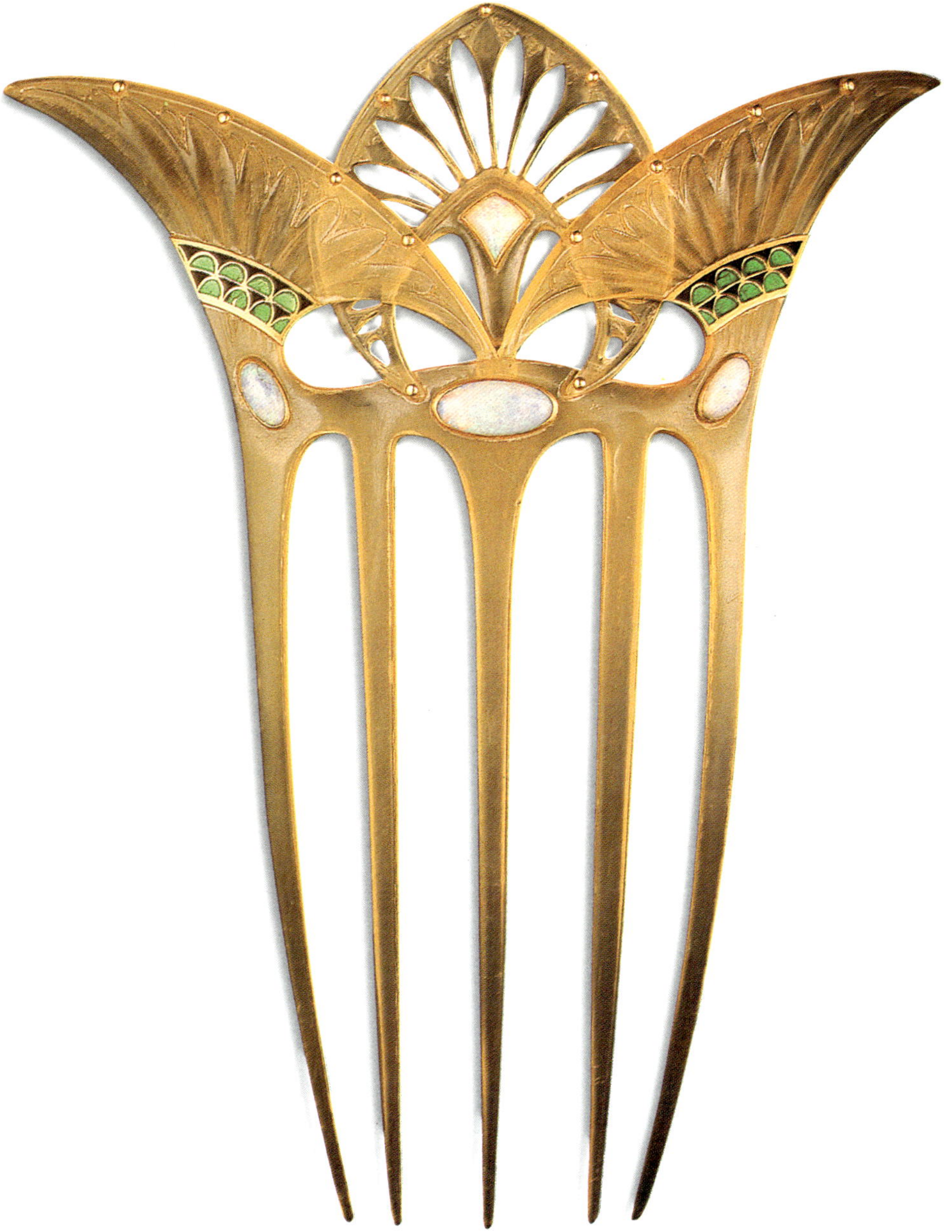

La Maison Moderne

Julius Meier-Graefe's shop, La Maison Moderne, was one of the outlets that retailed jewelry in high Art Nouveau taste by Paul Follot, Maurice Dufrene, and Manuel Orazi, while more traditional firms, such as those founded by Frederic Boucheron in 1858, made certain concessions to the fashions of 1900. Designs by L. Hirtz for Boucheron were published in the winter of 1901 in *The Studio* in a special number devoted to jewelry and fans.

Eugène Feuillatre

Having mastered the skills of enameling in Lalique's workshop, Eugène Feuillatre began designing and exhibiting independently. His forte was in large tours-de-force of enameling, including delicate plique-à-jour creations of unprecedented daring. The finest surviving example of his work is an 11in (29cm) diameter dish, now in the collection of Charles Hadley-Read, the design of which is of a grotesque fish in polychrome enamels within a silver framework.

Left: Horn and gold hair comb by Georges Fouquet.

NON-GALLIC JEWELRY

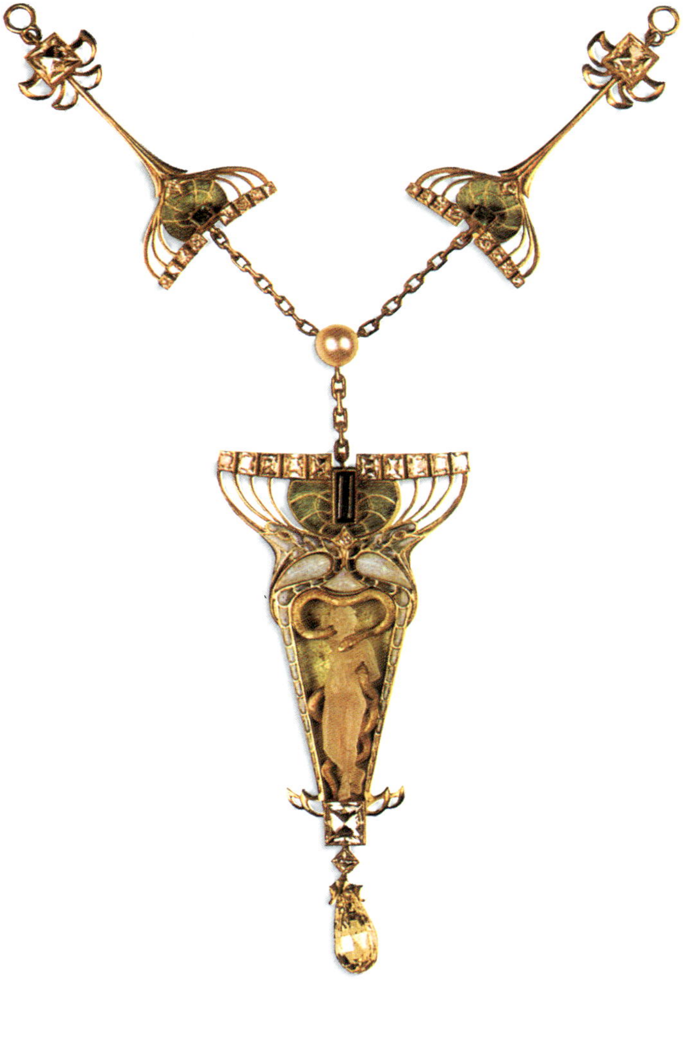

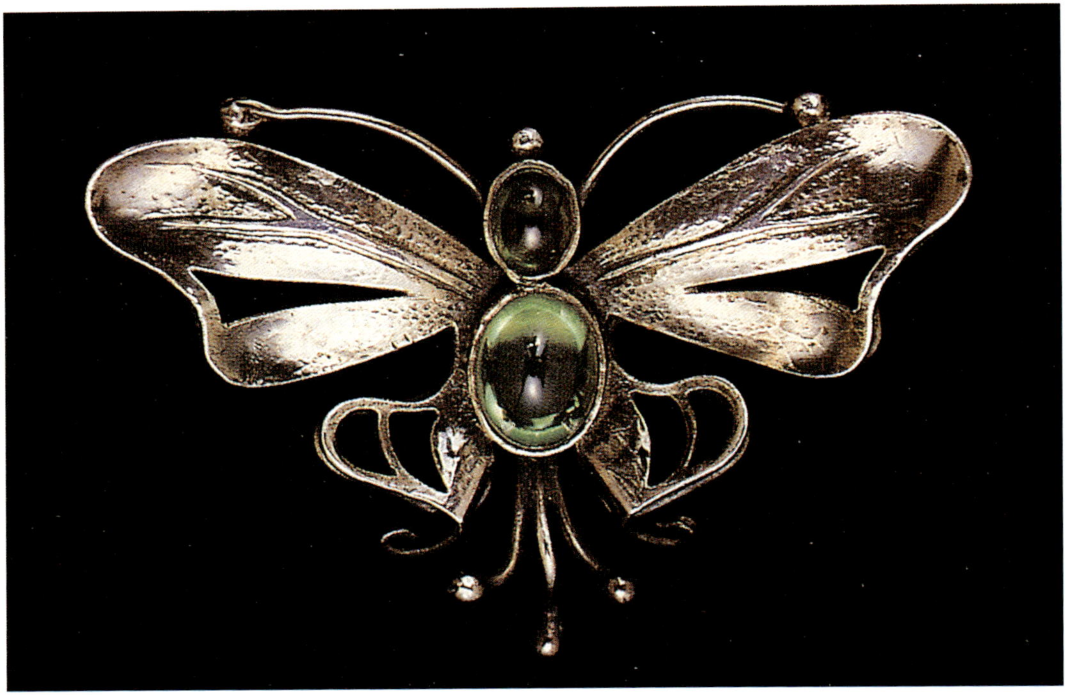

Above: Oxidized silver and cabochon moth pin by C.R. Ashbee.

Overleaf: Eve, a pendant designed by Philippe Wolfers in 1901.

The sinuous shapes and striking use of enamels and semiprecious stones gives a distinctive character to the jewelry of the late 1800s and early 1900s. Beginning with the Art Nouveau period, there was a fundamental change in the attitude toward jewelry in terms both of its design and its function. The aesthetic merits of form, color, and texture became increasingly important, rather than the financial value of the materials used.

Until this period, much of the jewelry made continued the use of precious materials. It was therefore the prerogative of the rich and its role was to demonstrate a person's position in society. When factory production began in earnest in the mid-1800s, many entrepreneurs and industrialists turned toward the indiscriminate use of ornamentation in order to satisfy the growing consumer market. Even the most mundane and utilitarian of machine-made goods were embellished to make them more desirable to the consumer. This was not a philanthropic exercise. More often it was done to disguise poor workmanship.

Individuals such as John Ruskin and William Morris questioned the effects of large-scale production on art and design. Their followers in the Arts and Crafts Movement of the 1860s were interested in reinstating the aesthetic values of the artist-craftsman in place of those of industrial production.

JEWELRY IN BRITAIN

At the end of the 1800s, British jewelry differed from that produced in France because it owed more to the traditions established by the Arts and Crafts Movement.

Perhaps the best known of the Arts and Crafts Movement jewelry and metalwork was the product of the Guild of Handicraft established in 1888 by Charles Robert Ashbee. Ashbee trained as an architect as well as a silversmith and jeweler, and he produced many designs in gold, silver, pearls, jade, and turquoise, often in the form of that popular motif in Art Nouveau, the peacock. For Ashbee, design was all important, and the gemstones are more often than not set into the metalwork instead of overwhelming it. The stones themselves reflect the expanding British Empire — the opals are from Australia, the pearls from India, the moonstones from Sri Lanka, and the diamonds from South Africa.

FRED PARTRIDGE

Among the other designers who produced jewelry at the Guild were Fred Partridge, whose work had much in common with the French Art Nouveau designers in his use of horn and steel, and May Hart, a skilled enameler, who later married Partridge.

Enamelers aimed to create a "people's jewelry" by substituting cheaper glass enamels for gemstones. Moreover, its laws of production appealed to Arts and Crafts idealists — enamel jewelry was made by, at most, three people, in place of a whole team of gem cutters, silversmiths, and polishers. To a large extent in Britain, enameling was also a woman's craft, but one which could be both a hobby and a professional discipline — Phoebe Stabler

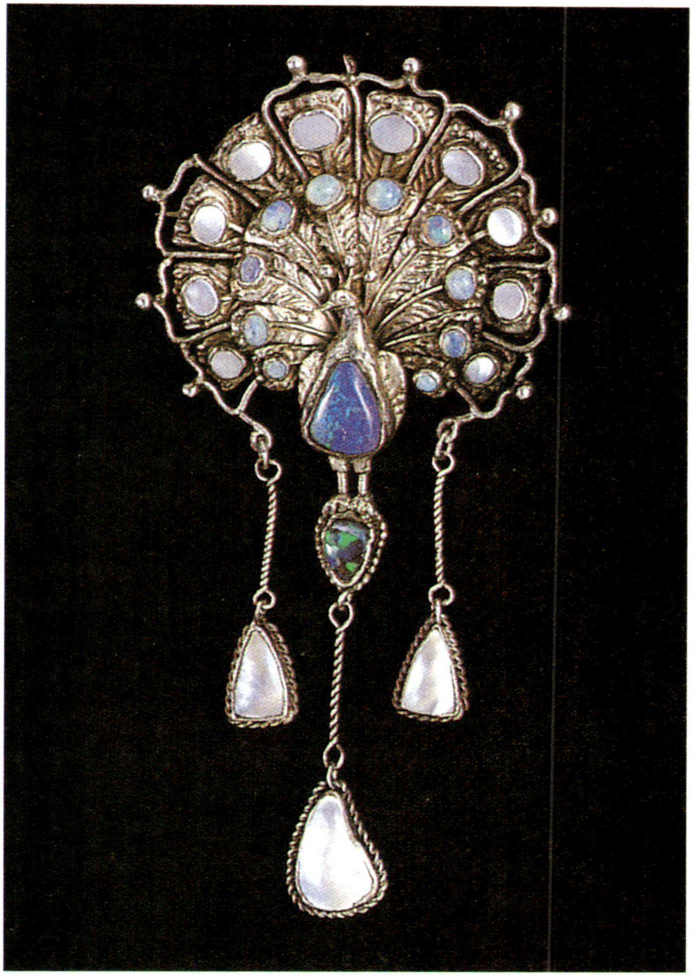

Above: Silver, opal, and mother-of-pearl peacock brooch designed by C.R. Ashbee.

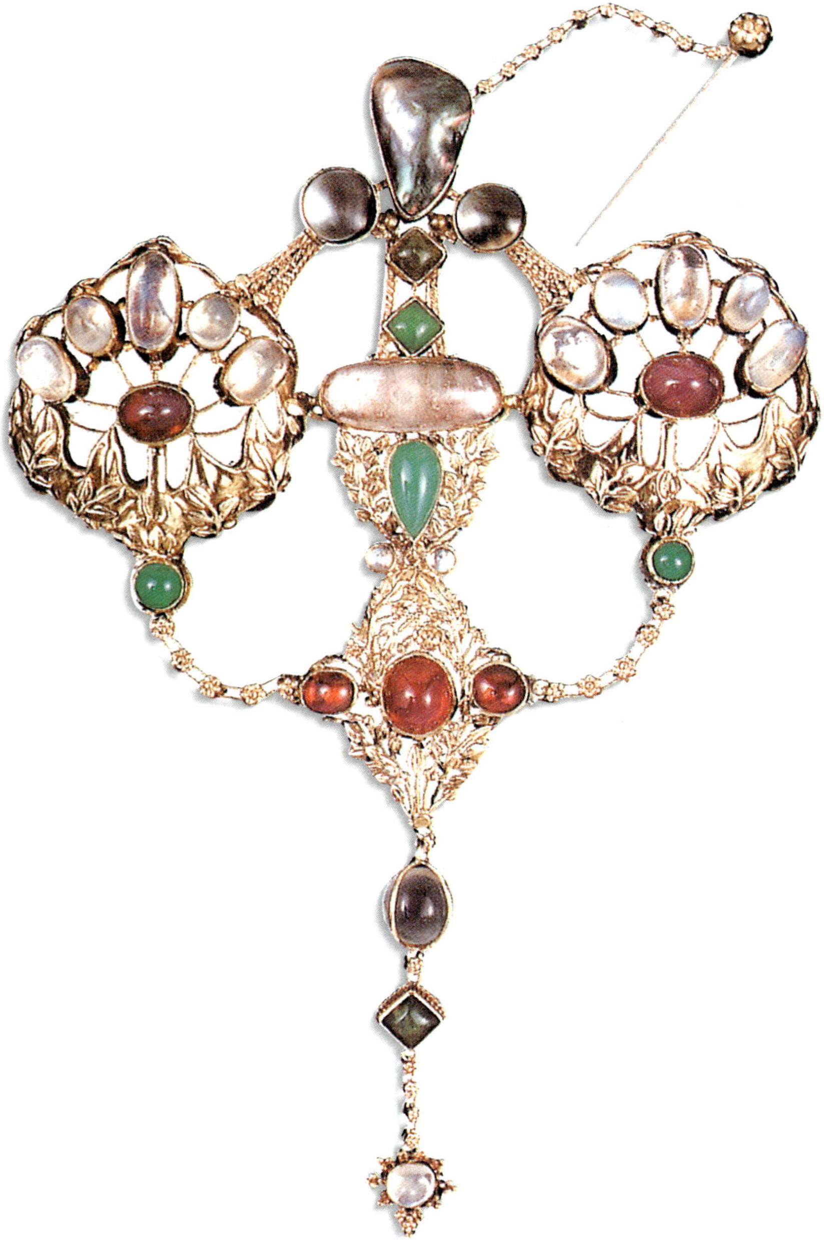

in Liverpool had in fact studied her craft with a Japanese enameler. Like potters, enamelers generally mastered their craft by trial and error and taught each other new skills.

INFLUENTIAL ENAMELER

Possibly the most influential enameler in Britain was Alexander Fisher. A former pupil of the French master Dalpayrat, Fisher taught enameling in his London studio to members of the aristocracy and the leisured middle class. Fisher actively promoted painted enamel as a jewel or art form in its own right. These were either in a single or multiple plaque form, set in gold, silver, bronze, or sometimes even steel, and formed belt buckles, coat clasps, brooches, pendant necklaces, and rings which were all designed to be worn with the new, simpler, more "Rational Dress" fashions of the time. Because it came closest to miniature or easel painting, enameling gained perhaps the widest acceptance of all the newly revived crafts, and was no doubt encouraged by Fisher's popular instructional book, *The Art of Enameling on Metal.*

BROMSGROVE GUILD OF APPLIED ART

Other guilds were to flourish in Britain, including the Bromsgrove Guild of Applied Art founded in 1890, and the Artificer's Guild of 1891. At Bromsgrove were Joseph Hodel, whose silver buckles, brooches, and pendants were in foliate and fruit forms and dotted with semiprecious stones. Arthur Gaskin's jewelry contained cabochon (domed, unfaceted) stones, rope borders, silver or gold filigree wires, and clusters of silver beads and tendrils. From 1899, Gaskin worked with his wife, Georgina Cave

Left: A pendant in gold, pearls, amethysts, and moonstones by C.R. Ashbee from 1902.

France, an extremely talented craftswoman in jewelry and metals. Mrs. Gaskin had been designing in silver since her student days at the Birmingham School of Art, and the Gaskins' pieces are marked with a capital "G."

The Artificer's Guild

Members of the Artificer's Guild, founded by Nelson Dawson with his wife Edith, produced work in a number of different media. They also explored the potentials in jewelry of base materials like horn and shell, cloisonné, champlevé, and the technically challenging method of unbacked, plique-à-jour enameling.

Other British jewelry designers included the Scottish jeweler based in London, Sybil Dunlop, Harold Stabler (a founder member of the Design and Industries Association, the forerunner of the Design Council), Henry Wilson, Omar Ramsden, and Alwyn Carr. But possibly the most significant contribution to British Art Nouveau was the jewelry marketed by Arthur Lazenby Liberty.

Liberty & Co.

Liberty had opened his shop in 1875, initially specializing in the importing and retailing of Oriental goods from India and Japan. By the turn of the century, its affluent clientele were to include the residents of the new garden cities and suburbs of London. Liberty's stocked one-off, handmade items as well as factory-made goods. Demand was such that the store, while continuing to use independent suppliers, also began to operate its own design studios and manufacturing workshops.

Designers from the Arts and Crafts Movement were employed to create innu-

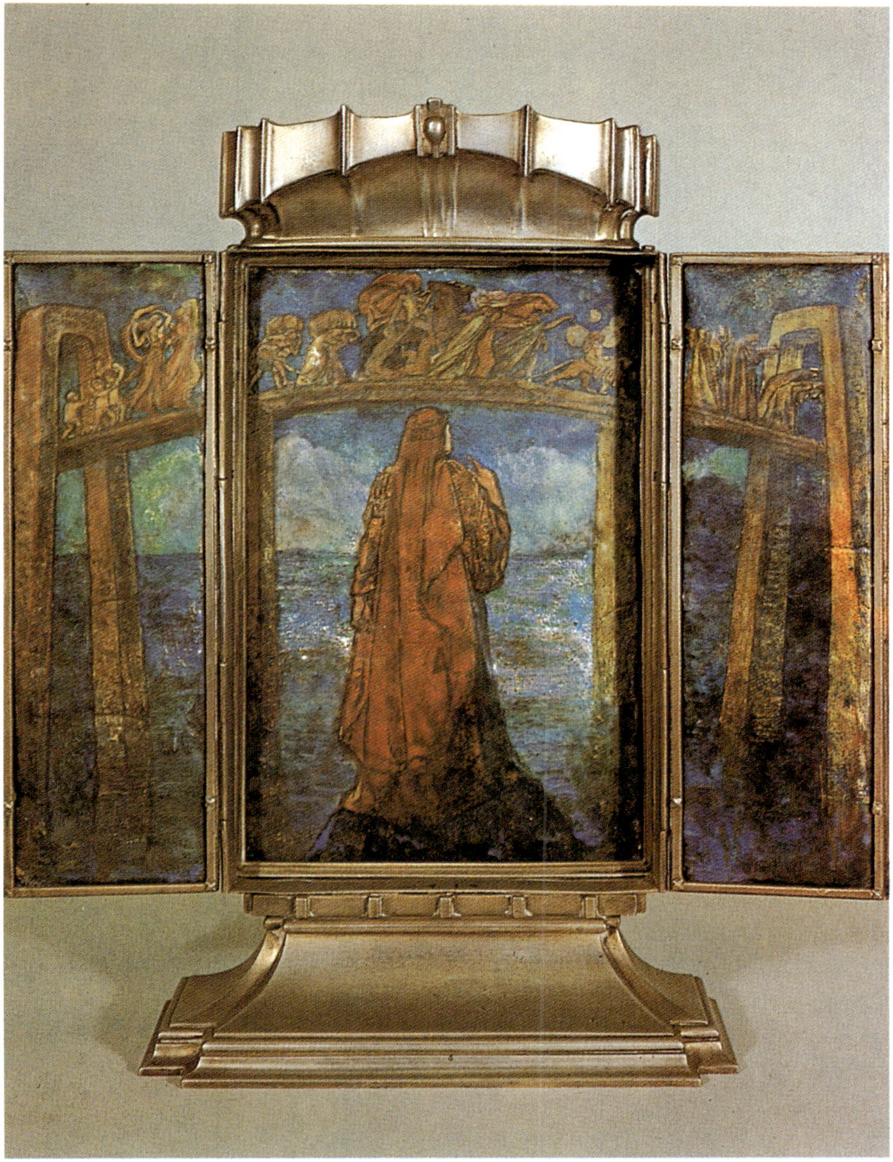

Right: Enameled triptych made by Alexander Fisher, ca 1900.

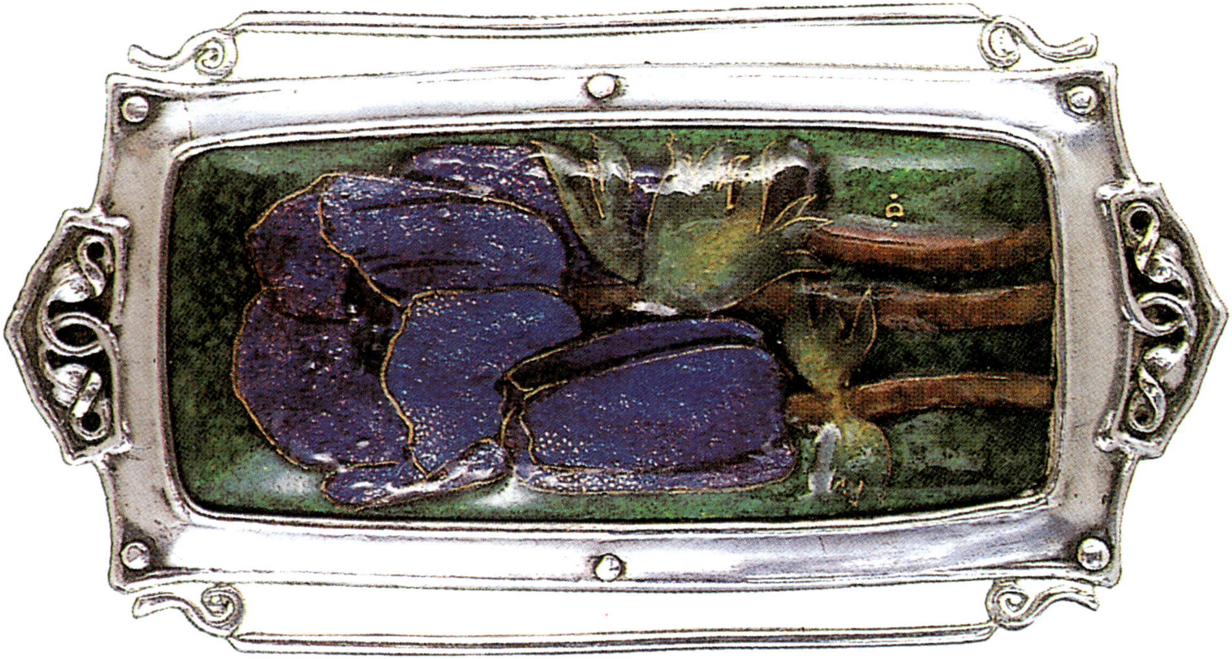

Above: Enameled silver buckle decorated with a floral motif by the Arts and Crafts jeweler Nelson Dawson, a founder of the Artificer's Guild.

merable products from furniture and textiles, to ceramics and silverware.

CYMRIC AND PEWTER

Liberty sold silveware under the name of "Cymric" (silver) and "Tudric" (pewter) from the 1890s. Both of these included a large collection of jewelry designed and manufactured by Jessie M. King, Rex Silver, Georgina and Arthur Gaskin, Oliver Baker, and Archibald Knox, who created more than 400 designs for the firm which were, for the most part, responsible for defining and determining the "Liberty style." Knox had studied Celtic design at the Douglas School of Art on the Isle of Man, and applied the Runic interlacing of forms in his designs. There is an affinity between the forms used by Alexander Fisher and Knox, but where Fisher used the style by way of decoration, Knox employed the form in a more integral, structural manner.

Initially their designs were made by hand, but by the end of the 1800s, jewelry and silverware were increasingly manufactured by machine and contracted out to various firms, including the Birmingham firm of W.H. Haseler. They included brooches, pendants, belt buckles and clasps, and necklaces. The designers favored the use of semiprecious stones such as peridot, tourmaline, moonstones, and chrysoprase, but in a few instances, precious stones such as rubies, sapphires, emeralds, fine

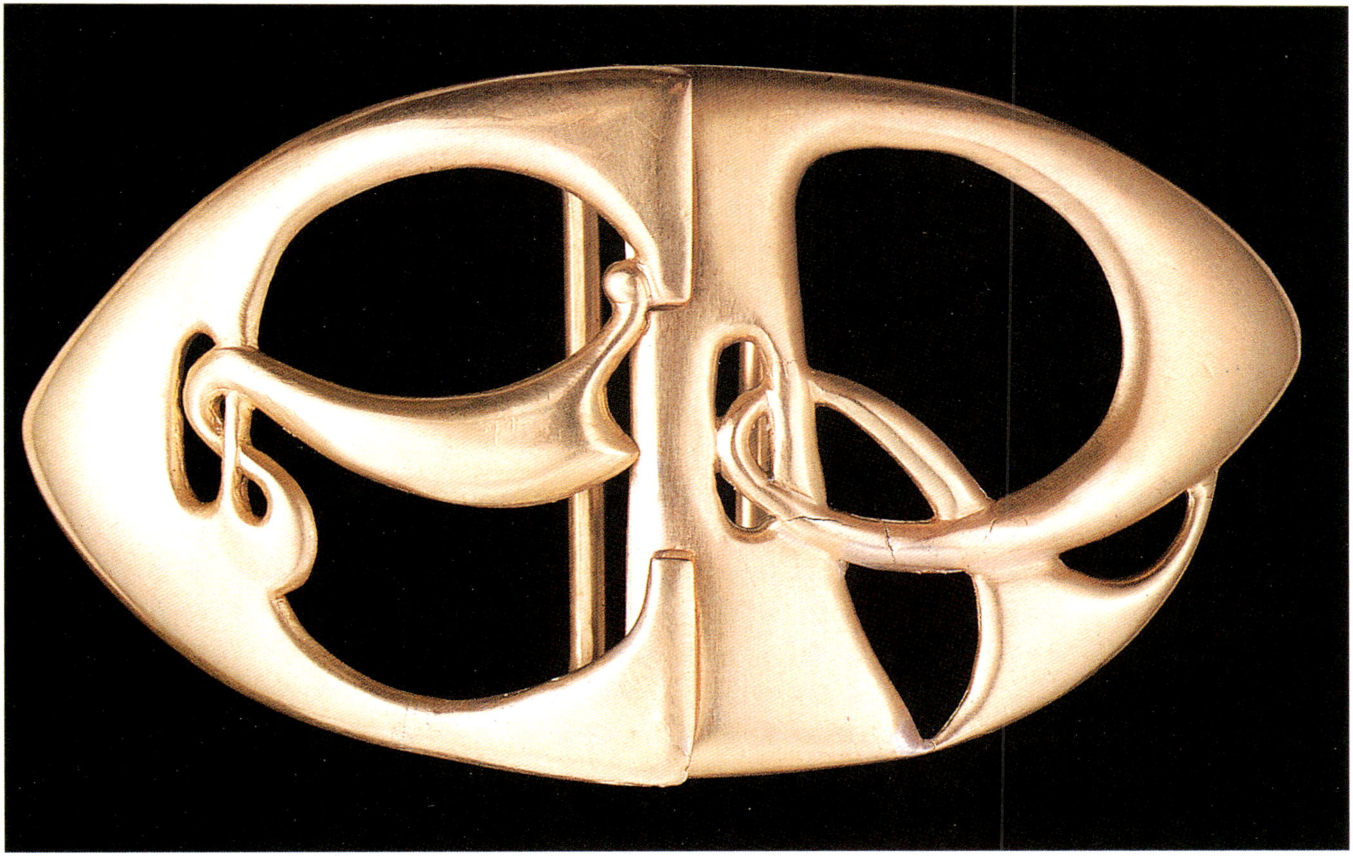

pearls, and diamonds were used. The use of gems, however, was often dependent on the commissions of the purchaser. Often less precious materials were preferred by the designers not just because of cost, but because individual creativity took preference over conforming to traditional aesthetic practices.

DRESS REFORM

The market for such jewelry was, however, limited to the more "enlightened" and artistic of Liberty's clients who appreciated the new aesthetic and moralistic qualities associated with the Arts and Crafts Movement, as well as with the dress reforms of the late 1800s. Dress reform was concerned with removing the restrictions imposed on the body by Victorian costume. In 1881 in Britain, the Rational Dress Society had been formed, which campaigned against the wearing of corsets and

Above: Silver belt buckle designed by Archibald Knox, who worked for Liberty & Co. in the first decade of the 1900s. This piece has the same stylized, abstract quality found in European Art Nouveau.

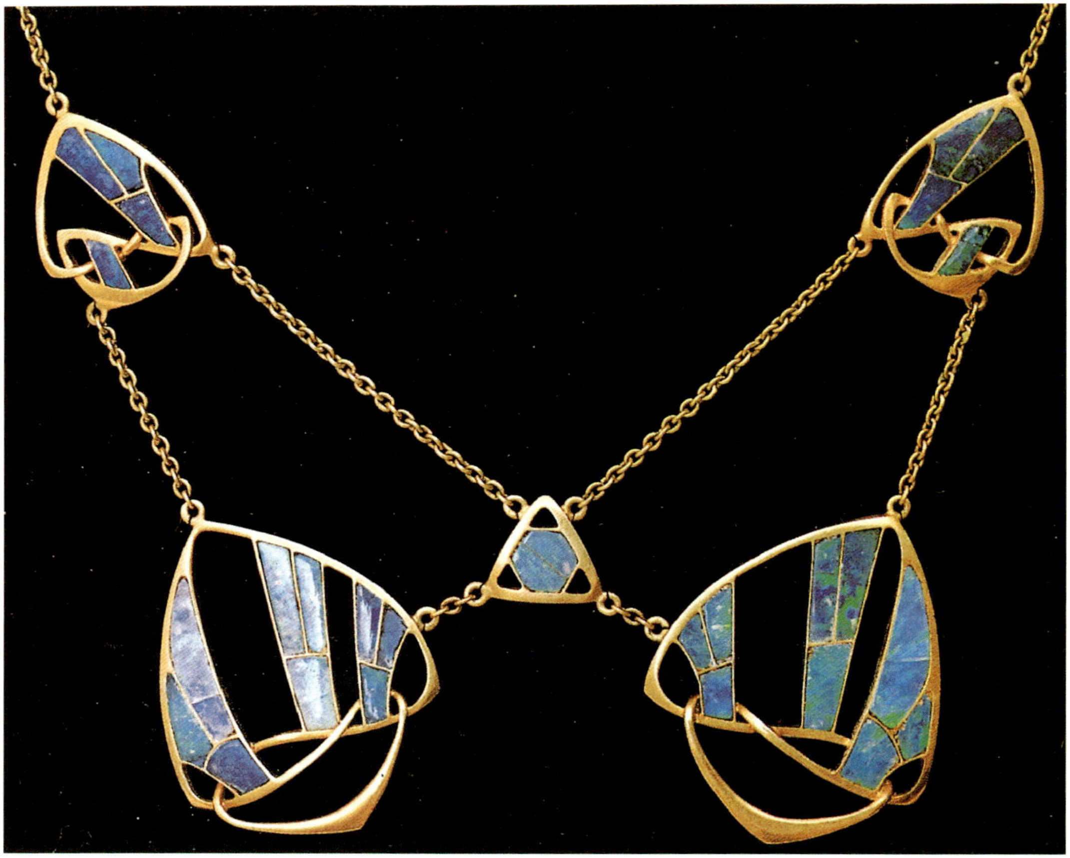

Above: A gold and opal necklace by Archibald Knox for Liberty & Co.

advocated the adoption of looser, simpler garments that could be adorned with large and eye-catching pieces of jewelry, such as a robe clasp. Elsewhere, there were important parallel developments — in Germany, the leading critic of contemporary dress was Dr. Gustav Jaeger from Stuttgart who introduced his Sanitary Woollen System in 1878, while in the United States, the American Free Dress Society had been founded.

Advocates of the new, free styles of dress for both men and women included the dancers Loie Fuller and Isadora Duncan, and the novelist and playwright, George Bernard Shaw.

THE GLASGOW FOUR

In Scotland, the foremost exponents of Art Nouveau were the "Glasgow Four," Charles Rennie Mackintosh, his wife, Margaret

Macdonald, her sister Frances, and Frances' husband James Herbert MacNair, who worked independently and together from the 1890s. Each was influenced by the formal organization and economy of Japanese art, and by their own Celtic heritage. The elongated, gaunt austerity of their work earned them the name of the "Spook School." Their jewelry bore some resemblance to English Arts and Crafts, but its repertory of motifs was very much its own and more in the spirit of Vienna Secession (Austrian Art Nouveau). Among the silver and jewelry designs of the Glasgow Four were stylized birds, leaves, blossoms, and hearts.

ART NOUVEAU OUTSIDE BRITAIN

The Arts and Crafts Movement assumed many different guises throughout Europe and the United States with some significant differences. While the British abhorrence of industrialization was not shared by many other countries — especially those who had not yet been industrialized and had no reason to reject it — two fundamental aspects of Arts and Crafts ideology were embraced. The first was the use of design to express a country's national identity, and the second, was the attempt to reform design by applying certain Arts and Crafts values to machine production.

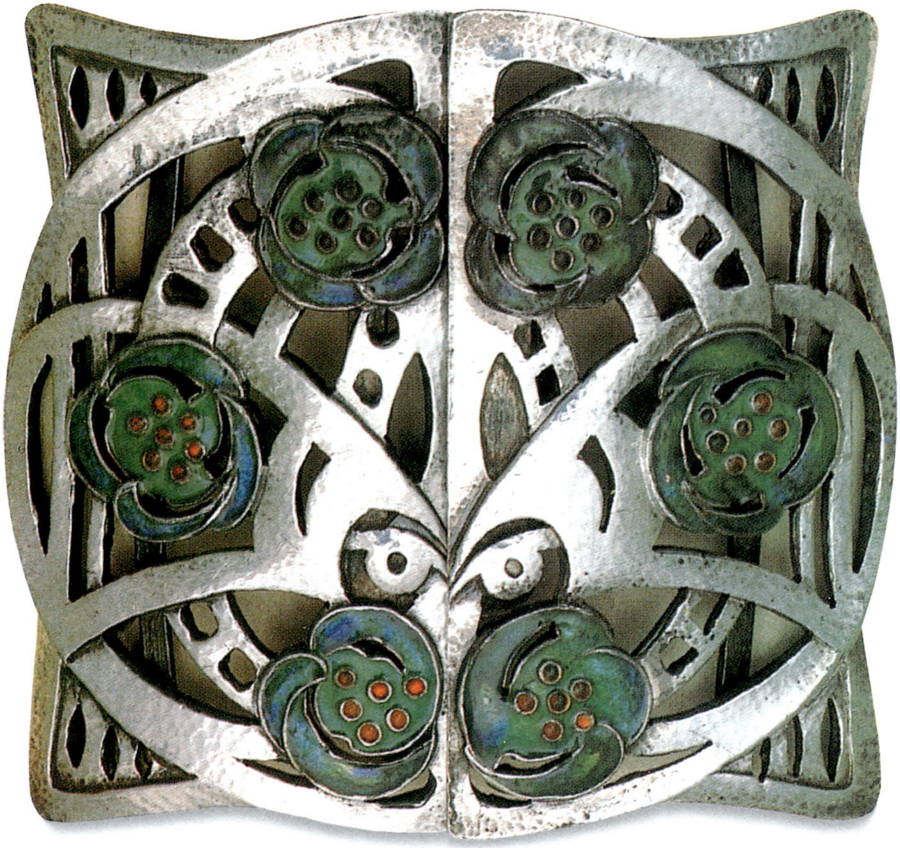

Left: A silver and enamel belt buckle designed by Jessie M. King for Liberty & Co. in 1906.

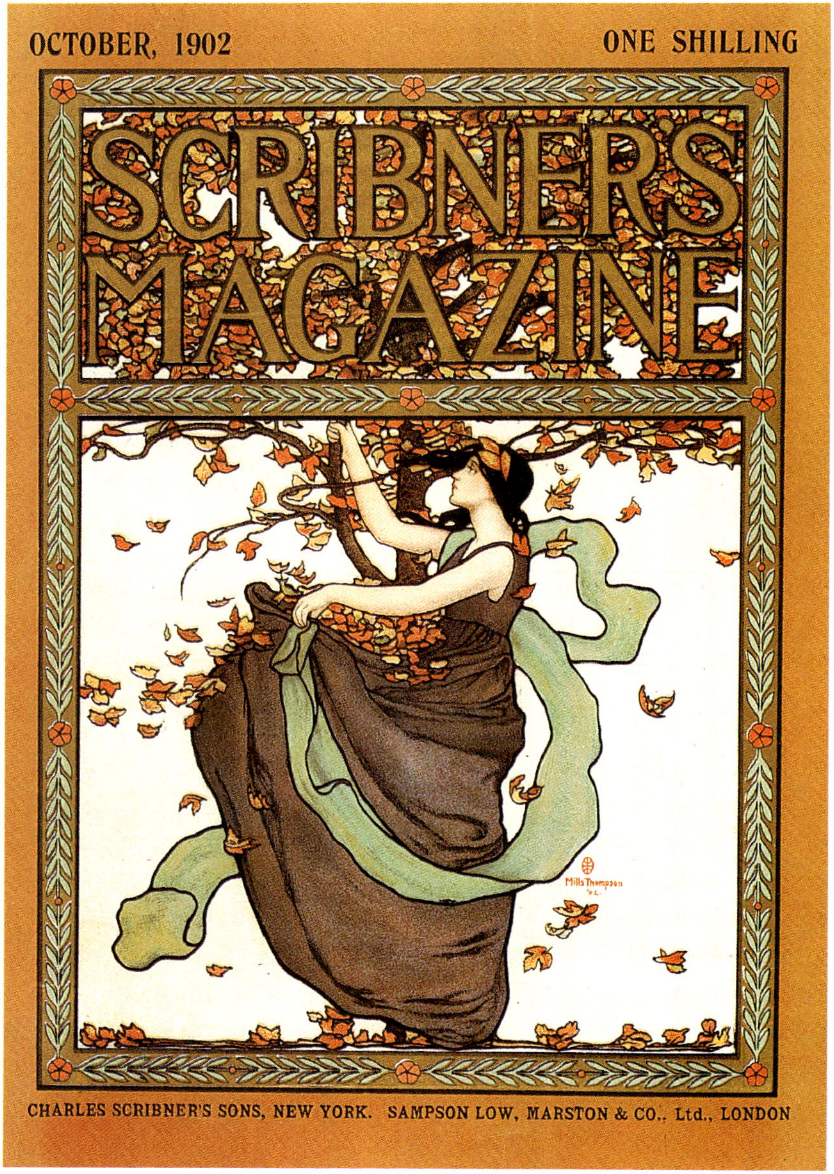

THE STUDIO

The two areas most influenced by the ideals of Ruskin, Morris, and the other leading lights of the British Arts and Crafts Movement were Scandinavia and the countries in middle Europe — Austria, Hungary, and Germany. Their leaders read the works of Ruskin and Morris, subscribed to journals like *The Studio,* and visited Britain and the major international exhibitions to see at first hand the British crafts on display.

SCANDINAVIA

From 1890 onwards, the Scandinavians were to emerge from being merely imitative in the field of the decorative arts to holding a major position in European design. In some fields and at certain points, their influence was to spread beyond their own countries.

These developments were led by Denmark and Sweden, which could build on centuries of independent nationhood and a long-established court culture with accompanying high standards of taste and workmanship. No such similar traditions existed in Finland or Norway, however, as both were to gain political and cultural independence only in the early 1900s. The political union between Norway and Sweden was dissolved in 1905 and that between Finland and Russia in 1919.

Returning to their own indigenous folk arts for inspiration, and seeking a naturalistic style to soften the edge of the nascent modernity, the Scandinavian countries drew on the idealized democratic principles of craft production and searched for an aesthetic formula in keeping with their cultural traditions. They rec-

Left: A cover for Scribner's Magazine, *by Mills Thompson. Magazines such as these helped spread the Art Nouveau style.*

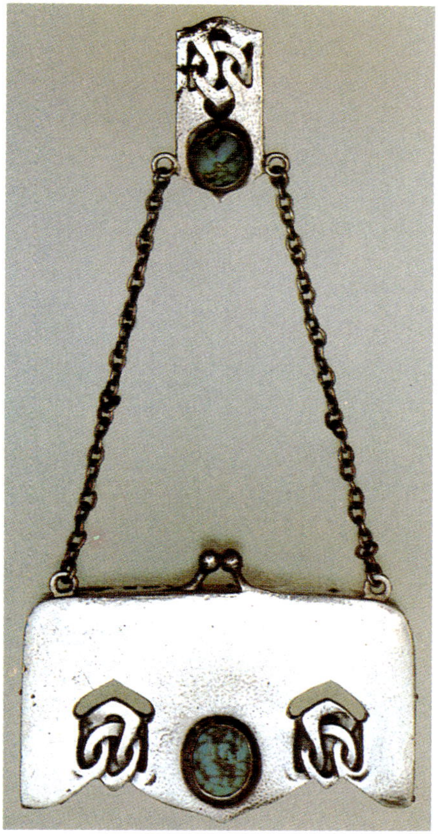

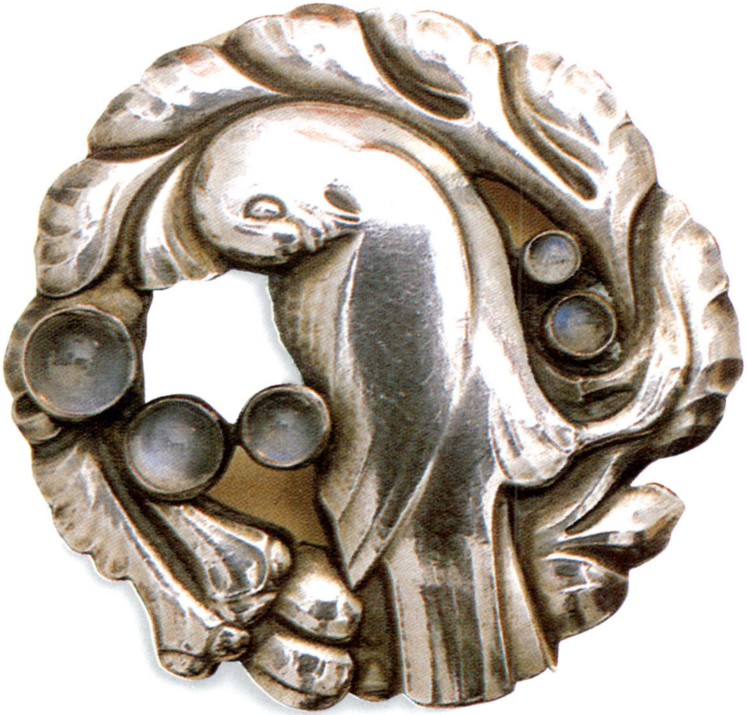

Left: A silver purse frame with Celtic entrelac motif, by Archibald Knox.

Above: A piece by one of the most famous names in Scandinavian design, Georg Jensen, known for his abstract forms.

ognized the need to invite industrial sponsorship, not only to maintain links with the market place, but also to provide support for the designers. They hoped that this would eventually lead to the widespread dissemination of well-designed and well-made goods.

The great name in Scandinavian silver and jewelry was, of course, Georg Jensen, an artist whose fascination with his craft resulted in the creation of some of the most outstanding pieces of silver and jewelry. His designs betray a remarkable sensitivity to form, while the celebrated, almost matt-hammered finish became an international hallmark of the Jensen style.

Austria and the Wiener Werkstätte

In Austria, the search for a new style at the beginning of the 1900s was led by the architect Josef Hoffmann and the members of the Secession group that had been organized as a rebellion against the official *Kunstlerhaus* (Society of Artists) and its narrow definition of what constituted art. The primary motive of the Secessionists was to bring Austria to the forefront of modern art. Their definition of modern art gave the applied arts equal status to fine arts, but Hoffmann wanted to take the goal of unifying art forms still further. After visiting Ashbee's Guild of Handicraft in 1902, Hoffmann was determined to establish a similar craft organization. In the program of the Wiener Werkstätte, which he founded with fel-

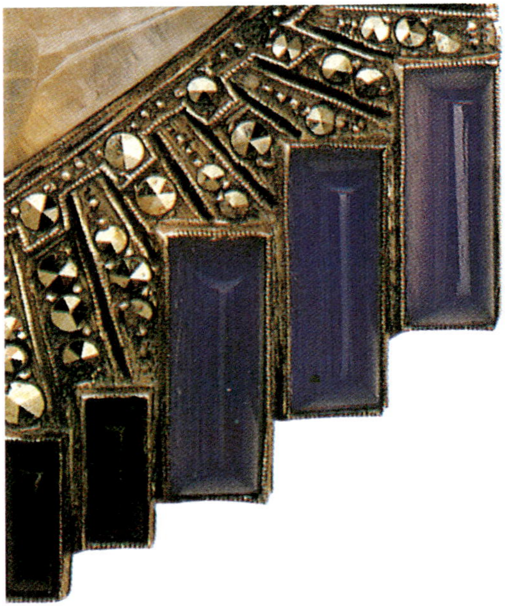

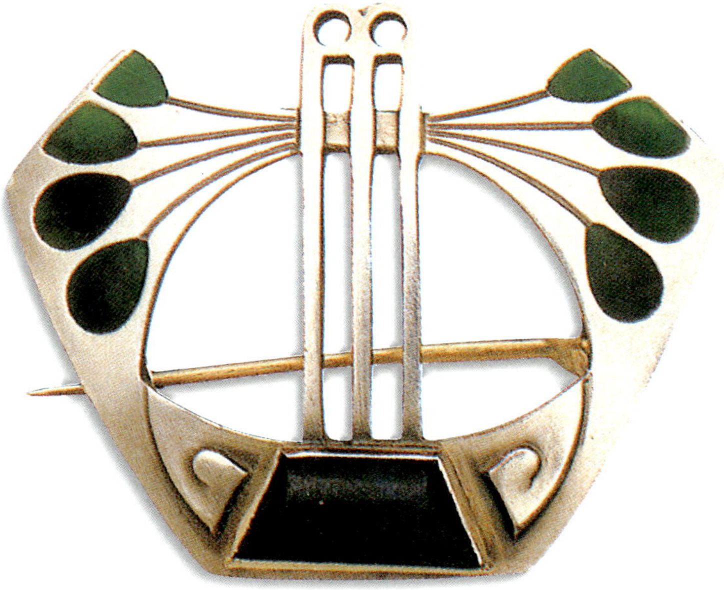

Above right: A later brooch in silver by Georg Jensen.

Above: Scandinavian design during this period was relatively formal, as seen in this silver clip by Georg Jensen.

low Secessionist architect Kolomon Moser, Hoffmann declared that their aim was to create an "island of tranquillity," which amid the "joyful hum of arts and crafts" would be welcome to followers of Ruskin and Morris.

But Hoffmann was selective in his choice of Arts and Crafts principles. Ignoring the aspects of social reform, Hoffmann adopted only those principles concerned with the reform of design — functionalism and craftsmanship which were rigorously combined in a reductive geometry of forms. Many historians credit this to the influence of Mackintosh, whose designs were greeted with wild acclaim in Vienna and who was also a close friend of Hoffmann. Regardless of the source of inspiration, the square would become the leitmotif of the Wiener Werkstätte designs.

Hoffmann and Moser also championed the use of more modest materials such as semiprecious stones for jewelry in the belief that exceptional design and craftsmanship were more important. Both were passionate about the highest standards of craftsmanship, but, when special commissions were to be undertaken, they were also passionate about the finest materials.

Whether plain and simple, patterned, or highly ornamented, privately commissioned or made in multiples, the products of the Wiener Werkstätte were expensive. Although they did not shun the use of machinery, the Werkstätte members would not compromise their high ideals of craftsmanship to make good design available to all.

THE CRAFT IN GERMANY

In Germany, the equivalent of Art Nouveau was known as Jugendstil, which became the

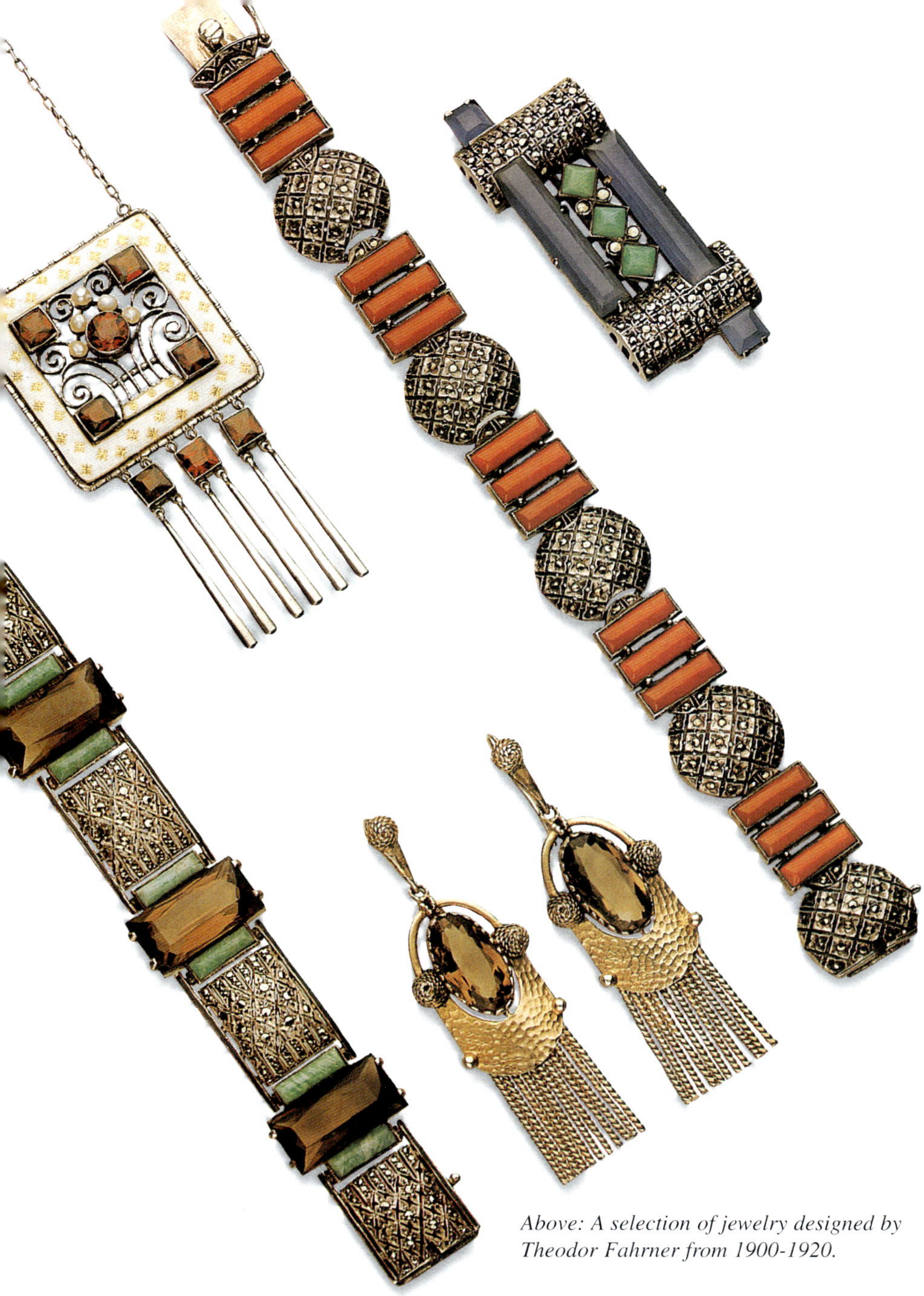

Above: A selection of jewelry designed by Theodor Fahrner from 1900-1920.

major influence on the decorative arts by 1900. The attitude of the Vienna Werkstätte was not one shared by most of the workshops established in Germany.

The first and most influential was the United Workshops for Art and Craftsmanship, founded in 1897 in Munich. While the members of this group looked to the example of Britain and its precedent in raising design standards by applying simplicity, integrity, and fitness of purpose to making everyday objects, they rejected the belief held by Ruskin and Morris about the sanctity of the handmade. Like their Viennese contemporaries, the German group was not interested in social reform, but they also differed strongly in that the German members were also indifferent to individualism in the work process.

Their aim was to make quality goods at an affordable price, and they supported any methods that would improve the standard of German goods to make them more competitive in the international and domestic market. By employing the latest technologies, the designer worked in close cooperation with the makers and manufacturers, a rejection of the Arts and Crafts idea that the designer was also the maker. In jewelry, designers such as Peter Behrens, Henry Van de Velde, Josef Olbrich, Patriz Huber, and Carl Otto Czeschka contributed designs for mass production by the firm of Theodor Farhner in Pforzheim, the center of the German jewelry industry between 1900 and 1930.

Jewelry in the United States

The Arts and Crafts reformers' designs were shaped by moral convictions and often prescribed how people should live. The moral aesthetics of American reformers were once again developed from the works of Ruskin

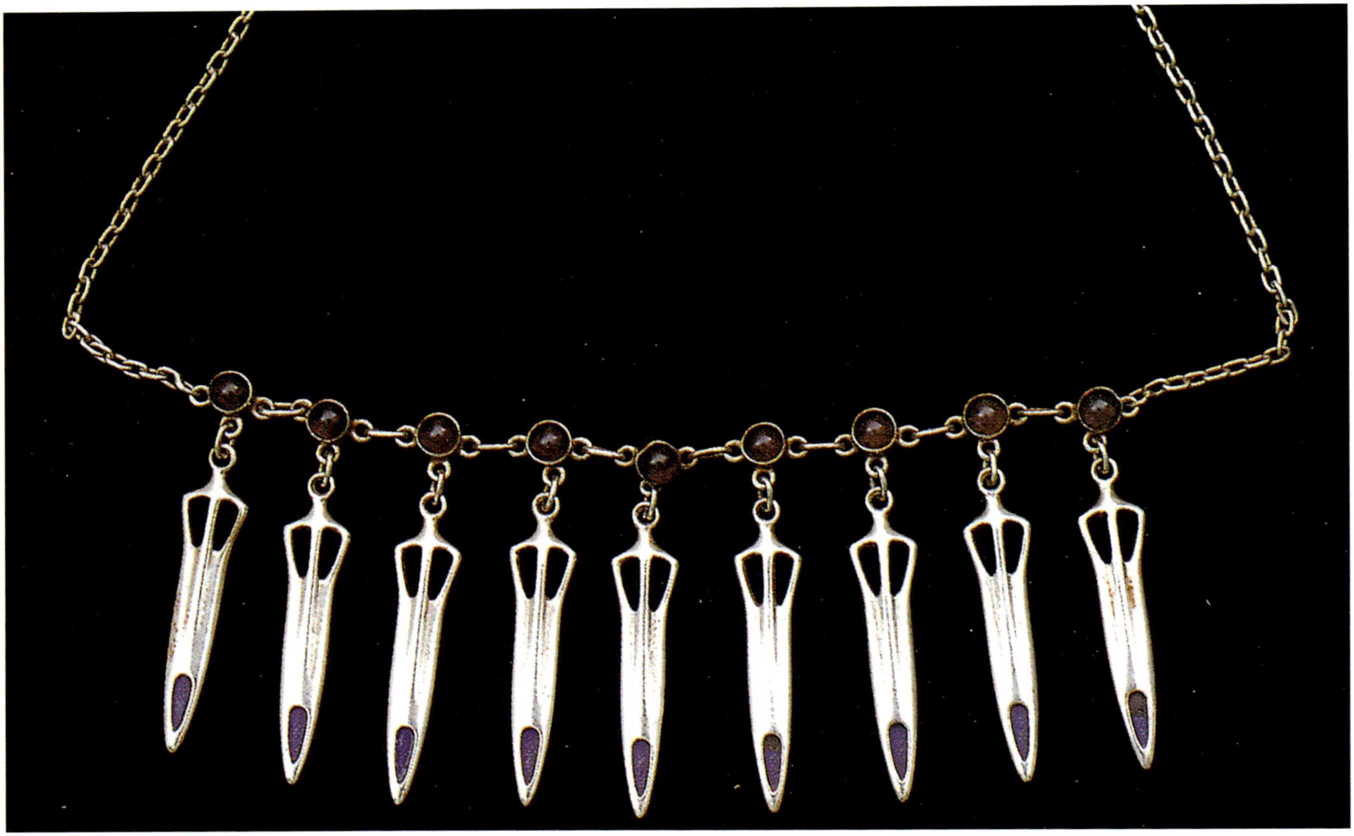

Right: Silver and amethyst necklace inspired by the rectilinear qualities of Art Nouveau. It was manufactured in 1905 by the firm of Theodor Fahrner in Pforzheim, the center of the German jewelry industry.

and Morris whose writings were bestsellers in the United States. Between 1859 and 1892, for example, Ruskin's only book devoted to the decorative arts, *The Two Paths*, was reprinted 19 times and many reading groups were established across the country to study the works of other writers. Joseph Twyman established a William Morris room in the Tobey Furniture Company of Chicago's showrooms and also founded a William Morris Society.

Although Morris and Ruskin never visited the United States, many other leaders of the British Arts and Crafts Movement made the journey. Among them were Walter Crane, Charles Ashbee, and Morris's daughter May, and all gave lectures and toured exhibitions of their work.

ELIZABETH E. COPELAND

Inspired by the movement, many individuals in the United States followed the British lead and turned to the professional practice of their crafts. In Boston, where the Arts and Crafts first took hold in the United States, Elizabeth E. Copeland, after studying in England, combined silver and enamel in her work which clearly showed the handicraft of the maker. Following her, Edward Everette Oakes, also in Boston, designed jewelry and showed at the Arts and Crafts Society's Exhibition in 1923. In Chicago, Florence Koehler made jewelry in the Art Nouveau style that owed a stylistic debt more to France than England.

Madeline Yale Wynne

During this period, *The Craftsman* magazine extolled the virtues of simplicity and practicality, and while the latter virtue is always questionable in relation to jewelry, these beliefs were to influence the works of artist-jewelers like Madeline Yale Wynne. Wynne explored the artistic potential of different non-precious materials such as copper, pebbles, and rock crystals. This would prove to be a more enduring influence on future jewelry design than those companies and individuals preoccupied with precious metals and stones, since the search for new forms indirectly reflected the modern world. Other American jewelers who practiced within the Arts and Crafts arena include Brainerd Bliss Thresher and Josephine Hartwell.

One name, however, that stands out in the design and manufacture of Art Nouveau jewelry in the United States is that of Tiffany & Co., which produced a prolific amount of jewelry from the latter half of the 1800s, at first inspired by British Arts and Crafts, and later by Continental Art Nouveau in the first decade

Below: A swordfish brooch, manufactured by Tiffany's during the 1930s, in diamonds, sapphires, emeralds, and rubies.

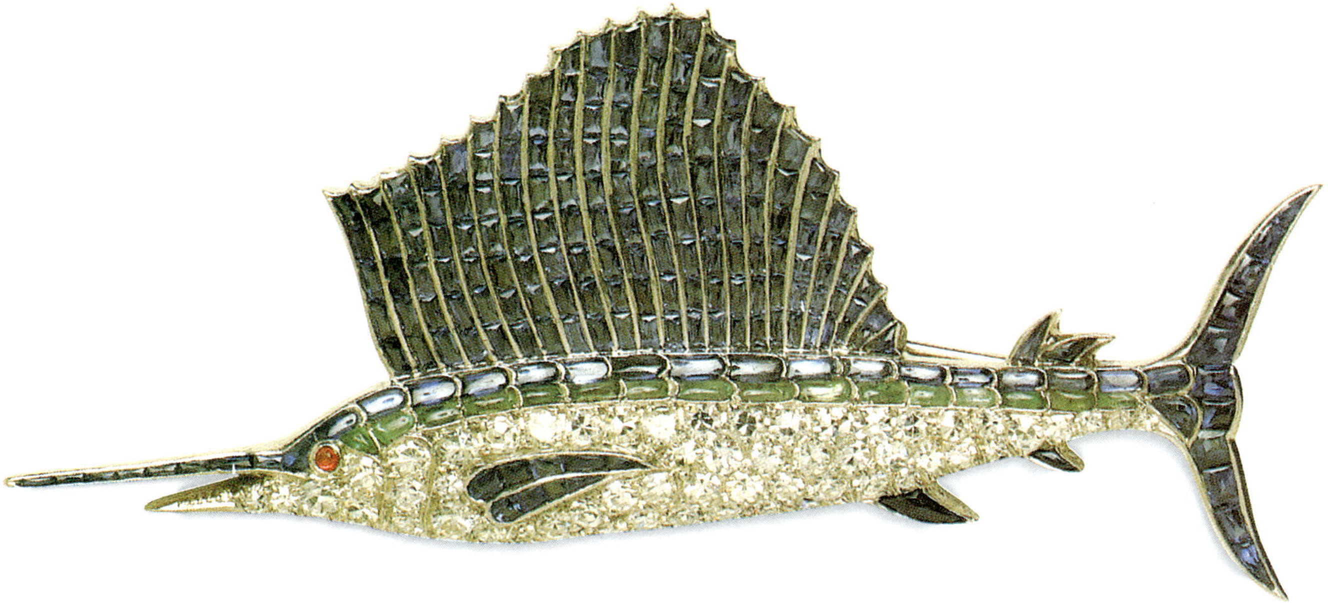

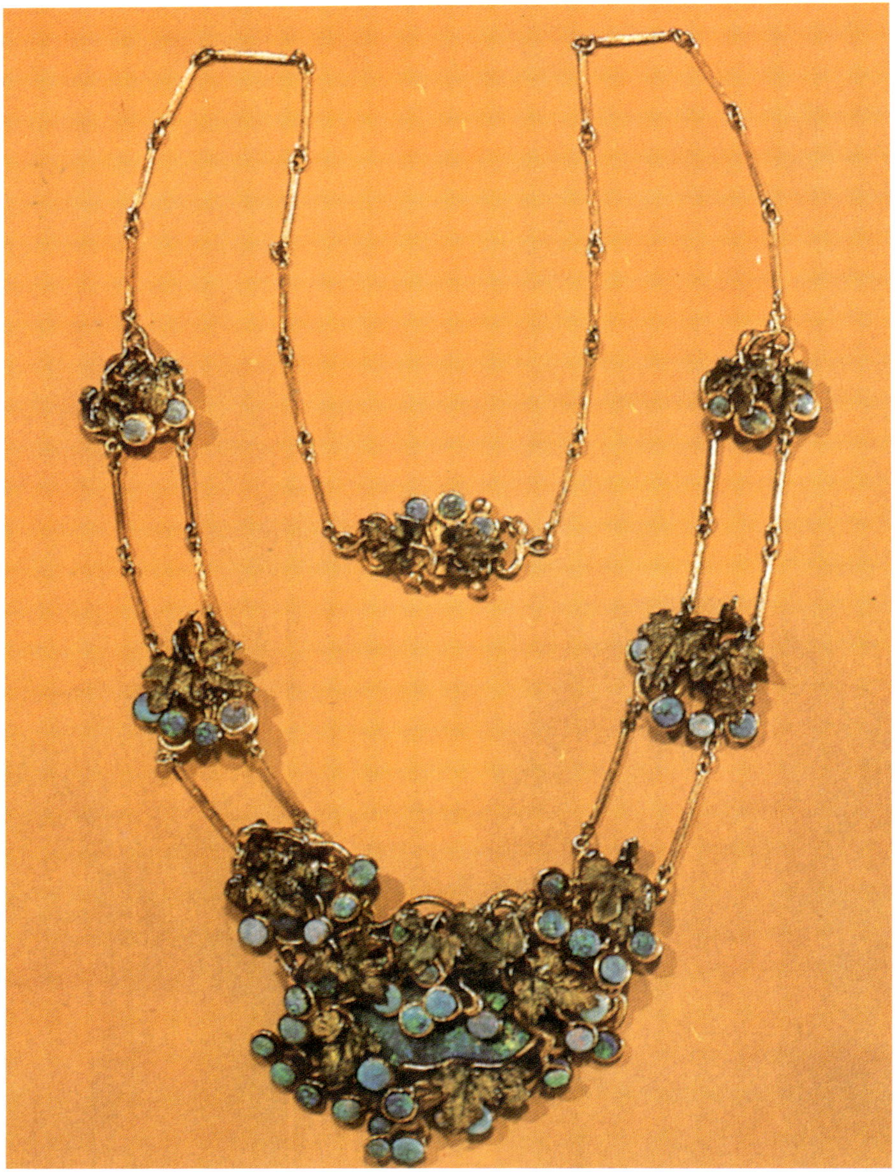

of the 1900s.

Louis Comfort Tiffany, famous for his masterpieces in glass, had been trained as a painter. Louis' father Charles had amassed an enormous store of precious stones over the years, and his craftsmen used them in designs for sword scabbards, tiaras, and coronets. In collaboration with Julia Munson, Louis opened an "art jewelry" department in the store and oversaw the production of luxurious Byzantine-inspired designs, utilizing such materials as opals and amethysts, rubies, diamonds, and emeralds. Jewelry designed by Louis Comfort Tiffany was produced under the auspices of Tiffany & Co. and bore their mark, so verification of Louis' own designs is difficult.

TIFFANY'S JEWELRY

What distinguishes Tiffany's jewelry from its European counterparts is that Tiffany did not make the gemstones subordinate to their settings, preferring instead a hard, clear design with unobtrusive settings. These pieces were perhaps too expensive and the "art jewelry" department closed in 1916, although the company of Tiffany & Co. continued to produce fine jewelry.

Above: Tiffany mixed opals with translucent glass in this necklace, but unlike his contemporaries, he did not submerge the gemstones in their settings.

ART NOUVEAU METALWORK

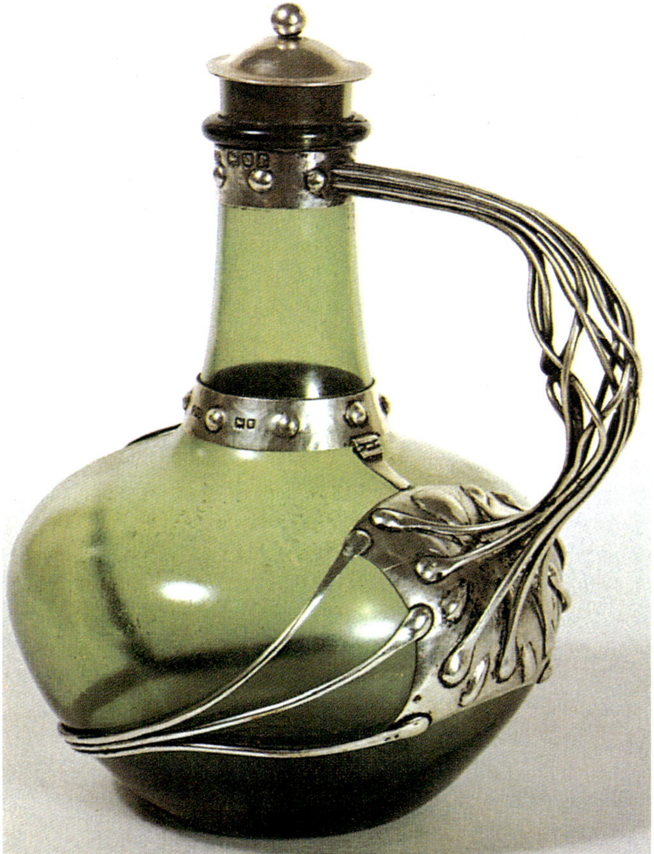

Overleaf: Silver mounted jug by C. R. Ashbee at the Guild of Handicraft, ca 1900. The green glass was made by Powell's of Whitefriars.

Below: The gate of Horta's Van Eetvelde House, whose intricate curving style is repeated inside.

The mid-1800s witnessed the beginnings of an age of individuality and innovation in terms of both precious and non-precious metalwork. The standards of Art Nouveau craftsmanship in this area were extremely high, and the period was rich in its constant variety of invention. Since the essence of Art Nouveau was the curving, sinuous line, its insubstantiality was best exploited in malleable materials.

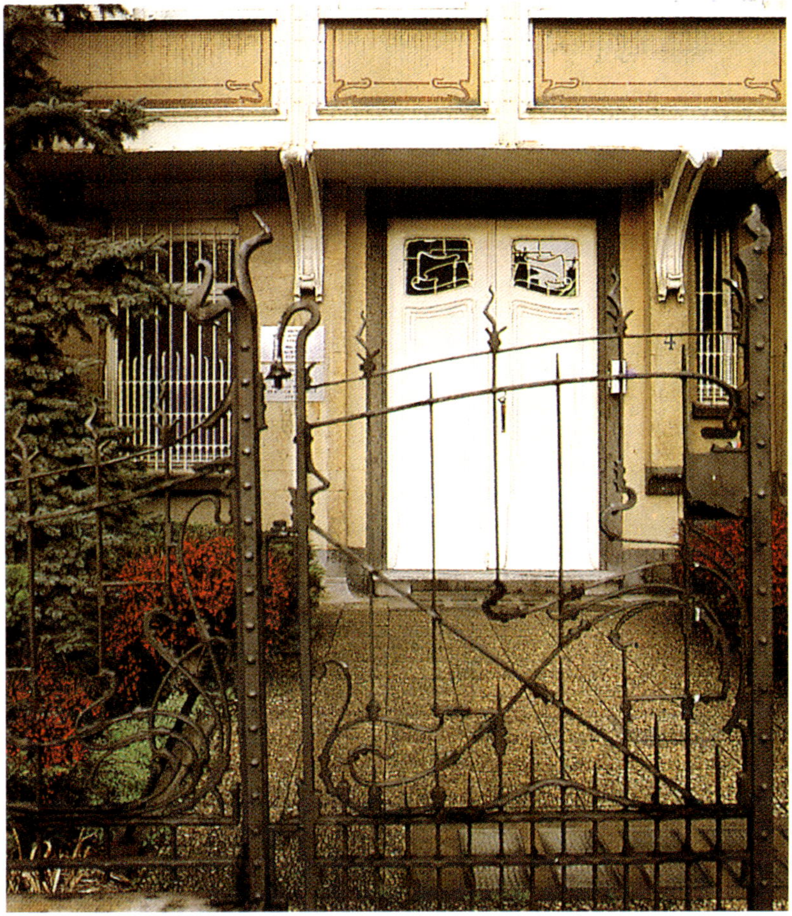

ART NOUVEAU METAL IN ARCHITECTURE

Metal, particularly wrought iron, was a significant part of Art Nouveau architecture, both structurally and decoratively. Victor Horta had made its structural role clear in his work in Brussels, and he had also used it decoratively, exploiting its relative malleability to provide lighter patterns in contrast to the weightiness of stone. In Art Nouveau architecture, metalwork serves as a link between the building itself and the style of its contents, which were often the product of the same designer. From exterior balconies, gates, and window mullions, the metal is continued into the interior in columns, beams, banisters, and door handles, and even to embellishments on furniture.

The versatile applications for metalwork and the range of metals available encouraged almost every Art Nouveau architect and interior designer to turn their hand to metal at some stage. As with glass or furniture, it is important to visualize metalwork as part of its context in the interior scheme. It could appear in the form of candlesticks, flatware, clocks, light fixtures, mirrors, caskets, and in fanciful, decorative sculptures.

EXTERIORS AND INTERIORS

Hector Guimard's Métro entrances emphasize the versatility of the medium, as they can be seen both as architecture and as sculpture, or even as enormous decorative pieces. They use

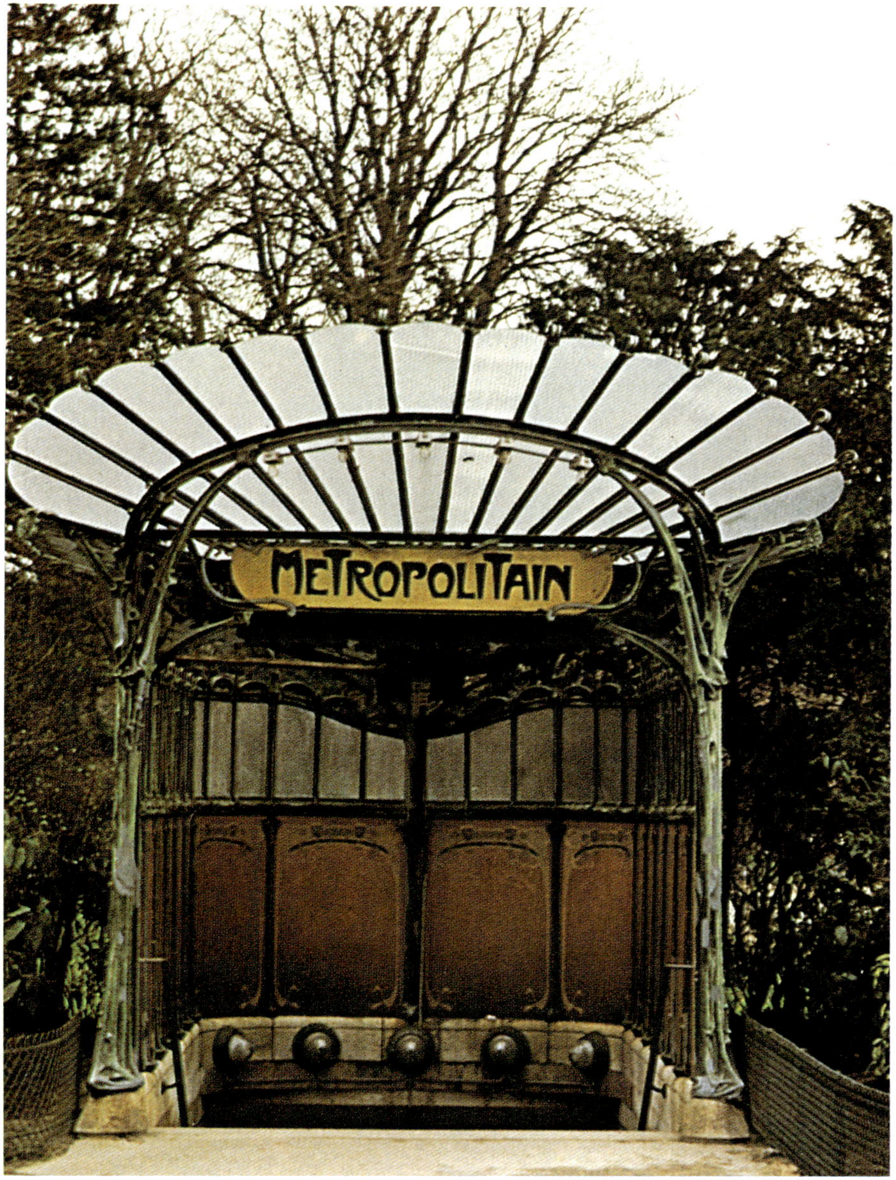

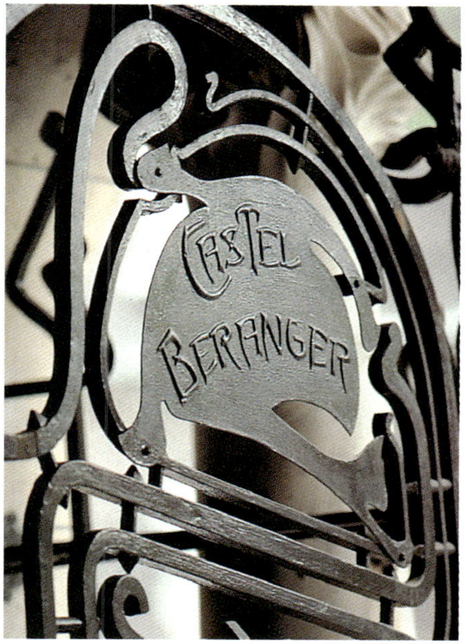

Above: The whiplash line is evident in Guimard's ironwork entrance to the Castel Beranger.

Left: The Paris Métro, Bois de Boulogne station by Hector Guimard, who also designed the typography.

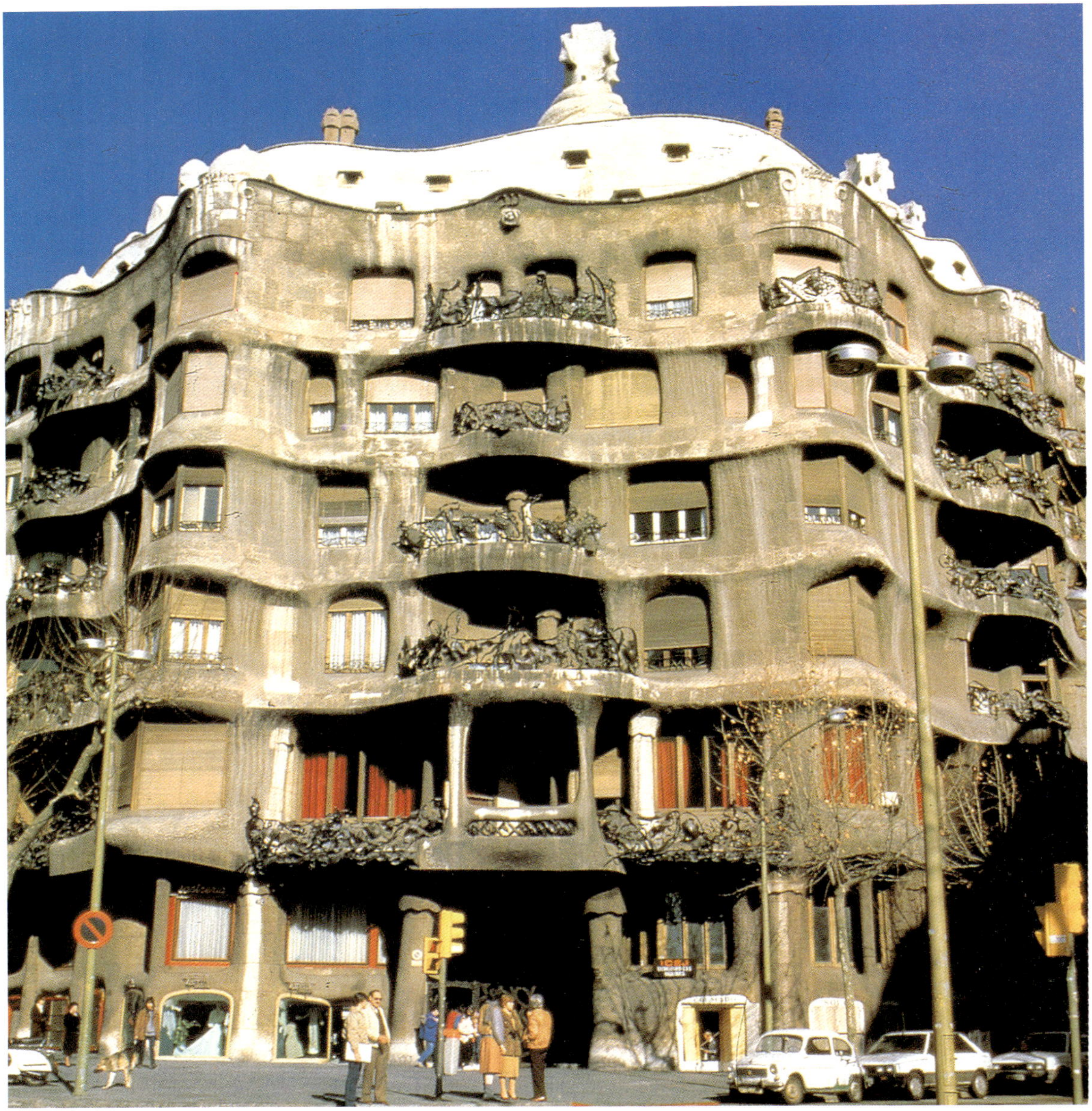

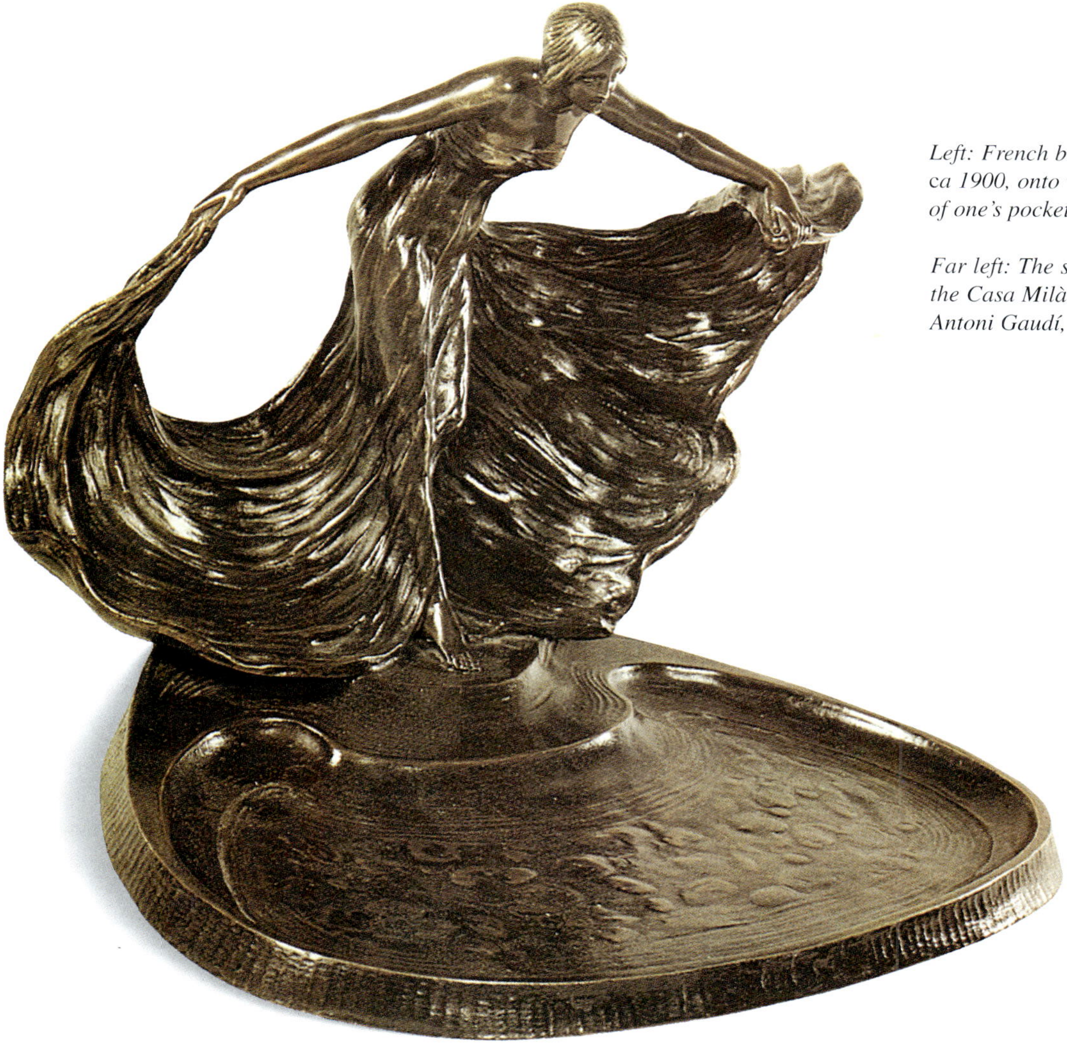

Left: French bronze vide-poche, ca 1900, onto which the contents of one's pockets were placed.

Far left: The sinuous lines of the Casa Milà, Barcelona, by Antoni Gaudí, 1905.

the same forms as the great iron gates of the Castel Beranger apartments, as well as for the banisters within. In Belgium, Horta carried the same continuity of form from the iron balconies to the banisters for the staircase, the main feature of his own home and studio in the Rue Americaine in Brussels.

Comparable in function, yet even more fantastic in form, were the balconies of Gaudí's Casa Milà, modeled like tangled seaweed. In his early work for the Casa Vicens, Gaudí achieved the effect of palm fronds with the spikes cut at the top bent in every direction as if they were dropping leaves. The entrance gate to the Güell Estate in Pedrables is even more outstanding. Here, almost the entire piece is treated in the form of a writhing dragon whose gaping jaw reaches out to ensnare the hand of the visitor who reaches for the handle.

Metal objects d'art

Work in the traditional precious metals, particularly silver, had, through the processes of industrialization and mass production, sunk

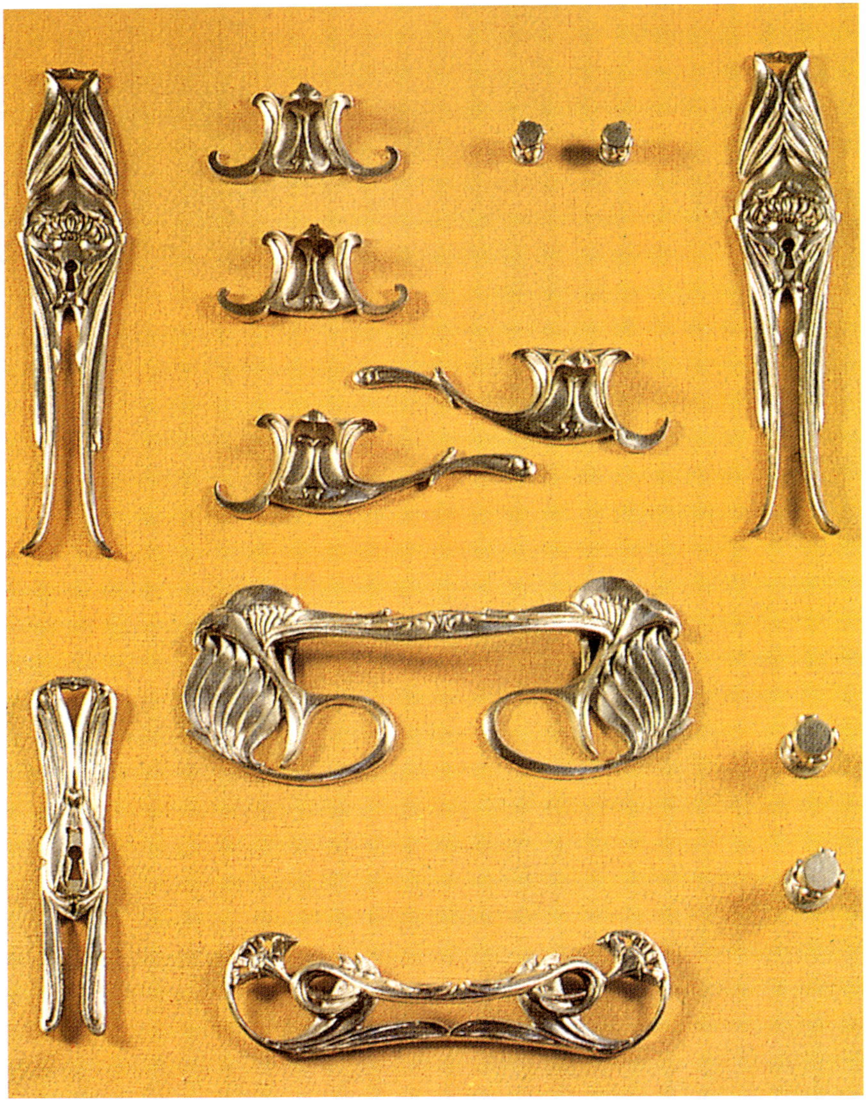

Above: An ornate set of metal fittings for furniture produced by Georges de Feure.

to a low level of design and workmanship until it was revived by the Arts and Crafts Movements, first in England and then later abroad.

These craftsmen emphasized the virtues of handmade objects, and at times even sought to underline this method of production by deliberately leaving the surface of their metal objects "unfinished" — that is, with their hammer marks left visible and unpolished. Less precious materials were also explored for their aesthetic qualities — bronze, brass, tin, and copper were all used, and a revival of interest in pewter also occurred. At times, Art Nouveau craftsmen combined a range of metals and mixed them with ivory, enamels, semiprecious stones, or any other material required to produce the appropriate effect. Some designers produced handmade and therefore very exclusive items, while others were to tailor their designs to large-scale production and found themselves more in tune with the future course of design in the 1900s.

Art Nouveau metalwork in France

Guimard was largely an isolated talent in France with regard to architectural metalwork, and the French reputation in metalwork is largely confined to the area of jewelry and orfeverie. In France, the Nancy school concentrated more on furniture, glass, and ceramics, although Louis Majorelle, who had used gilt trimmings on his furniture, produced some gates and banisters, as did Victor Prouve. More metalwork was produced by the Parisian craftsmen working for Bing, and Julius Meier-Graefe, who had opened his retail outlet La Maison Moderne in Paris in 1898. The elegant Georges de Feure was one of the most versatile of these designers and produced objects from candelabra to walking cane handles, based on stylized, fluid plant forms. Others, like Colonna and Selmersheim, turned to metalwork for a complete room setting, designing table lamps or chandeliers in the form of drooping plants whose flowers were the glass shades.

CARDEILHAC

The firm of Cardeilhac was a leading producer of exciting Art Nouveau designs, in particular by Lucien Bonvallet. The company also produced a series of mounts for vases by the leading glass makers and potters, and the firm's most characteristic pieces were those in silver or silver-gilt, decorated with stylized yet restrained plant motifs.

Like many Art Nouveau designers, Lucien Gaillard, a name most often associated with jewelry, also explored a range of media. Gaillard had studied in depth the various aspects of metalworking, patination, plating, and alloying, as well as Japanese techniques of decoration. He produced a variety of objects from parasol handles to hairpins which combined his fine workmanship with a strong sense of design, using precious and non-precious materials with equal respect.

SCULPTURE IN METAL

Another branch of the decorative arts which enjoyed a particular vogue at the end of the 1800s was decorative sculpture. Small, domestic scale sculptures could be found in a variety of functions, including supporting lamps, as well as being created in a purely ornamental capacity. This was principally a French-inspired fashion pursued by such figures as Eugène Feuillatre, Raoul Larche, Théodore Rivière, and Rupert Carabin, who generally produced nude or lightly-draped female figures whose hair and drapery was ex-

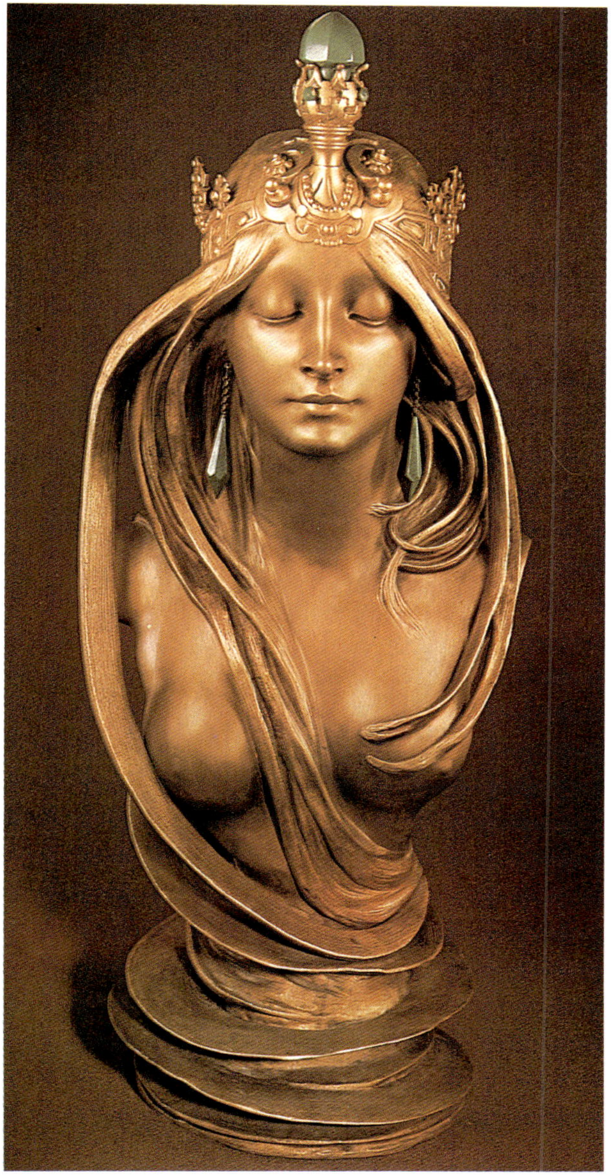

Left: Decorative sculpture enjoyed a particular vogue around 1900. One of the most popular motifs of the Art Nouveau period was the figure of a woman as the "dream-maiden."

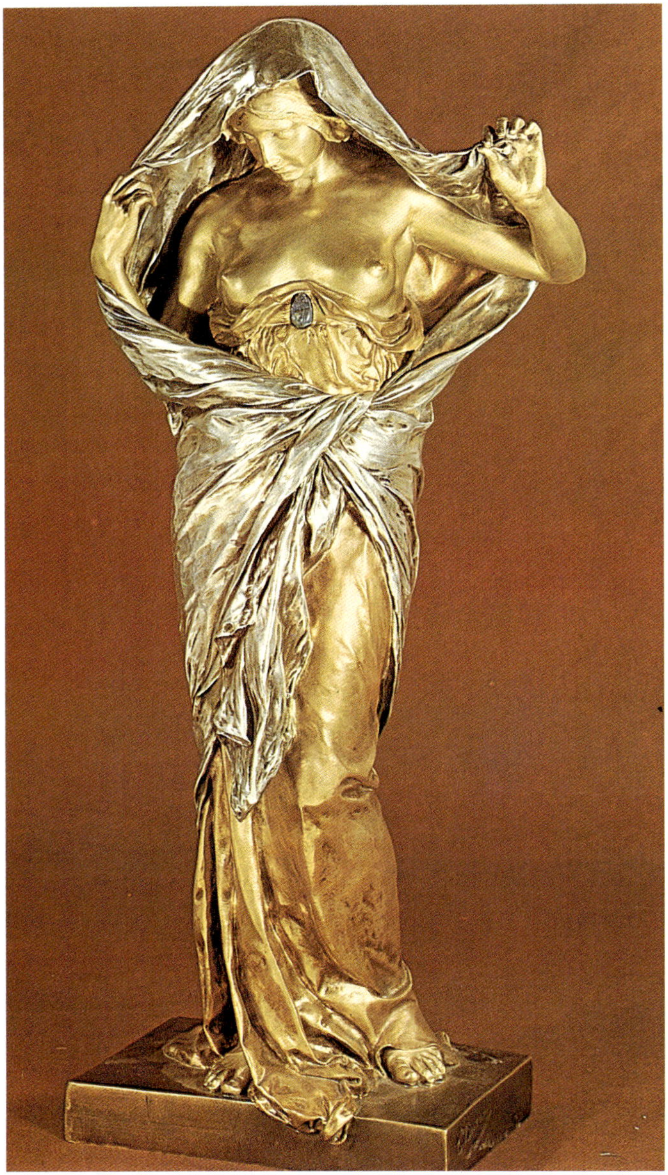

tended into extravagant arabesques.

French sculpture at the time was dominated by the aging genius, Auguste Rodin, whose work, principally in bronze, had exploited to the full that medium's possibilities for active poses and shimmering light. Rodin's work, however, was far too involved with symbolist and literary overtones to be described as decorative, yet his frequently twisting poses and erotic subjects do recall some aspects of Art Nouveau.

Folies Bergère

The main source of inspiration for Art Nouveau sculptors was undoubtedly the American dancer, Loie Fuller, who first appeared at the Folies Bergère in 1893, and triumphed at the 1900 Exposition Universelle where she was hailed as the living embodiment of Art Nouveau. Several sculptors captured the fluid magic of her dance movements in bronze.

Maurice Bouval

Some of the most sensual decorative Art Nouveau sculptures were modeled by Maurice Bouval. His works, which were conceived as paper knives, dishes, door handles, or purely decorative objects, were usually in gilt-bronze and always on the theme of the dream-maiden or femme-fleur so dear to Art Nouveau. A regional variant of this genre was produced in Belgium by the jeweler Philippe Wolfers, who, in 1904, devoted himself entirely to this form of decorative sculpture.

Sculptor and decorator Alexandre

Left: Gilt and silver-bronze statuette by E. Barrias called "La Naturese devoilant devant La Science."

Charpentier modeled low relief, sensitive, allegorical nude figures for door handles, furniture decorations, and lock plates. He was regarded as one of the best medalists during his active period at the turn of the century.

SIR ALFRED GILBERT

The British sculptor Sir Alfred Gilbert, the creator of the Shaftesbury Memorial fountain at Piccadilly in London, (better known as "Eros") was a sculptor in bronze who changed to working on a smaller scale with precious and semiprecious materials. In the detailing of his works — even those on a large scale — Gilbert was fascinated by intricate, twisting, and curving forms, often tinged with marine mythology taken from the 1500s and 1600s.

METALWORK IN ENGLAND

Silver was one of the materials which had received renewed attention due to the influence of the Arts and Crafts Movement. Silver design largely transferred from the established manufacturers to artists and architects who turned their hand to silversmithing. Perhaps the best known of the Arts and Crafts metalwork designers is Charles Ashbee, who had founded the Guild of Handicraft in 1888. Ashbee began working in silver and electroplate in 1889, although did he not register a mark until 1896. The first works produced by the Guild were in keeping with their high ideals. They avoided the abhorred smooth, mechanical finish produced by high polishing. Instead, Ashbee encouraged his craftsmen to leave the impression of hammer marks on the surface of their work. From 1890, the Guild began using gems and enameling, but

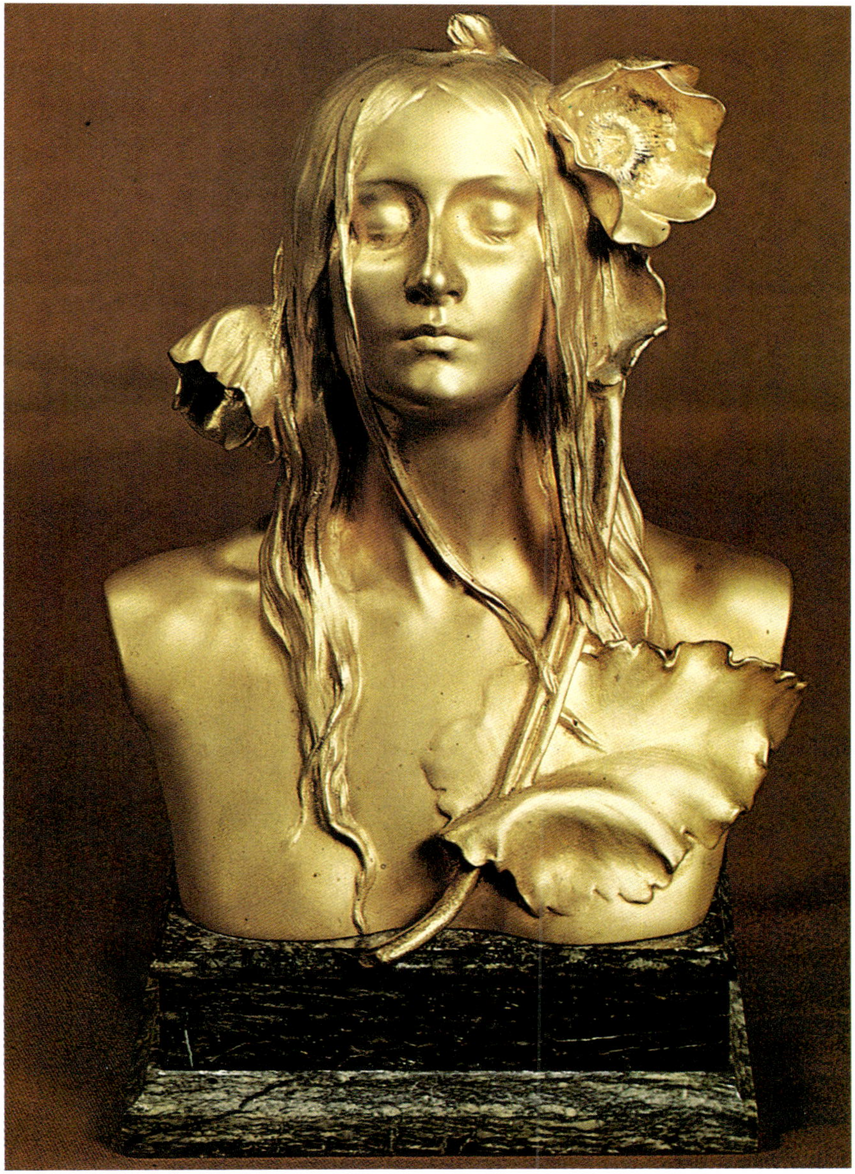

Right: Gilt bronze "femme-fleur" bust by Maurice Bouval, ca 1900.

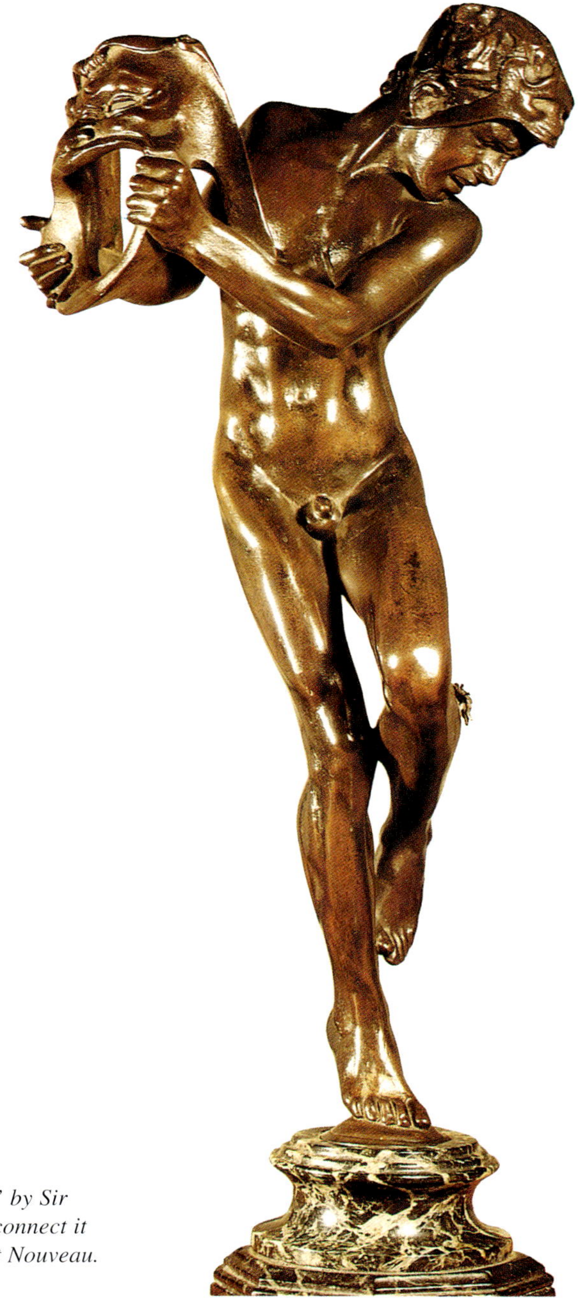

Right: "Comedy and Tragedy," by Sir Alfred Gilbert. The fluid lines connect it with decorative elements of Art Nouveau.

Ashbee's work is most recognizable from his wirework, which he perfected around 1897, and the delicacy of his designs which often incorporate green glass with silver.

With regard to design for industrial manufacture, it is the work of Christopher Dresser that represents the highest achievement. Dresser based his design ethic on "fitness for purpose" and most of them were carried out in electroplate, due as much to his concern for an economic use of materials as to the manufacturer's financial preference. One of the few designers to have visited Japan, Dresser's metalwork designs demonstrate a sparseness, and in some cases, a complete lack of decoration which is in complete contrast to many of the other leading Art Nouveau designers.

LIBERTY STYLE

Liberty & Co. was one of the leading English retailers of metalwork in the Art Nouveau style. Designs for silver and metalwork were commissioned from various designers, including Rex Silver, Oliver Baker, Bernard Cuzner, Arthur Gaskin, and Jessie M. King. The most outstanding of Liberty's designers, and the one who would largely determine the Liberty style, was Archibald Knox. Born on the Isle of Man, Knox had studied at first hand the Celtic design of the area's cultural history and applied the Runic interlacing of forms in his designs for silver and pewter. In 1899, Liberty's marketed the designs in silver under the vaguely Celtic name of "Cymric." At this time, Liberty's had stocked German pewter wares, but in 1903, following the success of Cymric silver, the store launched its range of "Tudric" pewter, again, designed largely by Knox.

THE GLASGOW FOUR

A similar mood was created by the work of

the "Glasgow Four" which centered around the architect and designer Charles Rennie Mackintosh. The two sisters, Margaret and Frances Macdonald, produced together, and individually, a great deal of relief work, either of beaten tin or silver, as mounts for objects such as mirrors, and as decorative objects in their own right. The pale coolness of their work perfectly complements the Mackintosh interior and adds a figurative and floral element to the Glasgow style.

GERMANY AND AUSTRIA

The majority of the members of the main German and Austrian Secessionist groups worked in both precious and base metals. The Wiener Werkstätte's metalwork was made in an extraordinary range of styles, something that was particularly true of Joseph Hoffmann's designs. The earliest examples, dating from 1903, are often very formal, with simple "modernist" shapes, and in some instances these pieces were left with a hammered finish. Pieces such as the silver-gilt tea set designed in 1904 rank among the greatest metalwork of the period.

INSPIRATION

Much of the early work of both Hoffmann and Kolomon Moser shows the obvious influence of Mackintosh, Ashbee, and Henry van de Velde. Highly respected by the Vienna Secessionists, Mackintosh's influence can be seen in the strongly geometric, open lattice-work baskets designed by Hoffmann, while Ashbee's work inspired some of Hoffmann's flattened, covered dishes, which date from around 1908.

Below: A silver bowl with wire-work handles by C.R. Ashbee of the Guild of Handicraft.

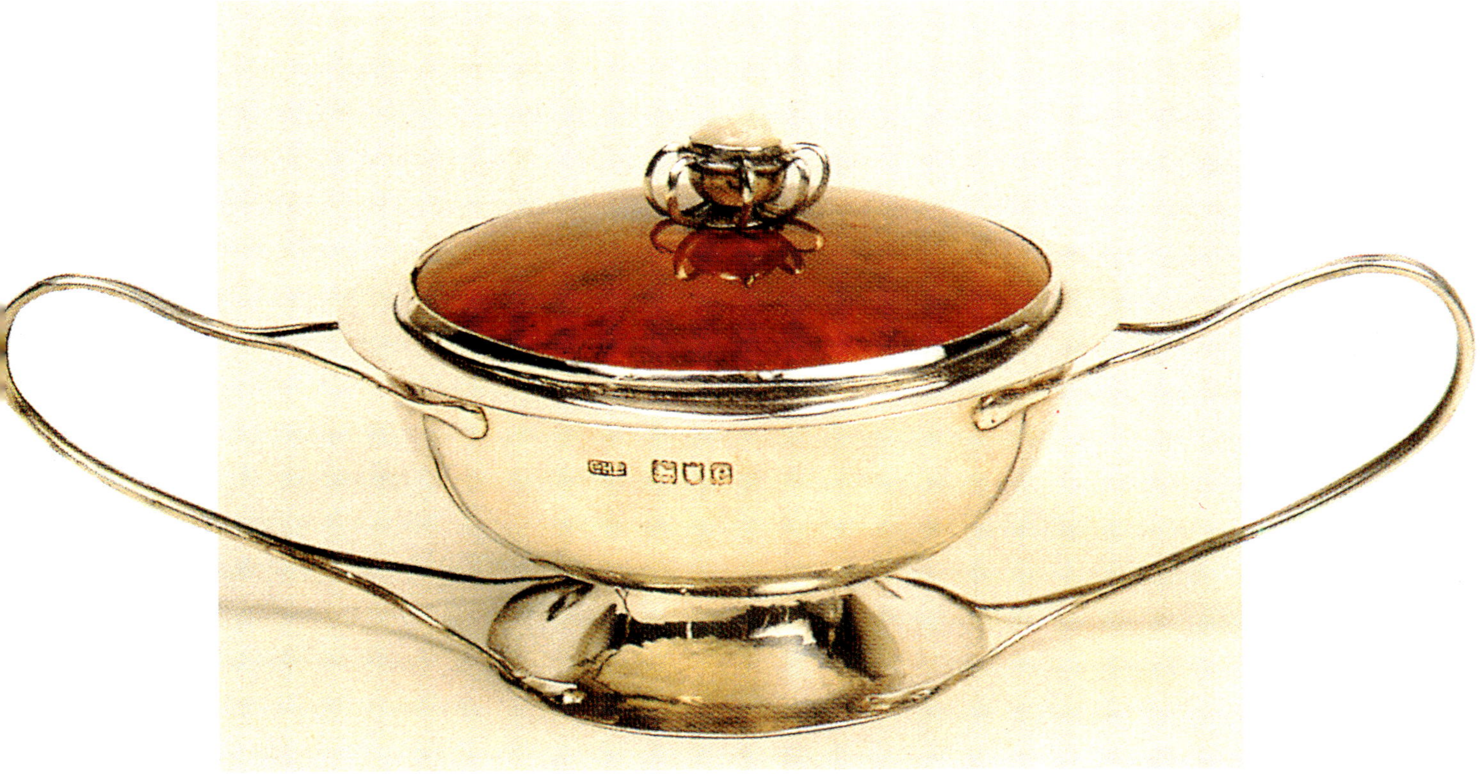

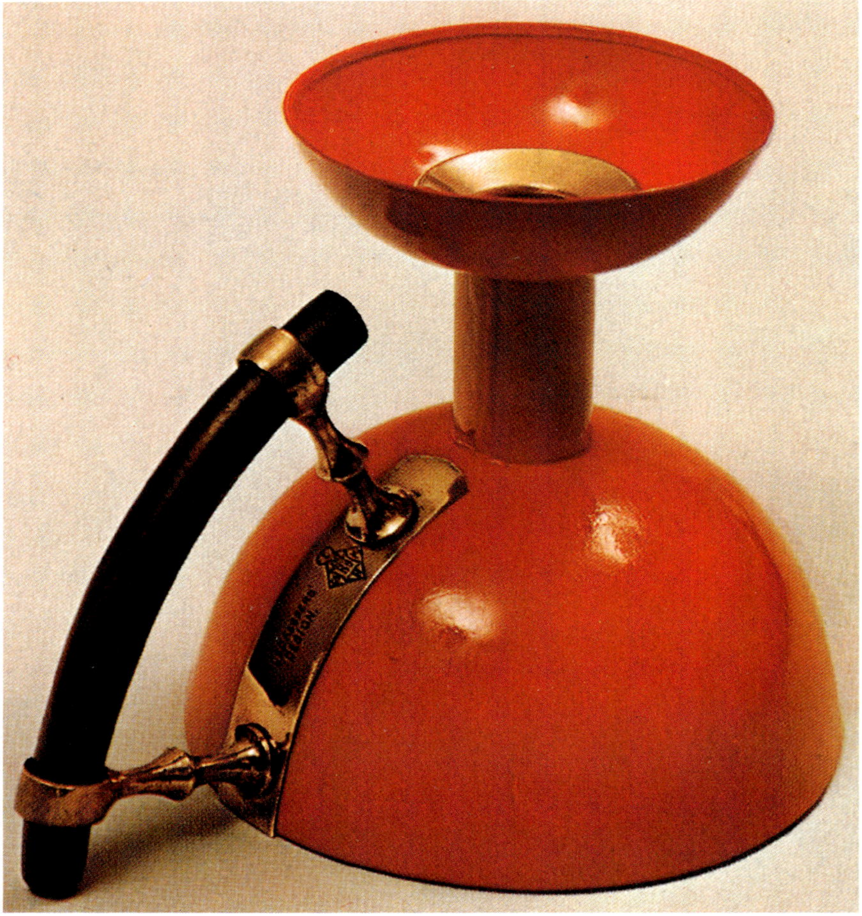

Right: A candlestick in painted copper, brass, and wood by Christopher Dresser, made by Perry & Co. in 1883.

Below: A teapot by Christopher Dresser in silver and wood from 1881.

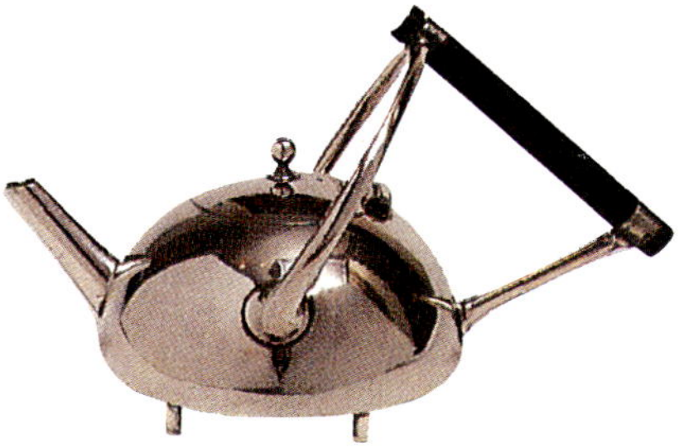

In Germany, there was a great deal of very ornate Art Nouveau metalwork, especially that produced by firms such as J. P. Kayser & Sohne of Krefeld who manufactured a range of pewter under the trade name of Kayser-Zinn. It was this pewter range, designed by Hugo Leven, that Liberty's in London sold until it developed its own Tudric pewter. WMF in Geislingen produced some of the most outrageous curvilinear Art Nouveau metalwork, usually in thick pewter or nickel-silver and often with green glass liners. On of the largest and most important firms was P. Bruckmann & Sohne of Heilbronn, whose designers included Peter Behrens, Friedrich Adler, George Roehmer, and Bernhard Wenig. Bruckmann

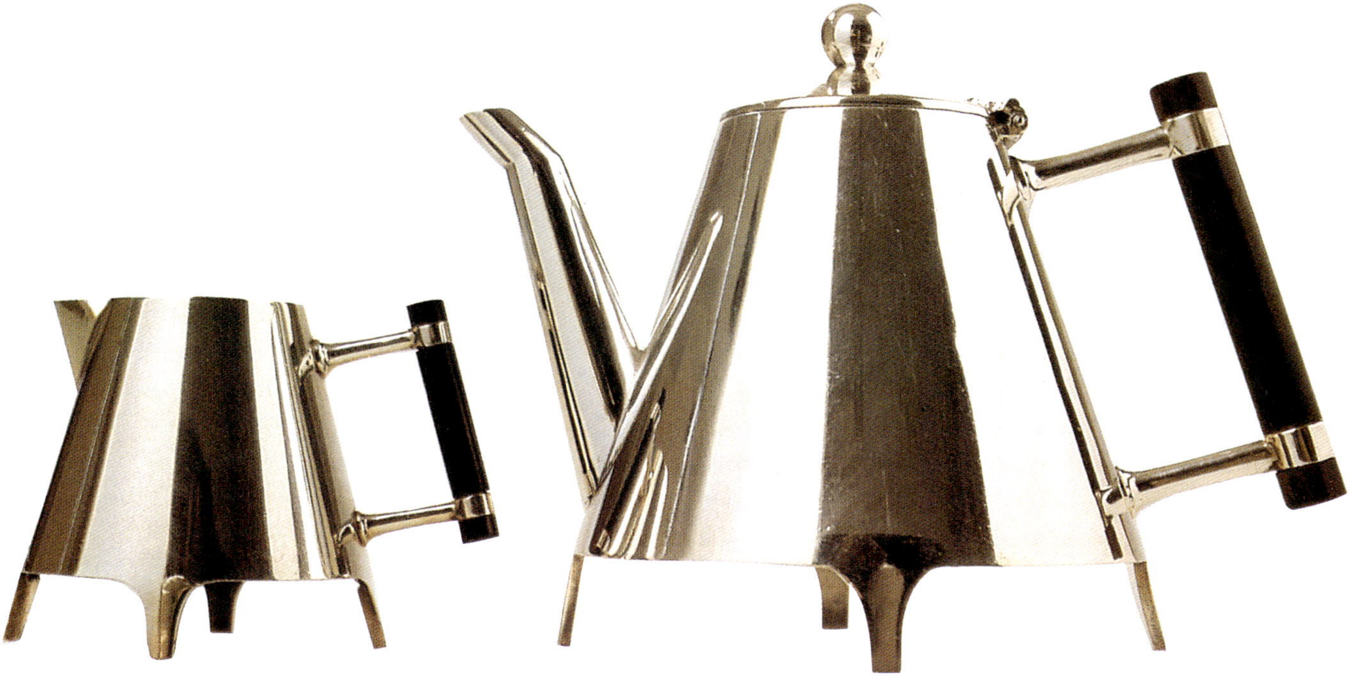

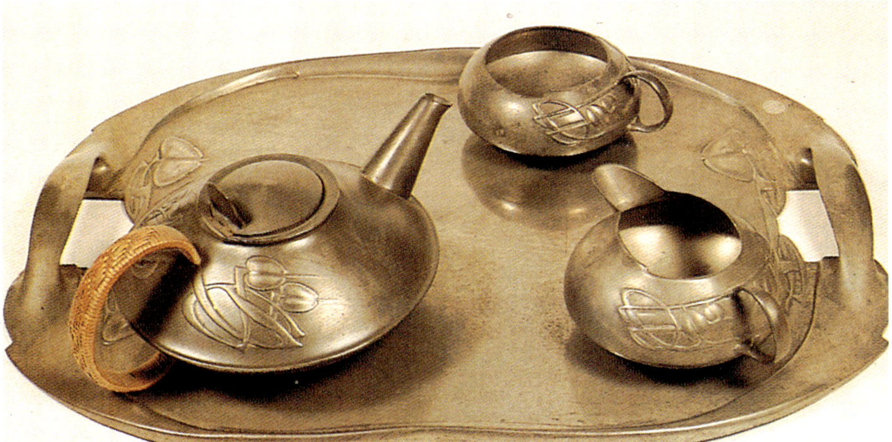

Above: A tea set of almost oriental refinement by Christopher Dresser.

Left: Tea set by Archibald Knox for Liberty & Co., part of the Tudric range he designed that continued the Celtic theme.

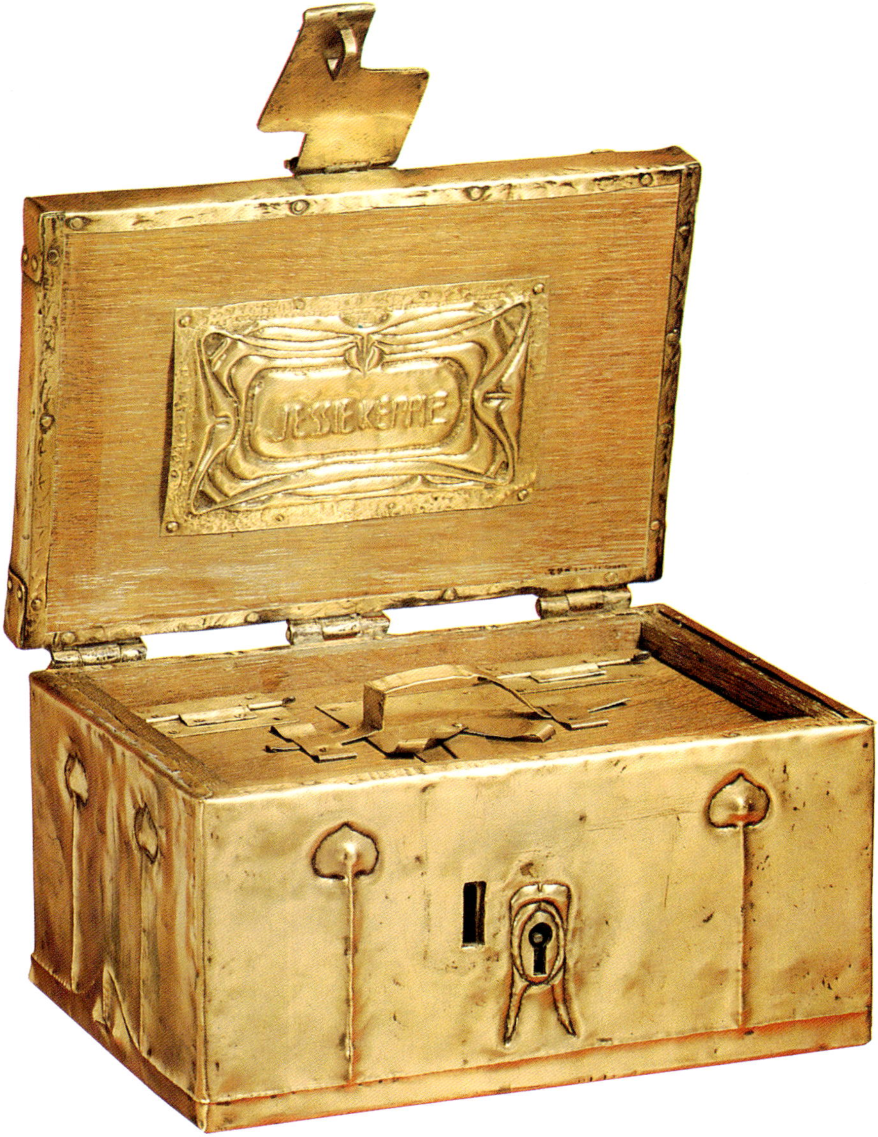

was also one of the major industrial firms to produce the designs of the Deutsche Werkbund.

Henry van de Velde

Possibly the most impressive of the metalwork designers active in Germany in the early years of the 1900s was Henry van de Velde. His early silver is in a style that is often described as "geometric-curvilinear" and can be compared to some of the earliest designs by the Dane, Georg Jensen.

Other European countries

Italian-born designer Carlo Bugatti created both outstanding furniture and magnificent silver objects which were made by the Parisian craftsman Adrien A. Hebrard. In true Art Nouveau style, they combined various subjects, materials, and techniques in an unusual manner. For example, one tea and coffee set comprised a long tray with a bizarre animal head at each end, both terminating in long, ivory tusks. The coffee pot, teapot, creamer, and sugar bowl were also in the shape of boar-like animal heads, also with ivory tusks.

In St. Petersburg, master jeweler Peter Carl Fabergé included Art Nouveau pieces in his outstanding oeuvre, including gold cigarette cases and flower- and leaf-shaped mounts for the glass made by Tiffany in New York and Loetz in Germany.

Metal in America

On the whole, silver in America had tended to be dominated by the old established firms such as the Gorham Manufacturing Co., or the internationally famous Tiffany and Co. At the luxury end of the market, these two firms

Left: A jewelry box designed by Charles Rennie Mackintosh.

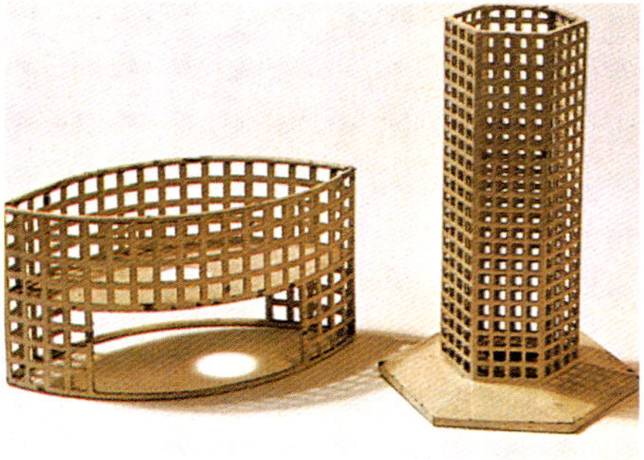

Left: Metal baskets designed by Josef Hoffmann, the founder of the Wiener Werkstätte.

Below: An electric kettle designed by Peter Behrens for AEG, ca 1908.

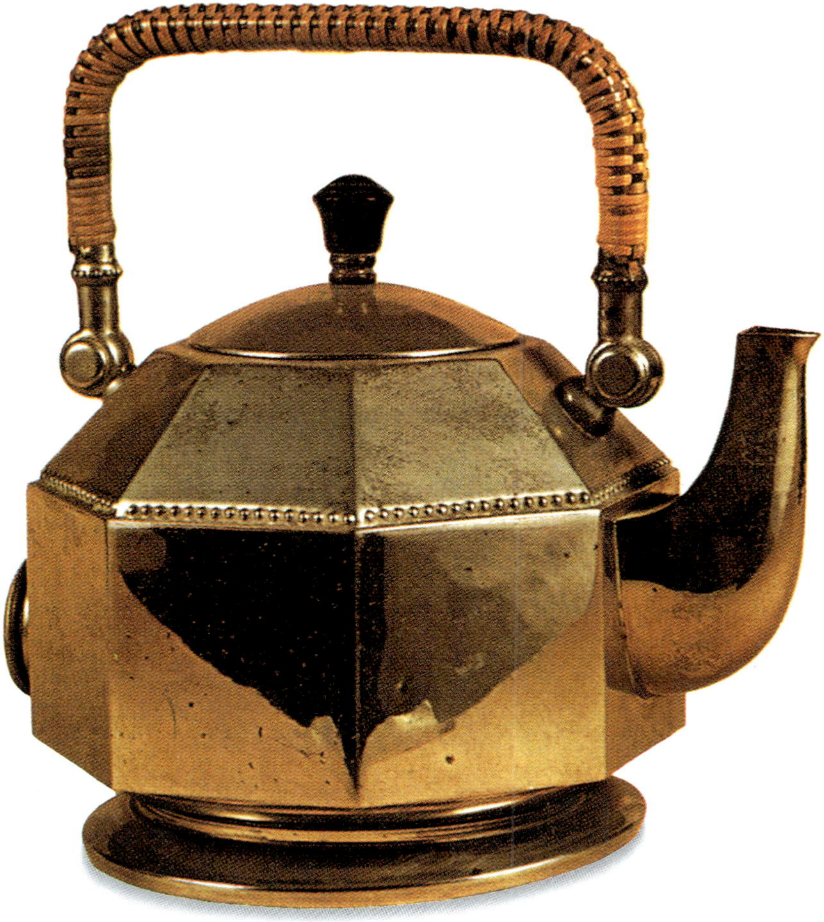

were the dominant force, and both were influenced by the changes in style created by the craft revival and Art Nouveau.

TIFFANY & CO.

Tiffany & Co., the New York jeweler, silver manufacturer, and retailer, was established in 1837, and it produced outstanding silver in Japanese, Indian, and Moorish styles, and, from the 1880s, in the Art Nouveau style. When Louis Comfort Tiffany opened his own Tiffany Studios, he began experimenting with enamels, often used on repousse copper bowls or vases. Opaque and translucent layers were used, fired separately and often finished with an iridescent coat which gave the pieces an effect similar to his glassware.

GORHAM MANUFACTURING COMPANY

The Gorham Manufacturing Company, founded in 1831, in Providence, Rhode Island, was Tiffany's chief rival in silverware, and also produced electroplated silver. In the late 1880s, its fine quality silver included Japanese-style wares, and later, hand-crafted pieces in the French Art Nouveau and English Arts and Crafts style which were marketed as "Martele" (hammered) silver.

The Arts and Crafts Movement inspired nu-

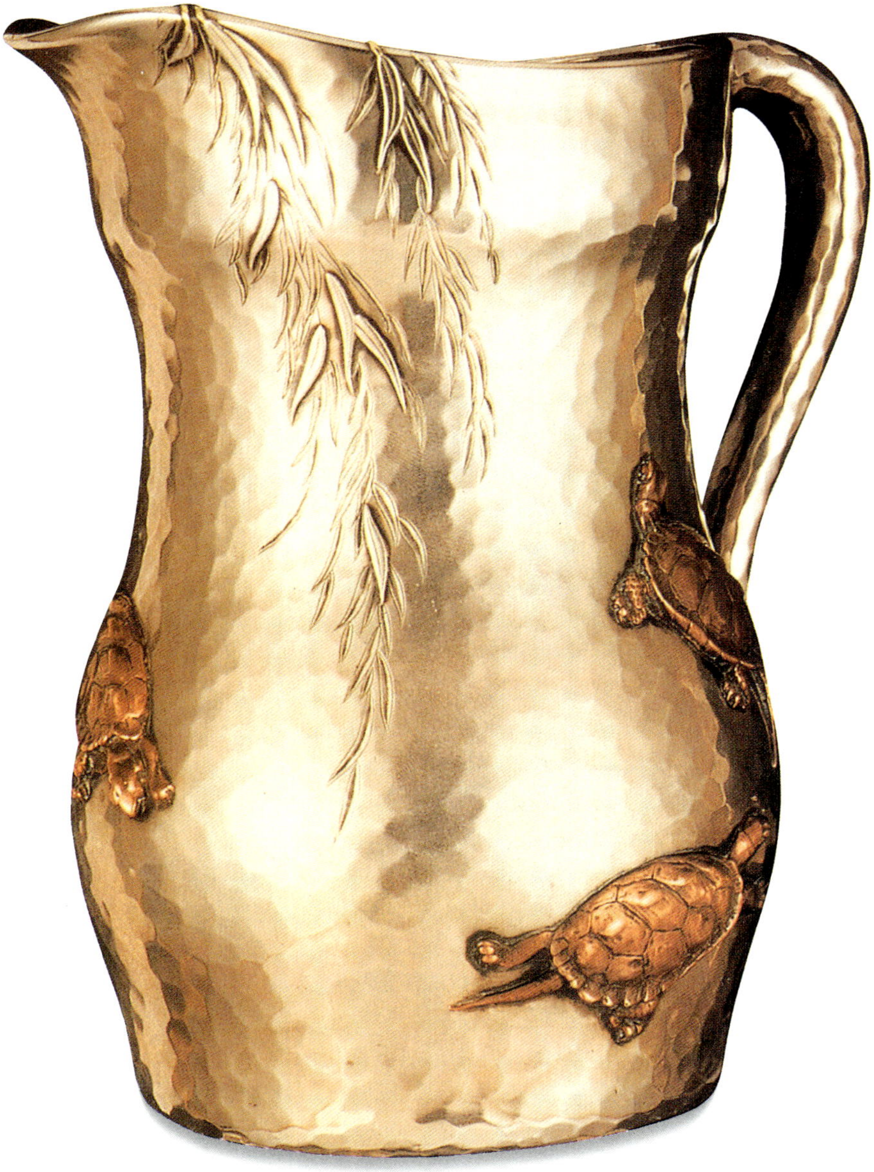

merous followers in the United States and several communities fostered a revival in metalwork. The Roycrofters made wrought iron, and the Roycroft Copper Shop was headed by Karl Kipp from Vienna. Kipp designed bookends, candlesticks, trays, vases, and other household items which were then made by other members of the Shop. The hammered copper was decorated with stylized designs, usually of flowers or trees, and was advertised and sold through the Roycroft catalogs.

Left: Silver, silver-gilt, and copper jug, decorated with hammered turtles by Tiffany & Company, late 1800s.

Below: A hammered bowl with the same applied turtles, typical of Tiffany's Japanese-style wares.

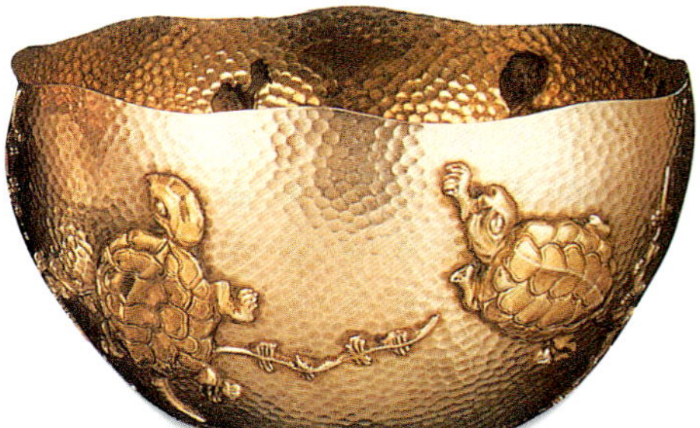

Art Nouveau
Glass and Ceramics

An Expression of Style

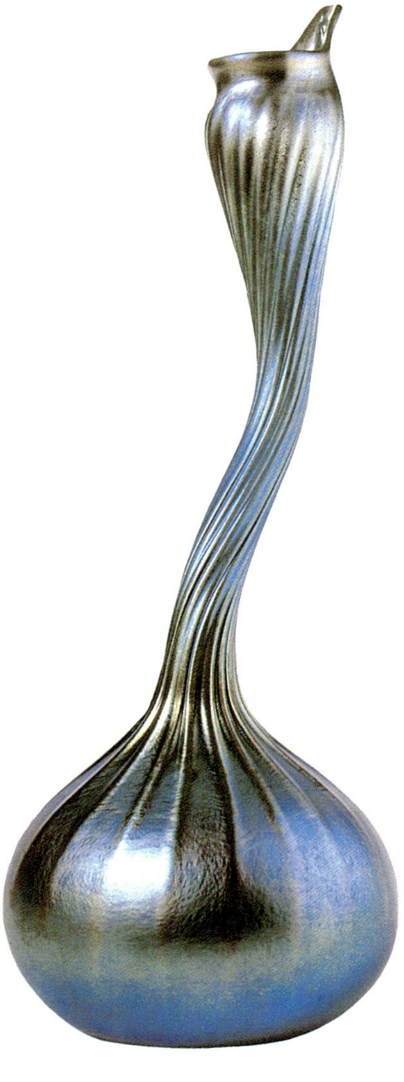

Art Nouveau glass and ceramics were closely linked in both style and technique, and much the same kind of ware was produced in each medium. In both crafts, the innovations of Art Nouveau increased the range of color and the possibilities for relief decoration, as well as changing the actual shape of the piece itself. For the Art Nouveau craftsman, glass and clay were, in their own way, as malleable and tractable as metal, and the fluid contours of the style could be equally well expressed.

Far left: A goose-necked vase by Louis Comfort Tiffany, inspired by a Persian perfume flask.

THE STYLES OF THE CENTURY

Art Nouveau developed in the late 1880s and was at its creative height in the subsequent decade. By 1905, it had declined into being a much diluted ingredient in commercial design, soon to be replaced by an aesthetic felt to be more in keeping with the new century.

The 1800s had seen enormous changes in society in both Europe and the United States, with the spread of industrialization resulting

Below: New machinery at the 1851 Great Exhibition, London, which had introduced the mass production of everyday artefacts and threatened the role of craftsmen.

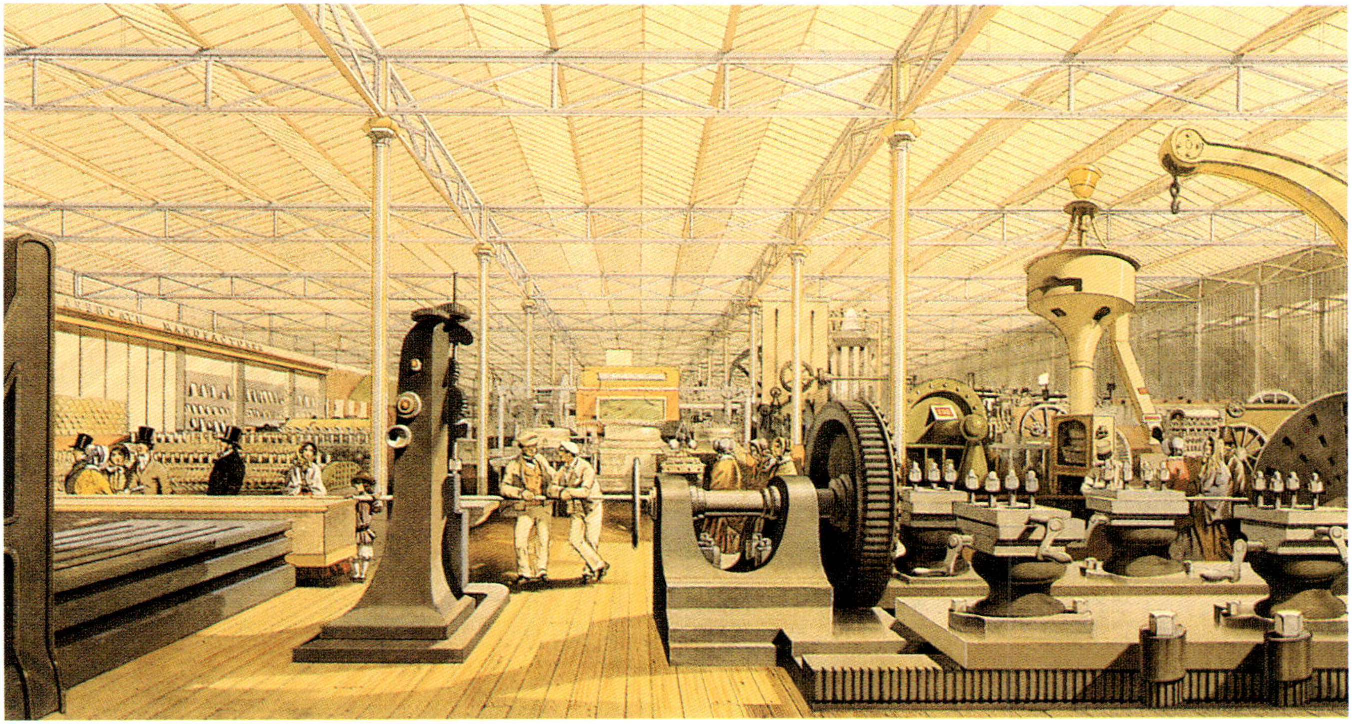

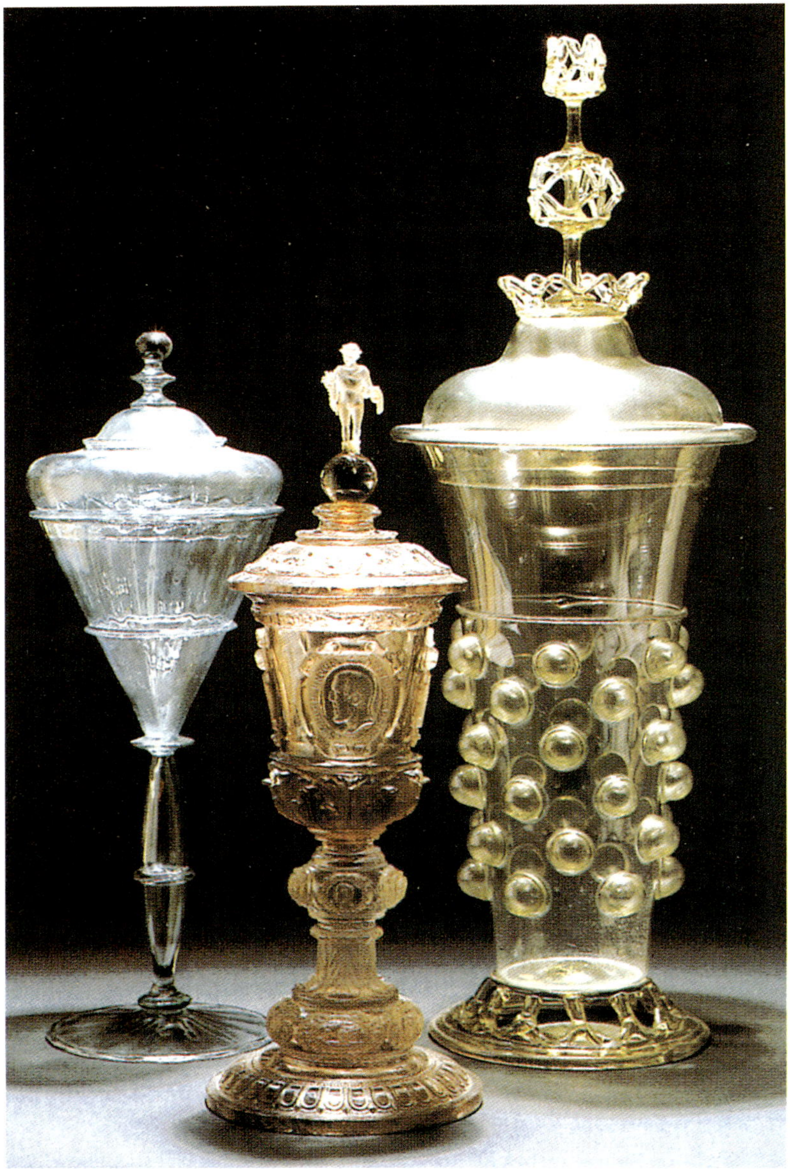

in great wealth mainly concentrated in the new manufacturing and commercial cities. Mass-production methods in factories not only produced a wider range of goods that were more widely available than ever before, but also created an entirely new class of workers. At the same time, major advances in technology such as railways, steamships, and the telegraph, were easing the problems of communication. The world had changed, yet it seemed as though there were no corresponding changes in the styles employed to shape its appearance. In the design of everyday objects, just as in the design of buildings, the new age was simply offering revivals of old styles — Classical, Gothic, Renaissance, Baroque, or Rococo. While technology advanced, the quality of design seemed to have stagnated, or even regressed.

NEW ART

The Art Nouveau — the "new art" — was the first style that did not seem to have its roots sunk deep into European history. Art Nouveau was the first new style of the 1800s — despite the fact that it did not emerge until its closing years.

ART AND INDUSTRY

The Art Nouveau style was made possible by a number of outstanding writers on aesthetics during the 1800s, notably John Ruskin and William Morris in Britain, and Léon de Laborde and Eugène Viollet-le-Duc in France. What all these writers had in common was a rejection of the crass materialism which had reached its peak in many of the exhibits that were on display at the 1851 Great Exhibition at the Crystal Palace

Left: Three "Historical Revival" Goblets from Germany, ca 1890.

in London's Hyde Park. The long-forgotten truth that art should be in harmony with the age which produces it was rediscovered around 1850 by these men.

John Ruskin was especially responsible for a number of advances in the field of aesthetics — he rejected the distinction between the so-called major and minor arts. Consequently, interior decoration, which had formerly been entirely in the hands of artisans, now took on the dimensions of a major social and artistic mission to be accomplished. According to Ruskin, the decorative arts should once again assume the central position in artistic concerns they had occupied at the time of the Renaissance.

INSPIRATION FROM NATURE

It was also Ruskin who called upon architects to draw their inspiration from nature. This concept was to be central to the movements in the decorative arts at the end of the 1800s. The translation of the "secrets" of nature into design are evident in the works of Art Nouveau architects like Victor Horta in Belgium and Hector Guimard in Paris, in the glass of Gallé, the Daum Brothers, Lalique, and Tiffany, and in the ceramics of Chaplet, Carriers, and Delaherche.

Count Léon de Laborde had been in charge of organizing the French participation at the 1851 Great Exhibition, and although many of the 1,756 French exhibitors won awards, Laborde was not uncritical of their works. Unlike many of his contemporaries, he did not make a cult of the past and he was against artists who killed art by making a fetish of copying the masterpieces of past ages. At the

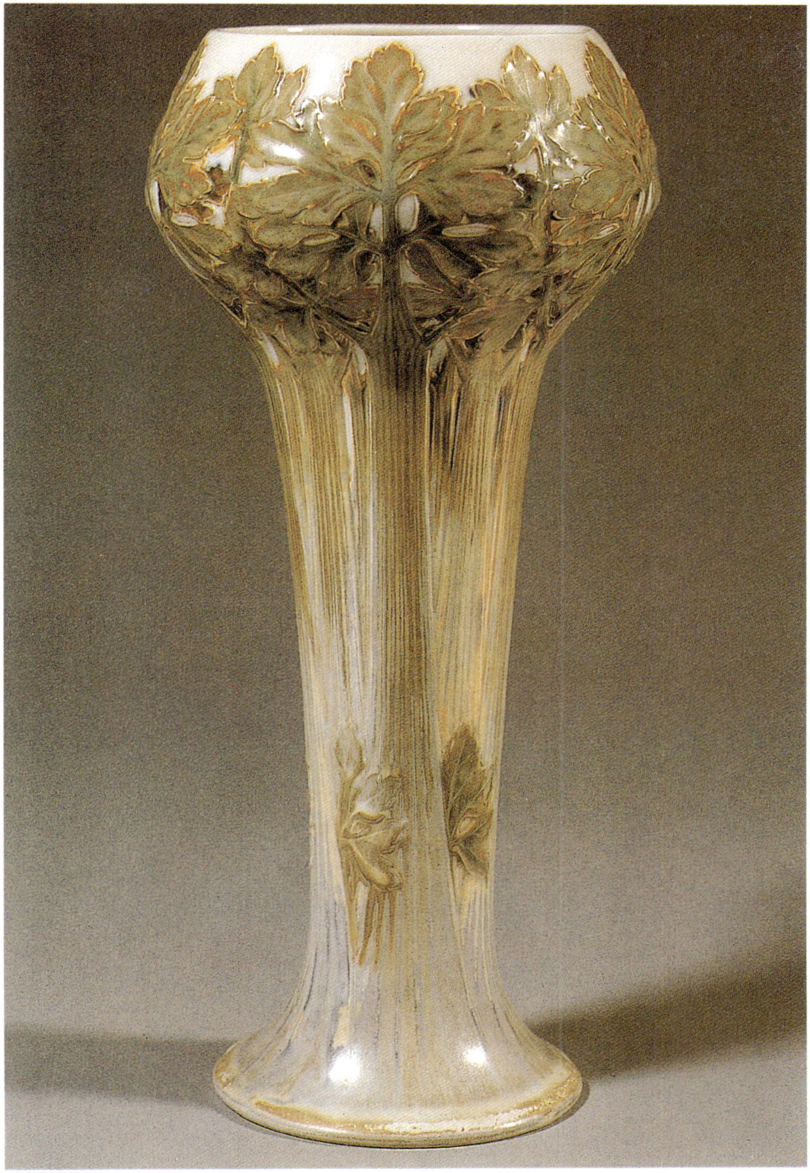

Right: Sevres "De Monteforte" vase, ca 1908, a fine example of the Art Nouveau style.

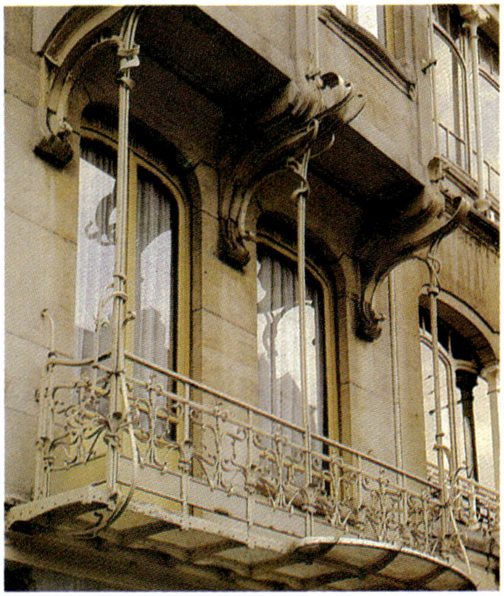

Above: In his own house and studio, Victor Horta's adventurous use of ironwork is demonstrated in the elaborate baclonies.

Right: Portrait of John Ruskin by T.B. Wirgman.

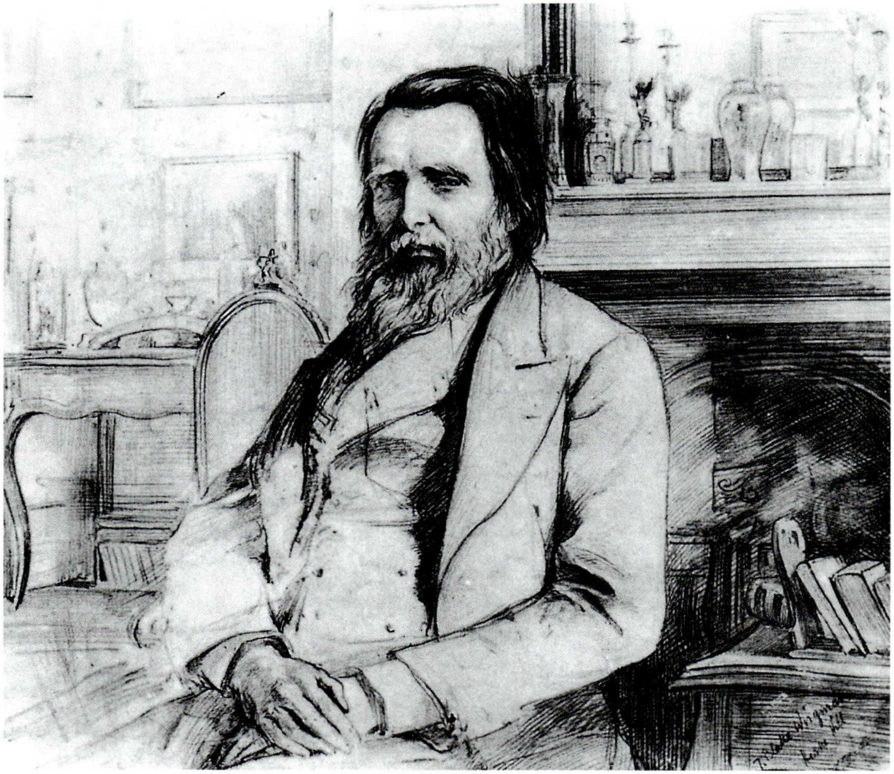

beginning of his report published in 1856, Laborde made a revolutionary statement: "The future of the Arts, of the Sciences, and of Industry lies in their association."

Transplantation

Eugène Viollet-le-Duc, in his *Entretiens sur l'Architecture*, suggested that it was barbarous to reproduce a Greek temple in London or Paris, since such a "transplantation" revealed an ignorance of the basic principles which governed its construction. He wrote further that interior decoration had lost its unity because the architect was not concerned with the paintings that would be hung in the rooms he had designed, the painter never took account of the rooms in which his work would be placed, the furniture maker completely ignored both the architect and the painter, and the man who made the curtains was only concerned that his work was all that was noticed anyway!

Through their writings, Ruskin, Laborde, and Viollet-le-Duc were to have a determining influence on the formation of the new modern style for which they had pleaded. Although they often contradicted themselves, they did at least try to resolve the dichotomy between Art and Industry, which was the major problem of their age.

Reform in design

To Ruskin, it seemed that the machine was at the root of the problem of design. Ruskin abhorred the products of mass-production and called for a return to craftsmanship inspired by a romantic view of the Middle Ages. By revitalizing the crafts, Ruskin hoped to develop an alternative to what he saw as the horrors of factory labor, as well as improving the aesthetic quality of everyday objects.

Morris and craftsmanship

Ruskin's ideas were taken up by his disciple, William Morris, the craftsman, poet, printer, textile and graphic designer, and occasional painter. Morris began his career firstly as a painter as a follower of the group of Pre-Raphaelite artists. As a student at Oxford, Morris had met and become friends with the painter Edward Burne-Jones, the painter and poet Dante Gabriel Rossetti, and architect Philip Webb. All shared Morris's enthusiasm for the culture of the Middle Ages and were inspired not only by its architecture, art, and crafts, but by the spirit of artistic cooperation which had fostered their creation.

Practical Victorians

Morris, however, had a practical Victorian view of the period when he came to recreate an idyll of painters, architects, and craftsmen working together on the same tasks. In 1861, he founded a company to produce the type of objects he wanted to see in every home, which became Morris & Co. Morris was able to bridge the divide between artists and craftsmen by employing his own friends to design and dec-

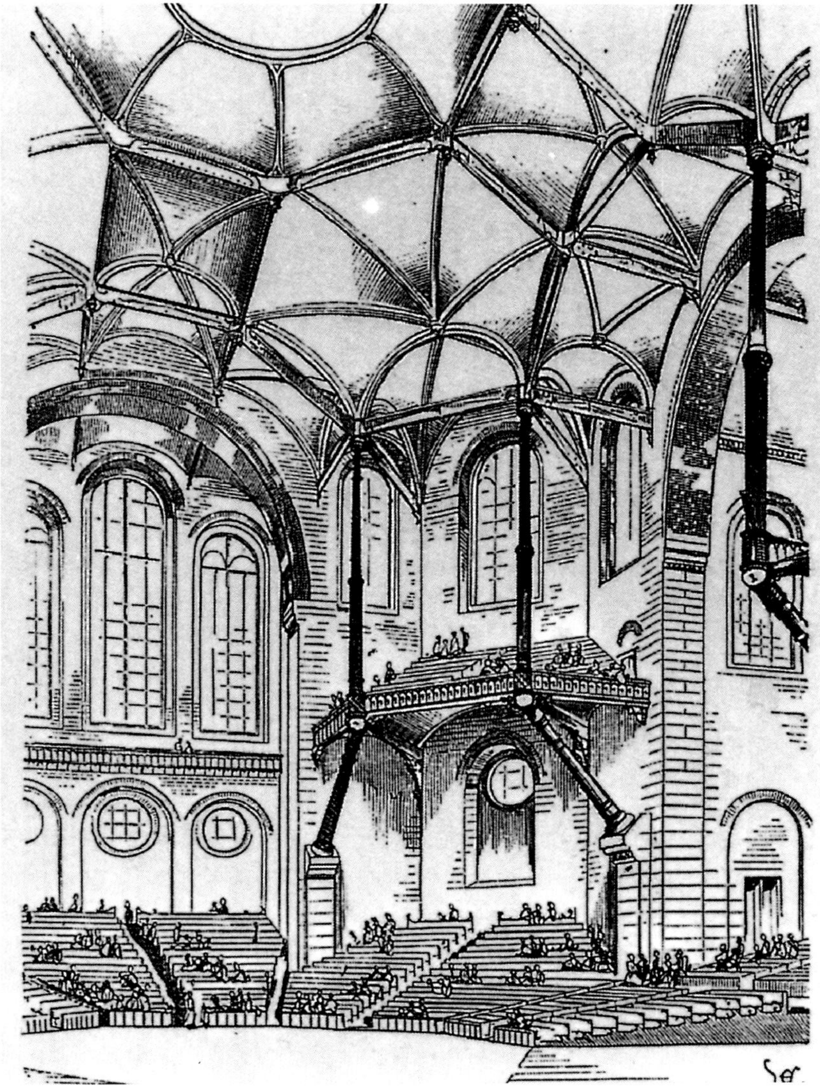

Above: A vaulted hall from Viollet-le-Duc's Entretiens sur l'Architecture.

Right: William Morris in 1877 when the Arts and Crafts Movement that he had created was beginning to revolutionize English design.

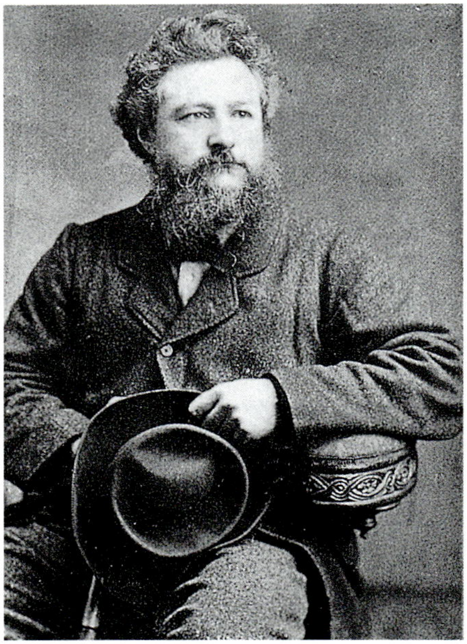

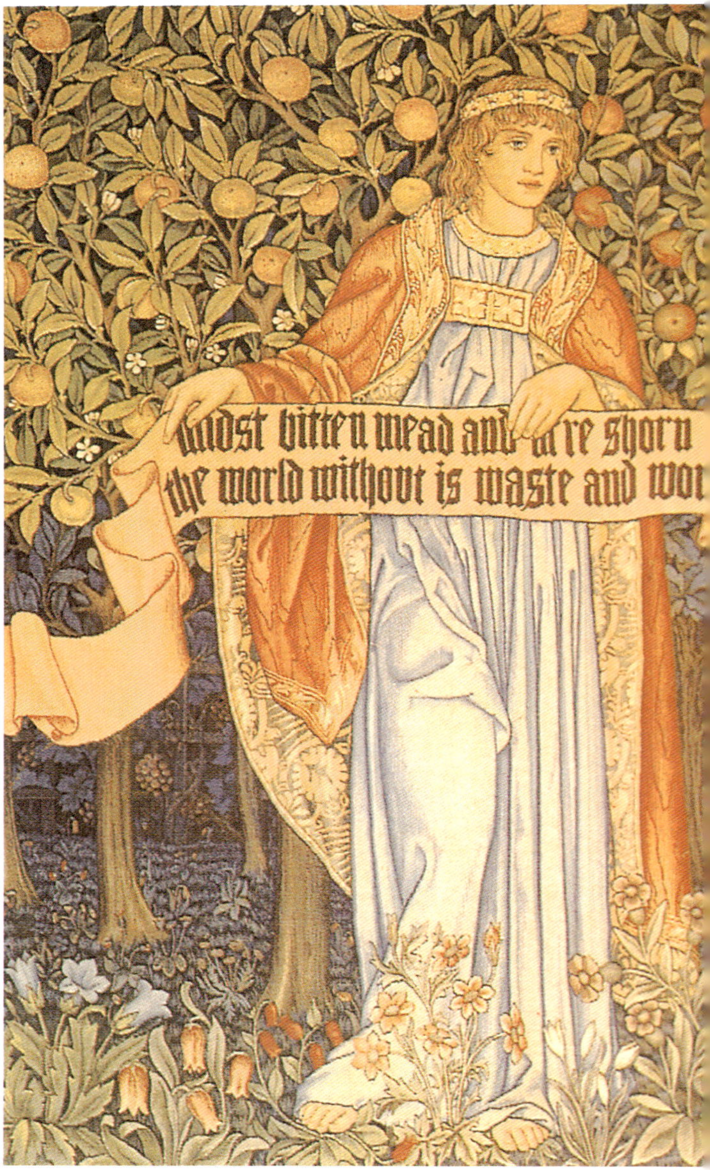

orate furniture, create tapestries, fabrics, printed books, and wallpapers. In doing so, Morris was able to produce a complete range of goods to furnish the home that were in a uniform style and created an overall harmony of effect. In this, and in his insistence that it was the observation of nature and its forms that was the basis for all design, Morris anticipated the versatility of the Art Nouveau artist-craftsman.

High ideals

Throughout his career, Morris struggled to reconcile his high artistic ideals with his social and political inclinations. His commitment to the creation of products that reflected the highest standards of design and construction were constantly at odds with his desire to produce them at a cost that consumers could

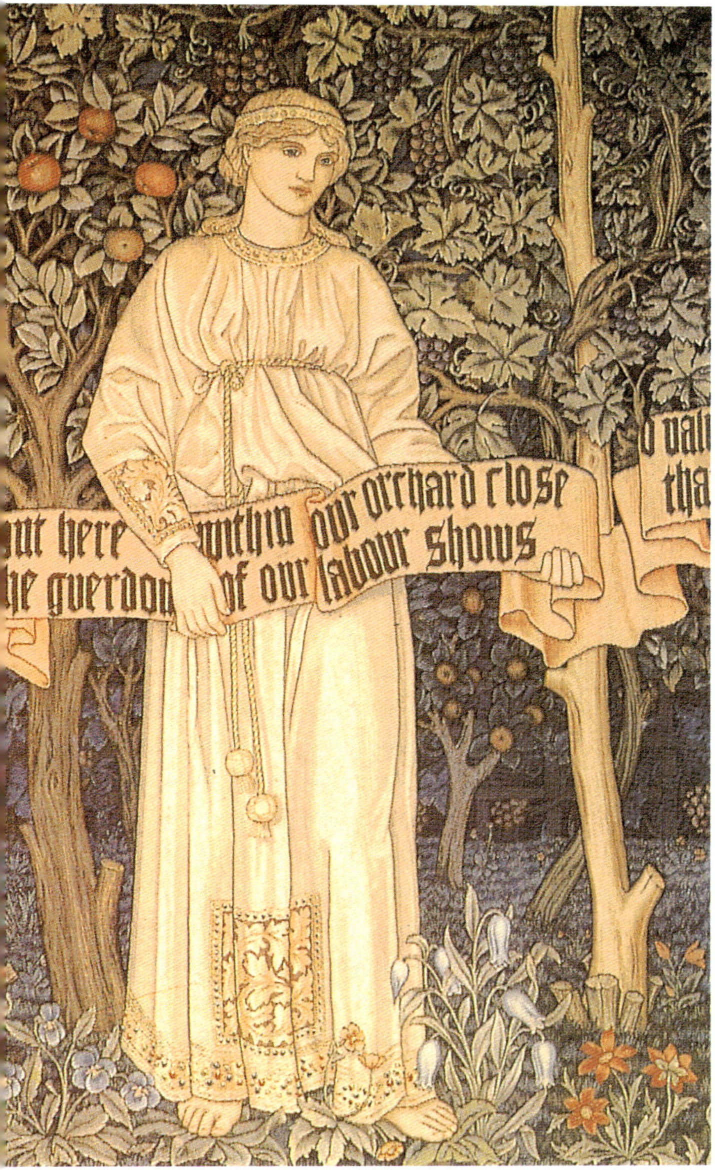

reasonably afford. His dedication to the principles of handcrafting conflicted with the need for machine production which could reduce the drudgery of certain tasks and reduce production costs. The successful marriage of art and industry was a dilemma that he was never to fully resolve. Nevertheless, his example encouraged many similar enterprises in Britain and overseas, usually referred to under the general term "Arts and Crafts Movement."

Left: The Orchard Tapestry, designed by Morris and woven at Merton in 1890 for Jesus College Chapel, Cambridge, is an example of Morris's use of high warp, or vertical, tapestry technique.

MACKMURDO AND THE CENTURY GUILD

Chief among the Arts and Crafts Movement groups was the Century Guild, formed in 1884 by Arthur Heygate Mackmurdo. Influenced by the flowing, natural forms used by Morris, Mackmurdo developed these further into more elongated, sinuous, and increasingly elegant patterns. In his illustration to the title page of *Wren's City Churches*, where the stems of the flowers undulate in an asymmetrical, rippling pattern like marine plants gently animated by unseen currents, Mackmurdo created the sinuous shapes and lines that were to become the hallmark of Art Nouveau for the next 20 years.

THE CRAFTS REVITALIZED

As with the other crafts revitalized by Morris and his followers, the histories of glassware and ceramics of the 1800s were the stories of technical advances which resulted in an impressively consistent quality of mechanical production. However, this was achieved largely at the expense of aesthetic distinction.

To the Arts and Crafts Movement, glass meant, above all else, the stained glass of their neo-medieval church windows. It was not until the 1890s, when Christopher Dresser began designing for the Clutha range of James Couper & Sons of Glasgow, that distinguished con-

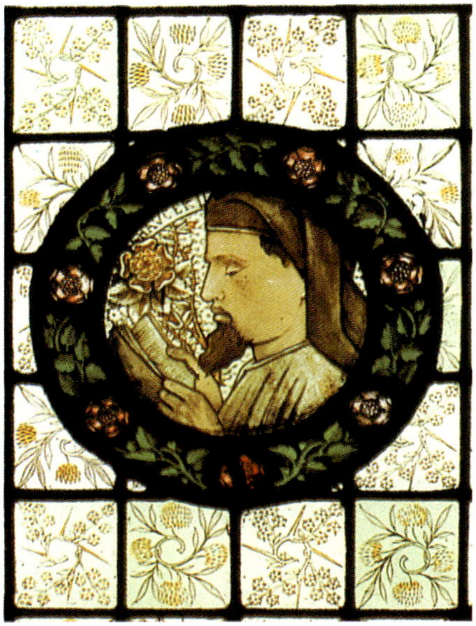

temporary glassware was to be seen in Britain with an Art Nouveau sense of line and color. In ceramics, the reaction against industrialization occurred a little earlier. In France, Théodore Deck, who set up his workshop in Paris in 1856, can be considered as the first of the "art-potter" craftsmen. Deck was inspired principally by Middle-Eastern and Persian designs and experimented with high-temperature glazes and oriental shapes and designs.

In England, this was echoed by W. Howson Taylor at his Ruskin Pottery near Birmingham, and by Bernard Moore in Staffordshire, but the first true art-potter, and the one most closely attuned to Morris's principles, was William de Morgan, who produced earthenware pieces in luster, and bright, Persian designs from the 1870s.

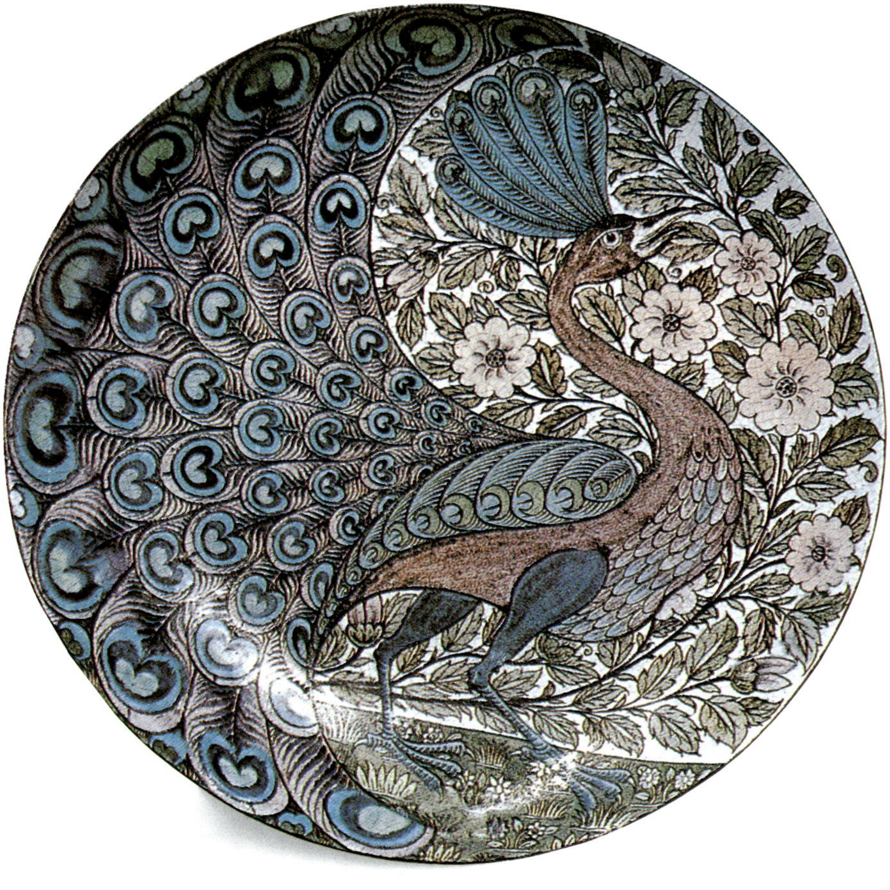

Above : Morris & Co. painted glass from Wightwick Manor. The figure of Chaucer emphasizes the medieval inspiration for Arts and Crafts glass.

Right: William de Morgan was associated with Morris, and in 1872 founded his own pottery and showroom in Chelsea, London.

Far right: Earthenware vase and cover by William de Morgan painted with a brightly-colored floral and foliate design, inspired by Iznik pottery of Persia.

ART NOUVEAU EMERGES

When he chose it as the name for the shop, La Maison de l'Art Nouveau, which he opened in 1895, Samuel Bing did not invent the expression "Art Nouveau." In fact, the term had been around since 1884 when the two Belgians, Octave Maus and Edmond Picard, who had created the review *L'Art Moderne,* proclaimed themselves as "believers in Art Nouveau," an art which refused to accept the prevailing cult of the past. At first, the term was attached to the works of painters who rejected academicism. The more specialized use of the term Art Nouveau, for architecture and art objects, was to come later. At the same time, different countries were to create their own specific versions of the term — Jugendstil, Sezessionstil, Modern Style, Stile Liberty, Modernismo, or even Belgische Stil.

Despite the different names, each movement has a number of common features. Firstly, there was the rejection of academic traditions. For anyone wishing to create Art Nouveau, the cult of antiquity was a thing of the past. The rejection of antiquity went hand-in-hand with a return to the observation and imitation of nature. The straight line was abandoned in favor of the curve — the essence of Art Nouveau. The characteristic curving forms of Art Nouveau which first appeared in England were to spread rapidly throughout Europe and the United States to a range of centers each with their own distinctive interpretations of the style.

THE NEW ART IN FULL FLOWER

While the 1890s saw the development of Art Nouveau, the fully evolved characteristics of the style which enjoyed their greatest success were to be seen at the 1900 Paris Universal Exhibition. It was here that the concept of Art Nouveau design as a "total" one emerged.

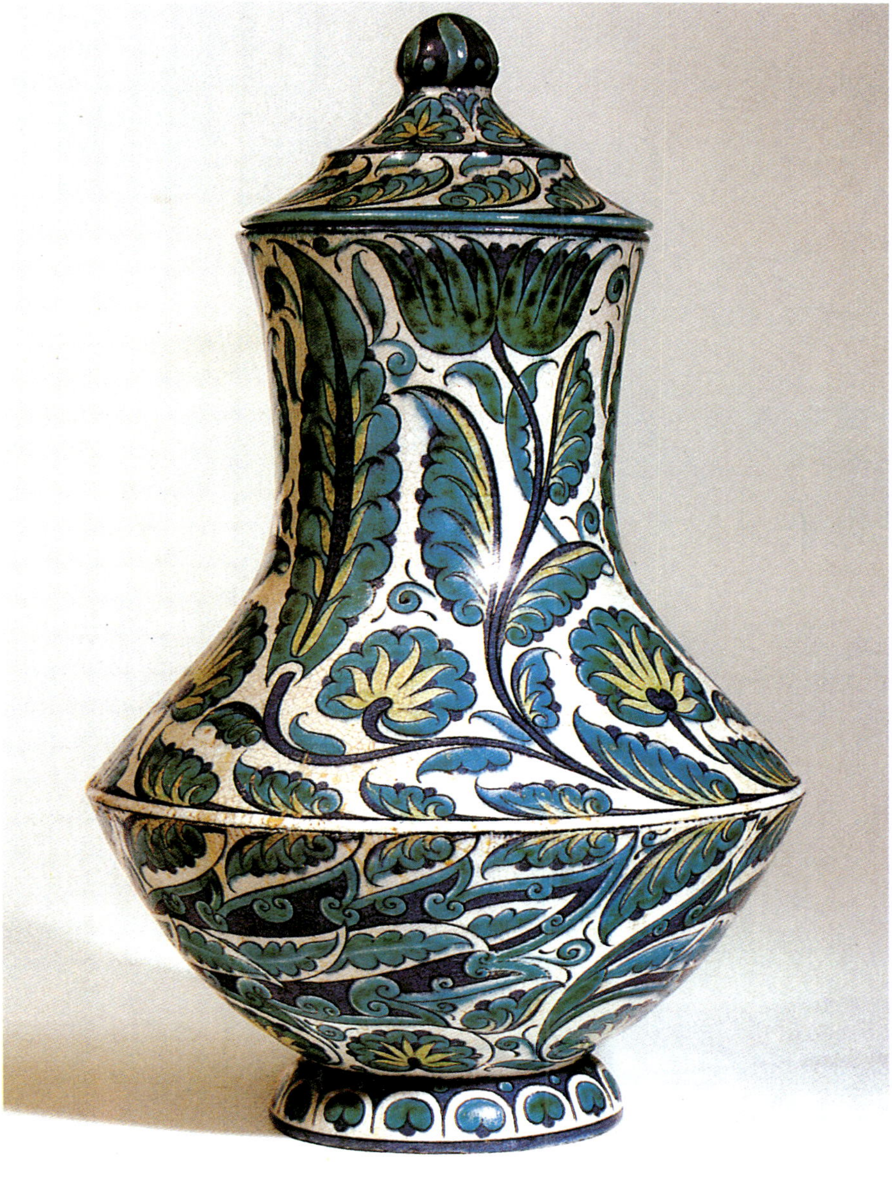

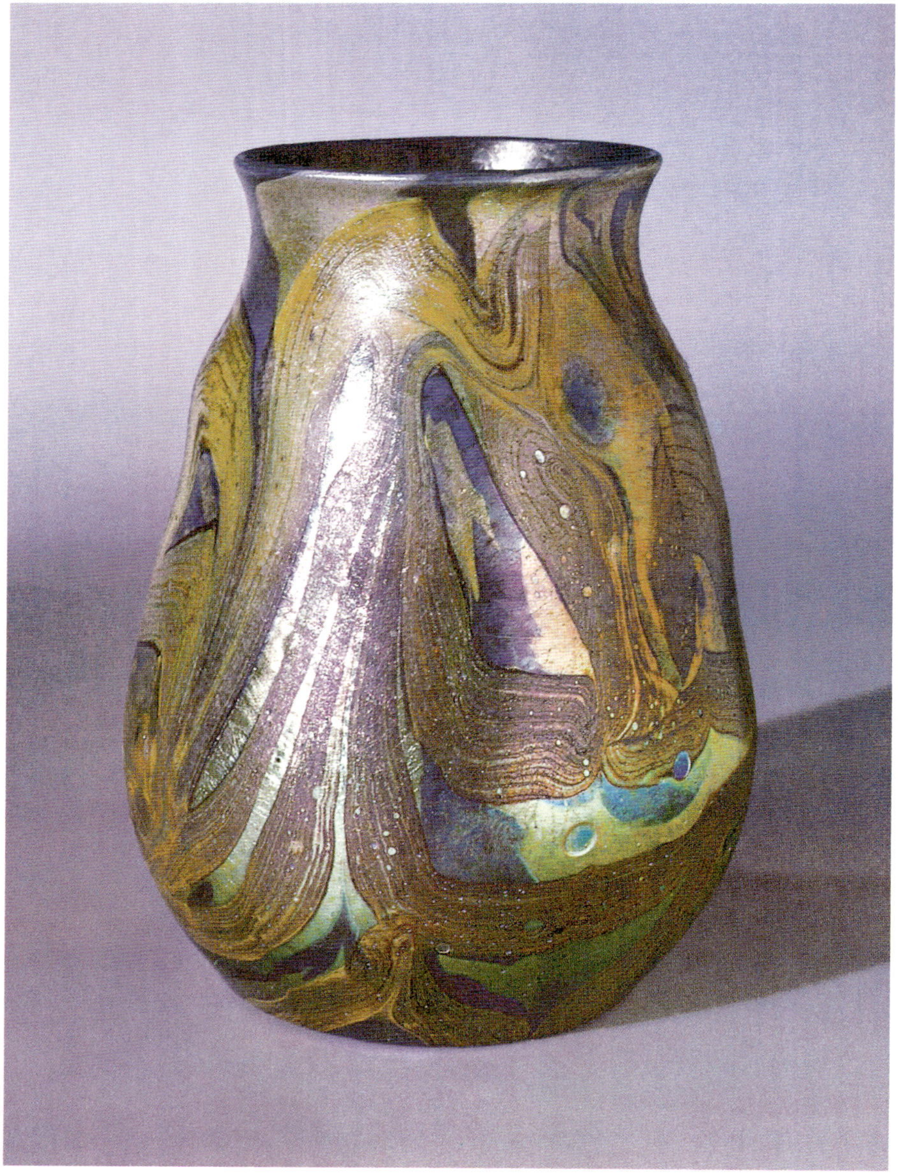

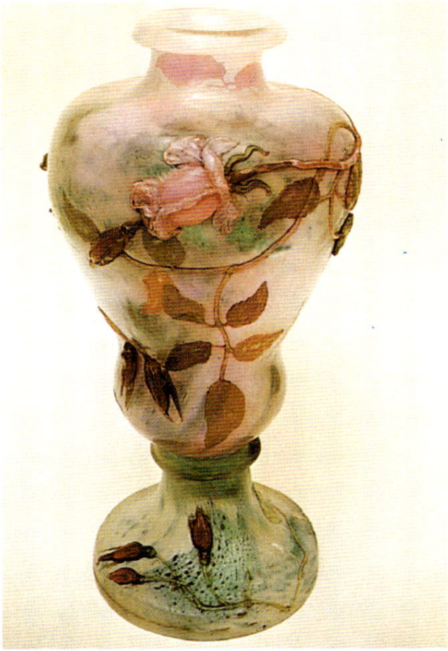

Above: "Rose de France" glass vase by Emile Galle, ca 1900.

Left: This Tiffany vase demonstrates his passion for the color and texture of glass.

Designers were seen as "ensembliers," rather than as creators of individual pieces. In truth, Art Nouveau could only be seen at its best in a complete ensemble, something, once again, that only a limited number of patrons desired or could afford. As manufacturers quick to cash in on the popularity of the style attempted synthetic versions for mass production, Art Nouveau was inevitably to deteriorate.

European Art Nouveau Glass

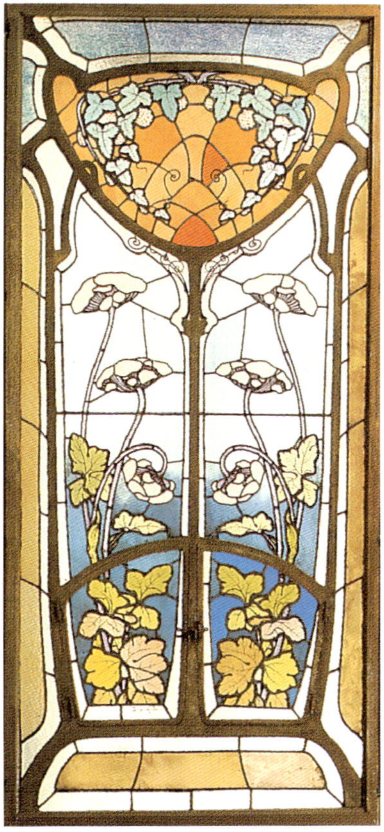

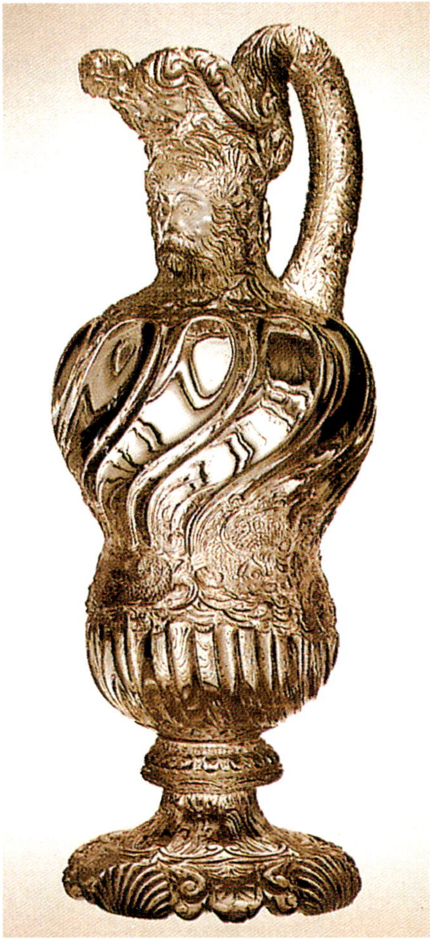

Above: Rock crystal ewer made in Stourbridge in 1886. The elaborate aquatic motifs were engraved by William Fritsche.

Overleaf: Art Nouveau stained glass. Sinuous lines end in a whiplash.

As with other crafts revitalized by the Art Nouveau, the history of glassware in the earlier part of the 1800s was the story of technical advances, resulting in an impressively consistent quality of mechanical production. The technique of press molding was invented in the United States in the 1820s, and steam power was applied to the process of glass cutting. More important was an accelerating interest in the chemical compositions of glass recipes and moves to increase the efficiency of firing. Stylistically, until Art Nouveau emerged at the end of the century, glass in the 1800s was once again marked by eclecticism and stylistic revivalism.

Art Nouveau glass in France

By the 1890s, French luxury glass production had reached a remarkably high standard of technical and creative inspiration. This major achievement can be traced back to a small, but significant number of talented artists — notably, Philippe-Joseph Brocard, Auguste Jean and Eugène Rousseau, and his friend and collaborator, Ernest Léveillé.

Rousseau began his career as an art dealer before starting up as a craftsman himself. In 1878, the year that Gallé unveiled his "clair de lune" glass with its delicate sapphire tinge, Rousseau created an equivalent sensation with his glass that imitated agates, jades, and other semiprecious stones, which were sometimes enhanced by internal craquelé effects. Jean showed enameled pieces, but his most notable innovation was in his free-form applications of glass, and in his vases of free-blown organic forms.

Above all, however, it was the genius of Emile Gallé who inspired an entire generation and made the Paris Universal Exhibition of 1900 a wonderful showcase for creations in glass of unprecedented technical and artistic virtuosity.

Emile Gallé

Although it produced furniture, ceramics, textiles, and metalwork, the Nancy School with Gallé as its chief designer, mainly based its reputation on the production of Art Nouveau glassware. Glass was in fact the traditional industry of the city, and Gallé had inherited his father's workshops in 1874. In addition to an extensive education which included botany and literature, Gallé also had a technical apprenticeship in glassworks at the Meisenthal glassworks (now in Germany). The inspiration for Gallé's own work was rich and varied. As with so many of the avant-garde of his generation, an introduction to Japanese art helped him to create a new visual language. His ability to create elegant, almost abstract graphic designs from the plant and insect life that were his most constant source of motifs owes a debt to Oriental art. The motto over his studio door, however, "My roots are deep in the woods," demonstrated that his greatest source of inspiration was nature.

Gallé's more personal creations also reflect his literary interests — he often used the works of contemporary French poets directly on his glass. His verreries parlantes (talking glass-

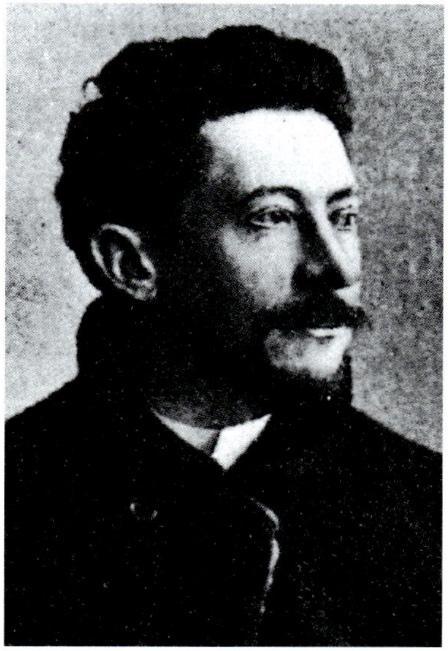

Right: Emile Gallé in 1889.

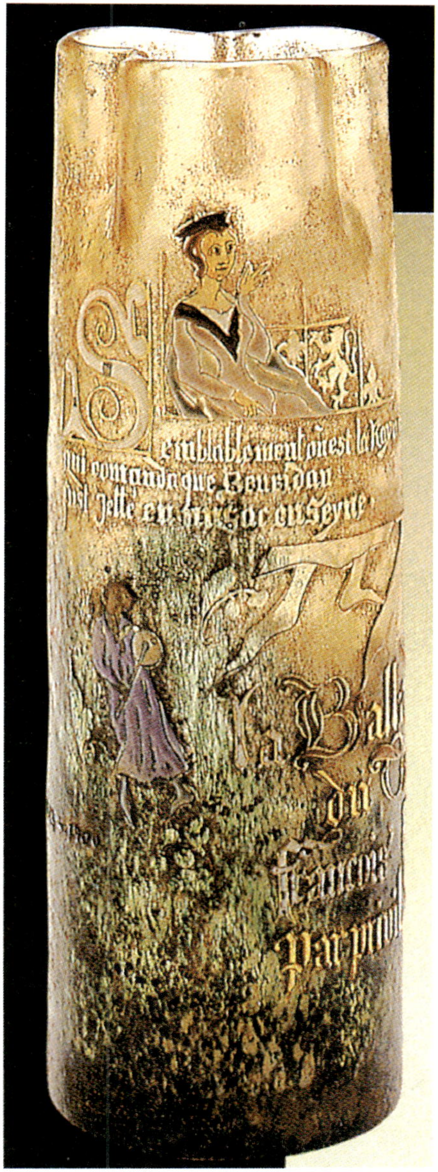

Far right: A brush holder that is also an early example of Gallé's verreries parlantes.

ware) were inscribed with extracts from the verses which had inspired their decoration — verses from Hugo, Baudelaire, Mallarmé, Verlaine, Gautier, and Rimbaud, as well as other sources as diverse as Shakespeare and the Bible.

Gold medal

Gallé's great success came in 1889, when he won a gold medal and the Grand Prix at the Paris Exhibition. His major innovation of this time was his cameo glass, whereby glass of two or more layers was carved or etched back, leaving the design in relief in one or more colors, against a contrasting background. The technique was copied from that of Chinese Chien Lung cased glass that Gallé had studied in the South Kensington Museum in London. It was on a mass-produced, acid-etched version of his cameo technique that Gallé was to base the prosperity of his business. The combined effects of color and translucence provided Gallé with the marvelous color effects which suggested submarine creatures against drifting seaweed, beetles crawling through long grass, or a butterfly settling on a flower.

1897 saw him introduce another new technique, marqueterie-sur-verre, which involved inlaying semi-molten glass details of decoration into the semi-molten body of the piece being worked on. A combination of several different ingredients might also be used, as in the example of champleve, in which the cavities created in the glass were lined with gilt before being filled in with layers of translucent enamels whose glow would be enhanced by the gold backing.

The 1900 Paris Universal Exhibition was perhaps the finest hour for Art Nouveau glass, it was also to be Gallé's last major showing before his death in 1904. By the turn of the century, Gallé was showing more sculptural

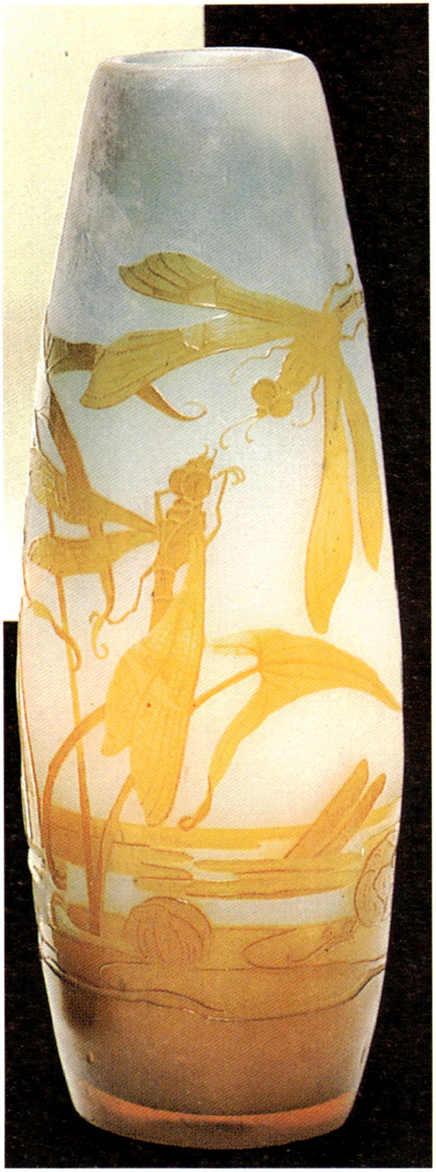

Left: Gallé's cameo glass, where two or more layers of glass were fused together and engraved.

freedom, producing pieces of completely organic form, or worked in high relief with fluid applications of glass. Two of his greatest masterpieces, the *Main aux Algues,* and the extraordinary and beautiful lamp, *Les Coprins*, date from this later period.

Functional design

In the best tradition of Art Nouveau, Gallé's glassware was prized far more as an artistic creation than for its functional design, and as such was collected by aesthetes and writers. His reputation rested upon a limited production of works which required an enormous number of man hours. A growing demand for his works encouraged him to increase capacity, but the more numerous workshop designs inevitably lacked the degree of finish of his earlier works. Nevertheless, Gallé's influence on contemporary glass makers was considerable, and he led a great renaissance of the industry in Nancy.

The Nancy school

In 1901, a group of artists allied themselves as the Ecole de Nancy, Alliance Provinciale des Industries d'Art. With Gallé as their guiding light, Louis Majorelle, Eugène Vallin, and the Daum brothers were vice presidents of the union. The Nancy School style of glass became prevalent in France, and was produced by local firms such as the Muller brothers, the Verrerie de Nancy of the Daum brothers, and that of Auguste Legras who had taken over the Cristaleries of Saint Denis and of Pantin.

The Daum brothers

Although Legras was operating the largest glassworks, employing around 1,500 people, the most notable rivals to Emile Gallé were the Daum brothers, Auguste and Antonin, who were also more dependent than Gallé on the creativity of their employees. Nevertheless, the Daums turned this to their advantage as they counted among their contributors Jacques Gruber (who later turned his interest to furniture making), Eugène Goll (their most talented glass worker who was responsible for some of the most sculptural and inventive pieces), and Alméric Walter, who developed the pâte-de-verre technique for the company.

ACID ETCHING

The Daum brothers were, like Gallé, concerned with opacity, color, and relief, and used acid to etch away layers of glass to reveal the colors beneath and create delicately modulated backgrounds for relief work. To produce a glowing, opaque finish in a variety of colors, powdered enamels were fused onto the surfaces of pieces during firing.

PÂTE-DE-VERRE

The Daum brothers were also involved in the development of glassware produced by a more lengthy process in which pre-manufactured, ground-down glass was used as an ingredient. By manipulating the oxidation process, an opaque glass known as pâte-de-verre, could be produced which had a similar appearance to alabaster. The technique of pâte-de-verre was first revived in the 1800s by artist-sculpter Henri Cros as a sort of mock marble. Cros made reliefs and free standing sculptures on a small scale and largely based on classical themes. The Daum brothers were the first to exploit the rediscovery on a commercial scale and produced designs by Alméric Walter — but the greatest exponent of the technique was François-Emile Décorchemont. His earliest pieces had thin bodies with trailing

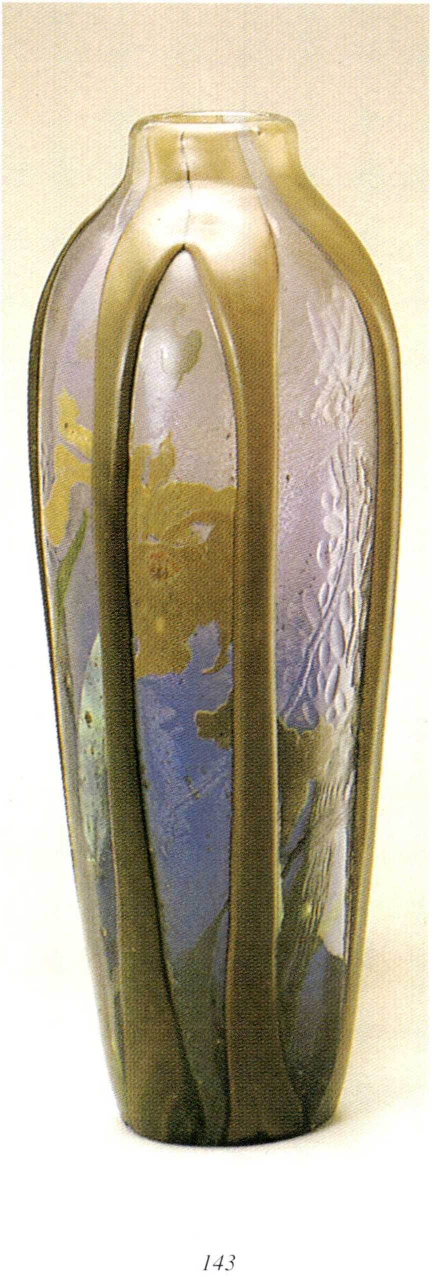

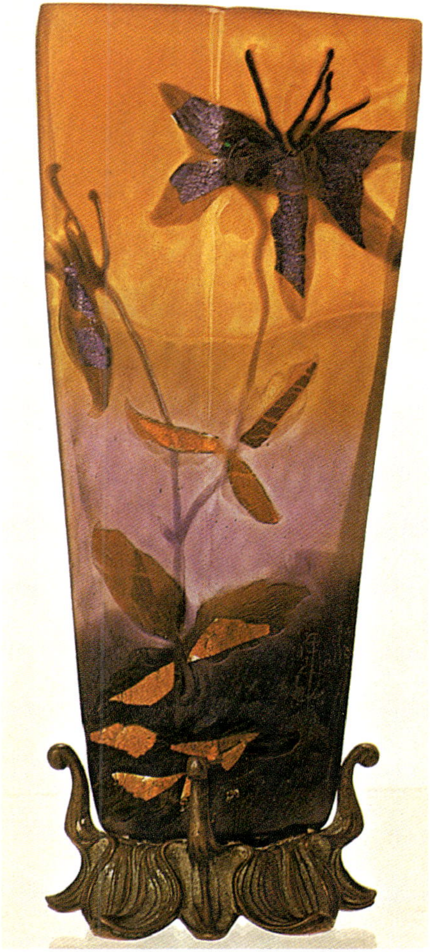

Above: Glass vase by Emile Gallé with decoration in marqueterie-sur-verre, ca 1900.

Left: Gallé vase with marqueterie-sur-verre on a translucent base engraved with irises.

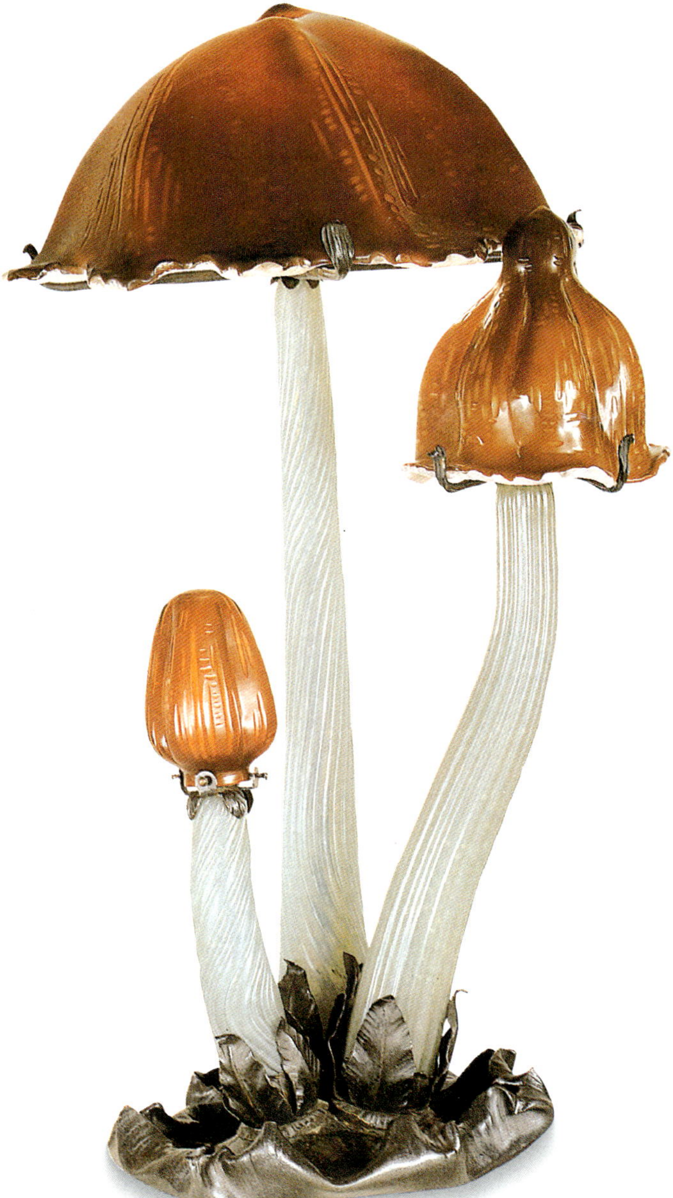

Right: Les Coprins lamp, ca 1900, by Emile Gallé illustrates three stages of growth in a mushroom.

Art Nouveau motifs such as seaweed and other natural forms.

RENÉ LALIQUE

The great maestro René Lalique's interest in glass also dated to the 1890s when he began using cast glass in multimedia works of art. Around 1900, he began to use glass in his exquisite jewelry, caring little for the lack of intrinsic value of glass if its qualities were appropriate to the design. Around this time, Lalique began experimenting with the creation of all glass cire perdue pieces, including vases and panels such as the ones he used as decorations in his own home.

In 1902, Lalique set up a small glassworks, and his first commercial commission was from the parfumeur, François Coty, who approached him to design scent bottles. Concentrating on large scale production, by 1912, Lalique's career as a jeweler was over and a new career in glassware design opened. Until the final close of production in 1939, the firm of Verrerie d'Art-René Lalique & Cie., at Wingen-sur-Moder, produced an extensive range of vases, glasses, and other tableware, as well as scent bottles and the famous car mascots. Lalique's greatest distinction was not for any remarkable quality of work, but the stylish repertoire of designs ranging from elegant evocations of the Art Nouveau age through the modern motifs of Art Deco. Combining modern techniques of mass production with a high level of artistic involvement, Lalique raised glasswork to the level of fine art in an idiom as appropriate to the 1900s as that of Gallé to the fin-de-siècle.

ART NOUVEAU GLASS IN BRITAIN

In England, while William Morris and his followers had sought to redress the imbalance between mechanical production and the poor quality of contemporary design by reviving traditional crafts, to a large extent, glassware did not benefit from the same outpouring of interest.

Stained glass windows

To the Arts and Crafts Movement, glass meant stained glass windows, and within the movement the two most famous makers of decorative glass were the firms of Powell's of Whitefriars, and James Couper & Sons of Glasgow. From 1890 to 1900, Powell's had pioneered forms of glass which relied more on firing techniques and upon the form itself rather than the decoration. The firm had earlier produced stained glass for Morris & Co. and simple, uncut table glass for the architect Philip Webb, and were happy to absorb the Arts and Crafts principles of beauty lying in shape and method of production rather than applied decoration.

Clutha glass

Truly distinguished glassware was developed by Christopher Dresser for Couper & Sons in the mid-1890s, when the firm produced a range called Clutha glass. Freed by the nature of glass from an adherence to strict principles of utility, Dresser's forms are irregular, following the sinuousness and rhythms of organic growth that is the central motif of Art Nouveau.

The blown Clutha glass uses opaque green glass, often shot with translucent streaks of gold or cream, and was the result of Dresser's interest in ancient Roman and Middle Eastern glass. Similar Art Nouveau forms were also used by the firm of Stuart & Sons of Stourbridge, which specialized in furnace decoration, and Stevens & Williams, also of

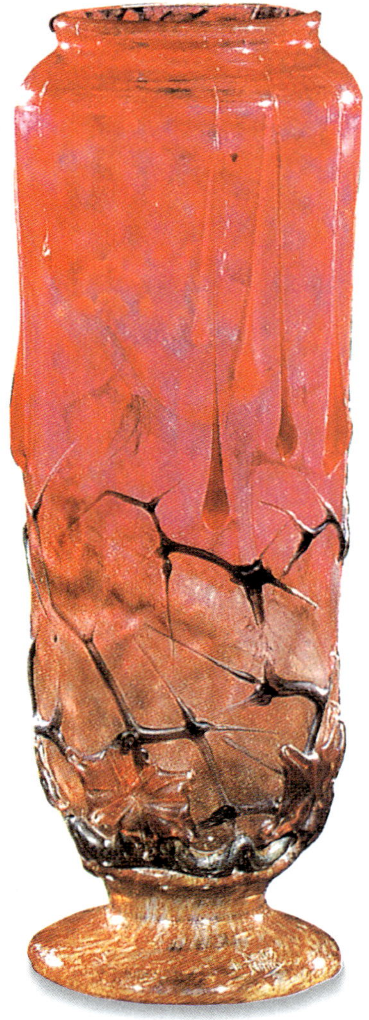

Above: The Daum Brothers' glass is clearly influenced by Gallé.

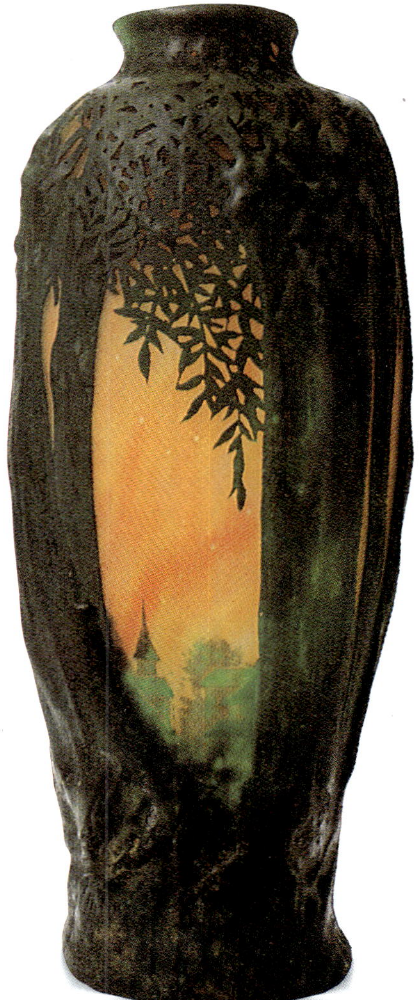

Above:The Daums achieved a consistently high standard, decorating their surfaces with a charming, light touch.

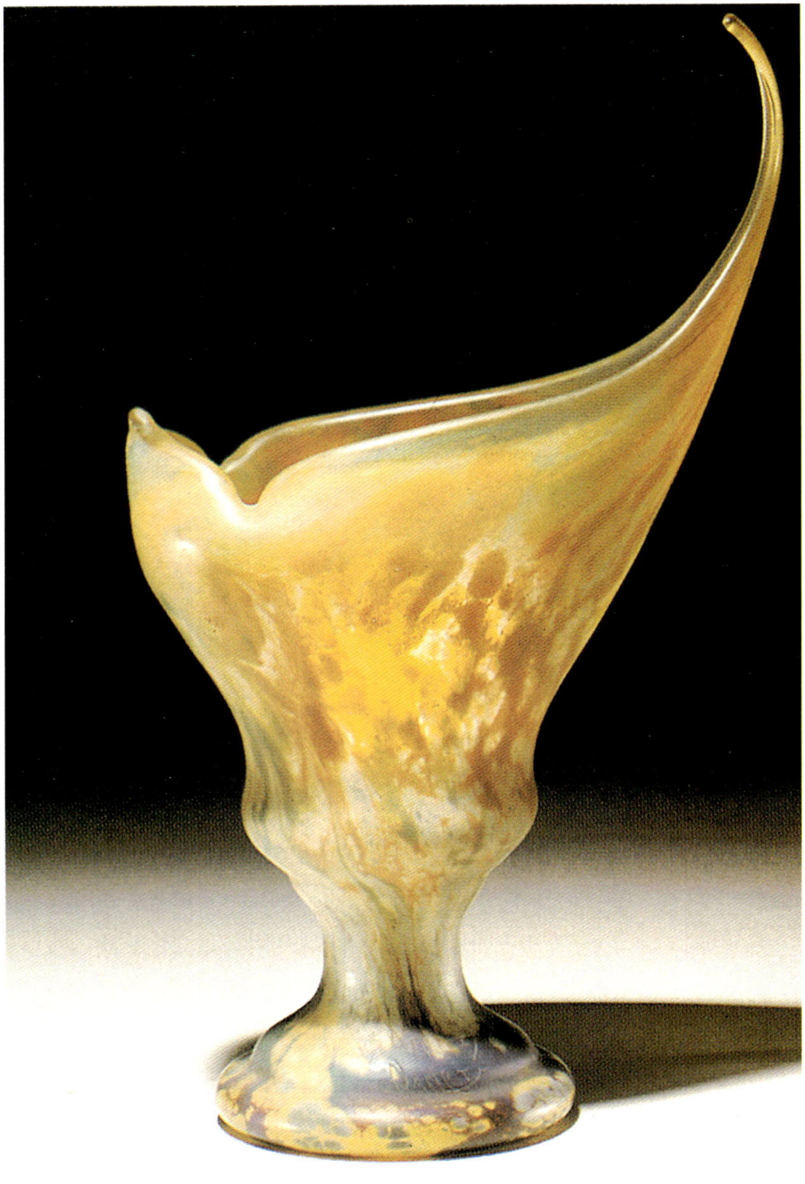

Stourbridge who experimented with crackled glass and silver deposit decoration.

Art Nouveau glass in Austria

If the great names of Art Nouveau glass in France and the United States are Gallé and Tiffany, in Austria, the greatest of the Art Nouveau glass makers was the Loetz factory. Surprisingly, it is the least highly valued today in terms of the art market, largely because the glass remains "anonymous" — it relates not to a named individual or personality, but to a corporate image.

The Loetz factory

This was founded at Klostermühle in 1836. In 1879, Max von Spaun became head of the Loetz factory, and for the next eleven years, he oversaw the production of seven varieties of decorative glass, many of which attempted to imitate the surface appearance of different types of hardstones. The firm produced its first iridescent pieces in the 1880s, and in 1898, at the Vienna Jubilee Exhibition, Loetz showed a major collection of iridescent glass. In addition to the designs by von Spaun himself, Loetz also commissioned designs from Joseph Hoffmann, Kolomon Moser, Otto Prutscher, Dagobert Peche, and Michael Powolny. The members of the Wiener Werkstätte were involved as designers with most of the leading Austro-Hungarian glass houses at this time, as they were with most of the potteries, and in this period, Loetz executed pieces on commission from members of the Werkstätte.

Two other prestigious firms in Austria, J. & L. Lobmeyr and Graf Harrach, were located in Vienna. Lobmeyr produced high-quality

Left: Daum Brothers' glass chalice.

table glass, but they also marketed decorative items including engraved and etched work on enameled pieces in a somewhat Middle-Eastern style. The company also produced pieces designed by the members of the Werkstätte and Joseph Hoffmann designed what is probably his best-known range of decorated glass for Lobmeyr. These pieces of clear or matt glass were decorated with opaque black or gray motifs in a type of decoration known as "bronzidecor."

Harrach glass house

In 1898, at the Vienna Jubilee Exhibition, the Harrach glass house showed glass that was obviously in imitation of the great American glass maker, Louis Comfort Tiffany. But, by 1900, the company had widened its scope to include cameo glass in the style of Gallé and enameled pieces decorated with designs inspired by Alphonse Mucha.

Below: Owls Bracelet by René Lalique, ca 1900-01, in gold, glass, chalcedony, and enamel.

German glass

In Germany, there were a number of important Art Nouveau designers, the most significant of whom was Karl Koepping. He had trained as a painter and etcher in Munich, but began experimenting in glass around 1895. To execute his designs, Koepping hired an expert glass blower — Friedrich Zitmann — but after a disagreement in 1896, Koepping's pieces were made by the impressively named, Grossherzogliche Sachliche Fachshule und Lehrwerkstätte für Glasinstrumentmacher und Mechaniker. Koepping's tall, spindly pieces with extraordinary curving stems, were greatly admired and were sold by Bing in Paris at La Maison de l'Art Nouveau. Zitmann continued his own glass-making enterprise, and around 1897 began making iridescent glass with bubbling and pitting which imitated the amazing surface effects of recently excavated ancient Roman glass. Glass of this type

Right: A Lalique "Styx" flacon for Coty, 1910-13.

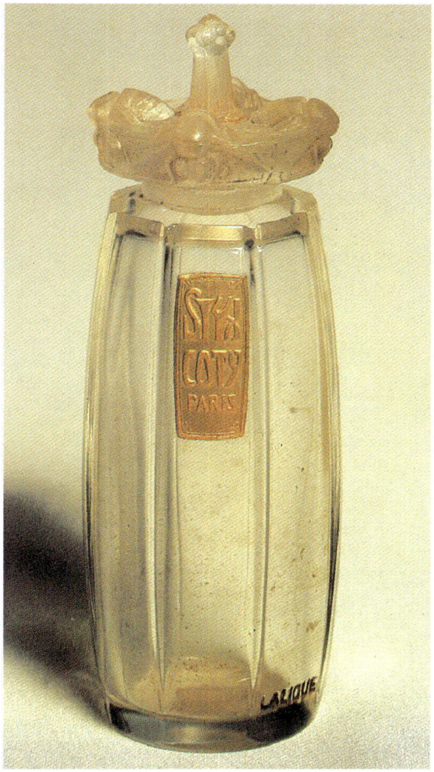

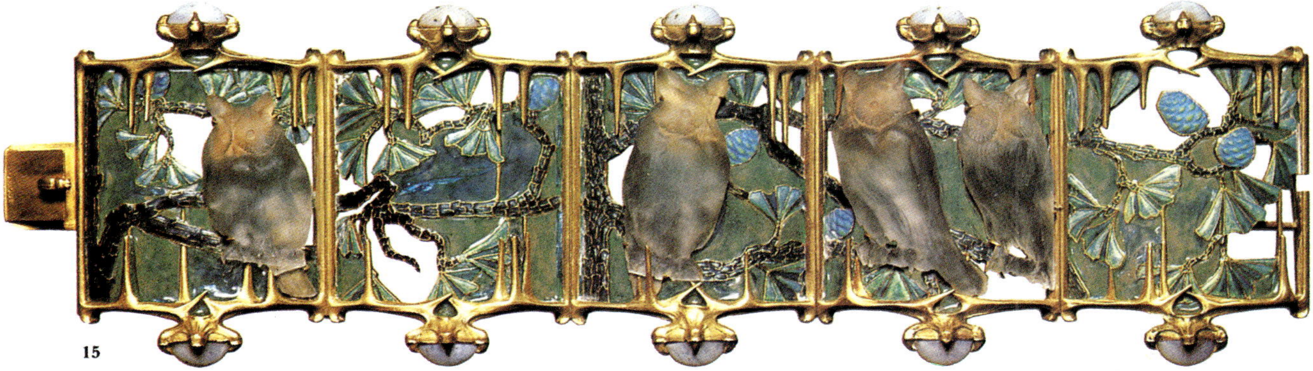

15

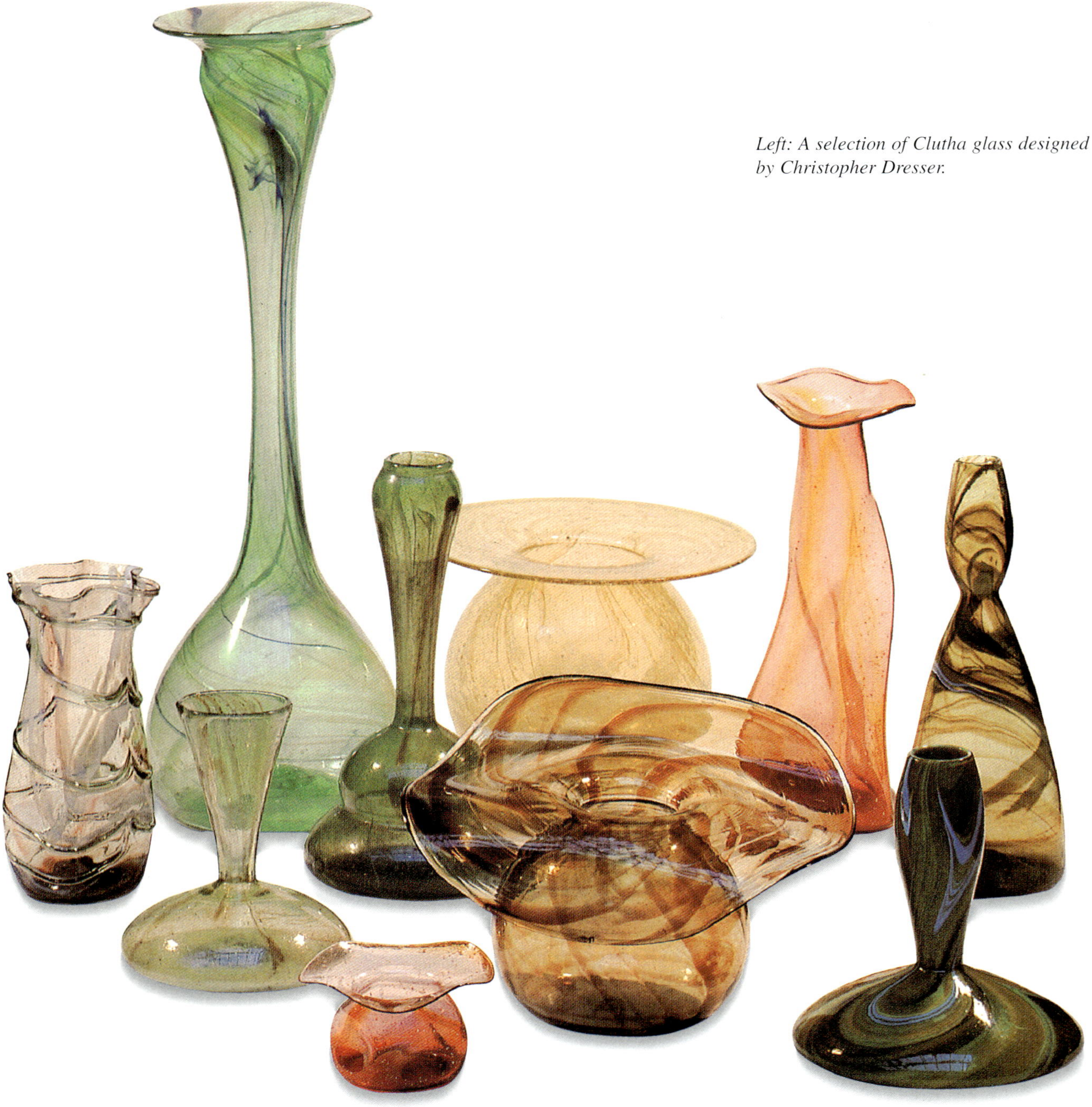

Left: A selection of Clutha glass designed by Christopher Dresser.

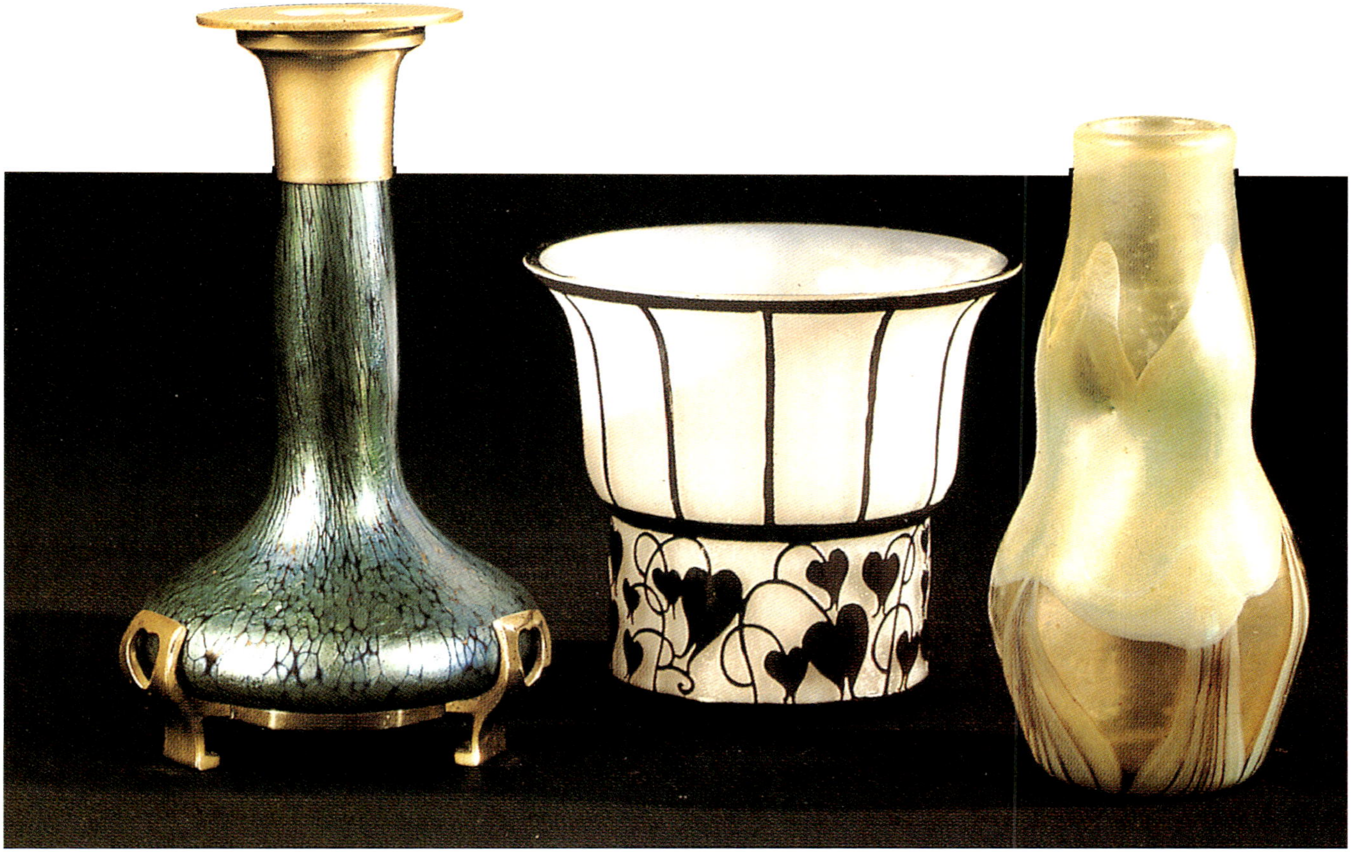

was also to be the inspiration for Tiffany's Cypriote glass which he first made around 1895-96.

The German Secessionist involvement in glass was not as influential or as widespread as in Austria. The WMF glass factory, established in 1881, mainly made glass liners for its metalwork. In 1883, it did establish a serious glass business, but did not produce art glass until the 1920s, when they marketed iridescent pieces called Ikora-Krystall and Myra-Krystall.

A new challenge

The invention of the incandescent electric lamp by Thomas Edison in the 1880s gave a new challenge to glass designers, who were no longer bound by the need to create lamps that could shield users from a flame. Louis Comfort Tiffany was among the first to recognize the potential of electricity for the Art Nouveau style and his name was to become synonymous with the style of lamp which used colored glass set into leaded panels much like a stained glass window.

Above: Austrian Art Nouveau glassware by (left to right) Zasche, Powolny, and von Harrach.

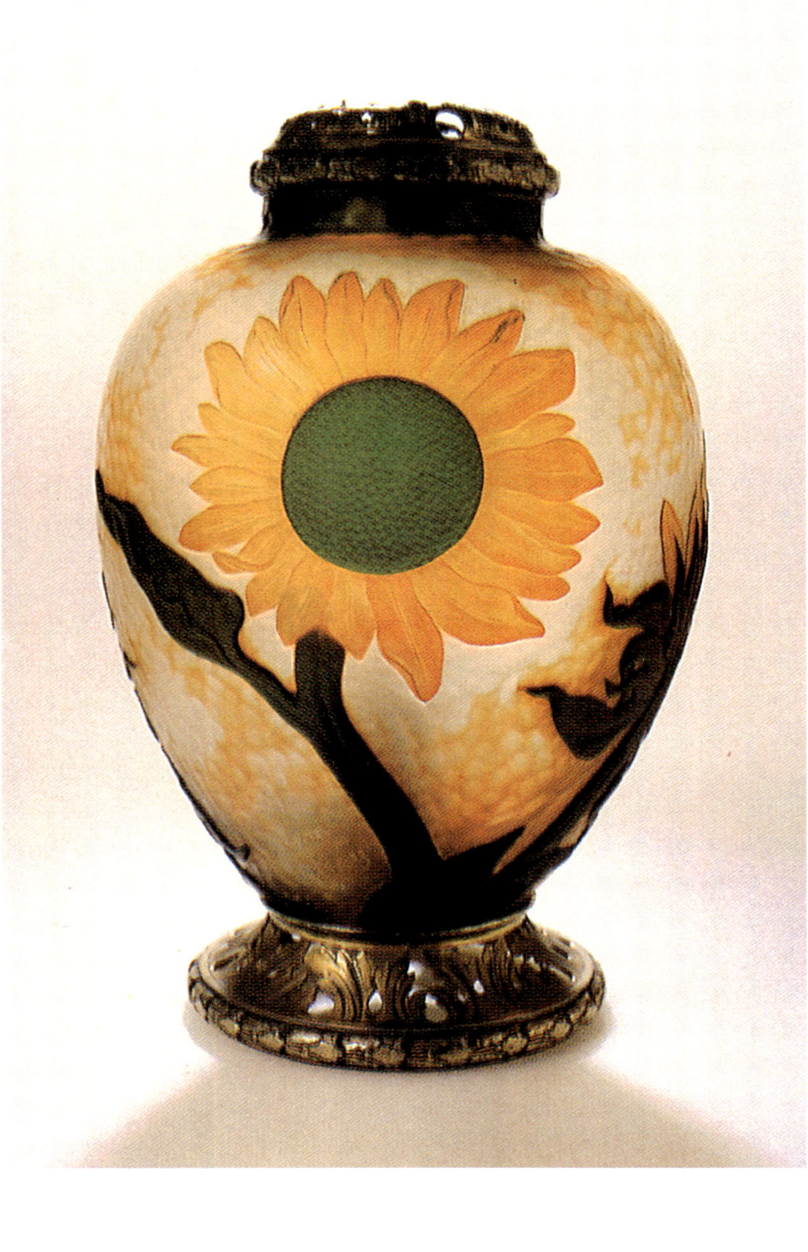

MIXED MEDIA

The opportunity for mixed media work in glass, metal, and ceramics was to give the electric lamp an instant appeal for Art Nouveau,very much apart from the bright, even light that it could harness as part of the overall composition. It is a typical tendency of Art Nouveau that the modernity of the electric light, with its startlingly technological aspect heralding the dawn of a new age, was to be ignored by many designers. Instead, filtered by colored glass, the electric light became a gentle glow, a part of the fantastic idylls of decorative lilies, swans, and butterflies that kept the Art Nouveau interior separate from, and unsullied by, brutish technology.

The treatment of the electric lamp in the hands of the masters like Gallé or Tiffany parallels the use of wrought iron in architecture by Horta or Guimard. It is used willingly, but, although playing a major part in the whole, it is masked by its conversion, against its very manufactured nature, into the organic world of Art Nouveau.

Both Gallé and the Daum brothers produced lamps in a style very similar to their other glassware. Glass figured as both base, neck, and shade, and, typically, the form of the mushroom was used as the most analogous form in nature. While other table, bracket, and standing lamps did use more metalwork, the plant form naturally remained part of the design.

METAL PLANTS

In works by Louis Majorelle, Hector Guimard, Eugène Vallin, and Emile Gallé, sinuous metal plants or tree saplings are created which flower

Left: A Daum Brothers' nightlight. The combination of glassware and electric light was irresistible to Art Nouveau designers.

into electric bulbs. These were used in the same way in which an Art Nouveau designer set a precious stone in a piece of jewelry — the whole setting, whether a vine, a tree, or a flower, constitutes the bulk of the work, while the light bulbs are scattered around the metalwork as highlights.

Lamps

While many Art Nouveau lamps feature glowing flowers, the bronze or gilt statuettes of nymph-like figures that were produced by many craftsmen could also be adapted to carry an electric light. In so doing, these pieces provide an interplay between function and ornamentation. The lightly-draped female figures which supported desk lamps are possibly an indication of Art Nouveau's retreat from the challenge of the new medium, as they have an escapist charm. To the next generation of designers, they revealed only a retreat into the impractical fantasies at odds with the nature of the artefact itself. From the wide range of Art Nouveau craftsmen and designers, only the Belgian Henry Van de Velde, commissioned by Bing, produced an electric lamp that took as its starting point the functional, practical, and scientific nature of the medium.

Architectural glass

If the 1900 Paris Universal Exhibition marked the high point for luxury and elaborately wrought glass into works of art, it was also the occasion for a prediction by Eugène Houtart that: "Steel and glass are without doubt the two elements which will characterize the 20th century and will give their name to it." After World War I, Houtart's prediction seemed to find its fulfilment when glass became the chosen material for designs of every scale, from the mass-production of Lalique's perfume bot-

Below: Tiffany lamp with a poppy motif glass shade from around 1900.

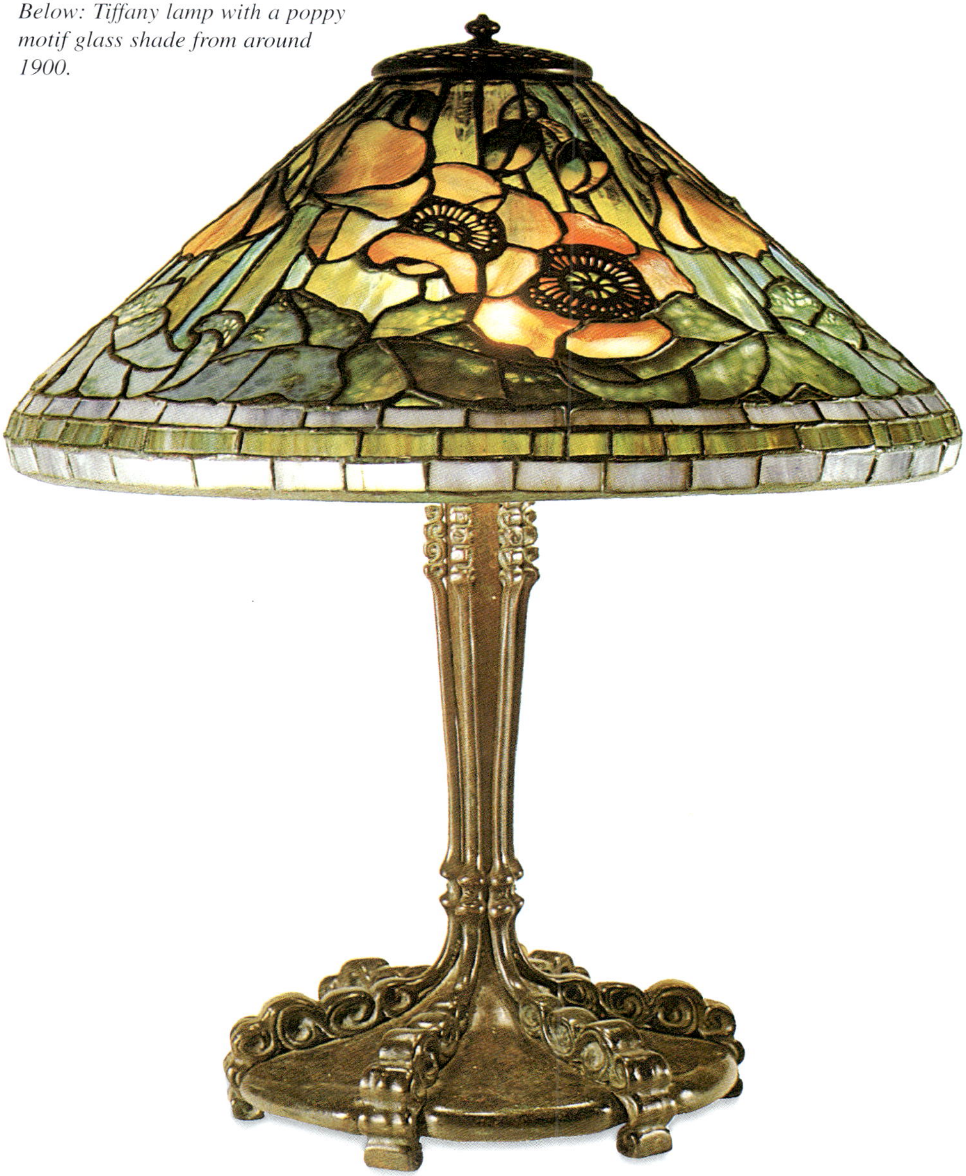

Right: A window by Georges de Feure. The elegant and alluring female is derived from the work of Aubrey Beardsley and relates strongly to de Feure's graphic work.

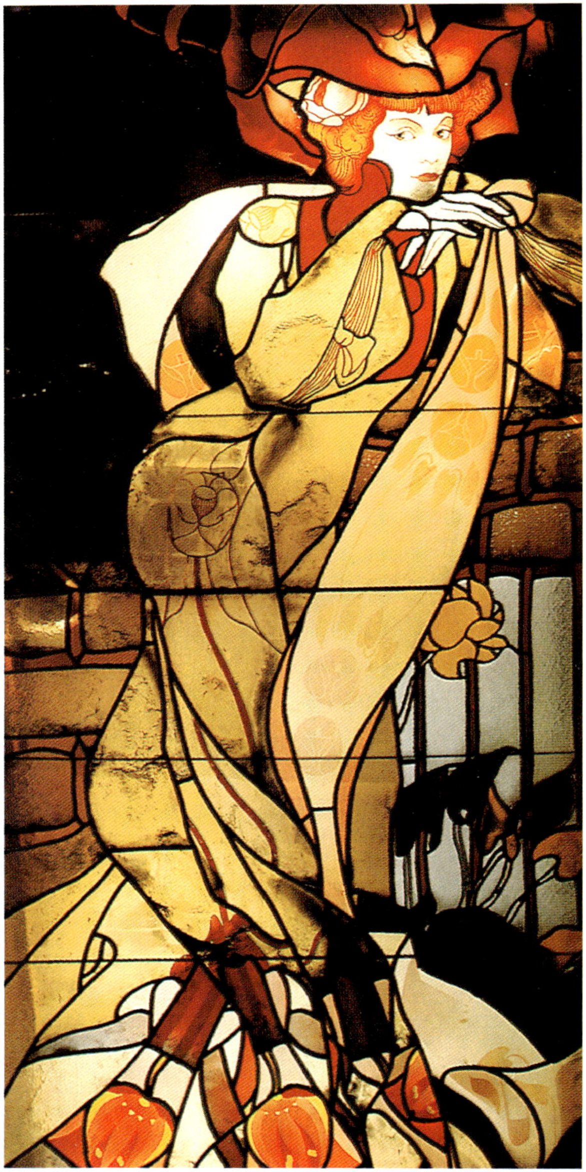

tle, to the glass curtain-walled architecture of the Modernists.

At the end of the 1800s, however, a more traditional part of glass design was that of stained glass. A huge revival of interest in its design and manufacture had accompanied the Gothic revival, and it continued to be an important art form with the medievally-inspired English Arts and Crafts Movement.

MORRIS & CO.

In its early years, the firm of Morris & Co. had depended financially on their stained glass. Dante Gabriel Rossetti, Henry Holiday, and William Morris had all designed stained glass to meet the ecclesiastical demand created by the Gothic revival, but the firms' most notable designer was the painter Edward Burne-Jones who adopted a free-flowing style in both lead lines and painting with strong, vibrant colors and naturalistic form.

INFLUENCES

The Art Nouveau treatment of stained glass grew from this revival, and profited from the growing decorative similarities between stained glass, embroideries, and paintings. The first two crafts, by their very nature, were concerned with two-dimensionality, and took their cue from the craftsmen, painters, and graphic designers of the 1890s such as Paul Gauguin, Toulouse-Lautrec, Aubrey Beardsley, Alphonse Mucha, Will Bradley, and Gustav Klimt were also exploring the flat decorative arrangement of color in their work.

For the Art Nouveau designer then, stained glass was not so much a revivalist anachronism, but a medium that was perfectly suited to the flatness, linearity, and love of light and color that were common to all the contemporary decorative arts. As an ensemblier, the

Art Nouveau designer often wanted to control the quality and strength of the light cast on his interiors by making it harmonize with the flowing plant forms of the furniture, wallpaper, and table ornaments. Tiffany even believed that stained glass in architecture played an important social role. In an age when city-dwellers were often looking out onto a bare wall, a stained glass window could shield the owner from such a brutal sight and provide him with an idyllic Art Nouveau world of flowers, butterflies, and birds to gaze upon instead.

Widely manufactured, stained glass was evident to some degree in almost every well-to-do home of the period. Yet most Art Nouveau stained glass did not represent the highest levels of craftsmanship, but rather, regularly shaped, painted, or enameled panes that were easy to produce and assemble. Only in the finest quality designs was the traditional method of production retained in which each motif was carefully outlined in lead, using panels of different shapes and sizes. In Nancy, Jacques Gruber produced his stained glass in this way, as did Hector Guimard in Paris.

For many of the Art Nouveau architects, glass was designed as part of an architectural whole. Charles Rennie Mackintosh's designs for Miss Cranston's Willow Tea Rooms in Sauchiehall Street, Glasgow featured five tea salons, a dining gallery, and a billiard room. All were decorated with a willow-leaf motif and abstracted forms related to tree shapes. The Room de Luxe was painted white with a dado, above which on three sides, was a mural made of mirror glass panels. The doors and windows were of leaded glass with the dom-

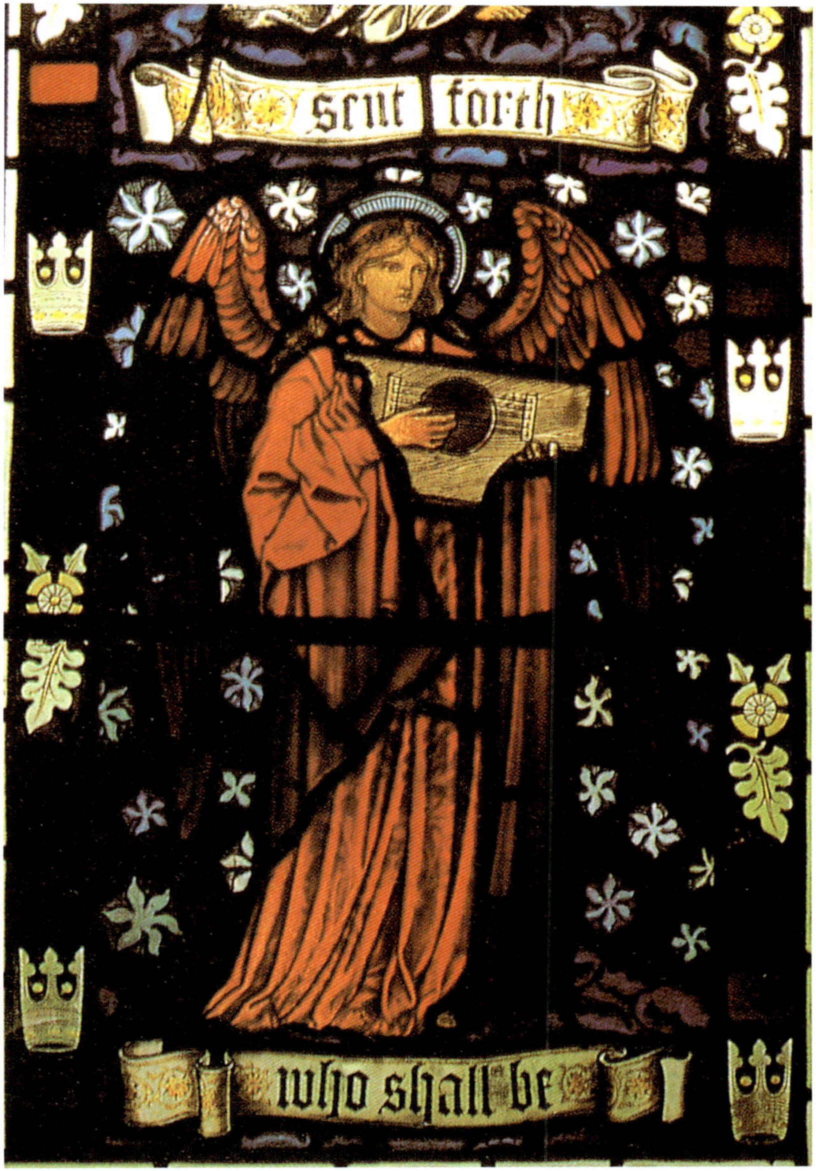

Right: The Angel Musician stained glass window designed by Edward Burne-Jones.

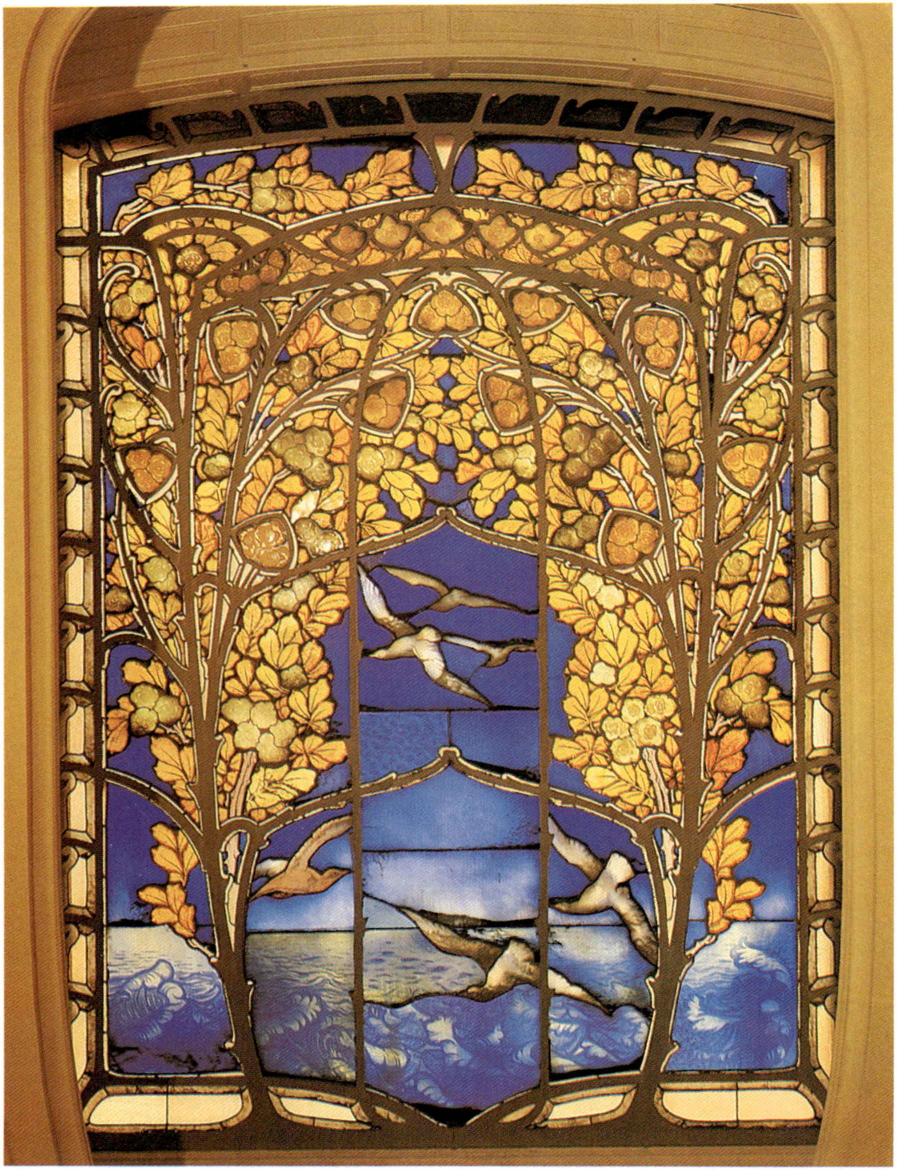

inant colors of purple and rose and a chandelier made of glass bubbles.

Hector Guimard

In Paris, one sees in Hector Guimard's stained glass the same abstract arches, bows, and ripples evident in his ironwork. The Swiss typographer Eugène Grasset, who was also based in Paris, produced stained glass designs, too. His, however, were more traditional in subject matter than Guimard's and were strongly related to his and other's contemporary graphic art — with Art Nouveau maidens idling in summer landscapes.

Left: A window at the medical school in Nancy, France, designed by Jacques Gruber.

ART NOUVEAU GLASS IN THE UNITED STATES

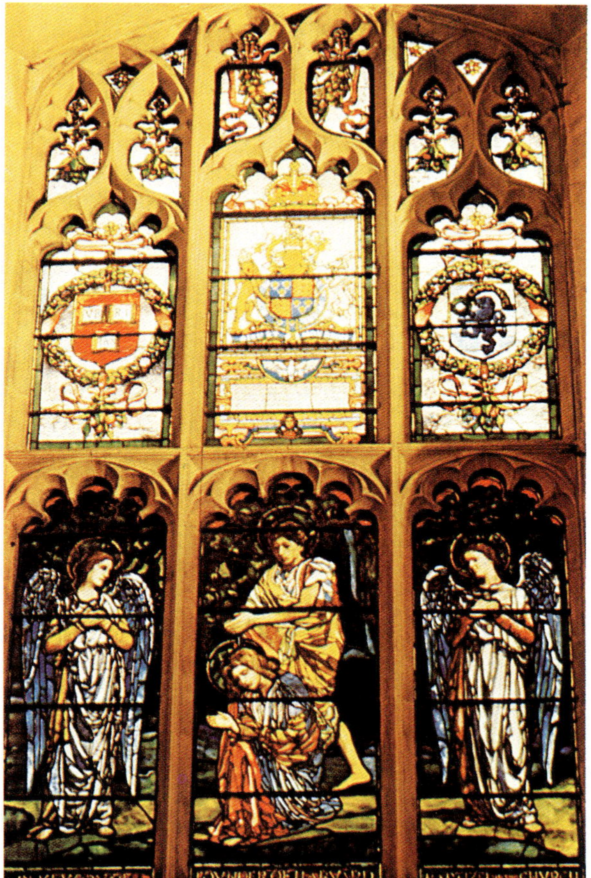

Toward the end of the 1800s, many contacts were made across the Atlantic in the decorative arts. In 1876, Christopher Dresser gave a series of lectures in Philadelphia. In 1882, Oscar Wilde arrived preaching not only aesthetic ideals, but also that the United States should find the inspiration for her art in her own lands and not copy the styles of the past from dissimilar countries — a healthy attitude for a relatively young country. In 1893, Samuel Bing, founder of La Maison de l'Art Nouveau, the showcase for the new style in France, visited the United States. In 1896, C.R. Ashbee made his first visit, and in 1901 met with Frank Lloyd Wright.

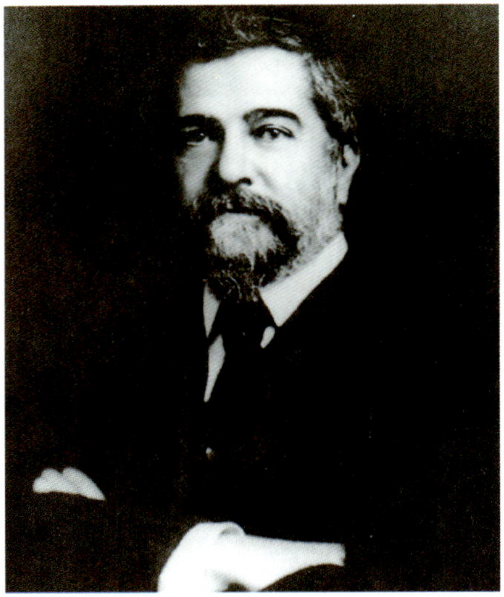

Above: Louis Comfort Tiffany in his middle years.

Overleaf: The John Harvard Memorial Window by John La Farge in St. John's Chapel, Southwark Cathedral, London.

The flow of ideas was not only one-way, however. In the same year that Wilde toured the United States, the Boston architect Henry H. Richardson visited England and met William Morris and Burne-Jones. In 1889, an exhibition of American arts, including Rookwood faience ceramics and designs by John La Farge, was held in London.

Glass in the United States

While the middle of the 1800s in England had seen a considerable revival in the art of stained glass, the United States had not had a Gothic revival that brought with it a re-emergence of ecclesiastical art. Consequently, in the United States, it was not until the end of the century that stained glass was seen as a promising art form.

In 1872, the illustrator and watercolorist John La Farge visited France and England where he not only admired, but met with some of the Pre-Raphaelite painters and saw the work of Morris & Co. La Farge produced his first stained glass in New York in 1876 and worked with Boston architect Henry H. Richardson and also Stanford White, who was part of the team of architects responsible for the Boston Public Library.

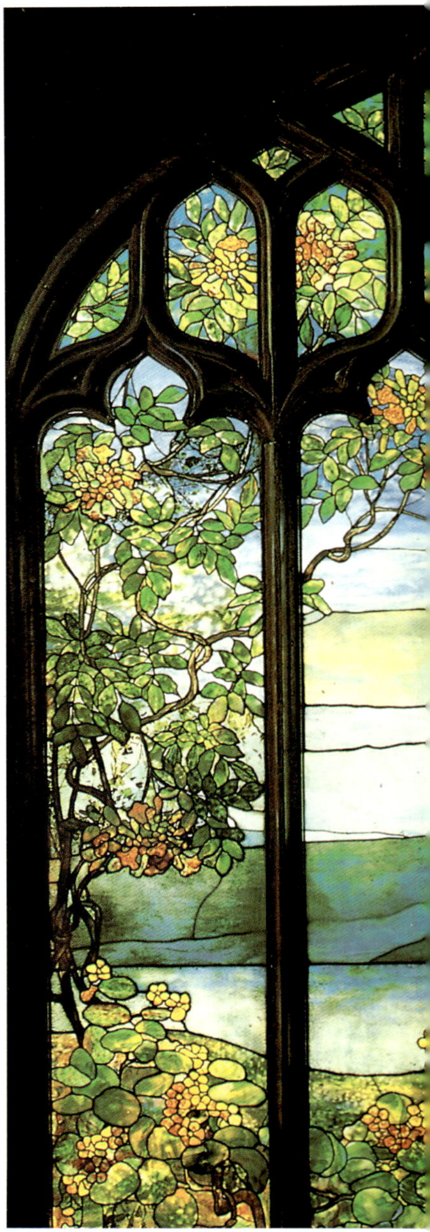

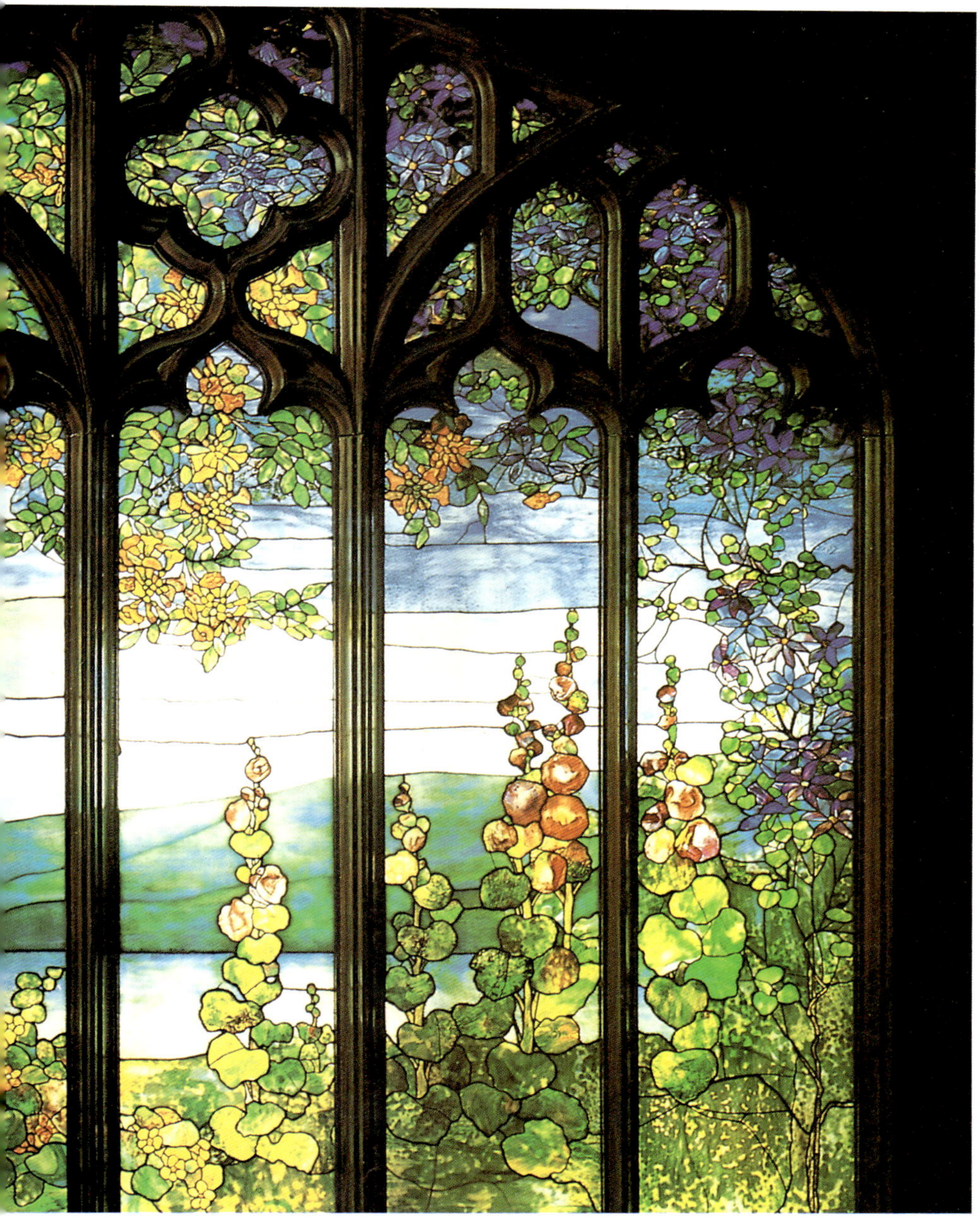

For Richardson's Holy Trinity church in Boston, often considered the finest example of "Richardson Romanesque," La Farge designed the panels. Around 1887, he began to experiment with different techniques which resulted in an opalescent glass which lent itself to Art Nouveau forms and no longer required painting or etching for its effects.

The undoubted leader — Tiffany

The undoubted leader in the medium, however, was Louis Comfort Tiffany. A true child of Art Nouveau, his designs and his sense of beauty matched exactly the ideals of his time. But Tiffany was no mere imitator of a fashionable artistic creed. Instead, he was one of the most original designers of the Art Nouveau style, and as such, his work set the standard for his peers.

Tiffany

Tiffany's technical virtuosity is compelling. In his stained glass windows, the stippling of a bird's feather, the roughness of the bark of a tree, and the gleam of water are all reproduced in the great pictorial windows he made, but none of these textures is drawn or marked into the glass. Tiffany used the mosaic system of the medieval craftsman, but his pieces of glass were not of pure color. Instead, they were a collage of colors — striped, mottled, patterned, and spotted — and the color variations themselves were contained within the glass. All the pieces in the designs are matched to allow the colors and textures to flow in a painterly manner, and the absence of brushstrokes allows the light to pass

Left: In this Tiffany stained glass window entitled, "Hudson River," plant forms dominate a vivid landscape.

unhindered through the glass.

Tiffany worked unceasingly toward the aim of creating paintings in glass, and it is in his abstract designs that he proved a master in stained glass. Before 1890, he designed stained glass windows that made perfect use of glass as an artistic medium. In his abstract work, in which the geometry of colored glass is delineated by the black line of the lead, Tiffany conveyed perfectly the use of light and design that made glass its own medium and no longer an imitation of painting.

The Tiffany Glass Company

Tiffany also perceived a social need for decorative stained glass to create interiors full of light and warmth, where otherwise a window, especially in the city apartments, might have looked out only onto a brick wall.

Tiffany was the son of the founder of the legendary New York store, Tiffany & Co. He had studied painting under George Innes and had traveled extensively in Europe before he set up L.C. Tiffany and the Associated Artists in 1879 with the help of Candace Wheeler. By the early 1880s, they were the most successful New York decorating firm, and in 1882 were commissioned to decorate the White House. By 1885, however, the Association had come to an end and the independent firm of the Tiffany Glass Company was founded.

Early influences

Louis Comfort Tiffany grew up in the shadow of the Tiffany workshops, and even as a child was privy to the techniques and methods of the craftsmen employed there. In particular, Edward C. Moore, a remarkable craftsman, designer, and art connoisseur of whom Samuel Bing said: "his country should forever enshrine him in grateful memory," was uniquely influential. Moore did not look to Europe for inspiration, but instead to the East. He admired Persian and Islamic art with their geometric abstractions of natural forms and sumptuous intricacy of design. Later, he became absorbed in Japanese art and its masterful use of metals. The first American to win a European award for his craft as a silversmith (the Gold Medal at the 1878 Paris Exposition), Moore was a great collector and amassed a significant collection of Oriental and antique glass which was to be of great interest in later years for Tiffany.

Society of American Artists

Tiffany began his artistic career as a painter and exhibited regularly. Although he rarely sold his paintings, he was also active in promoting the works of other artists and helped to found the Society of American Artists which included George Innes and La Farge. Among his closest friends, however, was Samuel Colman a watercolor artist whose real interest lay in textiles. It was Colman who was directly responsible for moving Tiffany away from painting into the field of applied art.

The first experiments in glass

Although he began as a painter, Tiffany's wealth allowed him to pursue other interests, and in 1875 he began his glass experiments in the Thill glass house in Brooklyn. He also traveled widely and collected antique Greek

Far right: Toulouse-Lautrec's painting translated into glass by Tiffany.

Right: Not painted on glass, but an opaque glass mosaic that contained color and texture within itself.

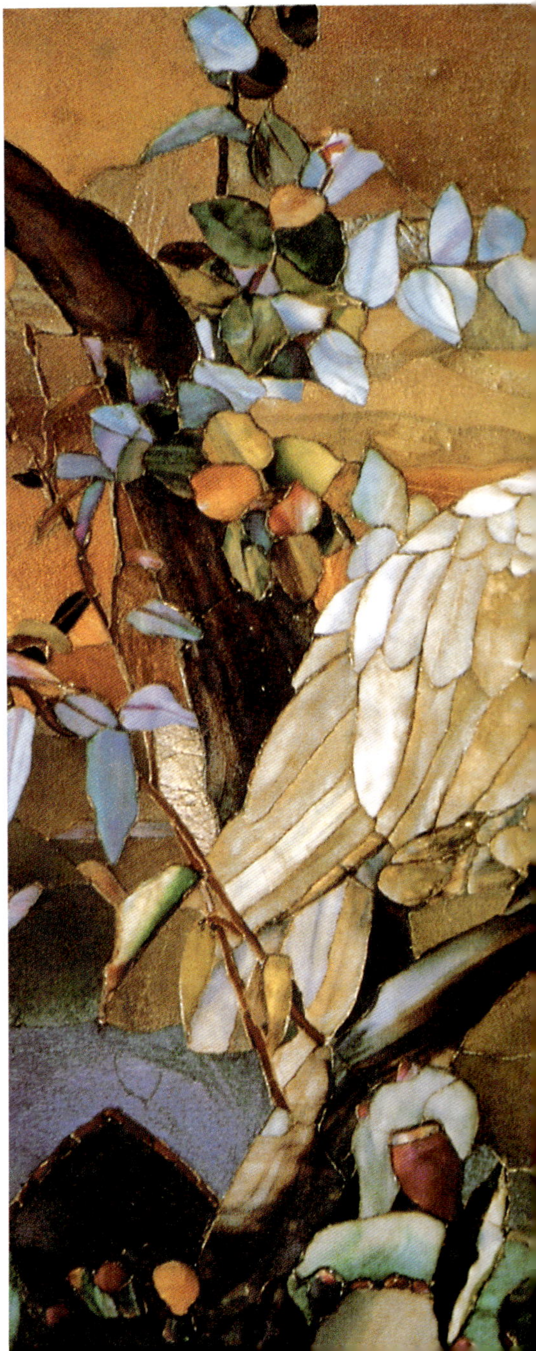

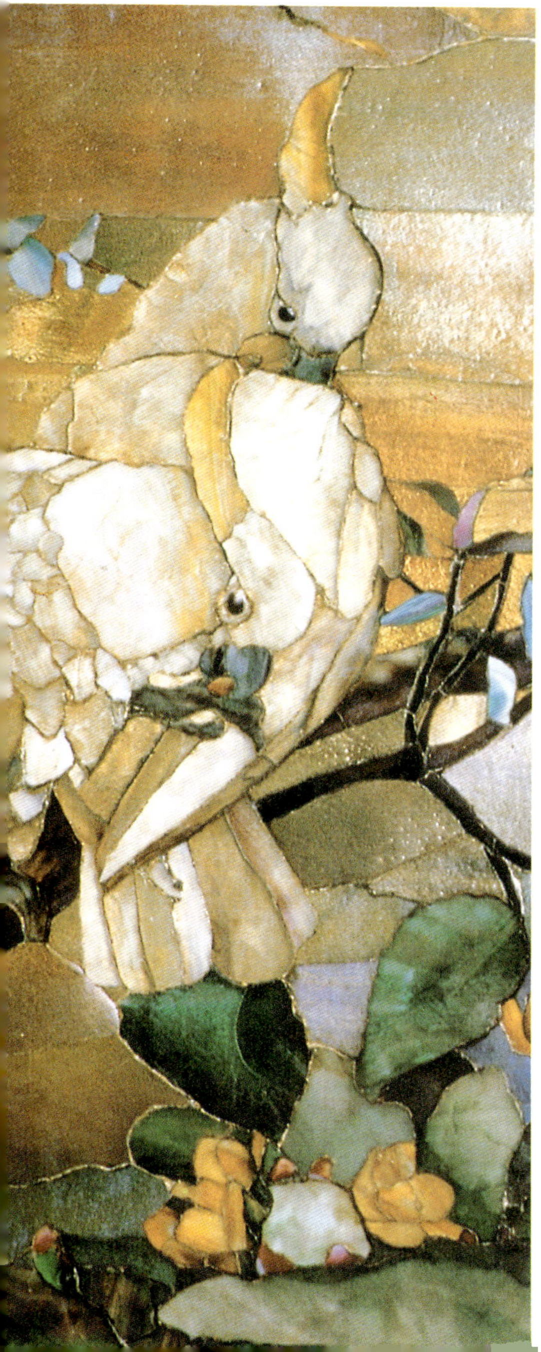

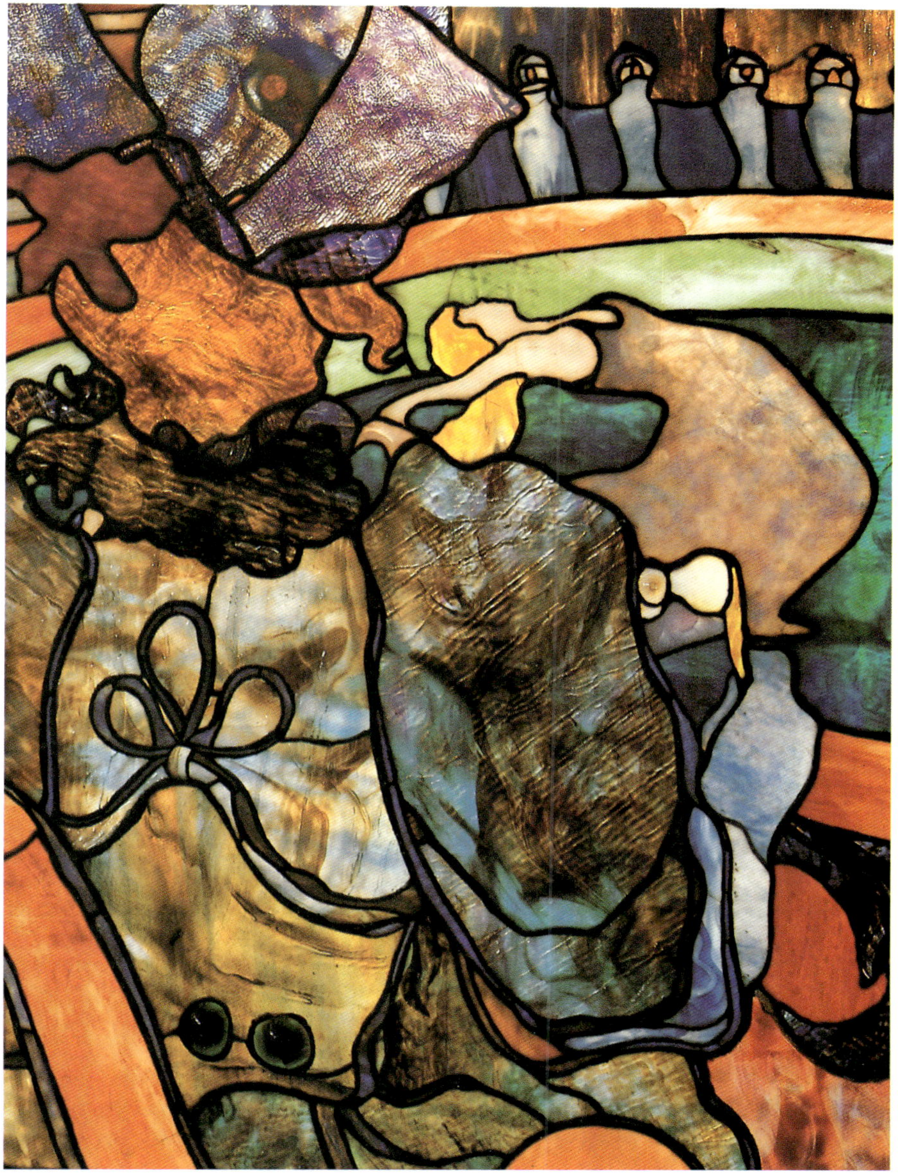

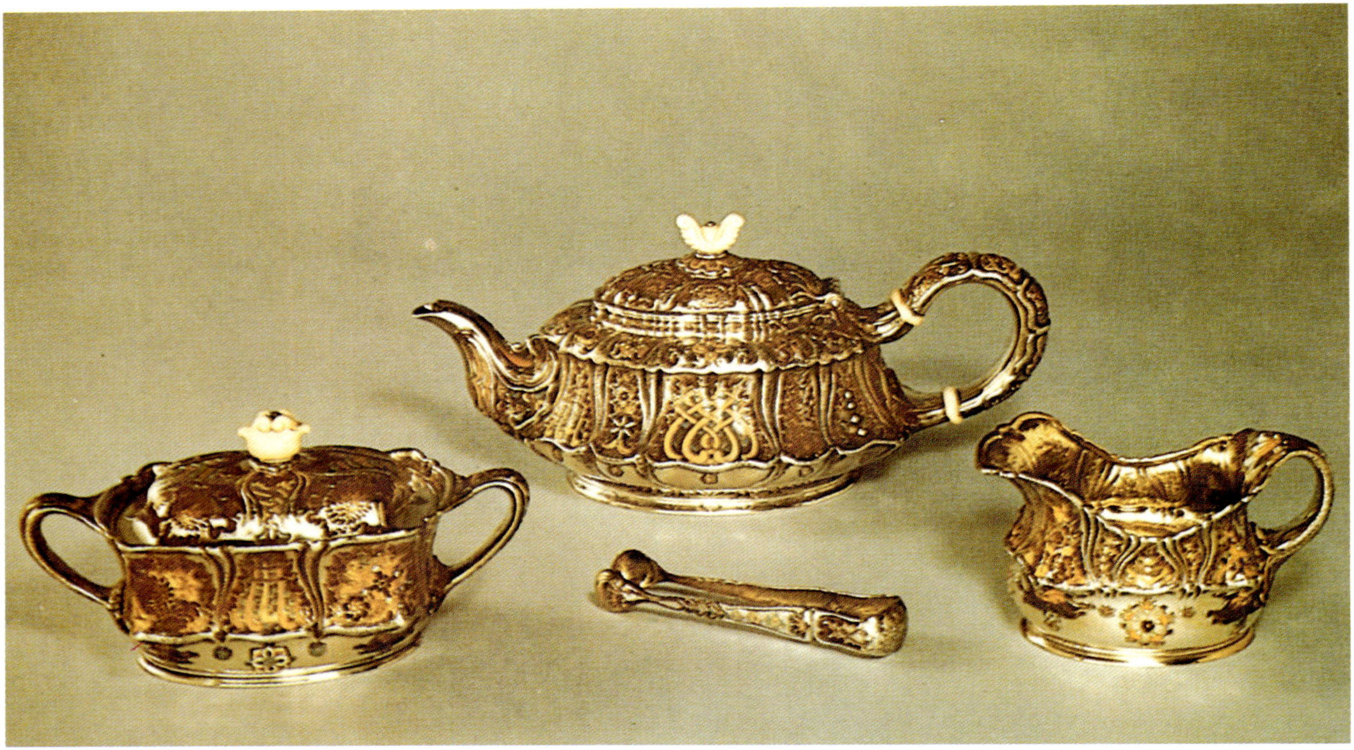

Above: A silver tea set, embellished with etching and enamels, is characteristic of the work of Edward C. Moore, the master silversmith whose taste was to influence the young L.C. Tiffany.

and Roman glass, and Oriental domestic ware which represented good craftsmanship or illustrated particular working techniques. Often they carried designs from nature and thus the objects were both functional and decorative.

Louis C. Tiffany and Associated Artists

In an effort to demonstrate his own ideas regarding the unity of the arts, and especially on the intermarriage of architecture and design, Tiffany invited Candace Wheeler, Samuel Colman, and the collector Lockwood de Forest to join him in a design venture. The group operated under the name of "Louis C. Tiffany and Associated Artists," and negotiated with the Society of Decorative Art for the exclusive rights to design, supervise, and sell the works of its members. The overall aim was to provide "perfect interiors," and among the many commissions they undertook were the private homes of Cornelius Vanderbilt II, the Metropolitan Museum's founder J. Taylor Johnston, the writer, Mark Twain, as well as decorating the White House. The piece de resistance of this scheme — unfortunately demolished in 1902 — was an opalescent glass screen that reached from floor to ceiling and which featured an intricate interlaced motif of eagles and flags.

Tiffany also continued his own work in glass, and in 1878 established his own glass house. Unfortunately, this burned down twice, and it was subsequently closed down. He then began experiments at the Heidt glass house in Brooklyn and applied for a patent for a new character of glass in colored windows. The glass tiles and lighting fixtures in many of the interiors he had designed had already attracted attention. In 1881, *Scribner's Monthly* devoted an article to glass mentioning Tiffany and La Farge as the leading exponents of the craft in the United States.

Glass tiles

Toward the end of the 1880s, Tiffany began to design a great deal of mosaic work, and the glass tiles were the results of his early experiments in opalescent and iridescent glass. In 1880, he made patent applications which specified three types of glass — one for use in tiles and mosaics, another for plating windows, and the third to give a metallic luster. This metallic luster developed into his famous Favrile glass, but it is important to remember that Tiffany did not invent the iridescent luster: in 1873, the Austrian glass makers Lobmeyr were selling iridescent glassware, and from 1878 in England, Thomas Webb & Sons were producing similar glass. Tiffany never pretended to invent it, but he did believe that he made the best glass of this type.

In his early experiments, Tiffany achieved many accidental effects which were quite beautiful, and later he deliberately produced irregularities of surfaces to vary and enhance the qualities of light transmission. Dissatisfied

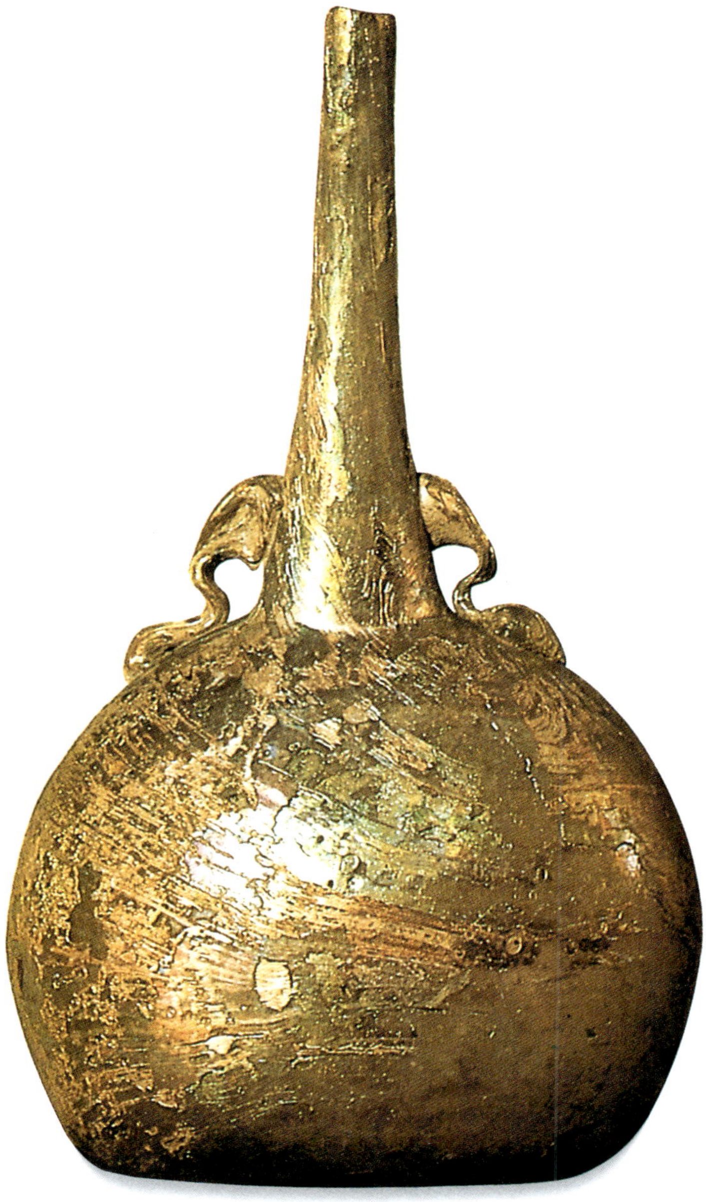

Right: Antique Persian glassware. Tiffany envied the flowing lines, luster, and textures.

with the "thin" colors produced by most commercial glass houses, Tiffany produced thick, dense colors ranging from ruby reds to emerald greens while abstract patterns or designs of rosettes and other plant forms were molded onto the surface of the tiles.

Tiffany and Art Nouveau

In 1888, Tiffany undertook the commission for the decoration of the Ponce de Léon Hotel in St. Augustine, Florida. The results met with high praise from the public and led to many more orders for the interior decoration department of Louis C. Tiffany and Co., the name of his company after he had parted from the Associated Artists. Many artists complained as they watched his workshops flood the market with ever more fashionable art glass windows, that Tiffany had betrayed his talent and opted for commercial success. But in 1892, Tiffany dumbfounded his critics when for Samuel Bing he executed and exhibited a stained glass window — Four Seasons. This piece was far removed from the popular designs heavy in pictorial content that Tiffany had produced in such quantities in the United States and marked the arrival of Art Nouveau in his work.

In 1889, Tiffany had visited Paris where he saw the work of the French master glass designer Emile Gallé. Gallé's engraved vases with their free-flowing shapes caught Tiffany's imagination, and in 1893 Tiffany acquired his

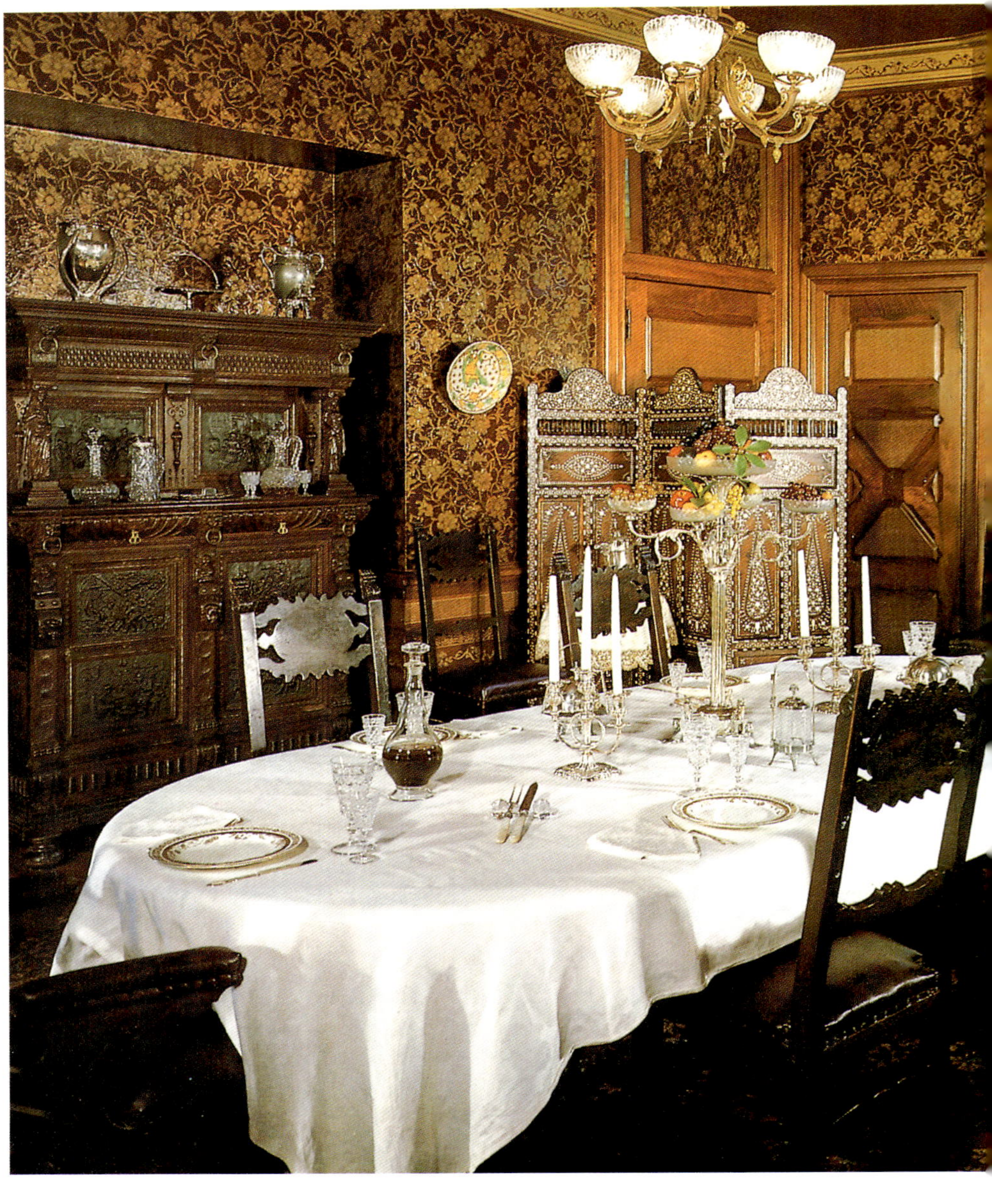

Right: Tiffany used glass wherever he could in his interiors. Glass tiles and stained glass dominate Mark Twain's dining room.

Far right: Tiffany's initial experiments in glass making were concentrated on glass tiles.

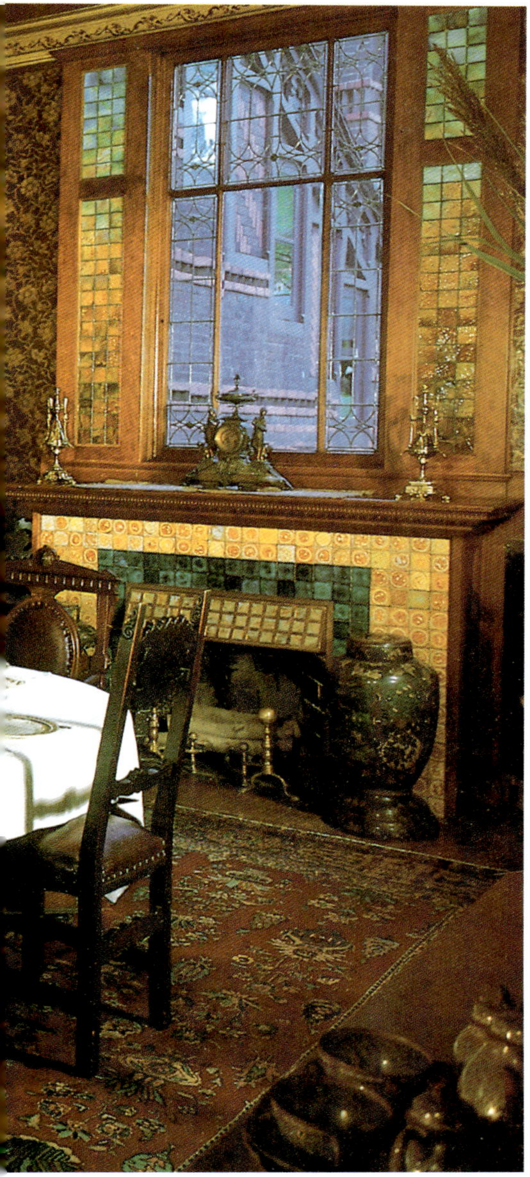

own glass house, the Corona furnaces on Long Island. Between this time and the end of the century, Tiffany was at his most creative and made his own unique contribution to Art Nouveau.

He turned to making what he called "small glass," which was varied, beautiful, and had a novel quality that expressed all the principles of Art Nouveau. Essentially organic forms abstracted into decorative surfaces were endowed with an asymmetrical linear quality. Tiffany's favorite motifs for vases were the peacock feather, the iris, morning glories, gladioli, tendrils, and trailing leaves. But no lines

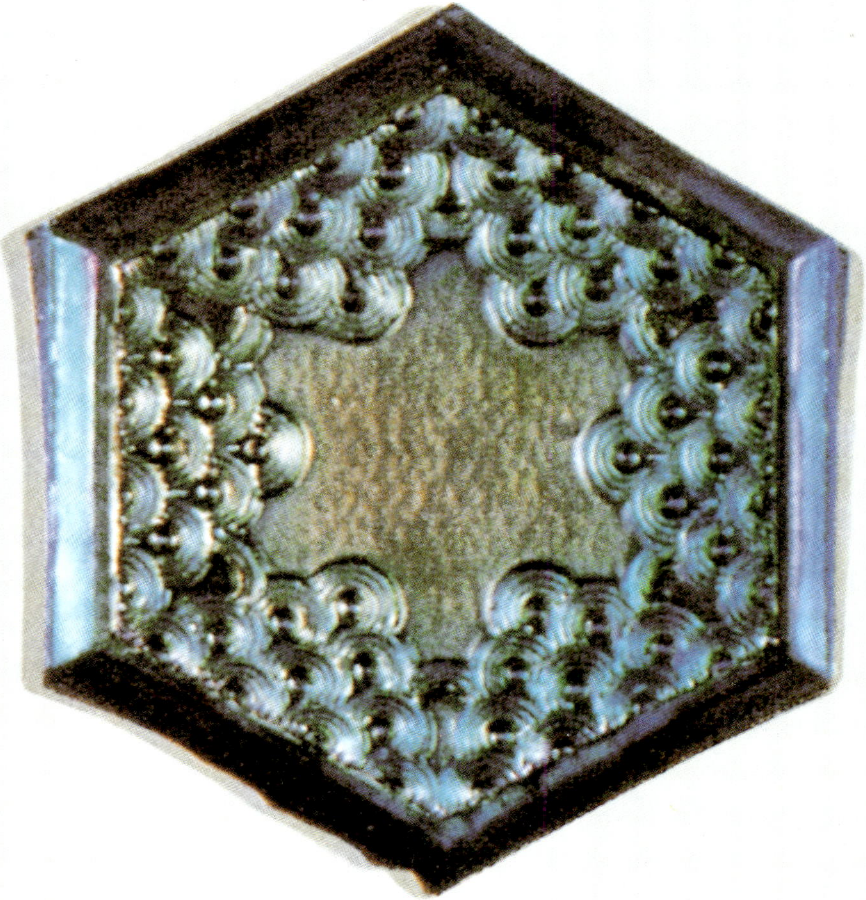

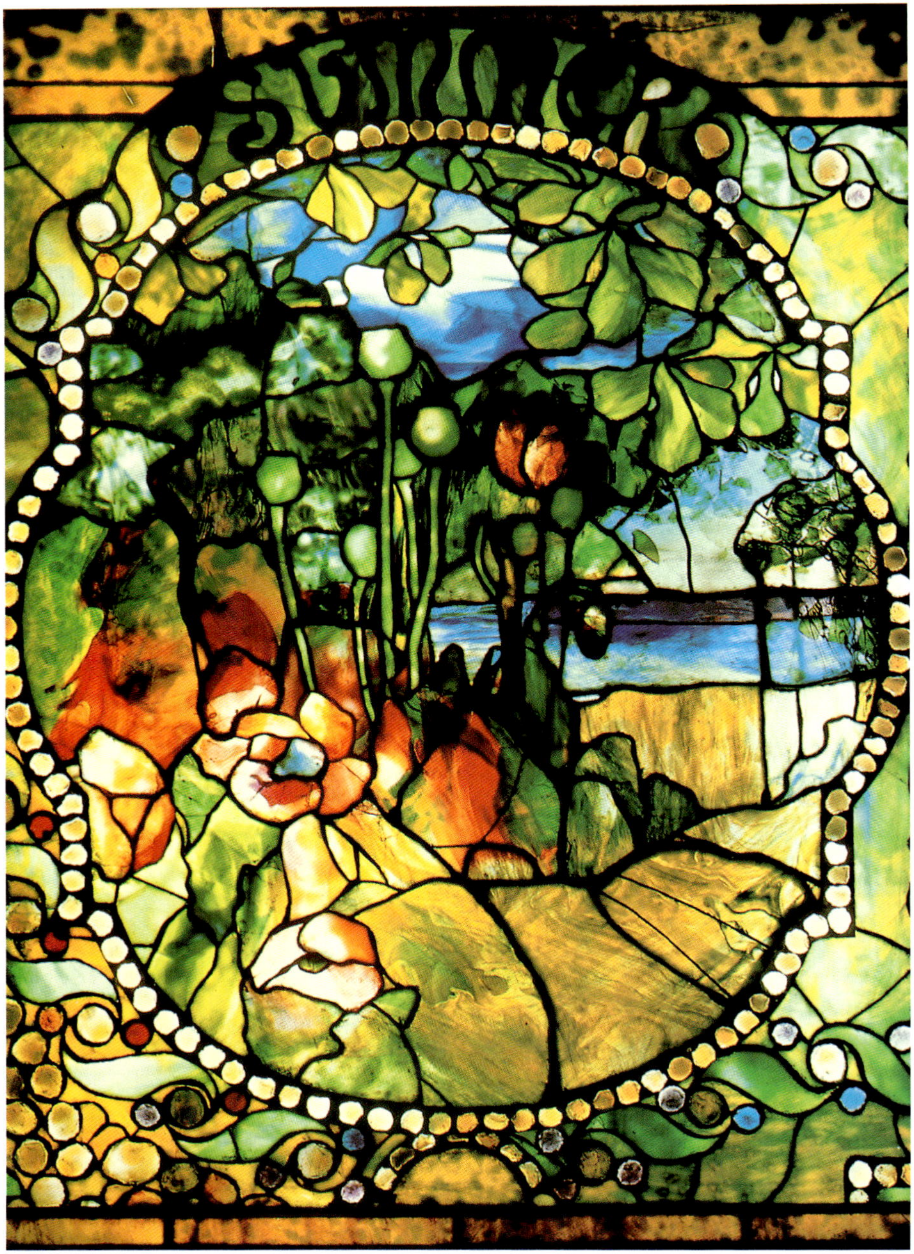

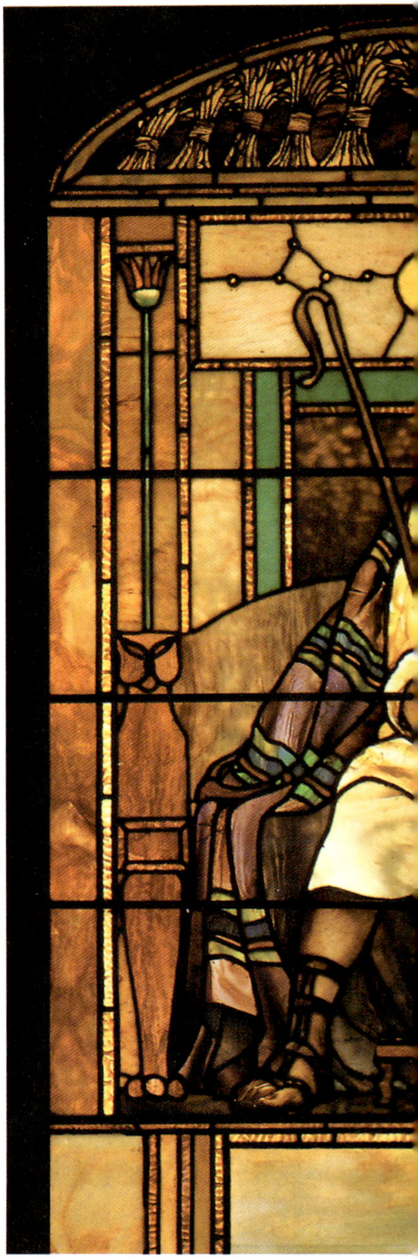

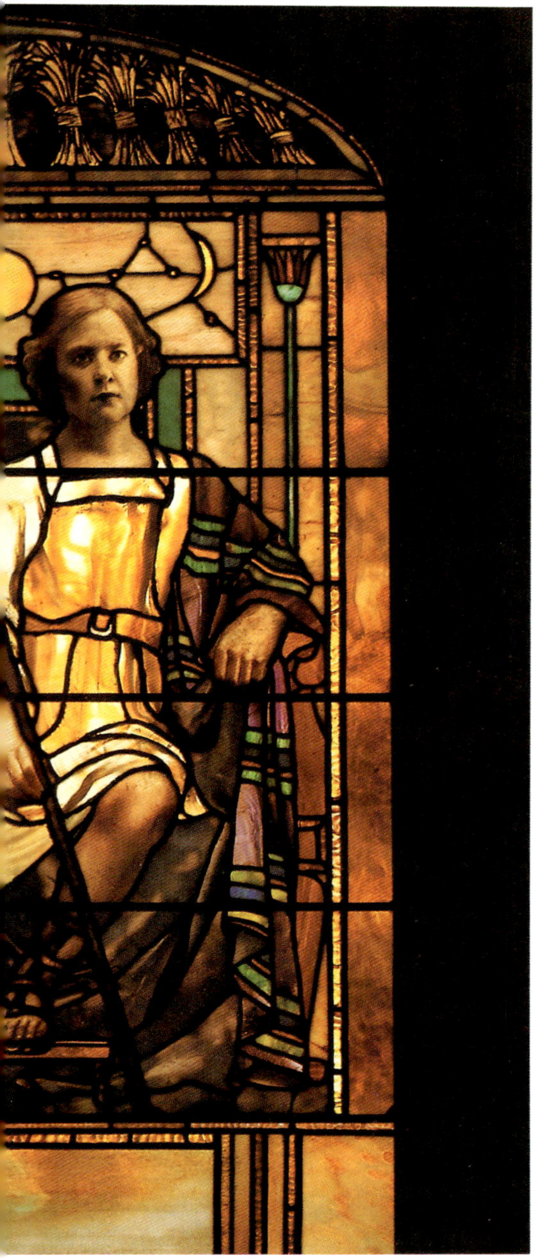

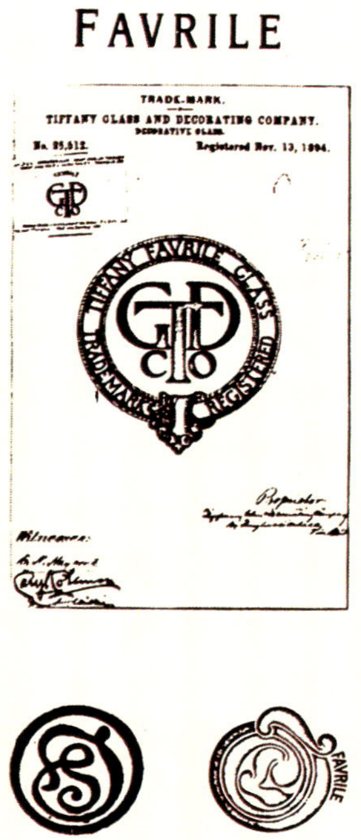

Far left: The "Four Seasons" window. Here, "Summer" is represented in Tiffany's masterly stained glass window.

Center: Equally popular were Tiffany's religious subjects.

Left: Tiffany registered several trademarks. He designed two seals for his Favrile glass and in 1894 registered a logo for the Tiffany Glass and Decorating Company.

were drawn or painted onto the vases, instead, the molten glass was blown with small amounts of colored glass of different textures, and colors were combined and manipulated to form the decoration.

Favrile Glass

In 1894, Tiffany registered Favrile as a trademark. The name is derived from the Old English word "fabrile," meaning belonging to the craft, or handmade. The first year's production had gone straight into museums and it was not until 1896 that the first Favrile glass was offered for public sale. Favrile glass exploited the use of chemical soaks or vapors to create different surface textures from a smooth matt to a burnished glow. Tiffany's glass rarely had the modeled plasticity of Gallé or Daum. Its decoration, much more abstract in its depiction of natural forms, rarely rises out in relief, but appears as more of an applied surface pattern.

Favrile glass

Favrile glass is a generic name — it can be divided into categories based on the various techniques used to make it. Types include Agate Ware, a thick glass which resembled marble; Lava Glass, a dark opalescent glass which had basalt or talc added to the molten glass and the surface then gold-lustered; Cypriote Glass, where the hot yellow glass of the object was covered with pulverized crumbs of the same material and then lustered. Paperweight or Reactive Glass is the term that is applied to all of Tiffany's translucent glass that had changed color and become iridescent when it was reheated in the furnace. This was Tiffany's most technically complicated glass and no other glass maker has ever sought to imitate it.

In addition to these, Tiffany also made another kind of Favrile glass called Cameo Glass. It was the only kind of Tiffany glass

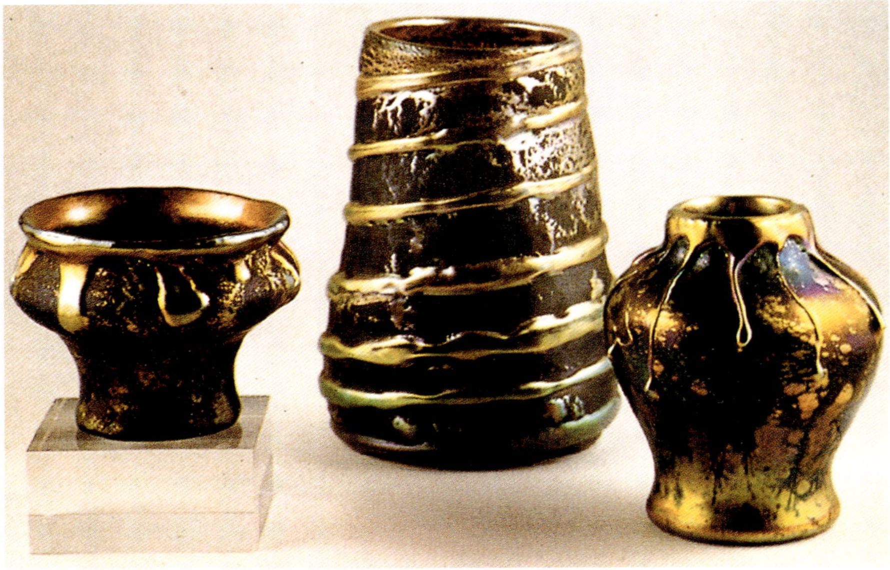

Right: Three examples of Lava glass. Molten glass spilt over a rough surface produces the volcanic effect.

Below: One of the popular Jack-in-the-Pulpit vases, which Tiffany made with numerous color effects.

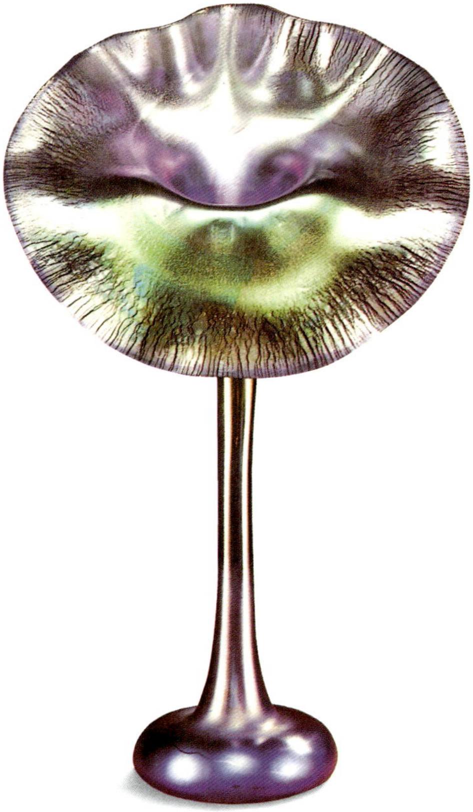

decoration not produced when the glass was semi-molten. Millefiori Glass was a type of glass that had been known since the 2nd century B.C., but the process was not revived until the 1800s. The decoration is composed of colored glass rods that contain a motif, usually a flower, which passes through its entire length.

The various techniques and the range of shapes that he devised meant that no two pieces of Favrile glass are exactly the same. There are elegant flower forms and "Goose-necked" vases inspired by Persian perfume flasks; "Jack-in-the-Pulpit" vases with bulb shaped bases and long slender bodies that flow into trumpet-shaped tops and the "Tel el Amarna" vases, named after the excavation of Pharaoh Amenhotep IV's capital, which retain the simple shapes of their Egyptian models, but with a more brilliant color tone.

Often imitated, never bettered

There have been many imitators of Favrile glassware. In the United States, Frederick Carder, who founded the Steuben Glassworks in Corning, New York, registered his iridescent glass as Steuben Glass and copied many of Tiffany's shapes. In Europe, many glass makers came extremely close to reproducing Tiffany's style, including Loetz in Austria. The Loetz glass, however, had a very limited range of colors and never really achieved anything like the tactile quality of Tiffany Favrile glass.

Reinforced by commercial success, Tiffany spared no expense in his experiments and could afford to be ahead of his competitors. But it was not just his range of colors and extensive experimentation that gave Tiffany the edge over his contemporaries. His distinctive designs, with their fluid and sensual, organic movement, put him even further ahead.

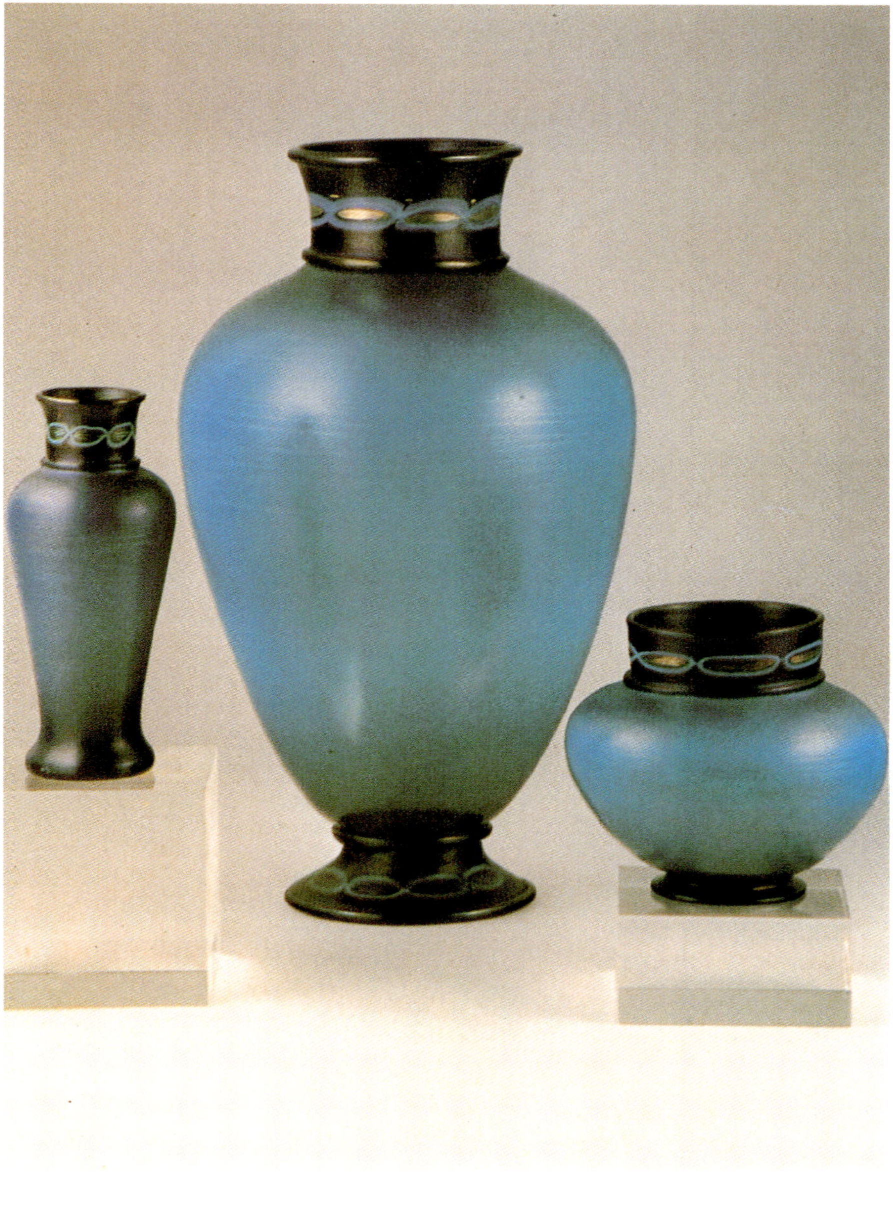

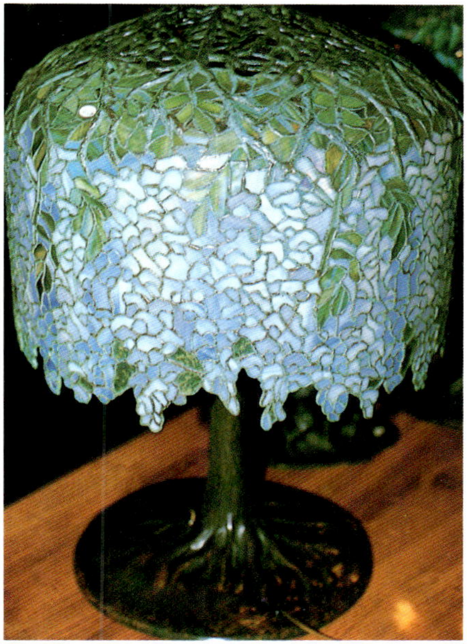

Above: The famous Wisteria lamp, designed by Mrs. Curtis Freshel, was an enduring favorite from the Tiffany workshops.

Left: Tel el Armana vases in aquamarine blue retain the simple shapes of the original Egyptian models.

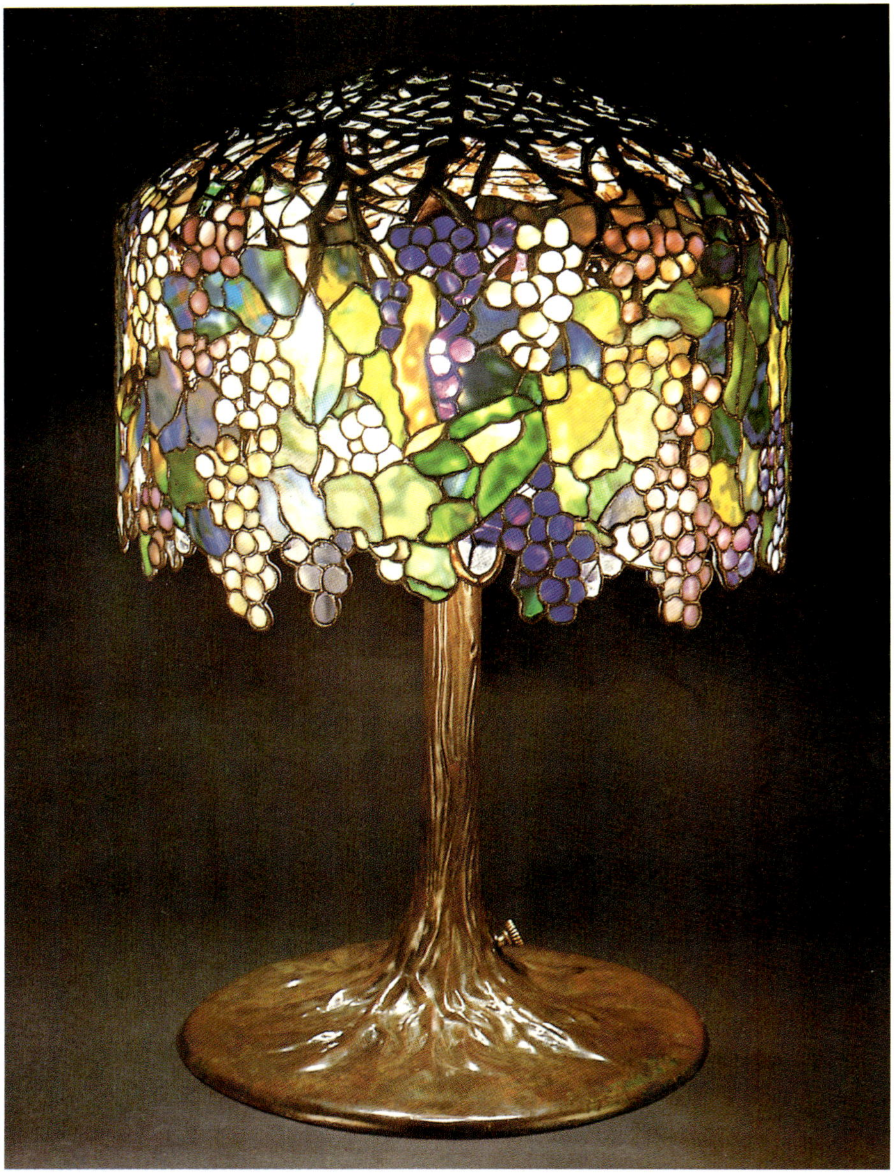

TIFFANY LAMPS

In 1900, Tiffany changed the name of his company to Tiffany Studios, the name it retained until its closure in 1938. Tiffany Studios continued to produce interior designs, Favrile glass, stained glass windows, and mosaics, as well as numerous household goods, including the most famous articles, the Tiffany lamps.

The lamps were a natural outlet for Tiffany's interest in glass and the effects of light on color. He considered the harsh brightness of electricity and softened its glare with lovely color. His designs were also technically well-considered — the electric lamps were given armatures to alter the focus of the light and the shades were interchangeable. In his lamps, Tiffany combined function with aesthetic appeal.

CANDACE WHEELER

Tiffany had started to sell lamps in 1895, although he had exhibited them earlier in the Women's Building at the World's Fair in 1893 in Chicago. Tiffany's former colleague, Candace Wheeler, was President of the Women's Building and, from this association, he recognized the talent of many women designers, a number of whom were to emerge from his studios. In the area of lamp design, Tiffany's two major designers were Mrs. Curtis Freschel and Clara Driscoll.

Freschel designed the famous Wisteria Lamp and Driscoll developed patterns for the Ivy, Rose, Geranium, and Butterfly lamps, among numerous others. While the leaded glass shades were not an innovation from the Tiffany Studio, the designs were, nevertheless, far superior to any other similar products. Tiffany

Left: Leaves and fruit tumble over the shade of the Grapevine lamp. Note the textured base.

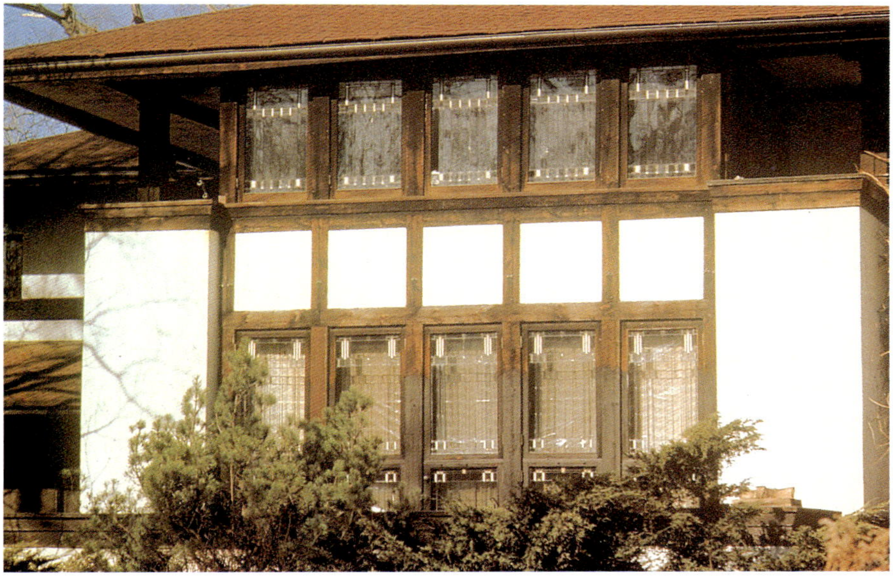

Left: The Ward Willits House, Highland Park, Illinois, designed by Frank Lloyd Wright. Stained glass was used in the windows to create colored light effects inside.

lamps are often thought of in terms of their glass, but the stands and bases were integral to the design and under Tiffany's guidance, these too became works of art.

Byzantine designs were sometimes used and an antique appearance given to them by the use of dark, mossy colors which complemented the organic shapes of nature — leaves, tendrils, cobwebs, stems of flowers, and roots of trees — that became the models for curving, sculptural forms. The leaded glass shades assumed the natural forms of branches and fruit and flowers or the circular spread of wings and spider's webs. Their titles confirm their origin and form — Pansy, Orange Petal, Snail, Queen Anne's Lace. All were realized in the jewel-like colors of Tiffany's stained glass.

Pattern molds were made so that the same lamps could be reproduced again and again and made in various sizes. This style became so widely popular in the United States that a "Tiffany lamp" is now the generic term for any lamp with a stained glass shade.

FOLLOWING THE LEADER

The popularity of Tiffany glass obviously encouraged many other manufacturers to follow his lead. In 1893, Handel and Co. of Connecticut began producing cheaper versions of the Tiffany lamp, and two former employees of the Tiffany Studio started the Quezal Art Glass and Decorating Company of Brooklyn in 1901. Other companies included the Fostoria Glass Speciality Company and Imperial Glass Company of Ohio, Fenton Art Glass Company of Virginia, Lustre Art Glass Co. of New York, and Vineland Flint Glassworks of New Jersey. The latter produced a much debased version of Tiffany Favrile glass called Carnival glass, a pressed glass with a sprayed-on iridescence of somewhat vulgar orange tones.

A NEW GENIUS — FRANK LLOYD WRIGHT

While Tiffany was the undoubted master of glass, another towering figure in the history of American design, and arguably the greatest influence on design in the United States in the first half of the 1900s, is Frank Lloyd Wright.

Born in 1867 — just 19 years after Louis Comfort Tiffany — Wright was to create a style that still seems fresh and relevant today. Best known as the architect of his Prairie and Usonian houses, Wright's architectural designs reflected a variety of influences that were frequently underlined in the decorative accessories that he designed to complete the interiors and complement the buildings.

Not content to simply design an attractive

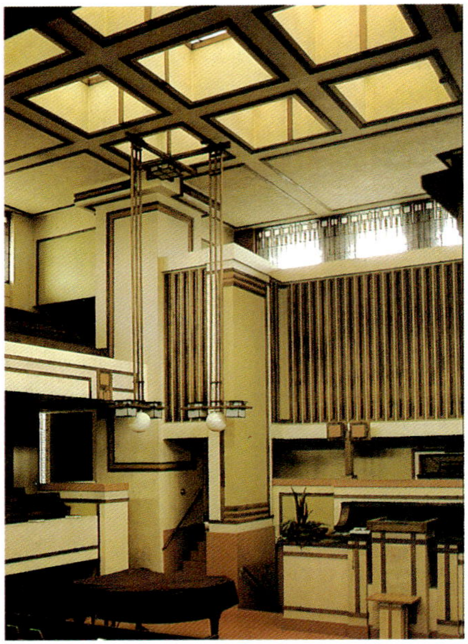

building, Wright also often designed the furnishings including light fixtures and art glass windows and screens. In 1894, Wright entered a competition to design an office building for the Luxfer Prism Company in Chicago, and instead of plate glass windows more typically used in commercial buildings, Wright incorporated the company's own glass blocks. Although not constructed, Wright's design made greater use of glass within its structural grid than any previous building, thus emphasizing the geometry of the iron skeleton frame. In 1897, Wright patented a series of glass blocks for Luxfer, the design of which incorporated a stylized flower of circles and squares. The fluid lines of the design recall not only the influence of Wright's mentor, Louis Sullivan, but also reflect the principles of English designers like Christopher Dresser and Owen Jones.

In his decorative schemes, Wright also used leaded glass, often made by the Linden Glass Company of Chicago. Plain glass in totally geometric designs echoed the central motifs used within specific houses. The repeated scheme of flowers and leaves — often of sumac, a plant native to the Prairies — is evident in the "Tree of Life" windows for the remarkable Darwin D. Martin House, and in the art glass designed for the Ward Willits House, the Dana-Thomas House, the Hollyhock House, and the magnificent Robie House.

NON-OBJECTIVE, GEOMETRIC DESIGNS

In the Avery Coonley Playhouse, the two-dimensional abstract designs of the art glass windows were based on Wright's observation of a parade with balloons, flags, and confetti motifs that were most suitable for a kindergarten theater. These windows, possibly Wright's greatest achievement in glass, were also some of his first non-objective, geometric designs.

Above: Interior of Unity Church, Oak Park, Illinois by Frank Lloyd Wright, 1906.

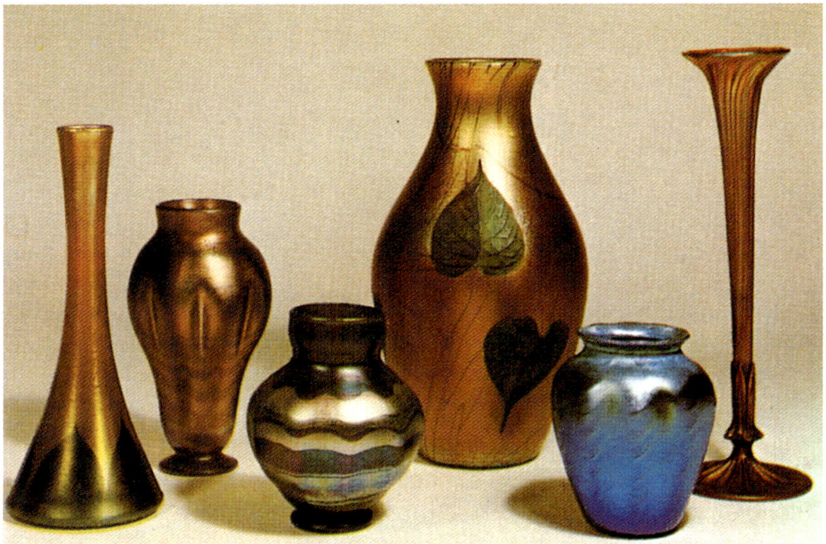

Right: A collection of Tiffany iridescent glass vases, ca 1900.

ART NOUVEAU CERAMICS

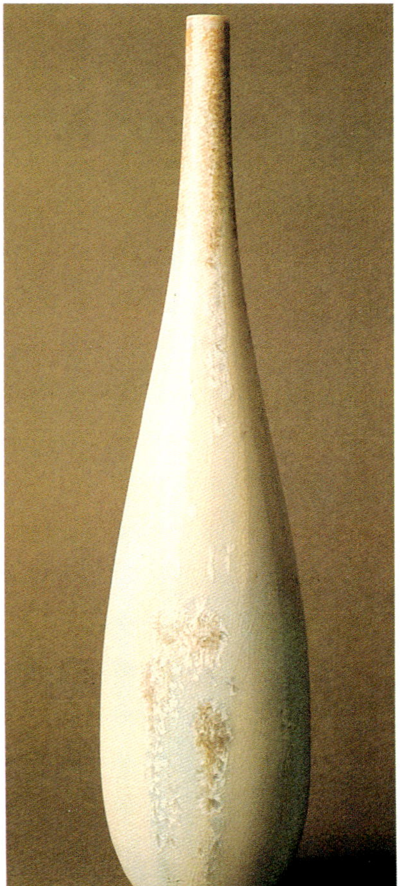

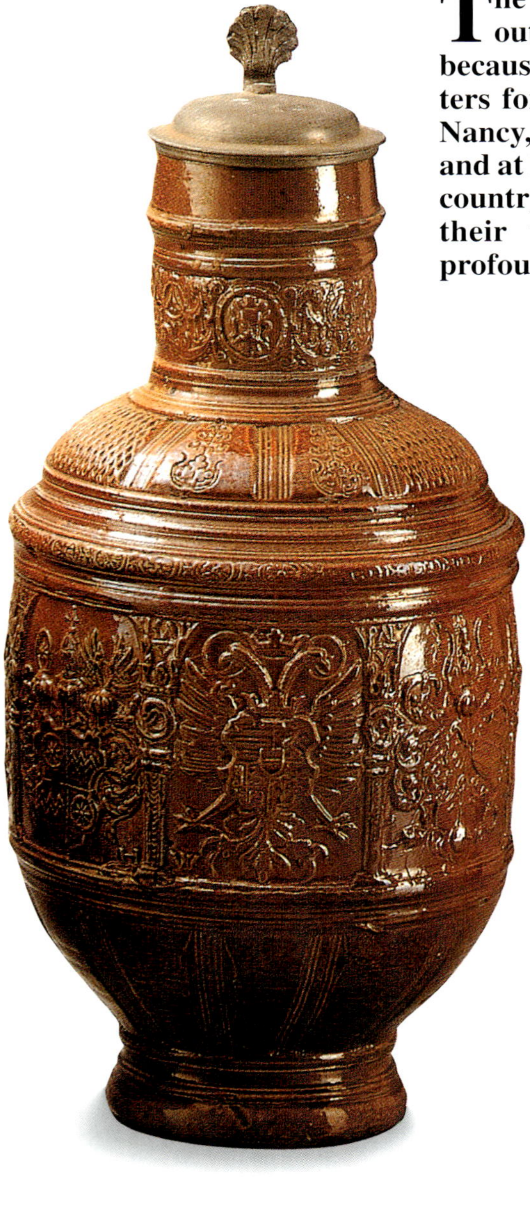

The ceramicists of the late 1800s remained, to a certain extent, outside the mainstream of decorative arts at the time, largely because of geography. In France, for example, the two main centers for Art Nouveau — except for ceramics — were Paris and Nancy, and although they participated in international exhibitions and at Paris Salons, French ceramicists were scattered around the country, using local clays, throwing, turning, glazing, and firing their works in an isolated way that demonstrated their profound love of their craft.

Overleaf: Vase by Taxile Doat, probably made before his departure for the United States.

Left: Glazed stoneware and pewter jug from Germany, dated 1606.

Art pottery

Many of the famous names in other fields of Art Nouveau design — Guimard, known for his ironwork for the Paris Métro, Gallé, best known for his work in glass, and de Feure and Colonna, best known as furniture designers — worked in ceramics as well. Often their work was more closely linked with the major porcelain factories — Guimard's ceramic designs were well suited to Sèvres porcelain. Instead of focusing on the natural warmth, texture, and color identifiable with stoneware, they were essentially hard-lined, abstract linear creations carried into three dimensions, in which the rising curve of the vase's silhouette is incorporated into the composition. George de Feure and Edward Colonna both designed for Limoges, an appropriate combination since both were sophisticated designers well-versed in 18th-century style.

Traditional stoneware

Many among the new generation of craftsmen, however, turned their backs on fine porcelain almost entirely, concentrating instead on the production of more coarsely grained, traditional stoneware which was the subject of an enormous revival in the Art Nouveau period.

Almost universally referred to as Art Pottery, the revival of stoneware created

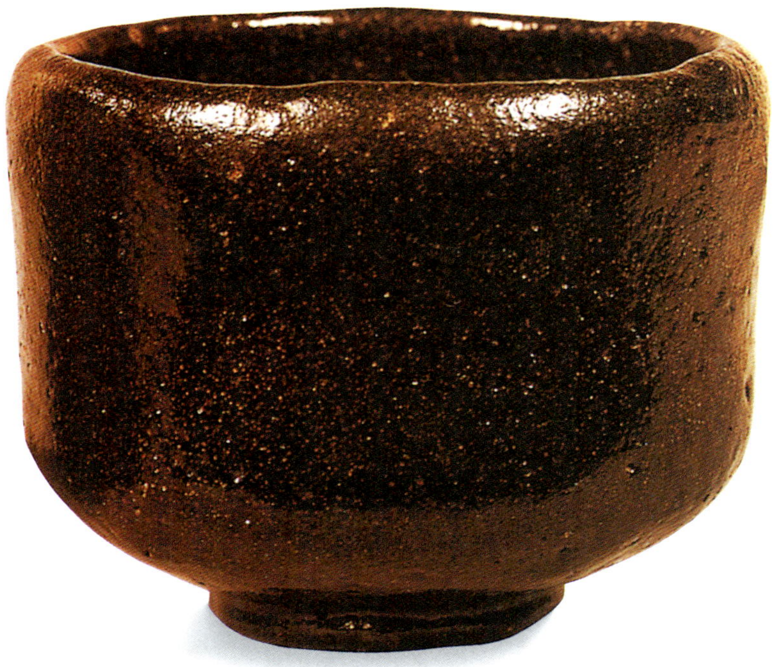

Left: A tea bowl of low fired Raku ware with black glaze from Japan, 1600s. Such pieces have had a powerful effect on European studio potters.

throughout Europe and the United States, a whole new or revitalized tradition quite separate from that of porcelain production, and one that still thrives today.

"HONEST" MATERIALS

The choice of such a "democratic" medium was influenced by the socially-conscious side of the Arts and Crafts Movement that preferred plainer, cheaper, "honest" materials that were free from association with wealth and social aspirations. While the exploitation of stoneware had begun before the emergence of the Art Nouveau style, it was primarily those artists who were working in the Art Nouveau idiom that were responsible for developing the full potential of the medium. In Art Nouveau design, the increased range of materials and the exploration of materials hitherto considered as "inferior," places the emphasis on the aesthetic qualities of a piece rather than on the economic criteria.

ORIENTAL INFLUENCES

It is arguable whether the revival of stoneware would have been so significant if it had not been for the example of oriental, in particular Japanese, ceramics. Japanese wares, including pieces decorated with cloisonné (a type of enameling), ivories, and bronzes, were shown at the Paris Exhibition of 1862, and the revelation of their simple shapes, sparse decoration, and asymmetrically placed motifs made a dramatic impact on those who saw them. The Frenchman Félix Bracquemond (1833-1914) produced possibly the best of the European japonaiserie in ceramics. Inspired by the discovery of a volume of sketches by the artist Katsushika Hokusai, he made a series of woodcuts that were copied onto an earthenware service produced in 1866 by the firm of F.E. Rousseau.

Chinese porcelain had already had a major impact on the west from the 1700s onward. Among 19th-century aesthetes such as James McNeill Whistler and Oscar Wilde, there was a great enthusiasm for blue-and-white porcelain, although working craftsmen were more excited by the technical possibilities of oriental stoneware. Warm, rich colors were as possible as glowing lusters. The chance effects of slip and glazes could be explored alongside a range of surface textures.

FRENCH CERAMICS

In addition to oriental models, advanced technical equipment and knowledge in Europe helped Art Nouveau designers to create new artistic effects in ceramics. Supporting the works of the pioneering French ceramicists, in 1881 the Haviland workshop moved from Auteuil to Paris where it was managed by Ernest Chaplet. Here, Chaplet rediscovered the technique for producing the much envied sang-de-boeuf (oxblood) glaze of Chinese stoneware, which was, as its name implies, deep red in color. Chaplet never divulged the secret of the process, but versions were developed by contemporaries such as Adrien-

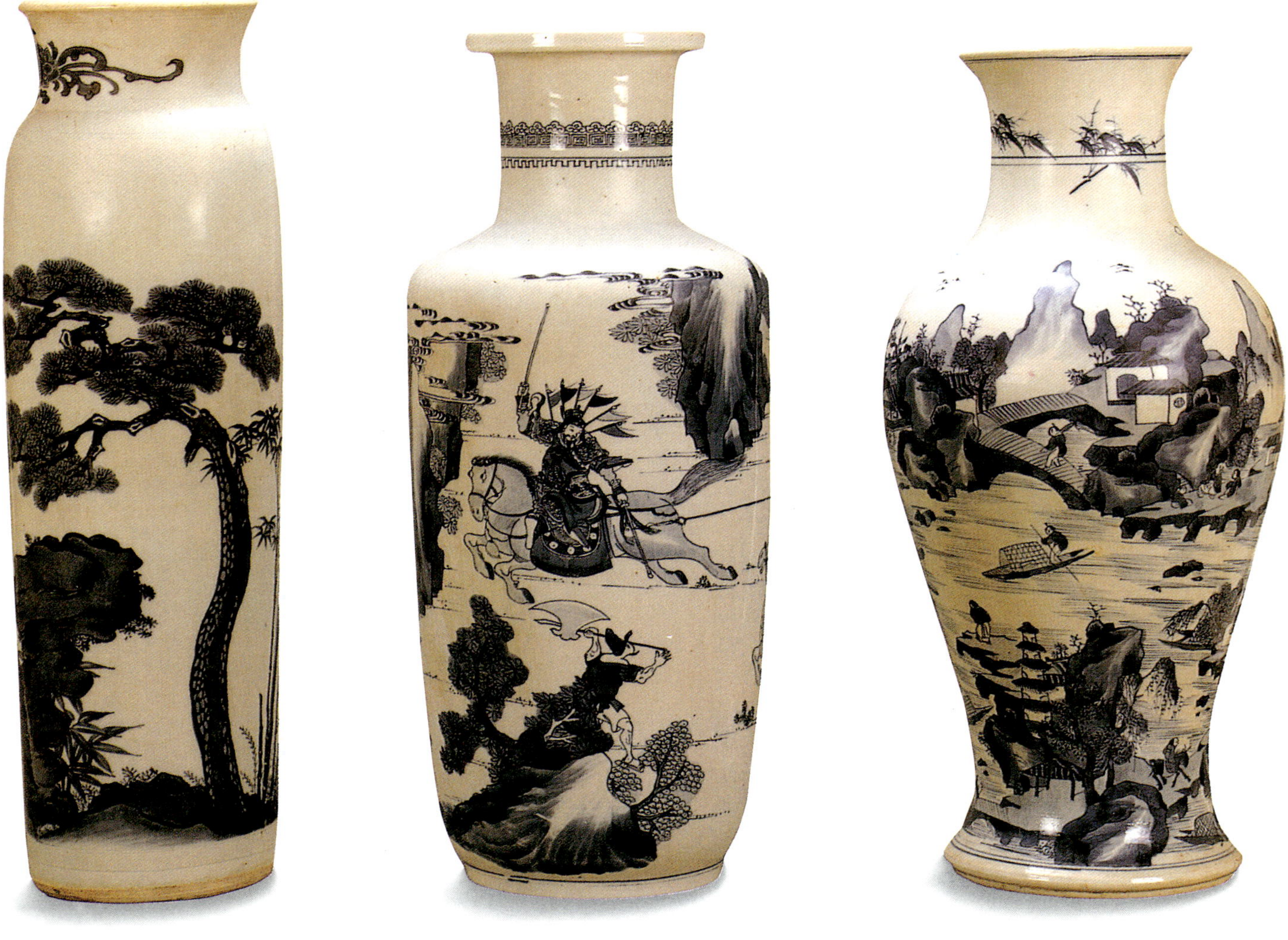

Below: Three Chinese blue-and-white vases dated ca 1640 (left) and 1662-1722 (middle and right).

Pierre Dalpayrat, the inventor of a similar, copper based "rouge Dalpayrat." Dalpayrat is best known for his stoneware vases, sculpted either in strange twisted shapes, or in the form of animals, fruit, or vegetables.

Chaplet and Haviland's

In 1885, Chaplet bought the firm from Haviland's and together with Edouard and Albert Dammouse, Ringel d'Illzach, Hexamer, and many others, Chaplet made dark red-brown stoneware with incised decoration, the colored glazes encircled with gold in the manner of cloisonné enamels. It was at this time that the painter Paul Gauguin started experimenting with ceramics that were fired by Chaplet. Gauguin produced works that were free from the conventions of a specialist. His lack of inhibition in handling the clay resulted in primitive vessels of swelling and flowing forms, many with gnarled and twisted handles. These works, which were few in number, were produced in the late 1880s, both before and after Gauguin's trip to Martinique, and predate the development of the Art Nouveau proper of the 1890s.

Pâte-sur-pâte

Dammouse, who trained as a sculptor before devoting himself to ceramics, began his career by decorating in pâte-sur-pâte (paste on paste) in which decorations were built-up in low relief with layers of porcelain slip. The varying thicknesses give the effect of shading in the design. When Chaplet sold Haviland on to Auguste Delaherche, Albert Dammouse set up his own studio in the village of Sèvres where he made stoneware, faience, and porce-

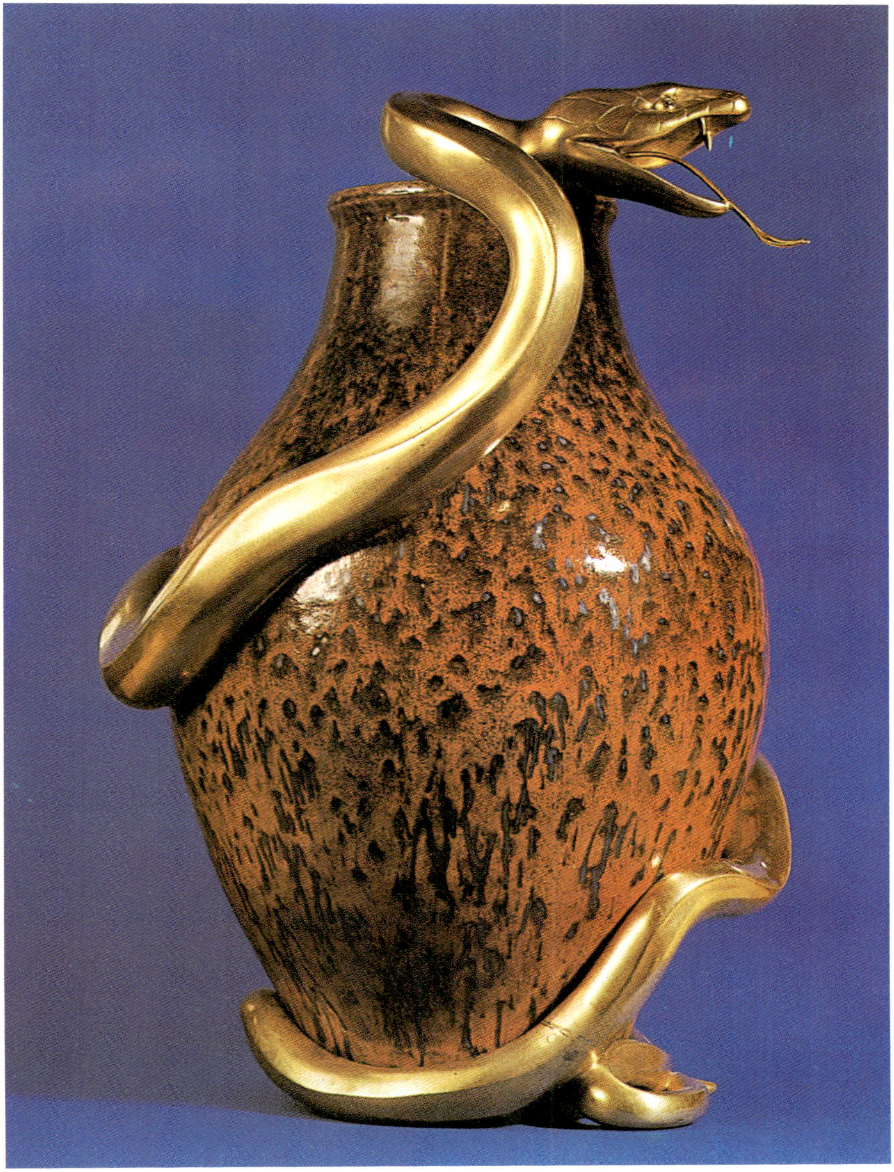

Right: Stoneware vase by Adrien-Pierre Dalpayrat, with ormolu mounts by Keller.

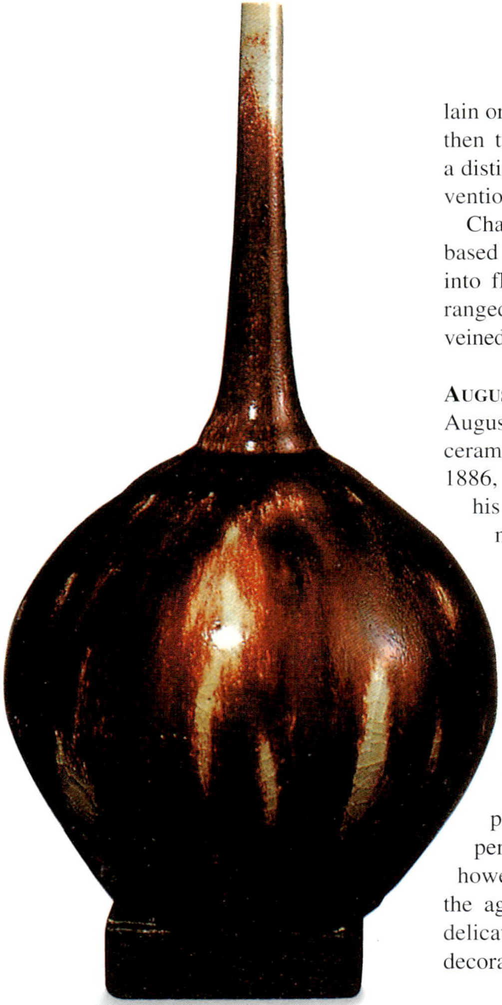

lain ornamented with flowers and leaves. He then turned to making vases and bowls in a distinctive translucent paste of his own invention, which were first exhibited in 1898.

Chaplet's decision to sell Haviland was based on his desire to continue his research into flambé glazes. The remarkable results ranged from the shiny sang-de-boeuf to veined, spotted, and pitted turquoise and white.

Auguste Delaherche

Auguste Delaherche was a more prolific ceramicist than Chaplet. Between 1883 and 1886, he worked in saltglaze stoneware, but his aim to sell art ceramics at low prices met with little success. He began to use drip glazes which he had seen on Japanese stoneware, with engraved or raised floral decoration, which won him a gold medal at the 1889 Universal Exhibition in Paris. In 1894, Delaherche began a ten year period of experimentation in deep, pure, monochromatic glazes on simple forms. After 1904, he made unique pieces, only keeping those which were perfect and refusing to accept any result, however beautiful, that was accidental. At the age of 68, Delaherche began to make delicate white porcelain vases with a pierced decoration of stylized flowers, now very rare.

Carriès and the School of Saint-Armand

A second center for the production of stoneware was in the Nivernais region at the School of Saint-Armand-en-Puisaye. The leader here was the charismatic but short-lived figure Jean Carriès, who died at the age of 39. Out of his hands grew grotesque masks, goblins, and fanciful animals. These bizarre creations are some of the best examples of the

Above: A hard-paste vase (1885-1904) by Ernst Chaplet, inspired by oriental sang-de-boeuf.

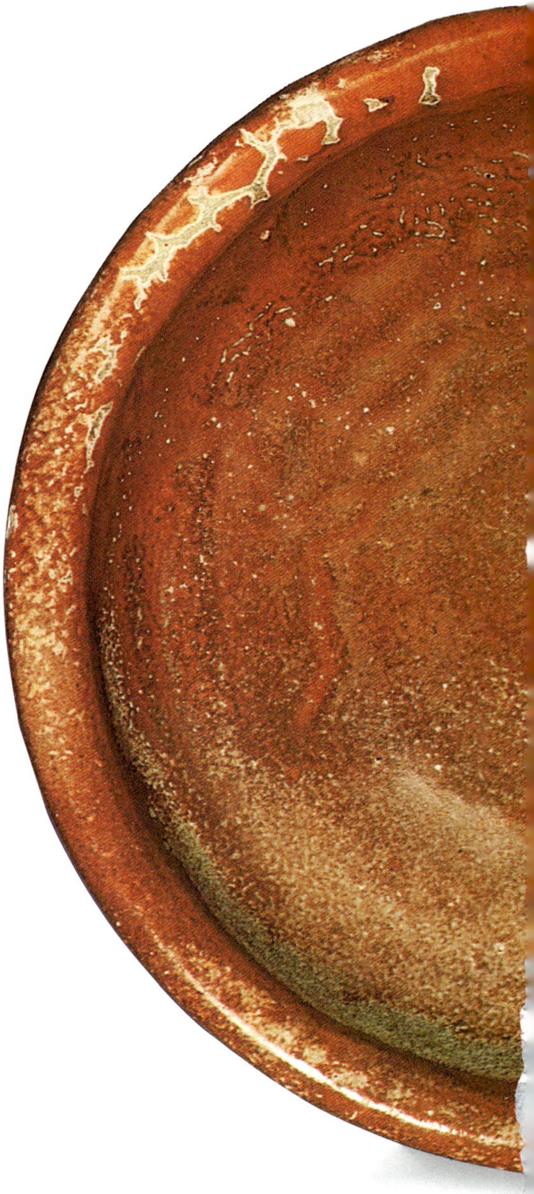

Right: A stoneware dish by Ernst Chaplet.

Far right: A stoneware vase by Albert Dammouse, ca 1900.

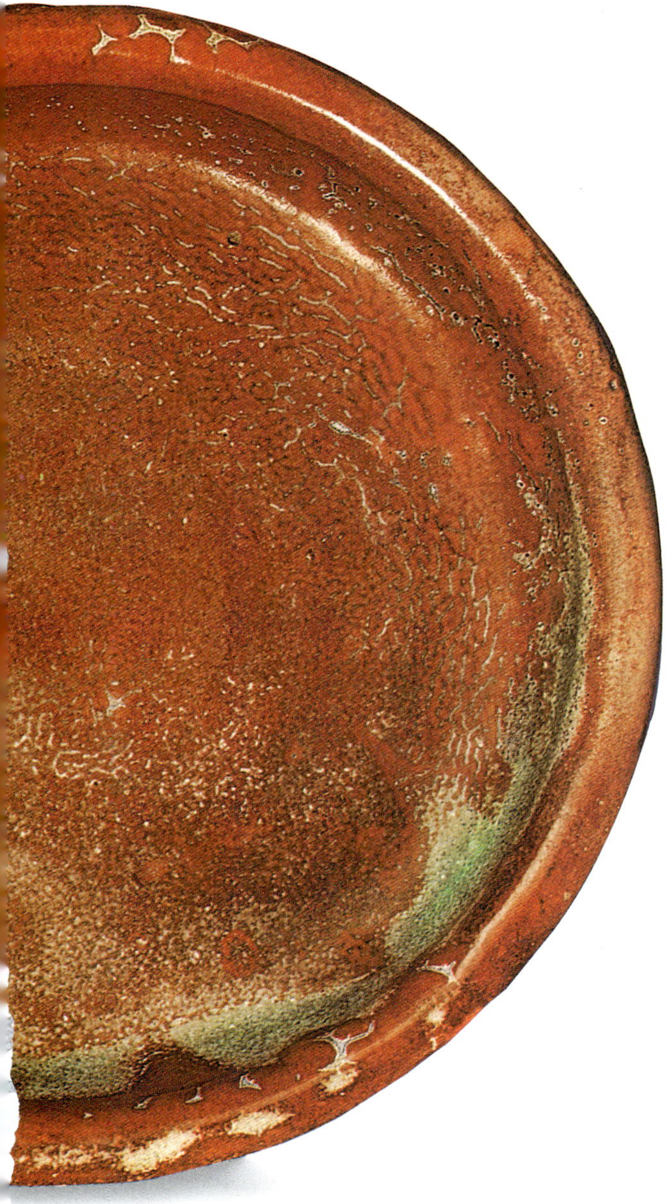

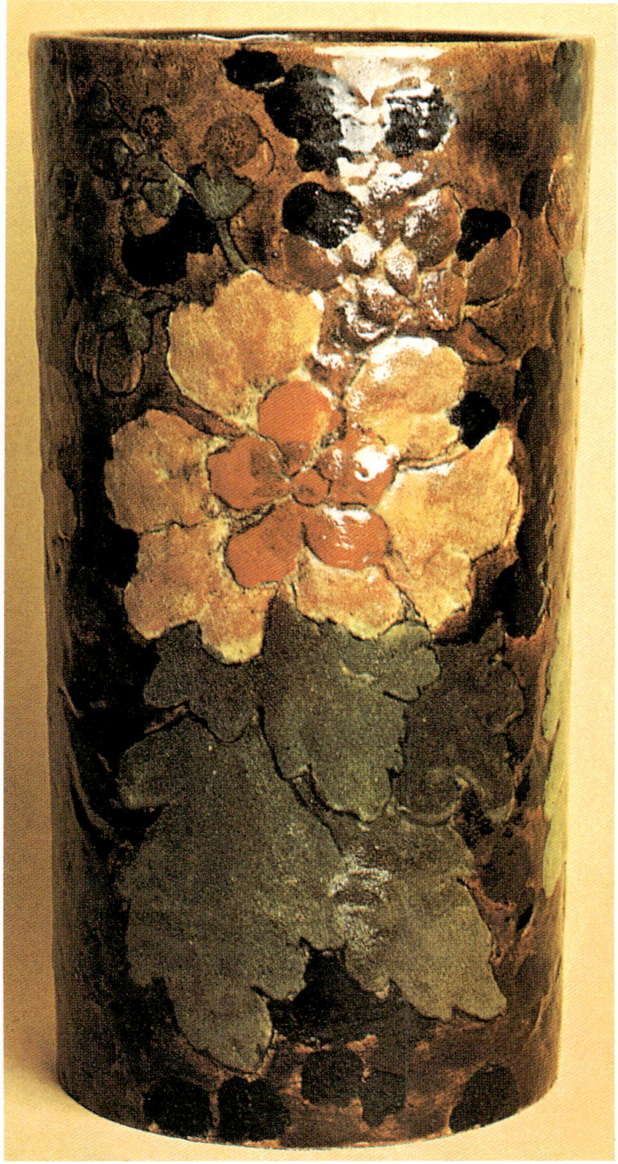

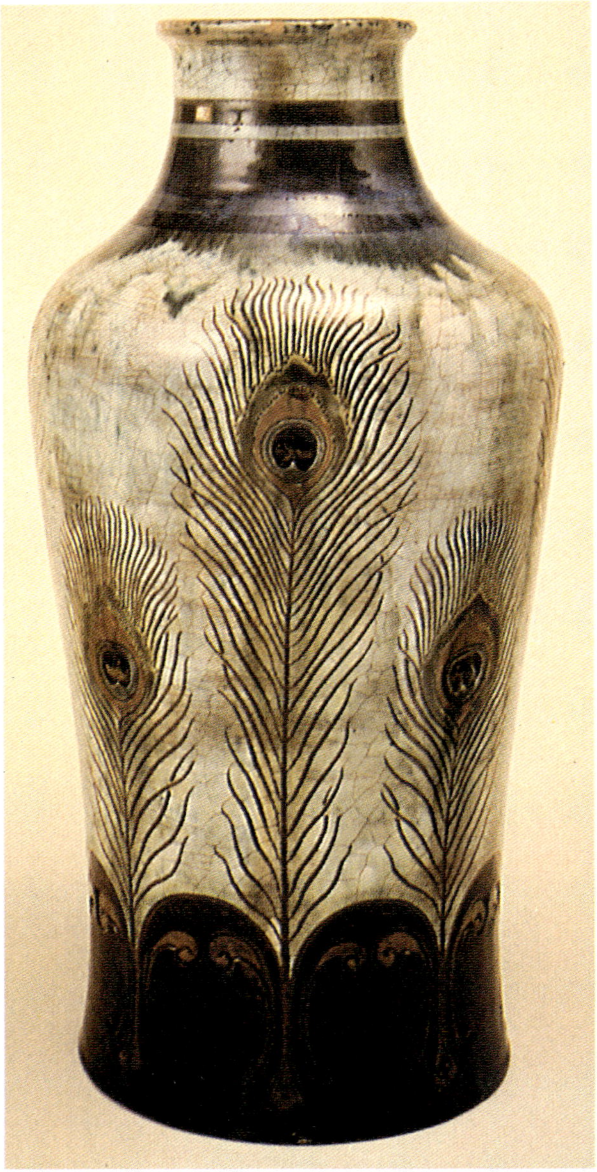

Right: Auguste Delaherche vase with blue drip glaze and peacock feather motif.

Far right: A selection of pierced stoneware vases by Auguste Delaherche.

fanciful and almost surreal side to much of the Art Nouveau borrowings from nature. All his work was left to his great friend Georges Hoentschel, a celebrated decorator, who also began to make stoneware for himself. Closer to the Japanese originals than Carriès, vases in sober blue, green, gray, and beige were sometimes finished with ivory stoppers, and others were sometimes mounted in ormolu.

Ceramic sculpture and architecture

Art Nouveau ceramic production was not simply limited to vases and bowls, but extended to the production of editions of sculptures. The application of stoneware to architecture was an important feature of the style. The leading figures in this field were Alexander Bigot, Emile Muller, and Edmond Lachenal.

From 1894, Bigot produced plates with newts, frogs, and mermaids in low relief swimming among deep translucent glazes, but from 1900, he turned toward making stoneware for both inside and outside buildings, among them Guimard's Castel Béranger, as well as editing sculptures.

Ivry

Muller's factory at Ivry produced stoneware sculptures, and he was responsible for the edition of the well-known portrait of Yvette Guilbert by Toulouse-Lautrec. Muller, together with the firms of Gentil et Bourdet and Hyppolyte Boulanger, made much of the architectural ceramics of the time. Lachenal was a painter, sculptor, and decorator whose stoneware vases ornamented with flowers and animals had a certain success, but he became particularly well known for his stoneware editions of Art Nouveau sculptures by Rodin, de Frumerie, Dejean, Fiz-Masseau, and Saint-Marceaux.

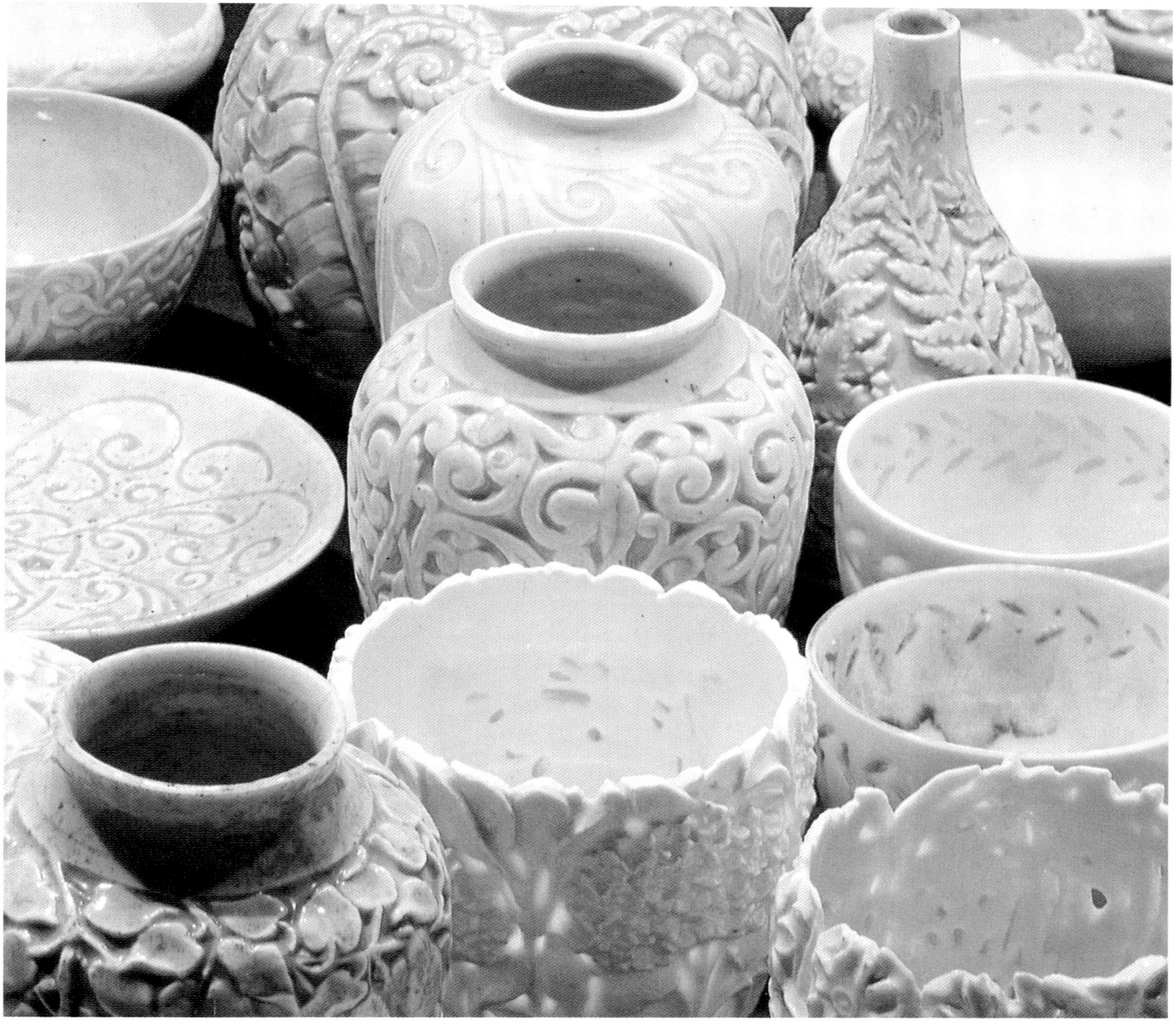

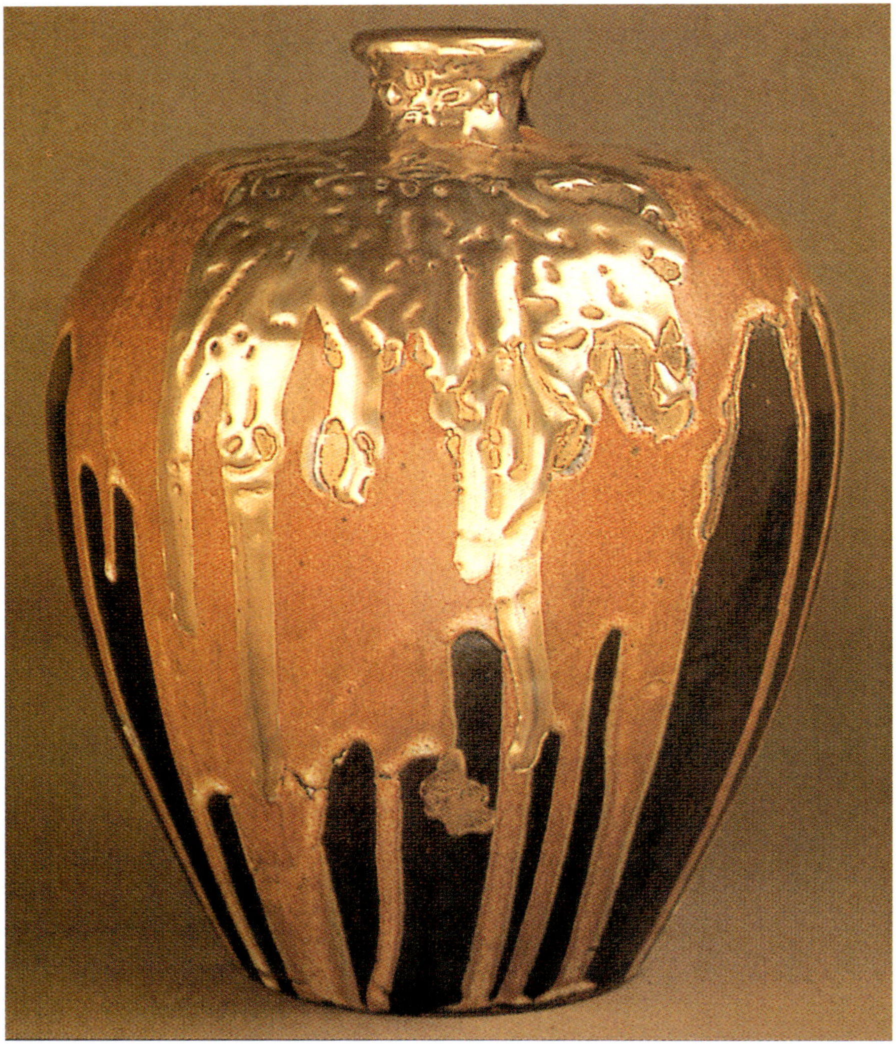

Above: A gourd-shaped vase by Jean Carries exploiting poured glazes and enamel rich in oriental colors.

Britain

The three principal influences in the applied arts in Britain in the second half of the 1800s were Gothicism, japonisme, and Islamic art, and British ceramics of the late 1800s show these three very strongly. The willowy "whiplash" curves of French Art Nouveau had a minor effect.

The 1870s had seen the foundation of a number of art-potteries that attempted to produce ceramics based on new ideas in design outside of the industrial factories. Of these, the most important were Minton's Art Pottery Studio in London, the De Morgan Pottery, the Doulton factory of Lambeth, London, and the Linthorpe Pottery of Middlesbrough in Yorkshire founded by John Harrison and Christopher Dresser in 1879.

Saltglaze

Doulton was concerned principally with the revival of medieval saltglaze stoneware, but also produced painted wears called Impasto and Faience, the latter based on the poster art of Alphonse Mucha. It was this type of pottery that was also the main product of Minton's Art Pottery Studio.

One of the most important British designers of the period was Christopher Dresser, who began his career as a botanist before designing wallpaper, furniture, textiles, metalwork, glassware, and ceramics for a number of companies. At the Linthorpe Factory, most of Dresser's ceramic pieces in dark, green-brown streaky abstract glazes, were influenced by his extensive knowledge of Japanese ceramics, while his monochrome yellow, green, or blue wares were influenced by Chinese examples which Dresser also designed for Ault in the 1890s.

Art pottery was possibly the area of design

where Arts and Crafts ideals were most widespread. Practically and financially, art pottery was — and is — a form where the artist-designer and craftsman could be one, and it is interesting to note that in the United States, many art potteries were established either for therapeutic purposes, or to provide a useful, but suitably lady-like occupation for women.

CERAMICS IN THE UNITED STATES

The initial impetus for American pottery came with the Philadelphia Centennial Exposition of 1876 where the first Oriental exhibits could be seen alongside works from the Doulton factory and Ernest Chaplet. Both the Robertson family from the Chelsea Ceramic Art Works, and Mary Louise McLaughlin, visited the ex-

Below: Stoneware vases and pears by Georges Hoentschel, Emile Grittel, and Henri de Vallombreuse, ca 1900.

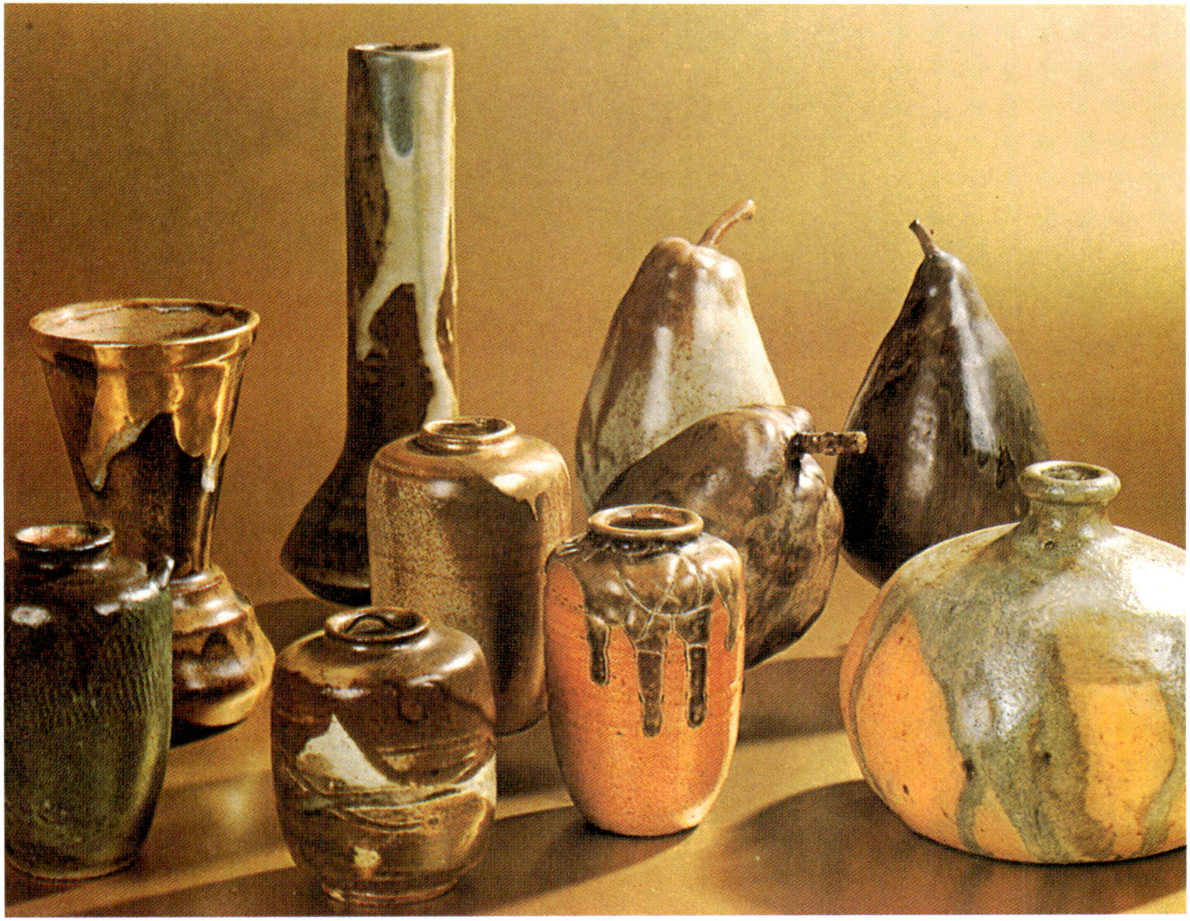

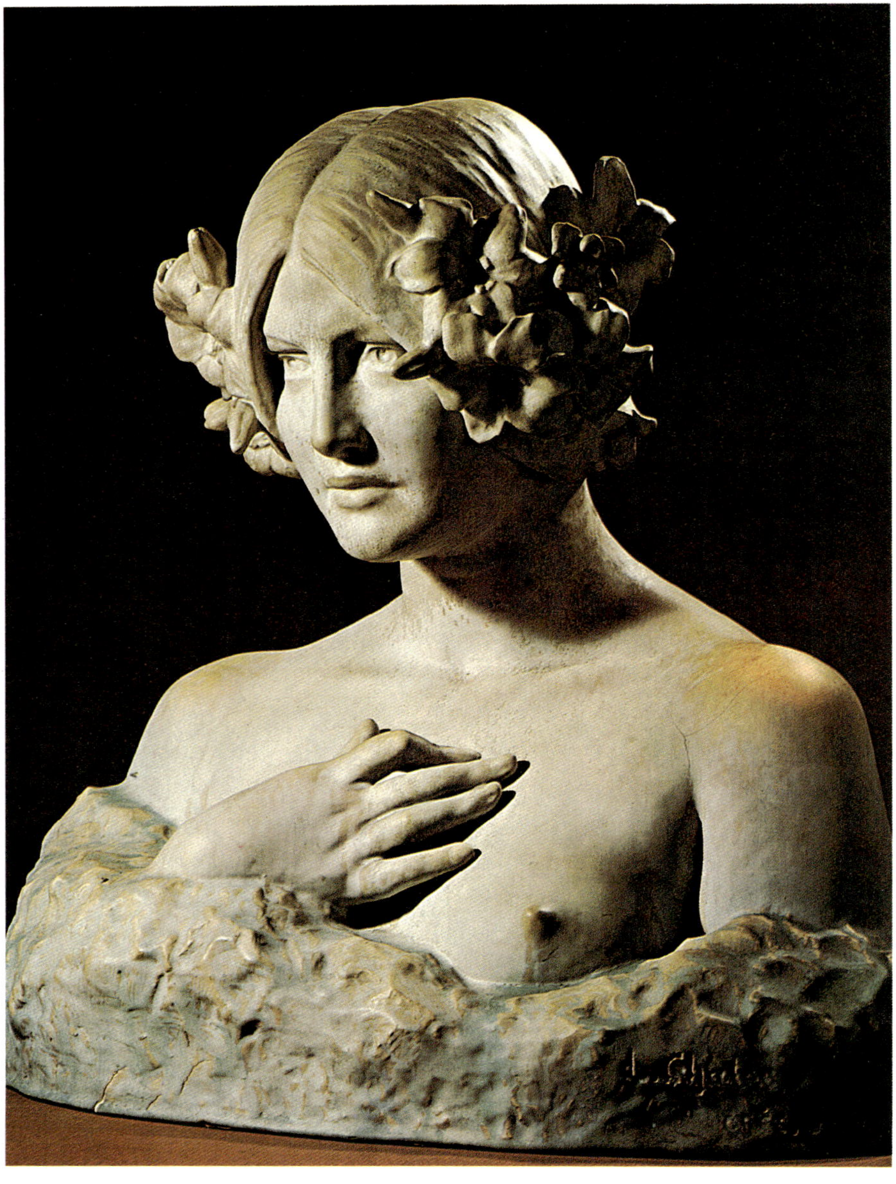

hibition of ceramics and returned to their home states of Massachusetts and Ohio to put what they had seen into practice.

The development of American ceramics ran parallel to experimentation with the use of exotic glazes on simple stoneware shapes that occurred in France. The Roberstons specialized in Greek terracotta forms at first, but by 1877 had introduced their Chelsea faience, using simple shapes and soft colors. Around

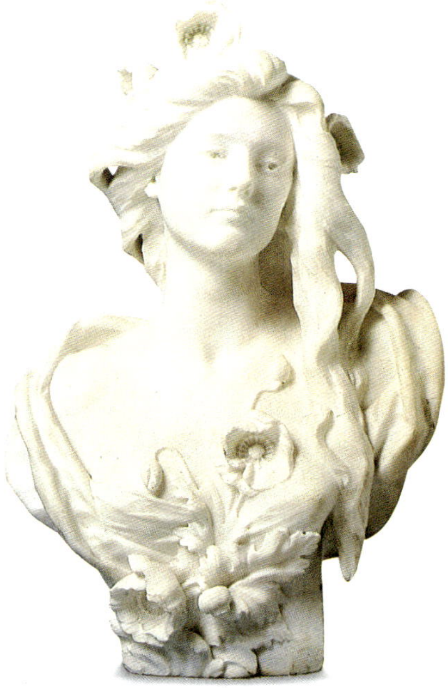

Above: A ceramic bust by Gustave Obiols. The dreamy maiden returns — this time in clay.

Left: Stoneware bust, "Flore," by Louis Challon and Emile Muller, ca 1901.

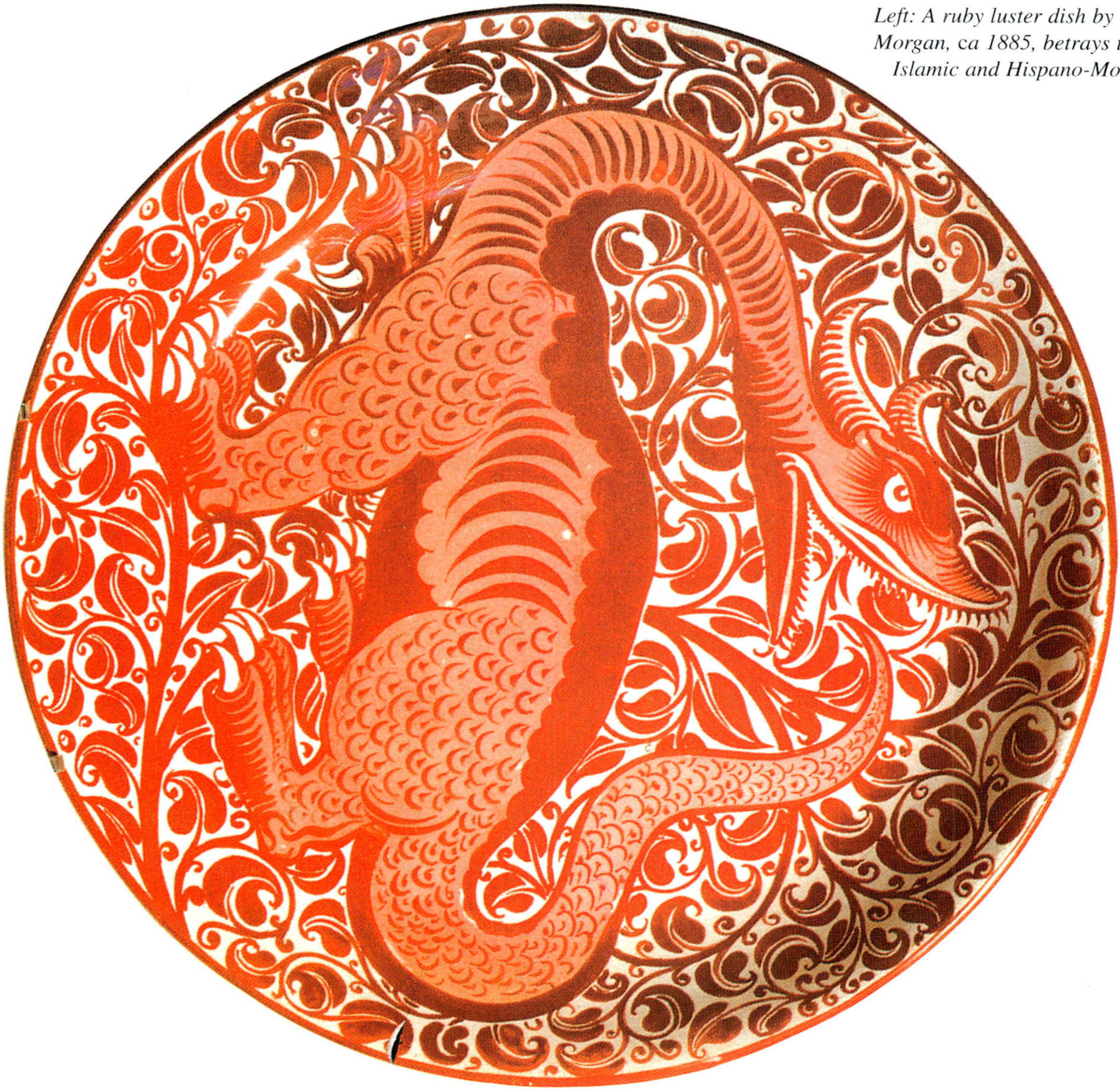

Left: A ruby luster dish by William de Morgan, ca 1885, betrays the influence of Islamic and Hispano-Moorish originals.

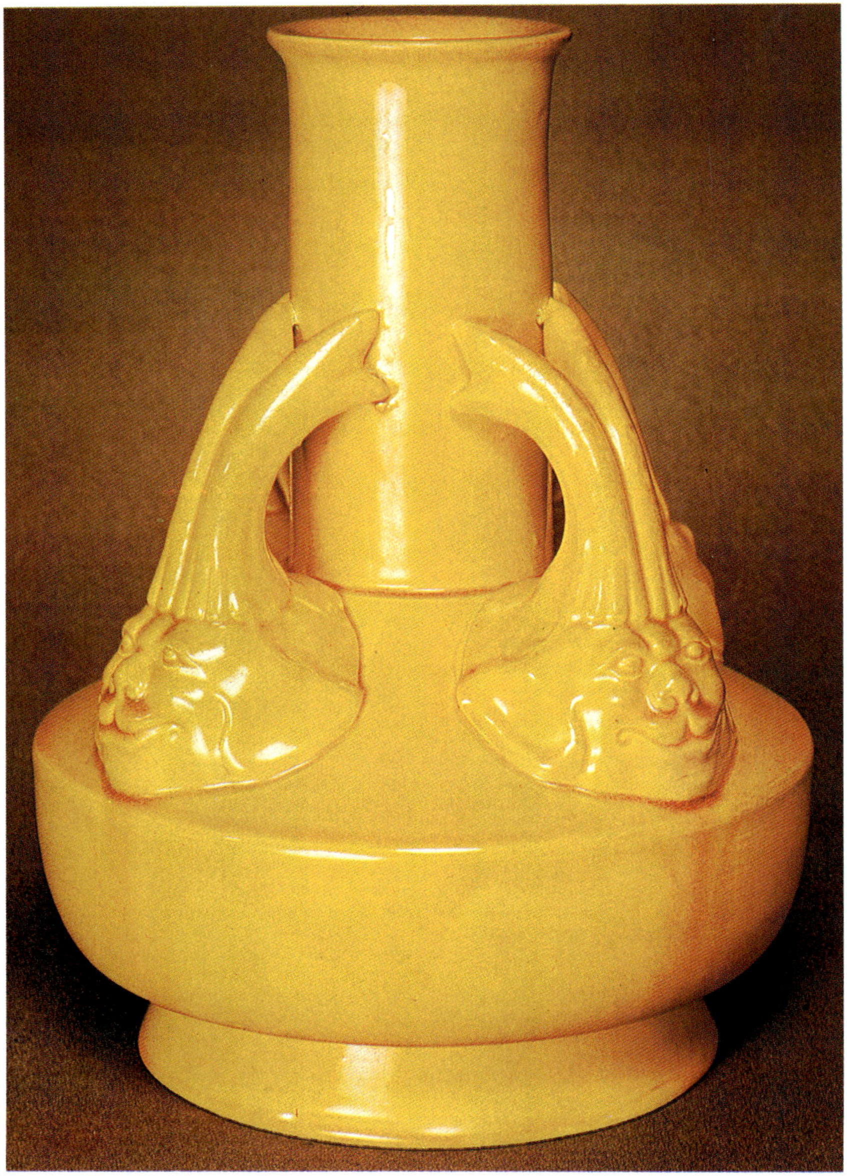

the same time the process known as barbotine, painting with colored slips, usually on a blue or green background was introduced. Further experiments resulted in an American version of sang-de-boeuf, but also in financial trouble. The Chelsea works closed, but were reopened in 1895 along more commercial lines as the Dedham Pottery, best known for its crackleware with blue-in glaze borders decorated with flowers and animals.

Underglaze

In Cincinnati, McLaughlin, an amateur enthusiast and another exponent of the underglaze technique, developed her Limoges glaze, which became known as Cincinnati Limoges. In 1879, she founded the Cincinnati Pottery Club to encourage other women in the craft. From 1881, the club used the firing facilities at the Rookwood Pottery, one of the most famous of the 30 or so potteries in Ohio. Rookwood was started by Maria Longworth Nichols Storer with support from the ladies at the Cincinnati Pottery Club, and from 1880 to 1884 the output at Rookwood mainly consisted of the ladies' experiments, usually with much gilding and heavy relief or incised decoration. After this, Rookwood was reorganized on a more commercial footing, but always maintained the tradition of allowing individual artists a free hand in their designs.

Rookwood ceramics were often characterized by underglazing, a difficult technique requiring mild firing to maintain the warm-colored glaze. When the pottery won a Grand Prix at the 1900 Paris Exhibition, a craze started for its elegant wares. Best known perhaps

Left: Grotesque vase designed by Christopher Dresser for William Ault, ca 1892.

are the vases, decorated with floral themes, animals and flowers — especially orchids and lilies — where the Art Nouveau style was seen to some degree in the elegant, elongated vase forms and curving plant-like handles.

DOAT

One of the most remarkable examples of the ascendancy of American pottery was the University City Pottery in Missouri. The pottery belonged to the Art Institute of the People's University, started by the entrepreneur Edward Garner Lewis. Lewis was himself interested in ceramics and self-taught using a translation of French ceramicist Taxile Doat's *Grand Feu Ceramics,* a treatise on new techniques in firing and glazing.

Doat was a ceramicist who made his name working in Sèvres, while at the same time maintaining an independent production. Doat treated porcelain to the techniques of the stoneware innovators using dripped glazes and even the vegetable shapes of gourds, pumpkins, and pears which had also been used by Carriès at Saint-Armand. Doat also varied the texture of his works by having pâte-sur-pâte medallions, like ancient cameos, applied to the surface, which proved to be popular.

Offered an extremely fine porcelain clay that had been found in the area, Doat was lured from his native Sèvres — along with his ceramics collection — by Lewis to University City in 1909, where he stayed for some five years, giving Missouri stoneware an international reputation.

Although more usually associated with glass, Louis Comfort Tiffany began experimenting with pottery in 1898 at his Corona works in New York — but from its inception, Tiffany's pottery was overshadowed by his Favrile glass and none of his ceramic wares

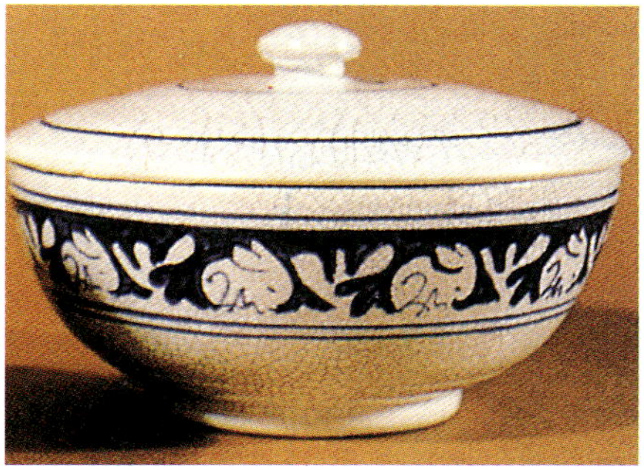

Left: Blue-and-white serving bowl by Dedham Pottery who were best known for their animal and floral border patterns.

Below: A Rookwood Pottery tile, ca 1911, features a pair of rabbits flanking a tulip tree.

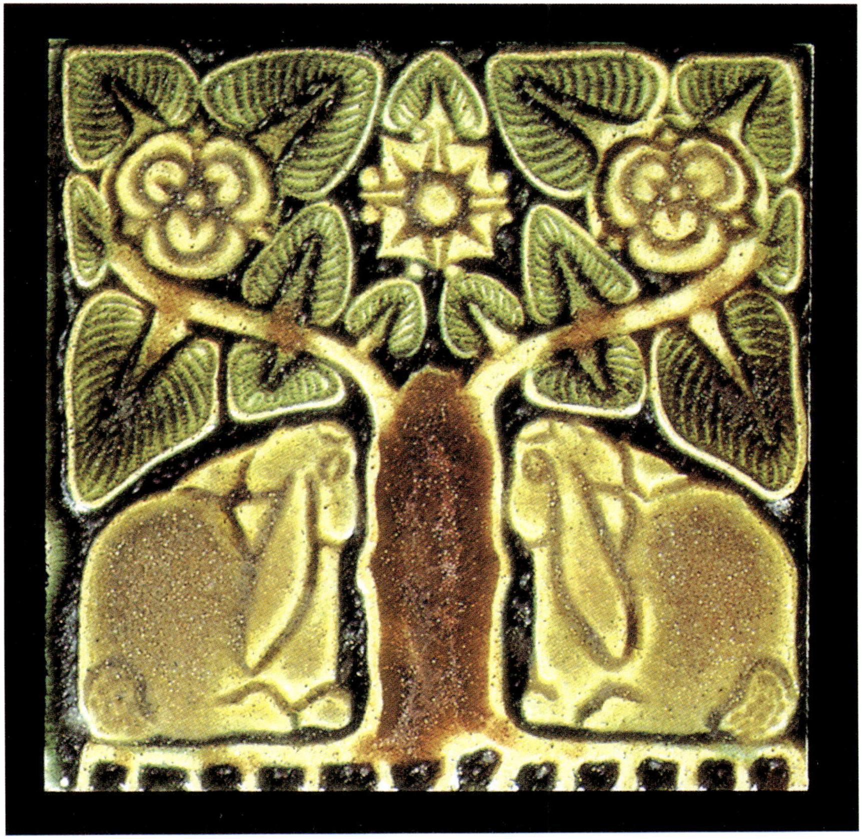

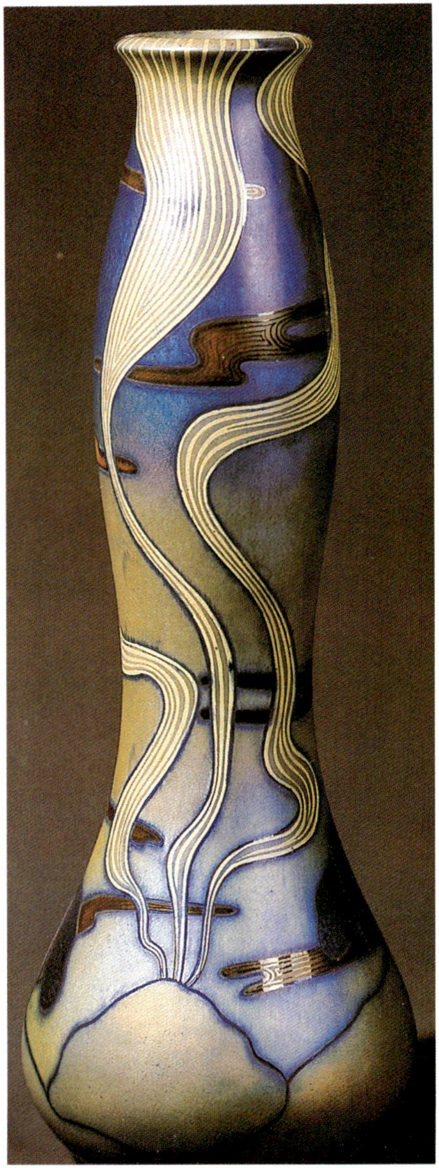

Left: A stoneware vase by Jószef Rippl-Rónai for Zsolnay of Hungary. The Hungarians introduced a distinctly central European element to forms and color.

Below: A Rookwood Pottery vase, exhibited at the Paris Exposition Universelle in 1900.

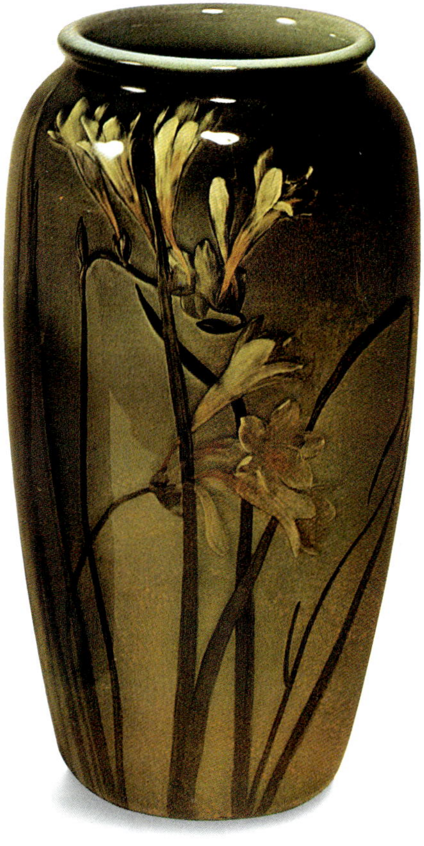

were offered for public sale until 1905. The pottery bases for his famous lamps were in fact purchased from the Greuby Pottery.

EASTERN EUROPE

Throughout the whole of Europe, ceramics followed much the same pattern as in most other countries. There were studio potters experimenting with new techniques, many small art potteries, as well as some fine work produced by some of the large, established firms such as Meissen and Berlin in Germany, Joseph Bock in Vienna, the Rozenburg pottery in The Hague, and the two great Swedish factories, Rorstrand and Gustavberg.

An outstanding example of Hungarian Art Nouveau ceramic production is Zsolnay Pottery. Founded in 1862 by Vilmos Zsolnay at Pécs, in its early days it produced earthenware in a semi-industrial, semi-folk style. In 1893, Vinsce Wartha was appointed artistic director, and it was he who developed with Zsolnay the famous iridescent luster glaze called Eosin.

Stylistically, Zsolnay's products can be divided into six groups — those in a traditional style; those in Luster resembling Tiffany or Loetz glass; the figures; the dishes painted with flowers and landscapes in red, green, and blue; the pots with animals sculpted in high relief and the pieces made early in the 1900s which show the influence of the Vienna Secession. In artistic terms, the designer Jószef Rippl-Rónai marks the high point in the factory's history, as his flowing floral patterns and designs are most evidently Art Nouveau.

MAJOR CRAFTSMEN AND DESIGNERS

ASHBEE, Charles Robert (1863–1942)
British Arts and Crafts architect, designer, and writer. He founded the Guild of Handicraft in 1888.

BAILLIE SCOTT, Mackay Hugh (1865–1945)
British architect and designer. He worked extensively abroad.

BEARDSLEY, Aubrey (1872–98)
British decadent writer and illustrator famed for his consummate graphic skill.

BEHRENS, Peter (1868–1940)
Austrian architect and designer and member of the Deutscher Werkbund.

BING, Samuel (1838–1905)
German writer and entrepreneur who opened his shop, La Maison de l'Art Nouveau, in Paris in 1895.

BRACQUEMOND, Felix-Henri (1833–1914)
French painter, etcher, and ceramicist.

CHAPLET, Ernest (1835–1909)
French ceramicist.

CHARPENTIER, Alexandre (1856–1909)
French Art Nouveau designer and decorator. He was associated with Samuel Bing.

COLONNA, Edward (1862–1948)
German designer and decorative designer working in the United States and France.

CRANE, Walter (1845–1915)
British designer, painter, illustrator, and writer. A socialist, he was president of both the Art Workers' Guild and the Arts and Crafts Exhibition Society.

CZESCHKA, Carl Otto (1878–1960)
Austrian painter, architect, and designer; member of the Wiener Werkstätte.

DAUM, Auguste (1853–1909)
DAUM, Antonin (1864–1930)
French glass designers, brothers.

DAY, Lewis F. (1845–1910)
British arts and crafts designer and writer. A founding member of both the Art Workers' Guild and the Arts and Crafts Exhibition Society.

DECK, Theodore (1823–91)
French art potter.

DELAHERCHE, Auguste (1857–1940)
French ceramicist in the Art Nouveau style. He was associated with Samuel Bing.

DOAT, Taxile (1851–1938)
French ceramicist working at Sèvres and the University City Pottery, Missouri.

DRESSER, Christopher (1834–1904)
British industrial designer who, after achieving a doctorate in botany, turned to design for industrial production.

DUFRÊNE, Maurice (1876–1955)
French designer in the Art Deco style. Worked for Julius Meier-Graefe who opened "La Maison Moderne" in 1898.

ENDELL, August (1871–1925)
German architect and designer.

FABERGÉ, Carl (1846–1920)
Russian jewelry designer and jeweler to the Russian Imperial Court.

DE FEURE, Georges (1869–1928)
French Art Nouveau decorative artist and designer.

FISHER, Alexander (1864–1936)
British Arts and Crafts enameler. He studied in France and subsequently set up his own school in Kensington, London.

GAILLARD, Eugène (1862–1933)
French Art Nouveau designer and writer, connected with Samuel Bing.

GALLÉ, Emile (1846–1904)
French designer. His Nancy workshops produced some of the finest examples of Art Nouveau glass and furniture.

GAUDÍ, Antoni (1859–1926)
Spanish Art Nouveau architect and designer.

GAUGUIN, Paul (1848–1903)
French painter, sculptor, and graphic artist — leader of the Pont-Aven group.

GRASSET, Eugène (1841–1917)
Swiss architect, writer, and designer working in France in the Art Nouveau style.

GUIMARD, Hector (1867–1942)
French architect and designer working within the Art Nouveau style to create the total environment.

HOFFMANN, Josef (1870–1956)
Austrian architect and designer — a founder member of the Vienna Secession, he founded the Wiener Werkstätte in 1903.

HOLIDAY, Henry (1839–1927)
British painter and stained glass designer.

HORTA, Victor (1861–1947)
Belgian architect and designer in the Art Nouveau style.

JENSEN, Georg (1866–1935)
Danish silver and jewelry designer.

KLIMT, Gustav (1862–1918)
Austrian painter and designer associated with the Vienna Secession.

KNOX, Archibald (1864–1933)
British silver designer who was the inspiration behind Liberty and Co.'s "Cymric" and "Tudric" lines.

KOEHLER, Florence (1861–1944)
American Arts and Crafts jewelry designer.

KOEPPING, Karl (1848–1914)
German Jugendstil glass designer.

LALIQUE, René (1860–1945)
French designer, trained as a goldsmith. He opened his glassworks in 1909 and was best known for his jewelry and glass designs.

LOOS, Adolf (1870–1933)
Austrian architect and designer and pioneer of Modernism.

MACDONALD, Frances (1874–1921)
Scottish artist and designer and a member of the Glasgow Four.

MACDONALD MACKINTOSH, Margaret (1865–1933)
Scottish artist and designer and a member of the Glasgow Four. Wife of Charles Rennie Mackintosh.

MACKINTOSH, Charles Rennie (1868–1928)
Scottish architect and designer — leading figure of the Glasgow Four.

MACKMURDO, Arthur (1851–1942)
British Arts and Crafts architect and designer. Founded the Century Guild in 1884.

MACNAIR, James Herbert (1868–1955)
Scottish artist and the lesser-known member of the Glasgow Four.

MAJORELLE, Louis (1859–1926)
French designer and cabinet maker in the Art Nouveau style.

McLAUGHLIN, Mary Louise (1847–1939)
American pottery and porcelain decorator.

MORRIS, William (1834–96)
British writer, poet, and designer. Founder of Morris and Co. and the Kelmscott Press; leader of the Arts and Crafts Movement.

MOSER, Koloman (1868–1918)
Austrian painter, designer, and graphic artist involved in the founding of both the Vienna Secession and Wiener Werkstätte.

MUCHA, Alphonse (1860–1939)
Czech artist and poster designer.

MUTHESIUS, Hermann (1861–1927)
German architect and designer. He founded the Deutscher Werkbund in 1907.

ORBRIST, Hermann (1863–1927)
Swiss designer working in Germany.

OLBRICH, Josef Maria (1867–1908)
Austrian Art Nouveau designer, architect, and artist. One of the co-founders of the Vienna Secession.

PECHE, Dagobert (1887–1923)
Austrian artist and metalwork designer. Co-director of the Wiener Werkstätte.

POWOLNY, Michael (1871–1954)
Austrian pottery decorator and teacher.

PRUTSCHER, Otto (1880–1949)
Austrian architect, furniture designer, jeweler, and designer. Worked at the Wiener Werkstätte.

REDON, Odilon (1840–1916)
French painter, lithographer, etcher, and an associate of the Symbolists.

RIEMERSCHMID, Richard (1868–1957)
German architect, designer, and founder member of the Deutscher Werkbund.

ROHLFS, Charles (1853–1936)
American furniture designer and craftsman working within the Art Nouveau idiom.

ROSSETTI, Dante Gabriel (1828–82)
British painter, poet, and leading light of the Pre-Raphaelites. He was also involved in the formation of Morris, Marshall, Faulkner, and Co.

RUSKIN, John (1819–1900)
Influential British social critic, his writings were the main inspiration for the Arts and Crafts movement.

STICKLEY, Gustav (1857–1942)
American writer and furniture designer. He founded *The Craftsman* magazine in 1901, publicizing arts and crafts ideals.

SULLIVAN, Louis (1856–1924)
American architect, the pioneer of the modern office block, and father to the Prairie school of architecture.

TIFFANY, Louis Comfort (1848–1933)
American designer and interior decorator. He specialized in stained glass and art glass as well as mosaics, jewelry, and metalwork. Acknowledged as a genius and innovator of the Art Nouveau style.

VELDE, Henry van de (1863–1957)
Belgian theorist and designer. He helped found the Kunstgewerbeschule in Weimar in 1906.

VOILLET-LE-DUC, Eugène-Emanuel (1814–79)
French writer and architectural theorist.

VOYSEY, Charles Annesley (1857–1941)
British Arts and Crafts architect and designer.

WAGNER, Otto (1841–1918)
Austrian designer and member of the Deutscher Werkbund.

WEBB, Philip (1831–1915)
British architect and designer. He was associated with Morris and Co. from its foundation. He designed many country houses.

WILSON, Henry (1864–1934)
British Arts and Crafts architect, sculptor, and silversmith.

WOLFERS, Philippe (1858–1929)
Belgian Art Nouveau jeweler and sculptor.

WRIGHT, Frank Lloyd (1867–1959)
American architect, writer, and interior designer, pioneering an integral, structural style of interior decoration. He was the first major "modern" American architect.

INDEX

ACKNOWLEDGMENTS

The material in this book previously appeared in:
Art Nouveau Architecture and Furniture, Art Nouveau Jewelry and Metalwork, Art Nouveau Glass and Ceramics, The Arts and Crafts Movement — Textiles and Interiors, The Art of Louis Comfort Tiffany, The Encyclopedia of Decorative Styles 1850–1935

Quantum Publishing would like to thank Siân Donovan for additional photography, Rod Teasdale for jacket design, and Dorothy Frame for indexing.